Is Comrade Bulgakov Dead?

Mikhail Bulgakov at the Moscow Art Theatre

In the same series

by Constantin Stanislavski
An Actor's Handbook
An Actor Prepares
Building a Character
Creating a Role
My Life in Art

Stanislavski: A Biography
Jean Benedetti

The Moscow Art Letters
*Selected, Edited and Translated
with a commentary by
Jean Benedetti*

Stanislavski: An Introduction
Jean Benedetti

Meyerhold on Theatre
Edward Braun

IS

COMRADE BULGAKOV

DEAD?

Mikhail Bulgakov at the Moscow Art Theatre

ANATOLY SMELIANSKY

Translated by Arch Tait

METHUEN

First published in Great Britain in 1993
by Methuen London
an imprint of Reed Consumer Books Limited
Michelin House, 81 Fulham Road, London SW3 6RB
and Auckland, Melbourne, Singapore and Toronto

This abridged translation has been prepared from the second edition
of *Mikhail Bulgakov v Khudozhestvennom teatre* by Anatoly
Mironovich Smeliansky, published by Iskusstvo Publishers,
Moscow, 1989 (ISBN 5–210–00336–1)
Russian text © Iskusstvo Publishers, 1986
© Iskusstvo Publishers 1989, with supplementary material
This revised edition © Anatoly Smeliansky, 1993

Translation © Arch Tait, 1993
The author and translator have asserted their moral rights.

ISBN 0 413 63070 6
A CIP catalogue record for this book
is available from the British Library

Typeset by Wilmaset Ltd, Birkenhead, Wirral
Printed in Great Britain by Clays Ltd, St. Ives plc

He died on 10 March 1941 at four in the afternoon. For some reason I always imagine it was at dawn.

The following morning, or perhaps it was the same day (I no longer remember the time exactly. I think it was the following morning), the telephone rang. I picked up the receiver. It was somebody from Stalin's secretariat. A voice enquired, 'Is it true Comrade Bulgakov is dead?'

'Yes, he is dead.'

The person on the other end of the telephone hung up.

(Sergey Yermolinsky,
Dramaticheskie sochineniia, Iskusstvo,
Moscow, 1982, p. 684.)

TRANSLATOR'S NOTE

References in the text to Michael Glenny's translations of Bulgakov's works are to the following editions:

The White Guard, Collins Harvill, London, 1989.
ISBN 0 00 271026 9.

The Days of the Turbins (translated as *The White Guard*), *Flight*, *Molière* and *The Last Days* (translated by William Powell and Michael Earley), all in *Mikhail Bulgakov: Six Plays*, Methuen Drama, London, 1991.
ISBN 0 413 64530 4.

The Master and Margarita, Collins Harvill, London, 1988, ISBN 0 00 271513 9.

Black Snow: A Theatrical Novel, Collins Harvill, London, 1991. ISBN 0 00 271139 7.

There is a translation of Bulgakov's biography *The Life of Monsieur de Molière* by Mirra Ginsburg, published by Oxford University Press, 1988. ISBN 0 19 282111 3.

Contents

List of Illustrations

I look intently at his likeness.

Average height, round shoulders, pigeon chest. Wide-set eyes in a swarthy face with high cheek bones. A pointed chin. Nose broad and flat. Altogether a thoroughly unprepossessing appearance. But look at his eyes. There I read a strange, unchanging sardonic smile but also a kind of constant astonishment at the world surrounding him. There is something voluptuous, almost feminine, in those eyes, and they conceal some very deep-seated malady. A worm, I can tell, is lodged in this twenty-year-old man and even now gnawing away at him. He is a stutterer, and his breath comes unevenly when he speaks.

I can see he has a fiery temper. He is subject to sudden swings of mood, passing rapidly from moments of merriment to moments of dark brooding. He sees the funny side of people, and likes to joke about it.

He is sometimes frank to the point of indiscretion. At other moments he tries to be secretive and devious. There are times when he is recklessly brave, but he can quickly lapse into indecision and cowardice. I can tell these characteristics promise him a hard life, and he will make many enemies.

But let his life begin!

Mikhail Bulgakov,
The Life of Monsieur de Molière

Preface

I study his likeness closely.

Above average height. Hair fair, golden hued, even. Brushed flat, but keeps coming adrift and needs to be brushed back. Walks rather oddly, with a kind of waddling gait, thrusting his right shoulder forward. Irregular features, nostrils deeply incised. Frowns when speaking. But look at his blue eyes . . .

Beyond that, almost nothing needs changing. Studying the face of the great French dramatist Bulgakov was also scrutinising himself. His pen portrait of Molière has a dual quality about it, the contours of a face overlapping the contours of a destiny, each discernible in the other.

Artists paint self-portraits the better to paint from life. Writers look intently at the faces of other writers for the same purpose. The book may be titled *The Life of Monsieur de Molière* but it is also a book about the biographer himself.

In his portrait of Molière Bulgakov predicts even his own fatal illness, and the course of his own literary destiny.

In the conversation with the midwife with which Bulgakov begins his book, the author of 1933 explains to the nurse of 1622 the kind of baby she is delivering. 'The child's words will be translated into English, Italian, Spanish, and Dutch. Into Danish, Polish, Turkish and Russian . . .'

The midwife is astounded. 'Can this be, Sir?'

Enumerating the languages in which Molière's plays will be heard, Bulgakov punctuates the list with a full stop in order to draw breath. If we were to list the languages which today serve as Bulgakov's own native tongue we should again have to pause for breath.

Boris Pasternak once remarked that only genius frees someone who writes from having a destiny during his life in order to have one after he dies. In the case of Bulgakov we need to add that his posthumous literary destiny was to prove as controversial and eventful as his destiny in life. For several decades now the secondary literature on Bulgakov has been proliferating throughout the world. Not only are Bulgakov's works much published and translated, but plays and poems, books and articles are written about him, films are filmed, and memoirs flow in a never-ending river. His real biography is gradually being turned into legend, the process intensified a hundredfold by the over-hasty dismantling of an empire carried through wholly in the style of his diabolical character Woland. Standing on the ruins of the great utopia, the detritus of a state which destroyed the author of *The Master and Margarita* even as it provided him with a source of bitter inspiration, Russians are closely studying Bulgakov's writing and his life all over again in the hope of drawing sustenance from them.

There are important lessons to be learned from Bulgakov's career in the theatre, and in particular from his relations with the Moscow Art Theatre. Not only is the art of the dramatist thrown open wide before us, but the topic opens up the history of the Russian theatre as a whole. Bulgakov's romance with the Art Theatre was the great romance of his life, a source of great happiness, much anguish, and ultimately of his downfall. His relationship with the Art Theatre went far deeper than the customary relations between a theatre and a playwright.

The legendary Pavel Markov, my predecessor as literary director of the Art Theatre, coined the term 'An Author of the Theatre'. By this he meant a dramatist who did not merely provide the Theatre with the occasional play, but one who worked in partnership with it with each new play he wrote to create his own theatre. It is he who shapes its destiny as much as he shapes his own. Markov named Chekhov and Gorky as the first 'Authors of the Art Theatre', and Bulgakov after them.[1]

The very notion of an Author of the Theatre is fraught with drama. A playwright and a theatre resemble magnetic poles generating the required creative field from the tension between their differently charged wills. So it was with Chekhov in his relations with the Moscow Art Theatre, so too it was with Gorky. In the case of Bulgakov a third force interposed itself: the brute force of the Stalin regime with its pretensions to remake the world. A state the like of which the world had never seen attempted to crush both the Theatre and its Author, to assimilate them to its ends and force them to work for it.

To the leaders of the Art Theatre at the time it seemed that his break with the Theatre in the autumn of 1936 was very much his own problem. Today we have a different perspective. We can see that the Theatre's break with Bulgakov, betraying its own author, signalled inner degeneration and moral collapse. If we recall the position that the theatre Stanislavsky created enjoyed in Russian and world culture, we can fully recognise the scope of the events which are the subject of our book.

That is what I wanted this book to be about: a man becoming an Author of the Theatre; the Theatre becoming his whole life; and that life then being drawn into a tight and terrible knot.

This is a book about a power which tried to destroy all that was alive in Russian culture. It is a book about a great Russian theatre seduced by the Stalin regime. It is a book too about one man who tried under conditions of absolute unfreedom to retain his own identity and soul.

Soon after breaking off relations with the Art Theatre Bulgakov began writing a book which had a variety of titles in manuscript, among them *A Dead Man's Notes* and *A Theatrical Novel*. That book was published a quarter of a century after its author's death, in Russian under the title *A Theatrical Novel*, in English as *Black Snow*. Bulgakov had, however, good reason for preferring his more testamentary title. In *A Dead Man's Notes* he drew up a literary balance sheet of his relations with the Art Theatre in which there is transparently light humour and unendurable pain, unrequited love and a sublime contempt shading over into sarcasm. The portraits of famous Russian actors and directors are as easily recognisable as are the conflicts in Bulgakov's own life. Over and above all this, however, there is an amazing ability to rise above the hurt and anger and see his relations with the Art Theatre in the free atmosphere of world culture. It raises his 'theatrical novel' to the level of a mirror to history.

May the same freedom with which Bulgakov wrote *A Dead Man's Notes* serve us, too.

One last thing: this book about Bulgakov at the Moscow Art Theatre was completed in the days before 1985, Gorbachev and *glasnost*. Those were difficult times for Russia, and this was the present author's personal response to the question, 'To be or not to be?' Life decided in favour of 'being'. The book was published in new and freer times, in 1986 and in a second edition in 1989. For the English edition, as for the Russian, I have felt no need to rewrite or radically alter anything to take account of the new political climate, beyond incorporating newly available documentary evidence. I say this not in any spirit of self-congratulation, but simply to mark the fact that the subject of this book was from the outset the ability of a human being to remain true to himself irrespective of the climate and pressures of the day. In this respect the book's subject and its own destiny have been firmly linked.

I

'This is My World!'

Carnival in Kiev

Bulgakov's writing is autobiographical from start to finish. This is a fact which has led to some curious misapprehensions, especially in the first years after the Master was returned to Russian literature. On the strength of *Black Snow*, for example, a number of critics have deduced that the dramatist who delivered *The White Guard* to the Moscow Art Theatre was a greenhorn, completely new to play-writing, who had magically intuited all the mysteries of the stage. Doesn't Maxudov after all admit in *Black Snow*:

Smashing a saucer in my enthusiasm, I tried to convince Bombardov how as soon as I caught sight of the golden horse I had instinctively grasped the secret of the stage and all its mysteries. How, long ago in childhood perhaps, or perhaps even before I was born I had dreamed of it and longed for it! And now I had arrived in that magic world!

'I'm a stranger in it,' I cried, 'I'm a stranger in your world – but nothing can stop me! I've arrived – and I shall stay!' (p. 140)

It is a tempting deduction, poetic, elegant, neat, but disproved, alas, by the sheer weight of long-established evidence. Bulgakov, unlike Maxudov, came to the Art Theatre already burdened with formidable experience of life, literature, and the theatre, derived in the main from the years of revolution and civil war. What really did go back to the years of his childhood and youth, to the general cultural background he inherited from his family, his home, and traditions which dated from 'before he was born', was his understanding and feel for the theatre; the way in which, as he later said himself, he had the stage in his blood.

How does someone come to start playing with the magic box? What makes a playwright?

Bulgakov gives his answer in his biography *The Life of Monsieur de Molière* with a brilliant and pithy sketch of the theatrical life of Paris which nurtured the great comic dramatist. It is an extended portrait which takes in the figures of two stage-struck upholsterers, a boy and his grandfather, victims of 'the passion for the theatre, of which no one has ever been cured'. They are portrayed against the background of a commercial Paris grown 'stout and bonny, and spreading out in all directions'. The booths, the market-place, the farce-players with their whited faces, twisting and turning like figures on a merry-go-round, pass before the eyes of the young Jean-Baptiste. They see Bellerose, the leading actor of the Hôtel de Bourgogne, 'painted like a turkeycock, soft and simpering'; the tragic actor Montdory astounds them with his thundering in the Marais. Most memorable, however, are Bulgakov's descriptions of the booth theatres set up at the market and beside the Pont neuf: 'Rage on, Pont neuf! I can hear the Comédie-Française being born, its father a charlatan, its mother an actress. Piercingly it shrieks, its coarse features powdered with flour!'

Bulgakov has left not a single line about the theatre of his own youth, but we cannot doubt that it was then, in Kiev, that the special sixth sense for the theatre was born and grew in him. In *Black Snow* Maxudov, himself a Kievan, knows how the stage breathes 'its cold, secret smell'. He notices the warm draught which inclines all the flames of the footlight candles in the same direction, and knows how laughter 'ripples through the house' (p. 140). Good acting brings him out in a 'gentle sweat'. The archetype of the theatre which had been building up in Bulgakov from the days of his youth, and the exceptional power and intensity of his first impressions of the theatre, were not to be displaced by later close acquaintance with the new stagecraft in all its varieties, from Meyerhold and Tairov to Vakhtangov and Mikhail Chekhov.

The Museum of the Theatre in Kiev has the memoirs of Vladimir Nelli in its archives. Nelli was well-known in the Ukraine as a producer, actor, and teacher. Coincidentally he went to the same High School as Bulgakov and also read medicine at Kiev University. In his youth Nelli came to know and love the theatre by much the same route as any other cultured Kievan. For him the pre-revolutionary theatre was the Solovtsov Theatre, 'a straightforward realist theatre with entertaining plays and good actors'.[1] The theatre of Bulgakov's youth was an actor's theatre. The repertoire was built round gala benefit performances, and dictated by the preferences of particular actors. This led to an odd, and sometimes barely credible, assortment of plays. Kiev had always been quick on the uptake, appropriating promptly anything that was proving success-ful on the stages of the Empire's two capitals. Over a period of years the Solovtsov's play-bill featured Gogol and Chirikov, Hauptmann and Urvantsov, Ibsen and Yushkevich, Rostand and Artsybashev, Strindberg and Kosorotov,

Amfiteatrov and Suvorin, Schiller and Protopopov and, of course, the *oeuvre* of Leonid Andreev in its entirety.

The repertoire changed frequently, with a new first night every Friday in accordance with provincial expectations. This obliged Stepan Kuznetsov to perform protean feats as Khlestakov and Charlie's Aunt, Jourdain and Semyon Semyonovich (in Artsybashev's *Jealousy*), Marmeladov and Ferdyshchenko, Plyushkin and Rasplyuev, Figaro and the third peasant (in Tolstoy's *The Fruits of Enlightenment*), all in quick succession, unhampered by lengthy rehearsal or preparation.

A revolution shook the Russian theatre at the turn of the century. Moscow acquired a new theatre in Chamberlain Street and the newspapers and magazines were filled with controversy and stories about it. It was beyond belief: they had done away with benefit performances, they were staging only three or four productions in a season, and people said they were achieving unheard-of results in a fearsomely complicated style known as *ensemble* acting. They didn't allow the audience to clap during the performance. They had installed a revolving stage and devised a new system of stage lighting. They designed a completely new set of stage decor for each new production. The venerable Kievan critic Nikolai Nikolaev verged on hysteria as he relayed to his compatriots his impressions of the first night of *The Cherry Orchard* at the Moscow Art Theatre: 'Like the author of "Letters from the Stalls", I too can now say, "I have seen *The Cherry Orchard*! I really, really have!" '[2] He compared his tremulous sense of anticipation on entering the Art Theatre to a Muslim's feelings on entering Mecca.

Stanislavsky might be in Moscow and Meyerhold in St Petersburg, but back in Kiev Orlov-Chuzhbinin, the Solovtsov's leading actor, was taking the director/producer Duvan-Tortsov to court for foisting a part on him unsuited to his *emploi*. At this time the Solovtsov Theatre had not the first idea of the role of a director. The nearest it came was in a few plays in two of its seasons which Konstantin Mardzhanov produced as he passed through and which were 'as staged by the Art Theatre'. They failed to evoke the least interest in their *mise-en-scène*. 'What need is there for all this clever gimmickry?' asked the testy Kiev correspondent of Alexander Kugel's *Theatre and Art*. 'It isn't even of the director's own devising.'[3]

In Moscow the Art Theatre had succumbed to and recovered from its first artistic crisis and was combing through the whole of world drama, opening Studios, inviting Gordon Craig as guest director, and dramatising Hamsun and Dostoevsky in an endeavour to restore its artistic impetus. In Kiev life went on much as before, with an orchestra entertaining the audience in the intervals, and the heavy blue velvet curtain rising equally affably on Shakespeare one day and *The Sleeping-Car Attendant* the next. The critics might curse and deride, but loyal audiences kept coming back to see their favourite actors and showing their delight in the traditional way by throwing their hats on to the stage. A special by-law of the Kiev Chief of Police obliged the theatre to return all headgear to its over-enthusiastic patrons.

In the capitals passionate debates had raged around 'The Crisis in the Theatre' and had generated much critical analysis before being satisfactorily resolved. Yevreinov's Theatre of Antiquity, presenting plays of other times and other lands as they would have been seen by their original audience, had come and gone. The classics had been stylised. In Kiev everything played alongside everything else: the old drama and the new, Shakespeare and Schnitzler, Rostand, Henri Bataille's urbane *La Femme nue*, and Ferenc Molnár's *The Devil*, featuring the Prince of Darkness himself. Stepan Kuznetsov, having chanced his arm in the Art Theatre, came back to Kiev and his native element of benefit performances and weekly first nights.

There was operetta in the Château de Fleurs municipal park, and musical evenings and symphony concerts in the hall of the Assembly of Merchants; there was the Viennese Operetta, and a Russian Operetta on Trukhanov Island. The much-loved traditional repertoire of the Kiev Opera House included *Boris Godunov* and *Faust*, *Aïda*, *Rigoletto*, *The Huguenots*, *The Death of Siegfried*, *Lohengrin*, and *The Valkyries*. Echoes of these immensely popular operas recur constantly in Bulgakov's writings, right through to the last works completed just before his death.

The rest of the country was in turmoil politically. The 1905 revolution boiled up and went down to defeat. Nothing seemed to have any impact on the theatre community in Kiev, with the exception of the member of the orchestra at the Kiev Opera who was wounded by a stray bullet during the assassination of the Prime Minister, Pyotr Stolypin. He subsequently demanded compensation from the government.

There were, certainly, disaffected elements from various parts of the political spectrum in Kiev in the first decade of the century. As yet there was little to suggest the impending storms and upheavals. Each season the theatre-going public of Kiev were treated to famous touring actors, including the Adelheim brothers and Meyerhold's company. Fyodor Shalyapin sang on tour, and Kiev thrilled to celebrated Italian opera singers like Titta Ruffo and Elvira de Hidalgo, Mattia Battistini and Giuseppe de Luca. Isadora Duncan danced for several seasons in succession, and there was always the Viennese Operetta, various visiting Italian tragic actors, and the best conductors of St Petersburg.

The pace of change gradually quickened. Like Paris at the beginning of the seventeenth century, Kiev grew 'stout and bonny, and spread out in all directions'. In the first ten years of the twentieth century the city's population doubled, new theatres opened, cinema theatres were built, and a huge new circus was erected in which, in the spring of 1912, Max Reinhardt presented *Oedipus Rex*. Tours by two 'theatres of short forms', *The Distorting Mirror* and Nikita Baliev's *La Chauve-souris*, resulted in the city acquiring first a Theatre of Farce, and then the Satiricon cabaret theatre.

In May 1912 the entire company of the Moscow Art Theatre arrived, bringing six productions with them. Vladimir Nemirovich-Danchenko informed *Kiev Thought's* reporter that they had brought their sets and properties in twenty-three goods trucks and railway carriages. The queue for tickets stretched the length of several streets, but the journalist reported the success of the tour with audiences as no more than middling.[4] One Kievan who managed to fight his way in to the first performance (of *The Cherry Orchard*) was astonished at their unresponsiveness, and wrote indignantly to Stanislavsky:

At first I thought the audience to have been intimidated by tales of the strict discipline imposed by your theatre, but then realised that this was not the case. Had you yourself seen all those unbuttoned waistcoats, sheep's eyes, and plump female bodies you would, I fear, have been unpleasantly surprised at the kind of audience to which you are feeding your pearls.[5]

Stanislavsky's feeding of pearls to the Kiev audience was happily not wholly profitless, since among the unbuttoned waistcoats and sheep's eyes were quite certainly also the bright eyes of Mikhail Bulgakov, medical student and future Author of the Moscow Art Theatre.

The Art Theatre's tour was duly recorded by the cinematograph, and the film shows it to have been a great occasion. We see the company sailing merrily down the Dnieper on a steamer. People are dancing, and Nemirovich-Danchenko walks in front of the camera twice and poses comically. Stanislavsky, a tall, prematurely white-haired dandy, skips down the ship's ladder with Moskvin close behind and then Artyom. We see Knipper-Chekhova's happy face in close-up, and a seething mass of delighted Kievans who cannot be made out individually.

Many aspects of Bulgakov's meteoric rise in the theatre remain obscure, but the starting point is quite clearly the provincial theatre of Kiev, the actors of the Solovtsov Theatre, and the Kiev Opera where he heard *Faust* and *Aïda* many, many times.

Shortly after Bulgakov's death Alexander Gdeshinsky, a friend of his years in

Kiev, recalled a letter of this period which Bulgakov sent him while away working as a doctor in the back of beyond: 'I picture you in my mind's eye passing along the front rows of the stalls in dinner jacket and starched shirt-front, treading on everyone's toes, while I . . .' Gdeshinsky goes on to explain that 'I was greatly taken at the time by Kosorotov's play *Dreams of Love*, *Autumn Violins*, and the like, and had written to Bulgakov to tell him as much.'[6]

This dinner-jacketed figure in his starched white shirt-front is the archetypal Kievan theatregoer, the 'denizen of the theatre's wings', and emblematic of the theatre milieu in which Bulgakov was raised. We know Bulgakov completely changed his appearance after the first nights of his own two plays in Moscow in 1926, emerging as the impeccably dressed playwright in starched shirt-front and bow-tie, and sporting a monocle. His resolutely old-fashioned appearance caused a certain amount of tittering even in literary and theatrical circles, which were on the whole sympathetically disposed towards him. The transformation had a logic of its own, however, as a sub-genre of 'theatre for itself'. Bulgakov was reconstituting a particular kind of theatrical behaviour in deference to the ethos of the Satiricon and the practical joking he had revelled in since youth.

We gain a good sense of the outward appearance of Bulgakov the theatre traditionalist from Sergey Yermolinsky, one of the people closest to him in the 1930s. Yermolinsky tells us that Bulgakov then liked nothing better than

to don a black suit, pin on the ribbon of a Tsarist order, and set off as 'one of the old school' to a performance, say, of the long-running, almost pre-revolutionary production of *Aïda* at the Bolshoy Theatre. Usually he went unaccompanied. He had a particular fondness for the creaking routine of this production with its by now very bored orchestra and assortment of third-rate actors, none of whom retained any spark of enthusiasm. There was a special poetry for him in this kind of ossified decrepitude.[7]

Some of Bulgakov's 'retrograde' remarks, recorded by Yermolinsky, are also of interest. 'It is so splendid when the curtain does not part, but rises, and has painted cupids hovering on it. Nowadays people are even known to present plays with no curtain at all.' Again, apropos of the design for Meyerhold's new theatre in which the audience was to 'merge' with a stage which would have neither curtain, wings, nor footlights:

'It's simply nauseating,' Bulgakov said, giving me a wink. 'The whole mystery of theatre is lost! . . . Personally, I would prefer to see orchestras re-introduced in theatres to play during the interval as they did in the old days in the provinces. There should be a conductor with a moustache wielding his baton and now and again looking over to the stalls to acknowledge acquaintances.'[8]

Nostalgia for the theatre of 'the good old days in the provinces' had a special place in Bulgakov's views on the theatre. All the clichés of the old romantic theatre, the backstage glamour, theatre as a magical room, the stage itself as a mysterious place of creation and transformation might have been living out their last days in the provinces, but they accorded with Bulgakov's most fundamental beliefs. His faith in the enduring nature of the organic, natural elements of life generated an image of the theatre of bygone years which closely coincided, in some detail at least, with his memories of the provincial theatre. Gaily costumed Valentine stepping up to the footlights in his time-hallowed way, the lights of the city, the warmth of his home and the 'Saardam tiles' beside which he read his favourite books, books which 'smelled of old-fashioned chocolate', the score of *Faust* lying open on the grand piano, all were attributes of a way of life, a routine, but equally of a culture at peace with itself. The old theatre as Bulgakov imagined it was part of his idea of comfortable everyday living, that norm of human life which, we are told in *The White Guard*, will unfailingly come into its own again 'because Faust, like the Shipwright of Saardam, is quite immortal' (p. 34).

It was a theme later to become tinged with tragedy, and to find itself waging an unequal struggle against other themes both in Bulgakov's writing and in his personal destiny. He was to pay dearly for his passion for *Faust* and Wagner, and for that monocle and starched shirt-front, and life would reveal abysses against which romantic stances of opposition would seem hopelessly inadequate. For all that, Bulgakov's theatrical conservatism and faith in the continuity of culture ('Oh, nexus of the passing years! Oh, currents of enlightenment!') were never to leave him. His pose as the non-Muscovite, the provincial with the temerity not to fit in to his own period in the theatre, was to be elevated into a statement of principle in *Black Snow*.

Chekhov had articulated the notion of the man whipped and beaten from childhood who has to spend the rest of his life wringing the slave out of himself drop by drop. It was much in evidence in Russian literature, but wholly inapplicable to the way Bulgakov's life developed. For him there was the large, happy family of a professor of Kiev Theological Academy, the family library, the family anniversaries, favourite catchphrases and quotations, and the staging of his own play, titled *On the Rails*, at the family's country dacha. He attended one of the best high schools in Russia, and this was followed by study at a no less renowned university. Life ran 'on the rails' of ideas which had stood the test of time and values which were unshakable.

For Bulgakov the theatre was an aspect of the world of his high-school days, a world which collapsed in ruins and ended among the shambles of the successive seizures of power in Kiev, with the descent on the City of Simon Petlyura's bands, and the corpses of those summarily hanged dangling from the lampposts.

Doctor Bulgakov, the admirer of Herbert Spencer's advocacy of gradual evolution, returned to his city at one of the most sordid moments of its history.

When the thunderbolts of Heaven (since there is a limit to even Heaven's patience) strike down every last contemporary writer and a new, genuine Leo Tolstoy appears in fifty years or so, a marvellous book will be written about the great battles in Kiev . . . For the present one can only say that the Kievans claim to have had eighteen seizures of power. Some of the cattle truck contingent make it twelve in their memoirs. I can state unequivocally, however, that there were fourteen, ten of which I experienced personally.

Bulgakov's newspaper article 'City of Kiev' was printed in the June 1923 issue of *On the Eve*, and written by an author who had already imagined, and largely managed to write, the book he forecast would appear only half a century later. The transition from one era to another is symbolised in the novel *The White Guard* by particular details of Kiev's cultural history which either supersede or conflict with each other. The City as it was, represented by the Opera House or the High School, continues to exist only in Bulgakov's imagination through his unexpected ironical similes and symbols. At one minute his Lieutenant Myshlaevsky is roaring like Radames in *Aïda*, the next we are told the turncoat Mikhail Shpolyansky resembles Yevgeny Onegin or Marcel in *The Huguenots*. In the midst of the panic and despair of the total defeat of his division Turbin notices a half-torn poster at the side entrance to the Opera House, proclaiming *Carmen. Carmen*. At the end of the novel all that had been written on the Saardam tiles, those domestic scrolls of history, has been wiped off, only one half-obliterated message by chance remaining: 'Lena . . . I've bought tickets for Aïd . . .' (p. 291).

The truncated title of Verdi's opera is all that remains from those enchanted times. No less charged are the details of a different culture which took root in the city in the course of those fourteen seizures of power. 'Operetta and farce were having a heyday,' one of Bulgakov's contemporaries recalls, 'with the aid of the notorious diva Victoria Kavetskaya and such *charmeurs* of the operetta as Ivan Grekov, and Dashkevich who staged *Silva*, the latest novelty from abroad, and the infamous *Pupsik*.'[9]

One further factor which had a crucial effect on the cultural and theatre life of Kiev was the wave of refugees from Petersburg and Moscow who came flooding into the city from the summer of 1918 onwards. Provincial Kiev suddenly became the swollen last refuge of the demi-monde of the twin capitals. In the course of a few months young doctor Bulgakov witnessed a quite incredible procession of famous names, trends, theatres, cabarets, and stars of the stage in wildly improbable combinations.

There came journalists from Moscow and Petersburg, corrupt, grasping and cowardly. Prostitutes. Respectable ladies from aristocratic families and their delicate daughters, pale depraved women from Petersburg with carmine-painted lips; secretaries of civil service departmental chiefs; languid young homosexuals. Princes and junk-dealers, poets and pawnbrokers, gendarmes and actresses from the Imperial theatres. Squeezing its way through the crack, this mass of people converged on the City. (p. 57)

Bulgakov's devastating hymn to the refugees is in stark contrast to Alexey Turbin's preceding dream. Turbin dreams of the City 'so familiar you could weep', and the City is quite separate from the fugitives, over them, and superior to them. It was not created by them, although it is they who are betraying it. The City seems to stand for a vanishing way of life and a vanishing kind of life. This is the meaning behind the opposition throughout the novel of lights and light to the fields, 'as dark as Egypt's night', which surround the City. 'Beautiful in the frost and mist-covered hills above the Dnieper, the City hummed and steamed like a many-layered honeycomb.' 'As far as the eye could see, like strings of precious stones, hung the rows of electric globes suspended high from the elegant curlicues of tall lamp-posts.' 'All night long the City shone, glittered and danced with light until morning, when the lights went out and the City cloaked itself once more in smoke and mist.' (pp. 55, 56) Bulgakov's hymn to Kiev is crowned with an opposition which is very important for him:

But the brightest light of all was the white cross held by the gigantic statue of St Vladimir atop Vladimir Hill. It could be seen from far, far away and often in summer, in thick black mist, amid the osier-beds and tortuous meanders of the age-old river, the boatmen would see it and by its light would steer their way to the City and its wharves. (p. 56)

People had lost their way. This was the underlying theme of Bulgakov's novel about 'the great battles in Kiev'. The City, still warm from sleep, was abandoned to the rapist Petlyura. A spectacle of culture become vacuous and degenerate accompanied its downfall, a culture truly feasting in time of plague.

Bulgakov was not the only writer to describe that feast. The following account is by Nadezhda Teffi, herself one of the refugees, whose short, sharp newspaper features were the delight of Bulgakov's generation.

Your first impression is that it must be a holiday. Your second is of a railway station, a terminus, just before the last bell rings for the train to depart.

There is too much anxiety and people are too grasping for this to be the bustle of cheerful holidaymakers. There is alarm in the air, and fear. Nobody is quite self-possessed enough, or able to see ahead to their next step. Everything is caught up hurriedly, as if people already sense that they will have to leave it all behind.[10]

Here is a further relevant observation by Teffi:

The streets teem with new arrivals. People are travelling in the most unexpected company: an actress from Rostov with a *Zemstvo* official from Moscow; a lady well known in public life with a balalaika player; the son of a rabbi with the governor of a province; an insignificant little cabaret actor with two elderly ladies-in-waiting. No doubt in just the same way the seven pairs of tame animals met up with the seven pairs of wild animals in Noah's Ark, sniffing each other over, and suffering from travel sickness.[11]

In the Noah's Ark that was Kiev at this time the most illustrious names of Petersburg and Moscow came together to a clashing of mordant journalistic pens. Theatre life took off in a blaze of cabarets, little theatres, and studios beyond number. Nikita Baliev's humorous theatre *Le Chauve-souris* was in town, as were the opera singer Leonid Sobinov and theatre critic Vladimir Doroshe-vich, the poet Osip Mandelshtam and chansonnier Alexander Vertinsky, the writer Arkady Averchenko and theatrical publisher Alexander Kugel, Pyotr Potyomkin the satirical poet and Nikolai Agnivtsev (another chansonnier), vampish film star Vera Kholodnaya and operatic bass Romuald Vasilevsky.

In that 'great and terrible year' dramatic performances and 'apotheoses' overflowed out of the theatres and on to the streets of Kiev. Mardzhanov staged *The Butting Comedians*, a street-theatre production written by Agnivtsev which to some extent anticipated Yevgeny Vakhtangov's *Princess Turandot*. There was a bizarre commingling of theatrical trends, genres and styles which eventually coagulated into the principal genre of the age which, following Mayakovsky, we may dub *Mistero Buffo*.

A further factor which was to prove no less fertile for Bulgakov was the detail of the local Ukrainian variant of the 'theatricalisation of life', from the farce of Skoropadsky's attempts at Ukrainianisation (he solemnly assumed the office of Hetman in a circus), to the spectacular transfiguration of the playwright and prose-writer Nikolai Vinnichenko into the nationalist government's prime minister. During the first night of his play *Falsehood* at the Solovtsov Theatre, Vinnichenko sat resplendent in his box side-by-side with his Secretary-General for Military Affairs, that long-standing champion of a Ukrainian national theatre who was so soon to find himself a role on the stage of history, Petlyura. Later during the march past in honour of Petlyura, Vinnichenko, playwright, prose-writer and, by now, former prime minister, drew frenzied applause from the townspeople as he bowed to all sides; 'Ovations the like of which,' as Nadezhda Teffi waspishly observed, 'he never received for his plays'.[12]

The succession of regimes was matched by a succession of celebrities, among them Ilya Ehrenburg, Victor Shklovsky, and that same young poet Valentin Stenich, who prompted Blok when he met him to write his article 'Russian Dandies', one of his most sorrowful meditations on the fate of culture.

Many people were tempted by role playing and tried on a variety of masks. The Russian dandy himself re-emerged as a grim-faced poet of the Cheka, complete with a black leather jacket and an enormous revolver at his hip. Ilya Ehrenburg, the habitué of the Rotonde in Paris, came to head the 'Section for the Aesthetic Education of Mentally Retarded Children'. Victor Shklovsky, later a celebrated philologist, managed to fit blistering journalistic attacks on the poet Valery Bryusov, 'a corpse who won't lie down', into the lulls between battles.

Shklovsky was sugaring the fuel tanks of the Hetman's military vehicles even as Armand Duclos, a clairvoyant boy from Odessa (of course) was reassuring frantic citizens from Petersburg that their furniture was 'quite intact'.[13]

'Great and terrible was the year of Our Lord 1918, of the Revolution the second.' (p. 9) For Kiev it was to be the year of the great exodus and, simultaneously, of the advent of new cultural forces. It saw the exodus of Russian dandyism, cabaret culture, the theatre of the refined non sequitur which aimed to evoke a wry expression and tight-lipped smile in place of laughter. They flowed away through the Kiev sluice along with the age which spawned them, while into the sluice new water poured, a counter current which grew in strength and volume and which was drawn not to foreign parts but to 'where Moscow had thrown her cap into the ring'.

There were many observers of the demise of the cabaret culture, already a much devalued version of what it had once been, by now 'baked with saccharine and margarine', as Osip Mandelshtam put it. Its decline was being separately monitored and interpreted by a great many people who would later become major Soviet theatre designers, directors, cinematographers, singers, compères, art historians, composers, critics, and journalists. Such politically diverse talents as Konstantin Mardzhanov and Konstantin Paustovsky were working in Kiev at this time; so were Les Kurbas and Reinhold Glière, Alexandra Exter and Boris Lavrenyov, Isaac Rabinovich and Alexander Tyshler, Anatoly Petritsky and Naum Shifrin. Alongside Grigory Kozintsev, Sergey Yutkevich and Alexey Kapler there were Mikhail Koltsov and Yefim Zozulya, Alexey Alexeev the stage compère and Mikhail Alexeev the future literary scholar and academician, Stefan Mokulsky and Valentin Asmus. For several months the two currents met head on, whirling and mixing together in an unprecedented carnival atmosphere which spilled over on to the pages of *The White Guard*.

Immediately before the coming of Petlyura the overblown city, already in winter's thrall, suddenly collapsed in on itself. Everything evaporated and dispersed as if it had never been. Clairvoyant Armand Duclos was killed during one of Petlyura's round-ups. Romuald Vasilevsky (ne-Bukva) and his wife Lyubov Belozerskaya, later to marry Bulgakov, headed for the open sea and Constantinople.

The hectic, overheated artistic life vanished and Kiev became empty, truly the abandoned nest of migrating birds. To the City's defence there would come, as Bulgakov puts it in his novel, 'fourteen officers, four cadets, one student and one actor from the Studio Theatre' (p. 130).

Like an exploding electric light bulb the vanishing elite culture flared brilliantly one last time before going out for ever, its end witnessed by a twenty-seven-year-old doctor who had opened a private practice on St Andrew's Hill.

It is generally accepted that the events of Bulgakov's two years in Kiev laid the foundations of his artistic beliefs and established the main direction of his writing. His first attempt to come to terms with these experiences is found in *The White Guard*. Bulgakov uses Kiev to provide a clearly defined setting for his image of Rusakov, the syphilitic poet who comes to Turbin's surgery; and for Shpolyansky, the chairman of the poetry association 'Magnetic Triolet' who also specialises in the 'sugaring' of military fuel tanks and is the author of that product of the burning of much midnight oil, *The Intuitive in Gogol*. The whole gamut of that theatrical intoxication, from *CRAP* to the *Lilac Negro*, is set not in bureaucratic Petersburg, to which the artists' confraternity was once a counterbalance, but in doomed, defenceless Kiev, and in this we may read Bulgakov's tacit condemnation of a culture which had degenerated and run to seed.

Plunged into the maelstrom of those fourteen coups, Bulgakov's reaction to the insanity and lawlessness was not that of many of his contemporaries, who flailed about desperately in search of a 'new outlook on life'. On the contrary, Bulgakov attempted to recall traditional, stable values, and to revive the austere, clear, authoritative tone of the greatest books in the world 'that smelled mysteriously of old chocolate with their Natasha Rostovs and their Captain's Daughters' (p. 11). As regards the theatrical sensibility of the future author of the play *Flight*, it was largely fed by memories of Kiev's year of blood when 'the twin capitals' most famous actors congregated there, and bent themselves into contortions to raise a laugh' on the boards of the doomed City's theatres (p. 57).

Bulgakov's Kievan conservatism in matters of the theatre had been subjected to unbelievable pressures but he was to deepen and develop it further. In that quest Bulgakov was to find a place for the aesthetics of the whole theatrical Satiricon which had erupted briefly in Kiev in 1918, although he would reinterpret them very much in his own ways. These range from ironic stylisation and the favoured device of a stage within a stage to the archaic acting of a *litsedei* with a mask, or the open revelation of how a production has been put together. The literary scholars have established other significant impulses, and we shall be looking at these later. Despite this, for Bulgakov the theatre was to remain a place full of the naive magic and mystery, colours and smells which were an inalienable part of the provincial theatre of his youth.

'The Written Word is Ineradicable'

Bulgakov's work in the theatre in Vladikavkaz gets short shrift in an autobiographical note he compiled in October 1924. He wrote, 'I was living in the remote provinces and staged three plays in the local theatre. On re-reading them in Moscow in 1923 I hastened to destroy them, and hope not a single copy survives.'[14] His hopes were confounded forty years later when meticulous historians ran to ground a prompter's copy of one of the plays, and succeeded in reconstructing at least in outline the general thrust of four more which he had not even included in his earlier tally. Tempted by the prospect of demonstrating a smooth evolution of Bulgakov's writing, dogged biographers and theatre historians have tried patiently, but in vain, to discern the contours of his future major works in the plays their author had destroyed.

We have to say that the project appears misconceived. Bulgakov's experiences in Vladikavkaz are of great interest, but in terms of the impact they made on Bulgakov himself. What we need to understand is what made him want to destroy those early plays, and why he subsequently referred to them with such marked distaste.

We need first to gain a general understanding of the cultural background and milieu in which the plays were written. One theme common both to *The White Guard* and to the impressions of Vladikavkaz which Bulgakov records in his *Notes on Shirt-Cuffs* is the sense of a complete overthrowing of old values.

A certain 'bold individual with an aquiline nose and an enormous revolver at his hip' turns up in the Cultural Subsection. He proclaims the following poetic manifesto:

> Drop that stuff about seagulls and peace.
> I'll sing you a song of the Secret Police.

Another no less resolute individual has views on the appropriate attitude towards the classics:

He stepped forward and declared:

'We got to follow a new parf, right? We've 'ad it up to 'ere, right, all that *Woe from Wit* and *Government Inspector* pornography, yer Gogols and yer Moguls, right? We're going to do our own plays.'

This said, he climbed into his motor car and was driven off. His face is etched for all time in my memory.

We know that it was in Vladikavkaz that Bulgakov took the momentous decision to abandon medicine for good and dedicate himself to literature. In Pavel Popov's record of what Bulgakov told him, 'literature' is to be understood to include various forms of work in the theatre. 'The fact of the matter is that my creative work divides abruptly into two categories: the genuine and the forced,' the beginning playwright informed his sister. 'I dream of Moscow and the best theatres in the country.'[5] The reality, however, was 'a cobbled square [. . .] on the left of which a squat, firmly rooted building rambled sideways. It was painted yellow, its walls were plastered with playbills, and on its pediment a faded red panel read "First Soviet Theatre".' (The quotation is from Yury Slyozkin's novel *Table Mountain*, which contains an abundance of detail about life in Vladikavkaz at this time.)[6]

This was the theatre where Bulgakov was employed, and on this cobbled square his earliest plays premièred in succession: on 16 June 1920, *Self-Defence*; in the autumn, *The Turbin Brothers*; and in January 1921, *The Communards of Paris*. We detect no hint of the exhilaration one might have anticipated. In February 1921 Bulgakov complained after the first performance of *The Turbin Brothers* to his brother:

You can't imagine how heavy my heart is at having the play produced in this God-forsaken hole [. . .] The audience yelled for the author to come out and clapped and clapped . . . I looked absently at the made up faces of the actors and the roaring auditorium and thought, 'I suppose really my dreams have come true . . . but in what a twisted way: instead of a theatre in Moscow, one in the provinces; instead of the drama about Alyosha Turbin I had been dreaming of, an immature, rushed piece of work.'[7]

He wrote in the same letter about *The Communards of Paris*, which had been entered for a competition in Moscow.

I am quite sure it won't get there by the deadline, and if it does I am quite sure that it will be a failure. That too is as much as I deserve. I wrote it in ten days. They're a motley crew,

'The Turbins', 'The Bridegrooms', and this play. I am doing everything in a rush, all of it. I am sick at heart.

But I am gritting my teeth and work night and day.

Clearly Bulgakov's attitude to his plays was a good deal less negative than he represented it in his 1924 autobiography. The fledgeling playwright is full of hope as he awaits the response of the Theatre Section of the People's Commissariat of Enlightenment, to which he had sent his plays for entry in a competition. 'For heaven's sake find out from the Theatre Section (9, Neglinnaya Street) where *Communards* has gone. Don't let anyone see it, as I wrote earlier, until I have sent the changes. Can the play really have been lost? That would be terrible.'[18]

These lines to his sister hardly suggest a man who regarded what he had written as having no importance, which makes us think that there is more to his later repudiation of the Vladikavkaz plays than a rapid rise in his expectations of his writing . . .

To date neither *The Communards of Paris* nor his 'drawing room comedy' *The Clay Bridegrooms* have been re-discovered. Neither do we have *The Turbin Brothers*, a play set in 1905 of which all that remains is the playbill.

Neither are we able to read *Self-Defence*, a 'one-act humoresque', whose characters included a flat-dweller called Ivanov and a residence committee chairman by the name of Commodorov, although it is not too difficult to imagine how it might have gone from the numerous journalistic sketches and short stories Bulgakov wrote on much the same theme.

By an irony of fate the only play to survive through all those eventful years is *The Sons of the Mullah*, a play Bulgakov in his short story 'Bohemians' predicted would win any competition open to 'the most imbecile, untalented, and brazen plays' created in the first years of the revolution.

The way in which the play came to be written is depicted not only in 'Bohemians' and *The Strange Adventures of a Doctor*, but also in *Notes on Shirt-Cuffs*, and there is every reason to suppose that it was a negative and hateful experience Bulgakov reacted against for a long time to come as he tried to find his own voice as a playwright. These were 'sorry words' Bulgakov could not expunge because they were deeply etched in the deepest and most private reaches of his intellectual experience.

There are in any case grounds for supposing that this clichéd and generally awful 'revolutionary play', which depicts the struggle of the Ingushi people against the Mullah Hozbat, is one of the sources for Bulgakov's later lampoon *The Crimson Island*. The latter with its red natives and white blackamoors surely drew in part on his own earlier 'native play', which he wrote in seven days. We now realise that Bulgakov's theatrical lampoon, written at the height of the frenzied critical campaign against *The Days of the Turbins*, was also in part a covert self-parody.

Even this is not the end of the matter. In order to gain a clearer understanding of what it was that Bulgakov learned in Vladikavkaz, let us look at his fictionalised account in *Notes on Shirt-Cuffs* of the writing of *The Sons of the Mullah*:

A hundred grand . . . I'd really made a hundred grand! . . .

The barrister's assistant, who was a native of the region, put me up to it. As I was sitting there with my head in my hands, brooding, he came over and said:

'I also have no money. The only way is you must write a play, about the life of the Ingushi, and revolutionary, and sell it . . .'

I looked at him stupidly and said, 'I couldn't write a play about the Ingushi, revolutionary or otherwise. I know nothing about their way of life. In fact I am incapable of writing anything at all. I am tired, and anyway I don't think I'm any good at writing.'

'You speak no good thing,' he replied, 'because of hunger. Be man. The way of life make no problem: I know the way of life very well. Together we write this play. We share the money.'

We can pass over the details of the joint labour, one author 'grinding his pen' while the other, snuggled up by the stove, would keep saying, 'I like create'. Let us proceed directly to the finale.

Seven days later a three-act play had been completed. Reading it over in my unheated room that night I am not ashamed to admit I started crying. In terms of sheer lack of talent this play was exceptional, indeed sensational. There was something brazen and moronic staring out from every line of this product of collective playwriting. I could hardly believe it. What hope could there be for the future, fool that I was, if this was how I wrote? The sheer disreputableness of it stared at me from the damp green walls and the terrible blackness of the windows. I started to tear the manuscript up, but stopped as the realisation dawned on me with wonderful clarity that when people say the written word is ineradicable they are absolutely right. You may tear it up, you may burn it, you may hide it away from the rest of the world, but there is no hiding it from yourself, ever! The deed was done, there was no going back. I was the creator of this uniquely remarkable piece of work, and that was that!

There we have it. With that 'wonderful clarity' Bulgakov discovered the law of literary gravity which today probably every literate Russian knows: 'Manuscripts do not burn'. In a flash that felicitous thought which slips from the lips of the Prince of Darkness in *The Master and Margarita*, the novel Bulgakov wrote at the going down of the sun, links up with his first book and establishes a unity and integrity in his fictional world which we shall more than once observe in the pages ahead.

The extraordinary, 'wonderful clarity' which visited the beginning playwright has an easily overlooked sting in its tail, and this is no less important for Bulgakov's attitude towards life and letters than the meaning most obviously encapsulated in his celebrated aphorism. It is not only that which is beautiful that does not burn, but everything created, or even thought, by a writer, including everything disreputable, false, cowardly, and untalented.

Students of Bulgakov are often perplexed by a particular crossed-out line in 'Funérailles', an unfinished poem in which he attempted in December 1930 to summarise his life as a writer:

> More than once with shameless falsehood
> My lips I have defiled . . .'[19]

We know of no facts which could remotely justify such self-condemnation, just as, in all likelihood, there are none relating to Pushkin, who wrote in his *Remembering*:

> I read with grief the pages of a life misspent,
> I shake and rage, and disavow them,
> and bitter is my plaint and bitter tears I shed,
> and yet cannot expunge the sorry lines there.

The sense of disreputableness staring in at the novice playwright from the terrible blackness of his windows is the first intimation of a sense of vocation, an understanding of the responsibility of literature and the theatre which, beginning with Pushkin and Gogol, is to be found running through all of Russian letters. Bulgakov became aware of this heritage in Vladikavkaz, and was later to defend it unswervingly and without compromise.

Fear of disgrace is a writer's guarantee of 'safe conduct' as he proceeds with his mission. As we embark on our account of Bulgakov's life in the theatre, let us remember not unkindly *The Sons of the Mullah* with which it began in 1921, a misbegotten attempt at collective playwriting, with a barrister's assistant and a famine for co-authors.

Prehistoric Times

In late September of that crucial year of 1921 Bulgakov travelled to Moscow. 'I arrived with neither money nor luggage . . . and stayed for good.'[20] Until he began work on his play *The White Guard* we find no attempt to continue the playwriting so vigorously embarked on in Vladikavkaz, except for an effort at a further drawing-room comedy, *White Clay*.

Bulgakov recalled his first years in Moscow in an unfinished novella of 1929, *To a Secret Friend*. Here he writes, 'Before you can write at night you need to find some means of existing during the day. I shan't bother writing to you of how I made ends meet during the period from 1921 to 1923, firstly because you would not believe me, and secondly because it is beside the point. By 1923, however, I had found a way of keeping body and soul together.'

This involved joining a peripatetic actors' collective which played the outskirts of the capital. 'The pay is 125 roubles per performance,' he wrote, 'which is desperately little. Of course, the performance will leave me no time to write. A vicious circle.' He even tried getting a job as a compère in a tiny theatre, perhaps remembering what he had seen of the cabarets in Kiev.

Having survived, and able now to keep body and soul together, Bulgakov set about realising the literary projects he had been nursing. For three years these were confined to prose. He set down his Kiev experiences in the form of a novel in *The White Guard*, and accompanied this by seeking to gain an understanding of the new post-revolutionary realities by writing novellas, short stories, and journalistic sketches.

It undoubtedly makes sense to analyse this great cycle of writing from an unorthodox angle: its treatment of the theatre. It is valuable to understand the place of the theatre in Bulgakov's prose at a time when the future playwright had as yet no direct contact with the theatre world.

The theatre crops up constantly in one form or another in Bulgakov's early prose. Chronicling life in Moscow in these 'prehistoric times', he never ceases looking attentively and with evident concern for signs of an unambiguous revival of the theatre; and from these he often forms his judgement of the processes taking place in the aftermath of the revolution deep down beneath the surface.

In his 1923 newspaper article 'Forty Times Forty' Bulgakov compares the images of two contrasting faces of the Bolshoy Theatre. The first:

[. . .] in the twilight a fiery inscription lights up on the building. The red flags sprout in their brackets. On the pediment there is a pale reverse shadow where the double-headed eagle has been cast down, and the dark mass of the green quadriga, its outline becoming indistinct in the twilight. The square is empty. Files of forbidding figures wearing sheepskin jackets over their greatcoats cordon it off. They are helmeted, the bayonets in their rifles fixed. Figures in black helmets wait on horseback in the sidestreets. Lights burn in the windows. In the Bolshoy the Congress is in progress.

Here, however, is a different aspect, with the light of a time long past breaking through:

[. . .] at seven-thirty, the hour beloved of the dramatic muse, we see no illuminated star, no flags, no long cordon of sentries by the square. The Bolshoy looms four-square as it has for decades, dim pools of yellow light between the pillars, welcoming theatre lights. Black figures stream towards the pillars. In a couple of hours inside the darkened auditorium heads will be ranged in the dress and upper circles. In the boxes parted hangings form rows of light triangles and diamonds against a dark background. There are waves of light on the material, and the triumph of Radames is like a breaker coming in on the blaring of the brass and the paeans of the choir. During the intervals with the house lights up the Theatre shines as gold and red and sumptuous as it did in days gone by.

That affecting phrase 'as it did in days gone by' does not indicate any sentimental weakening of the author's vision. The sharp-eyed Kievan theatregoer notices a glaring violation of the ritual proprieties of the interval. The wife of one of the New Economic Policy's nouveau riche NEPmen 'leaned over the barrier of her dress circle box . . . and cupping her hands excitedly bawled right across the stalls, "Dora! Come on up. We've got Mitya and Sonya here in our box!" '

But even a Dora can't discountenance Radames's admirer. The signs of theatrical revival are constantly measured against and derived from signs of economic and political recovery: 'Moscow is a cauldron in which a new life is being cooked up. This is a far from simple matter, with people having to be willing to allow themselves to be cooked. Among the Dunyas and the illiterate a new organisational skeleton is being born which reaches into every nook and cranny.'

The welcoming lights of the theatre, the triumph of Radames to the blaring of the brass and the paeans of the choir are signs of the return of normal life no less important than the militiaman who has appeared on the street corner with a baton in his hand, or the warden who fines people for nibbling sunflower seeds and spitting in public places. A train running to time and not festooned with bagmen is as unexpected as the 'unearthly sight' of a small boy swaying sedately from side to side, imperturbable in a fine, warm winter hat. From the satchel on his back the corner of a dog-eared book of maths problems protrudes. He is on his way to primary school.

The theatre's return to normality is part of a wider theme of a return to order, tradition, and historical propriety. The unearthly schoolboy is being followed down the road by an amazed crowd of men and women and a string of empty cabs. Immediately after this little vignette of the capital's new life Bulgakov gives us another, no less portentous. A section of his article 'The Capital in a Notebook' is titled 'The Man in Evening Dress', and brings us back full circle to the starting point of our account of Bulgakov's evolution as a man of the theatre.

Zimin's Opera House. *The Huguenots.* Just as they were in 1893, in 1903, in 1913. Still the same in 1923! It was exactly ten years ago, in 1913 that I last saw *The Huguenots*. At first sight you are knocked sideways. Two spiralling green pillars and an infinite number of light blue thighs in bodystocking. A tenor begins to sing and you immediately feel a desperate urge to head for the buffet. [. . .] This must be true beauty if these last turbulent years have been unable to drive *The Huguenots* from their theatre painted in toad-like hues.

Not only have they not managed to drive them out, but there's not a seat to be had in the stalls, the boxes, or the circles. All eyes are focused on the yellow boots of Marcel, and he, glancing wrathfully into the stalls, warns,

'Expect no mercy!

None shall you receive.'

Rumbling bass notes. The soloists turn blue beneath their grease paint as they cut their way through the thunderous roar of choir and brass combined. The curtain crawls down. Lights.

And in the interval the feeling that 'nothing has changed, everything is as it was five hundred years ago', is confirmed by the unexpected and defiant spectacle of a man in evening dress among the throng of dubious-looking jackets and old army tunics.

Credit where credit is due, everything was in place, from the dazzling starched shirt front, the trousers long ago ironed into submission, and the patent leather shoes to the dinner jacket itself!

It would have done the Comédie-Française proud, and indeed I thought at first its wearer might be a foreigner, they get up to all sorts of tricks. But no, he turned out to be one of ours.

More interesting even than the dinner jacket was its owner's face. An expression of wretched anxiety quite darkened the flabby Muscovite countenance. You could plainly read in his eyes, 'Yes, sir, it's a dinner jacket. Are you going to bite me? Nobody has any call to say anything to me about it. There is no decree against wearing dinner jackets.'

And in truth, nobody did lay a finger on the wearer of the dinner jacket. [. . .] There he stood steadfast as a rock, and the streams of jackets and tunics washed by him.

The man in evening dress evokes the same historical interest in Bulgakov as the boy with the dog-eared textbook on his way to school. The 'naked years' were coming to an end. The era of Lenin's New Economic Policy was beginning, which many cursed, and which caused the poet to lament the coming of an age not red but dyed a carroty henna colour. NEP engendered quite different feelings in the author of this article. 'Moscow seems to be buzzing again. [. . .] It's NEP. Don't use that damnable word! . . . It's life!'

That requires little commentary, unless to add that the revival of the theatre was the surest sign that life was buzzing and getting back on its feet.

The wind twists the cinema advertisements on banners across the streets. The fences have disappeared beneath a million colourful posters urging us to see new foreign films, proclaiming the 'Trial of the prostitute Zaborova for infecting a Red Army soldier with syphilis'. There are debates, lectures and concerts by the dozen; a 'literary tribunal' on Artsybashev's *Sanin*, on Kuprin's *The Pit*, on Saint Sergius of Radonezh. Wagner is to be performed without a conductor, the production of *The Earth Agog* is to use military searchlights and motor cars. [. . .] The kiosks are piled high with magazines and dozens of newspapers. [. . .] And sitting in my room on the fourth floor, a room piled high with old books, I dream of climbing the Sparrow Hills in the summer to the spot from which Napoleon looked down, and of seeing the golden domes of the forty times forty churches ablaze on seven hills, and Moscow, Mother Moscow, breathing, and sparkling in the sunlight.

From his Napoleonic vantage point Bulgakov also looked closely at what was being done in the theatres of Moscow, both newly revived and new. There are markers of his ideas about the theatre to be found in Bulgakov's early prose. These were becoming increasingly definite, and received a final polish in the theatre capital of Russia. Meyerhold's theatre was the focus at this time of the hopes and aspirations of the 'Left Front', and indeed more generally of the young revolutionary theatre. Bulgakov, the Art Theatre's future playwright, followed what was going on there particularly closely and jealously. Only recently a wholly unknown dramatist from Vladikavkaz bombarding Meyerhold's Theatre Section at the Commissariat of Enlightenment with his plays, Bulgakov now emerges as an irreconcilable critic of *The Magnificent Cuckold*. In his review of Meyerhold's celebrated production Bulgakov 'made it strange' by seeing it through the eyes of a factory-floor worker. A convinced archaist, he put his point of view forward with the obstinate determination of a man swimming against the tide, heading his piece with the defiantly sarcastic epigraph: 'Call me a vandal, I deserve it'.

Here is a draft of Bulgakov's parody, in which *The Magnificent Cuckold* gets much the same treatment as Tolstoy meted out in *Anna Karenina* to the opera he so detested.

In a peeling, derelict, draughty theatre a hole does service for a stage. There is of course no sign of any curtain. At the back two tomb-like windows punctuate a bare brick wall before which there stands a construction. By comparison with this Tatlin's structure must seem a model of clarity and simplicity. Cages, inclines, bars, doors and wheels. The wheels bear the inverted letters 'C R', and 'M L'. The stage joiners stroll back and forth quite at home, and for a long time it is unclear whether the action has begun.

Bulgakov the Vandal goes on to describe the performance itself, apparently overlooking the acting of Maria Babanova and Igor Ilyinsky:

The action: a woman gathers up her blue skirt. She slides off an incline on what men and women both sit on. The woman is cleaning the man's bottom with a clothes brush. The woman rides piggy-back on the man, modestly covering her legs with the skirt of her Meyerholdian 'prose-garb'.

'That's biomechanics,' a friend explained.

Biomechanics, my eye! The incompetence of these blue-clad biomechanics, who at an earlier stage in their careers were being taught to pronounce saccharine monologues, has to be seen to be believed. All this, be it noted, is going on not a stone's throw from the Nikitsky Circus where you can be amazed by the monster saltos of Lazarenko the Clown!

Somebody is hit boringly and repeatedly on the same part of the anatomy by a rotating door. The mood of the audience is what you might expect them to feel in a cemetery at the grave of a loved wife. Wheels rotate and creak.

'Not enjoying our performance, sir?' the usher enquired at the end of the first act with a smile so patronising I desperately wanted to biobox his ears for him.

Bulgakov contrasts the master clowning of Vitaly Lazarenko with the 'biomechanical dreariness' of the new theatre, and also the adulterated 'saccharine and margarine' slapstick of ex-Doctor Dapertutto to the genuine article as demonstrated by Grigory Yaron, the new star of the Moscow operetta: 'The moment he fell to his knees before Count Luxemburg, who had struck him on the shoulder, I understood the real meaning of that wretched word "biomechanics"; and when the whole operetta started revolving around Yaron like galloping fairground horses I understood the meaning of slapstick.

Grease paint! Mime! The tumult of an audience, the bursts of applause. You couldn't help but roar with laughter. It was wonderful beyond expressing.'

Ten years later, in the process of gaining an insight into the sources of Molière's theatre, Bulgakov would describe the entertainments of old Paris with the same relish. That tumult and applause are the accompaniments of real comedy in every age. Somehow Bulgakov manages to combine the direct, unmistakable democratic appeal of theatre with that predilection of his for good, old-fashioned opera and the starched white shirt front. The pleasure he took in brass wind instruments, Wagner and symphonic music are perfectly compatible with his enthusiasm for Yaron, operetta, and the monster saltos of Lazarenko. They were, indeed, to be the ingredients which would largely determine the nature and composition of Bulgakov's theatre.

The Pianist's Right and Left Hands

Bulgakov's ironical comments about his own journalistic output are well known. It was a means of survival, and it provided for his nocturnal, real work. Bulgakov initiates us into the secret of how to write for the newspapers in *To a Secret Friend*. He is reminiscing in 1929, his 'year of catastrophe', about how he became a playwright, and mentions in passing Novzikat, a well-known editor with a very individual understanding of journalism and writing in general. 'He supposed that a journalist could write anything that was required, and that it was all the same to the journalist what he wrote.' Before each revolutionary holiday Novzikat would say to his employee, 'I want you to knock out a good, heroic story for the holiday the day after tomorrow.' His employee 'would first blench, then blush, and be evidently discomfited'. The hero of Bulgakov's novella already has behind him the experience of the man who wrote *The Sons of the Mullah*, and tries to explain to Novzikat what later, in different words, Maxudov tries to explain in *Black Snow*, namely that 'Before you can knock out a good revolutionary story, you need to be a good revolutionary, and glad to see the dawning of the revolutionary holiday. If you are not, any story knocked out for financial or other gain is guaranteed to be a flop.'

Bulgakov describes the baleful influence of Novzikat's approach on his employee's writing.

The satirical sketches in the newspaper began to exact their price. My standards fell sharply. You were expected to be uproariously funny in every sketch, which made for vulgarity. In the end I said to hell with it all, and tried to write in whatever way would make Novzikat laugh. The sordid little sketches I perpetrated would make your hair stand on end, my friend.

His early prose, including what he wrote during his 'Novzikat period', goes a long way towards explaining where Bulgakov's precocious talent as a playwright disappeared to. It was not a question of the gift being lost, but of its being swallowed up for a few years by the sketches, good and bad, which endlessly poured from the pages of *The Hooter* and which Bulgakov put together in 'from eighteen to twenty-two minutes, including time taken whistling to myself and having a giggle with the typist'.[21]

What dominates in his feature articles on life in Moscow, in the extended satirical novellas which were collected as *The Diaboliad*, and finally in *The White Guard*, is the confident voice of the author-narrator. The overriding tone of the book derives from a forthright, judgemental authorial presence. The narrator's speech is refined, literary and austere, and contrasts sharply with the chaotic 'revolution in the printed word', that explosion of form which sought to articulate the period in linguistic forms appropriate to it. Bulgakov had the creators and craftsmen of a new literary language working alongside him. These were not authors but the 'literary processors' of an unruly new linguistic medium whose claim to be heard in art and society was legitimated only after the revolution. Despite his occasionally straying in their direction, and despite his evident assimilation and inward digesting of what may be called the style of the time, Bulgakov remained very much his own man. In his major prose he proceeds from the Russian classical tradition, with its retention of an implied author undiluted and uneroded, with a personal presence and a persuasive and committed voice, within the constraint of firmly literary language.

Exclusive to Bulgakov's newspaper contributions, good and bad, in *The Hooter* is his use of an impersonal, anonymous point of view. He is a mirror reflecting the life and language of new Russia as it happens. While agreeing that in his newspaper work Bulgakov was 'making marginal use' of what he had discovered in his major prose, it seems a mistake to view all his short-form journalism as no more than literary spin-offs. His years of hard labour on the newspaper had a hidden agenda which became apparent when at a crucial moment in his literary career Bulgakov began work not on a second novel, but on a play. The stage required of the prose writer the ability to objectify life without recourse to an authorial voice or directly expressed judgement. At this moment he really did need the reserves of dramatic language which had become second nature to him during his years of toiling on the newspaper.

In 1926 Bulgakov was to tell Pavel Popov that prose and playwriting were for him what the left and right hands were to a pianist. Developing this simile, we can imagine that while the right hand was playing the main theme, the left was not idle. To some extent the corpus of Bulgakov's journalistic pieces can be seen as a supporting 'theatrical accompaniment' to his major prose in the days before his involvement with the Moscow Art Theatre.

The first thing that strikes us is that many of the satirical pieces are virtually dramatic sketches, and sometimes one-act playlets. With the authorial presence confined to functional 'stage directions' and explanations, the fantastic, splintered life of the period is moulded into a broad spectrum of living voices and characters. Bulgakov often goes so far as to supply generic subtitles such as 'A Scene', 'An Episode', 'A One-Act Play', 'An Agonising Death from Thirst in One Act and Eight Scenes', 'The Government Inspector, with the Sacking of the Same (A New Production)', 'A Scene from Life', 'A Play to Substitute for *The Empress's Plot*', 'The scene takes place at dead of night on Rzhev II Station' and so on.

This of course is just our first and most obvious foray into the theatricality of the 'minor prose'. A second and more substantial aspect is that more often than not the newsworthy action develops within a recognisably dramatic setting. As in Gogol, reality is first dramatised, that is, it is transformed in accordance with the laws of the theatre. The author places that 'magical little room' between himself and the life he is depicting, a stage over whose boards he makes his innumerable heroes strut. The majority of the sketches are constructed in accordance with the *étude* method familiar to theatre directors. Real life presents a topic which, in the form of a letter from a 'worker correspondent' provides the epigraph. On this topic the author, Al Wright, G. P. Ukhov, Emma B., Mikhail M. or Anon, aka Mikhail Bulgakov, presents the reader with a theatrical sketch constructed in accordance with the rules of minor dramatic forms.

Here is a typical demonstration of Bulgakov's theatrical way of thinking, a satire titled 'The Dead Arise'. The topic is stated in a letter from Worker Correspondent No. 2121: 'The infant daughter of boilermaker Severnykh of Section 2 of the Torsion Assembly Line died. The Medical Officer insisted the child should be brought round to him to have its death certified.' Immediately after thus stating the theme Bulgakov provides a brief stage direction: 'A surgery. A Medical Officer is seeing patients.' He volunteers no further details. Life reveals itself to us at its own pace. The dialogue abounds with twists and surprises of a kind later found in Bulgakov's plays *Madame Zoyka* and *Ivan Vasilievich*.

'I have to have it confirmed, so I can bury her.'

'Ah, certified I expect you mean . . . You'd better bring her in then.'

'But Fyodor Naumovich, she's dead, poor little lamb. She's just lying there. You're alive.'

'Indeed I am alive, but there's only one of me, whereas there's piles of you dead people.'

And we're off, racing ahead with Bulgakov's dramatic imagination heaping up scene after scene. The orderly soon has a queue of people carrying coffins and waiting for him to confirm, or rather certify, the deaths. The climax comes when a breathless old man arrives. He has decided to obtain his death certificate in advance because, 'You see, Fyodor Naumovich, I'm on my own. I haven't got anyone to carry me along to the surgery. The neighbours said, "Pafnutich," they said, "you'd better get yourself down there and get registered with Fyodor Naumovich. We haven't got time tomorrow to sort you out, and you certainly won't last more than another day."'

Those half-hours he spent on producing sketches saw Bulgakov sharpen up his command of dialogue to pinpoint accuracy. Many tricks of the theatre, techniques of plot construction, and even individual stage directions which we recognise from the later plays, were first tried out in that endless newspaper output of minor prose which sapped the novelist's imagination.

Here, by way of example from 'In the Accountant's Clutches', is the description of one of his characters from that assembly of the just, the Area Communist Party Committee:

Guzenko, a member of the Area Committee. The usual attributes: eyes expressive of strong sympathies for the Communist Party; on his left breast, two portraits, on the right the badges of the Society for Voluntary Aid to the Soviet Chemical Industry and ditto the Soviet Navy. In his pocket he carries a copy of *The Children's Friend*.

And who can doubt that the sketch 'Mademoiselle Jeanne' was to prove fruitful. The topic was again suggested by a worker correspondent: 'We had a performance in our club by a fortune-teller and lady hypnotist called Jeanne. She could tell what other people were thinking, and earned 150 roubles in one evening.' The satire this suggested to Bulgakov undoubtedly looks forward to his magnificent fantasy, the black magic sequence at the Variety Theatre in *The Master and Margarita*

The 'stage directions' of this 1925 sketch are worth looking at closely:

A hush falls on the audience. A lady with restive, heavily made-up eyes and wearing a mauve dress and red stockings appears on stage. A boisterous, moth-eaten looking individual in striped pants and with a chrysanthemum in his jacket buttonhole follows her in. The latter glances gimlet-eyed to left and right, before bending over to whisper in the lady's ear, 'Front row, bald man with a cotton collar. An assistant deputy stationmaster. Proposed recently. Turned down. Girl called Nyurochka.'

There follows a telepathy session complete with fainting fits, people carried from the auditorium, and all manner of other thoroughly theatrical trappings.

Bulgakov's imagination was being fed by an unheard-of diversity of real-life material, both infinitely sad and blindingly vivid which literally leapt off the page at him from all these letters, complaints and documentary materials sent in by worker correspondents via the railway network spanning the Republic. A stream of satires fantastically rich in local colour and subject matter flowed from his pen, paving the way for his later major works and building up a reservoir of vivid detail for them. In one sketch, instead of helping his patients a Medical Officer gleefully informs them they are suffering from galloping consumption or a hole in the heart. In another, books published by the People's Commissariat for Land are being sold by weight. Someone asks to have a stone of World History wrapped 'to try it out'. In one sketch a jubilant crowd ties up the blameless Pyotr Wrangel because he happens to bear the same name as the White General and drags him off to the bridewell at some remote Russian halt. (Compare the rounding up at the end of *The Master and Margarita* of black cats and anybody whose surname begins with a 'W'.) In another sketch, 'The Main Committee for Political Services', a school is relocated in a church, and the teachers find themselves holding forth in mystical counterpoint to a church service. In one story rats chatter and dogs talk, in another Ivan the bathhouse attendant is obliged to work in the women's section ('Ivan the Bathhouse Girl'). Everyone gets so drunk in one tale that a locomotive is itself affected, and the very moon in the sky seems 'to be winking woozily'. In another an individual is working simultaneously in a canteen and a library ('The Libruffet Assistant') and greets his customers with a choice: 'This way, please. Will this table suit? Let me just give it a wipe. And what would you like, a nice beer or a nice book?'

From time to time among all the verbiage we catch a gleam of the gold of phrases, lines, and details familiar from later works: 'They'll weep roomfuls of tears, and I'm the one'll have to mop it all up!' an old woman laments.

We come across unexpected parallels and anticipations. In 'The Guard and the Member of the Royal Family' Khvostikov, a pathetic little train guard, dreams he meets the Tsar himself and the latter questions his former loyal subject with great interest about everything that is going on in Rus. Is everything in order? 'How is the Mutual Aid Society getting along?' How are the 'general assemblies' (i.e. the Soviets)?

'Everything is satisfactory,' Khvostikov reports.

'You haven't joined the Party yet?' the Tsar asks.

'Certainly not, your Majesty.'

'But you are a bit of a Communist sympathiser, eh?' the Tsar enquires, with a smile which sends a chill down Khvostikov's spine.

The Tsar then commands that ropes should be taken from the luggage and Khvostikov hanged from the brakes.

Khvostikov's dream, written on the level of *Hooter* prose, has resonances with another imagined scene at a railway station, the scene in *Flight* where the hapless stationmaster, holding a child in his arms, is trying to explain something to General Khludov and receives the curt response, 'Hang him from the signal-gantry' (p. 167).

In the minor prose a way of looking at the world fostered in Bulgakov by the traditions of Gogol and Saltykov-Shchedrin received a great deal of raw material to reinforce it. Bulgakov was later to define himself as a 'mystical' writer, and there is surely considerable significance in the way themes and motifs from classical Russian literature are brought together here with burning topical issues. 'Wondrous the Dnieper when the weather is settled, but more wondrous still the Moscow Regional Insurance Office of the B-Baltic Railways.' Thus Gogol. No less obvious are borrowings from Saltykov-Shchedrin: 'Enlightenment is to be introduced, but as far as possible without bloodshed . . .'

Reading the hundreds of pages of these sketch fragments as a single text full of manifest theatricality and generic variety tells us a great deal about Bulgakov, the future prose writer and dramatist. Most importantly it pinpoints the source of that deep, ineradicable melancholy without which none of Bulgakov's major works is imaginable. In the minor prose the soil on which that melancholy grew is documented and inescapable. *The Hooter* with its floods of data from every quarter, *The Hooter* with its sense of the endless *versts* of Russia, of railway tracks and halts and passing places imparted a painfully acute awareness of the coming of a new Russia and the departing of old Russia; a sense of journeying, which had been so important for Gogol, and which in many ways was to prove central to Bulgakov's writing.

In January 1925 the author of *The White Guard* began a new life. The 'theatre' hand which had been a secondary accompaniment to the melody of his prose began to play the main theme. Breaks occur in Bulgakov's journalistic work with increasing frequency, sometimes lasting for three to four months at a time, until on 3 August 1926 the last sketch Bulgakov was ever to write for *The Hooter* appeared. It was called 'The Wheel of Fortune', and two months and two days later, on 5 October 1926, the wheel of fortune was indeed to turn for Bulgakov's writing career when he became an Author of the Moscow Art Theatre. No longer would he dream at night of drunken locomotives and libruffet assistants, talking dogs and telepathists, sadistic medical orderlies and bathhouse attendants from Rzhev II Railway Station. Now his dreams were to be the dreams of theatre.

Strange Liaisons

Tolstoy had a favourite device in his narration of epic which allowed him simultaneously to narrate and develop different elements of the plot, making them cross over each other in unexpected juxtaposition. 'Just at the moment when everyone was dancing at the Rostovs', Count Bezukhov suffered what was now his sixth stroke.'

'Just at the moment when . . .' It is time for us to introduce the second hero of our book, the Moscow Art Theatre, and to try to collate two synchronous verticals, the biographies of a Theatre and its Author.

The story begins in October 1917, with days from which we must begin the account of a new life both for local government employee Doctor Bulgakov, and for a great Russian theatre.

Just at the moment when, from late September 1917 until February 1918, Bulgakov was working as a doctor in Vyazma Municipal Hospital, only to be sucked in February 1918 into the vortex of the coups in Kiev for a year and a half, a difficult process was under way at the Moscow Art Theatre as it sought to change its way of thinking and functioning, and its everyday routine. On 26 October 1917, the day after the Bolshevik coup, the Theatre was obliged 'as a consequence of political events' to cease its performances. 'It does not occur to people to talk about performances and rehearsals,' Vasily Luzhsky noted in his diary. 'Everybody is talking about what they have experienced and what it was like.'[22] There is an entry by Vladimir Nemirovich-Danchenko on 3 November in the Duty Roster for members of the theatre company: '12 noon. The corner of Great Nikitsky Street and Skaryatinsky Lane is the epicentre. Shooting along Great Nikitsky, Little Nikitsky, and Skaryatinsky. Kudrinsky Square under heavy artillery bombardment. All safe and well.' Olga Knipper-Chekhova entered, 'I'm alive. Came in 3 November.'[23]

Those days saw the Moscow Art Theatre riven with internal dissension. Some saw in the revolutionary events no more than barbarism, the destruction of monuments, antiquities, and Russian culture, and advocated 'protesting in the strongest possible terms'. Others proposed 'the complete repudiation by all active in the arts of any involvement in politics'. The meeting of members of the theatre company which discussed this issue inclined to Stanislavsky's view that 'The Art Theatre is unswerving in its efforts to present performances for the broadest circles of the democratic public without regard to political coups, whatever their complexion.' It was, however, impossible to have no regard to this one.

The first month after the revolution passed, and the doors of the theatres reopened. Once more Chekhov, Ostrovsky, Griboedov, Maeterlinck's *The Bluebird*, and Dostoevsky's *The Village of Stepanchikovo* were acted on the stage of the Art Theatre. The Theatre continued its performances, believing it was essential to maintain the cultural tradition unbroken. A few years later in a *One-Day Newspaper of the Academic Theatres Committee*, Stanislavsky wrote:

The theatre is not a luxury in the life of the people, but part of its bread and butter. It is not something one can quite well do without, but something incontestably necessary for a great people ... You can't postpone the art of the theatre for a while, padlock its workshop, and suspend its animation for a time. Art cannot go to sleep and then, when it suits us, wake up again. It can only go to sleep for ever, by dying. Suspend it, and it will perish ... returning to life only centuries later, if then. The death of art would be a national catastrophe.[24]

He might have written the same in 1917.

Life changed for Stanislavsky. Just at the moment when the refugees were sitting in the cafés of Kiev and wine from a German barter agreement was flowing like water; when dozens of little cabarets and little theatres were opening their doors there for the art of old Russia to live out its last days in them; just at that precise moment War Communism's regime of extreme austerity was being introduced in Moscow. Stanislavsky's house on Carriage Row was already changed out of all recognition. Some of the rooms were now rented out, and some had been adapted as rehearsal rooms for the actors of the Art Theatre's Studio workshops by whom Stanislavsky set great store. The Art Theatre itself presented no new productions, lending its stage to Studio performances. Its twentieth anniversary was marked quietly and without fuss in the autumn of 1918, Stanislavsky and Nemirovich-Danchenko each being presented with the precious gift of a loaf of white bread. Stanislavsky wrote to his old friend Lyubov Gurevich in April 1919, 'My life has changed completely. I have become a proletarian and am not so far in dire straits only because I engage in hack work (that is, I act on the side) almost every day when I am not occupied with the Theatre.'[25] That expression 'hack work', which comes so unexpectedly from Stanislavsky, soon became a familiar term in the actor's vocabulary, and was to become loathed by Stanislavsky virtually above all else.

On 31 December 1917 Doctor Mikhail Bulgakov wrote to his sister:

On recent trips to Moscow and Saratov I have had the misfortune to witness things the like of which I hope never to see again. I have seen mobs breaking train windows; [. . .] houses in Moscow wrecked and burned out; hungry queues at the shops; army officers hounded and pitiable. I read the flysheets of newspapers where they write of almost nothing but the shedding of blood: in the south, in the west, in the east. It will shortly be the New Year.[26]

On that same New Year's Eve, in similar mood, a general meeting of the Art Theatre company was held to discuss a plan of reorganisation. Stanislavsky unveiled what for several years was to become an *idée fixe* for the future of the Moscow Art Academic Theatre, right up until their departure for the tour of the United States in 1922. He proposed that all the Theatre's productions should first be staged in the Studios on a workshop basis and that the best results should then transfer to the Principal Stage. In effect, the Art Theatre as previously constituted would cease to exist. This startling idea came from Stanislavsky's sense of a need for renewal which was almost obsessive at this time. Just how unexpected the suggestion was we can tell from Vladimir Gribunin's reaction in a letter to Nemirovich-Danchenko, who also found the idea unacceptable. Gribunin describes the proposal of 'our Bolshevik K.S.' as 'destructive and devastating'.[27]

Stanislavsky was motivated not by Bolshevism, but simply by the fact that he could see no other way for the theatre he had created to grow, progress artistically, and retain its place as a focus and protector of art in the new Russia.

In May 1918 Stanislavsky again put to the Theatre a plan for radically reorganising its artistic practice.

The most outstanding work of each of the Studios would be thoroughly revised before being brought to the Moscow Art Theatre's Principal Stage, which would be the pride of each of the companies. [. . .] This would not be the Art Theatre we know at present, let alone the old Art Theatre. It would be different, better, indeed the best we can create out of our present strengths. It would be a Pantheon of Russian art against which today's Moscow Art Theatre with its *Autumn Violins* and its *In the Claws of Life* would appear banal and vulgar.[28]

'Our Bolshevik K.S.' was even prepared to become the dictator following an artistic coup in the Theatre, but was spared the necessity of that, or indeed of becoming the director of a Pantheon of Art, because things in general were moving in a different direction. The Studios on which Stanislavsky laid such great hopes were straining for independence and had no time for his Pantheon. Accustomed to thinking about the life of their Theatre a season at a time, Stanislavsky and Nemirovich-Danchenko found themselves unable to get back to their old rhythm. Not a single new play or playwright was to break through into the Art Theatre. The old plays continued to be performed, along with productions which came up through the Studios. In October 1919 the Art Theatre found itself split in two when a group led by the actor Vasily Kachalov, which was on a summer tour of the Ukraine, found itself cut off from Moscow by Denikin's troops. The Theatre faced catastrophe that autumn. Once again Stanislavsky addressed the company, and once again he tried to persuade them that a Pantheon of the Theatre was the only way out.

Is the Theatre aware that I can never abandon this dream, because I surely know that without it the Art Theatre is destined to fall apart in the very near future. The Pantheon is a means of preserving at least something of what we have achieved over the course of a lifetime. Is the Theatre aware that we have no strength, and can see no point, in contributing further to what is occurring in the Theatre at the present time, particularly knowing that we have not that much longer to live? The best thing to do with the present Theatre would be to close it down with its reputation intact. Is the Theatre aware that without an ideal and an aim I have neither the physical nor the moral strength to continue to work . . .?[29]

In November 1919 in Vladikavkaz, now re-named Grozny, Bulgakov published 'Prospects for the Future', a first article which was to prove prophetic in many ways. The revolution is portrayed as a national catastrophe whose consequences will be felt for a century to come. At this fateful moment Bulgakov abandoned 'the vocation of Physician of Note'. He was conceiving his first plays, and writing them. He was gradually developing the outline of a major novel about 'Russia's strife' in his mind.

In those same months in Chamberlain Street in Moscow the Art Theatre was hectically preparing *Cain*, its first new production since the revolution. Stanislavsky had planned his production of Byron's mysterium on the grand scale, but it was to fold in April after only eight performances.

In autumn 1920 Vsevolod Meyerhold became head of the Theatre Section at the People's Commissariat of Enlightenment, his appointment heralding a period of storm and stress during which furious attacks were mounted against the traditional 'academic' theatres, which were declared counter-revolutionary. A nucleus of 'Left' critics formed, the 'furious zealots' who over the next decade were to do their utmost to destroy the Art Theatre and its new playwrights.

The trouble was that the newly designated Moscow Art Academic Theatre still had not a single play about post-revolutionary life in its repertoire which it could counterpose to what Nemirovich-Danchenko described as 'this rabid onslaught'. The Theatre itself was divided, and four years after the revolution Gogol's *Government Inspector* was, in Nemirovich-Danchenko's words, the only trump in its hand. This had been revived in spring 1921 with Mikhail Chekhov in the role of Khlestakov.

In a letter to Kachalov, who was still stuck in the Ukraine, Nemirovich-Danchenko directly raised the question of the Art Theatre's continued existence.

The Art Theatre is finished unless we merge with you. Some new theatre may perhaps arise in its place, but the Art Theatre we know will sink beneath the waters of Lethe. [. . .] Some urged that we should *demand* your return. Who knows what that would have led to. The view currently favoured is that we should *propose* that you return. How about it?

Without you the Theatre will most probably go under; with you it might, perhaps, regain its old sparkle. Let each consult his conscience.[30]

. . . At approximately this moment Bulgakov was taking the most important decision in his life, leaving Grozny for Moscow, there to 'stay for good'.

Nemirovich-Danchenko made no attempt to conceal from Kachalov the many difficulties and disruptions that life in the aftermath of the revolution entailed. He warned him that payment of regular salaries had been discontinued; the housing crisis had reached new extremes, and Stanislavsky had been evicted from Carriage Row. Only after a great deal of trouble had a house been obtained for him in Leontiev Lane. Eight cubic metres of firewood cost around 120,000 roubles, and were expected to cost 150,000 by the autumn. Many of the actors were taking up residence in the Theatre complete with their children in order to keep warm. There were no new textiles to be had and everyone was looking terribly shabby. 'For better or worse, they (i.e. you) will have to share with us the burdens, the cares, the suffering – and the pride in our victories.'[31] But then Nemirovich-Danchenko goes on to articulate beautifully what it is that makes up for all the everyday inconveniences, the cold and hunger.

There are times when we long terribly for the trappings of an orderly life, and would willingly give up everything just to have things properly organised. Life is so dingy that you can fall into a torpor which it is difficult to fight against. Then at other times we have a feeling of pride and are at peace with our conscience in a way we never knew before. To be truthful, life is getting no better, rather the contrary; but we have that feeling more and more often, and more and more strongly, both because so many young people are coming to the Theatre, and because the atmosphere has so changed for the better. The inanity of so much theatre criticism has vanished. Something demeaning which used to choke the artistic atmosphere has been blown away. You find your intellect constantly pushing forward to a realm where everything must be straightforward, earnest, and noble.[32]

'An immense restructuring of basic ideals is under way throughout the world', a restructuring in which the Theatre is trying to find its place.

In all these past decades we have never faced such a sharp, visible divide between the spiritual ideals of the Russian people and material reality. It is a cruel divide, and one that makes itself felt at every step during the day. This makes these abrupt changes of mood so painful, from the contemplation at one moment of what is most precious and heartening, to having to cope at the next with things which are immensely irritating, annoying and petty, and which make you petty-minded yourself.[33]

In late September 1921 Bulgakov arrived in Moscow. Faced with choosing between the spiritual and the material, he, like the Art Theatre, chose the former. When salaries ceased to be paid to employees of the Art Theatre, they ceased also to be paid to Bulgakov, a civil servant in the Literary Section of the Commissariat of Enlightenment. With the coming of the New Economic Policy major cuts in government spending were the order of the day. Like the hero of his *Diaboliad* Bulgakov received his last salary in the form of a box of matches.

In the autumn of 1921 Russia was suffering the consequences of unusually severe drought, 'a famine and the panic it caused,' as Gorky wrote to Nemirovich-Danchenko.[34] The situation of the Art Theatre became critical, and Nemirovich asked Gorky to intercede with the Government for financial assistance to enable it to 'escape from the noose around its neck'. On the very day that Bulgakov was arriving in Moscow for good, Gorky replied. 'It would be a disgrace indeed if this fine torch of the art of Russia were to go out, choked by a want of forethought on the part of some and by culpable stupidity on the part of others.'[35]

The autumn and winter of 1921 when Bulgakov took up residence in Moscow were a great time for the theatre. Pavel Markov writes that 'the cultural legacy of the immediate pre-revolutionary period was tentatively coming to fruition in a very promising way. That winter the arts were as much at odds with themselves and as disturbing as the unstable and rapidly changing society around them. This was art at a time of major change, an art which was taking stock even as it dreamed of the future.'[36]

In November 1921 the Art Theatre's Third Studio opened on the Arbat. Five years later Bulgakov's *Madame Zoyka* would be staged there. In the First Studio, on which Stanislavsky and Nemirovich had laid such hopes that they had even wanted it to take over the main Theatre lock, stock and barrel, there was disorder and disputation. That month a meeting of the Board of the First Studio was held to decide whether to unite with the main Theatre. In an impassioned speech Yevgeny Vakhtangov urged that the best thing Stanislavsky could do for Russian art would be to leave the Art Theatre behind him, as Tolstoy had abandoned Yasnaya Polyana. He should turn his back on it and 'on a new site on the open road' start building a completely new collective based on the First Studio. The meeting continued with outbursts of hysteria through the night, but without reaching any conclusions. The next day a member of the Studio company related all this back to Stanislavsky and 'K.S. wept'.[37]

His vision of a Pantheon of Russian art was in ruins. The Studios, his babies, had grown up and wanted their independence, regardless of what their parents might think. Within the walls of their institution Stanislavsky and Nemirovich-Danchenko stalwartly maintained their ethos of discipline, dignity, and honourable conduct. Stanislavsky continued to give his attention to every last detail, and to find fault at the least suggestion of negligence or 'hack work'. Even during the revolutionary days of October 1917, when the actors were walking on shattered plaster and window glass, Stanislavsky had given instructions for the pavement outside the theatre to be sprinkled with sand and asked for the thickest floor mats which could be found to be laid down in order to minimise the dirt. In 1920 he went out to the audience before the beginning of the second act of *Uncle Vanya* in full make-up and costumed as Astrov to explain to them how important silence was for the success of the performance and how distracting the cracking of nuts was during the play. After the 'naked years' were over and the New Economic Policy arrived, with its relentless appetite for the high life and the opening of restaurants and bars by the hundred, Stanislavsky and Nemirovich continued their unflagging efforts to maintain the excellence of their Theatre and the honourable status of its actors. As 1921 drew to its close Nemirovich-Danchenko gave the following strict warning to his company:

Actors of our Theatre and Studios will undoubtedly be receiving proposals from various restaurants and other organisers of New Year parties to perform 'turns' for the benefit of dining speculators and new Soviet bourgeois. They will offer very good money, as well they might. It's very good for their clients' ego: 'You will be entertained at dinner by actors of the Moscow Art Academic Theatre or its Studios.' Money is no problem: what are a few millions nowadays? Alas, I cannot be sure that it is clear to everyone just how humiliating and disgraceful such performances would be.

I do not know whether the Directors of this Theatre are within their rights in banning such engagements, but if anyone considers that we are not I will beg him on bended knee not to tarnish the Art Theatre's reputation in this manner. And I give notice that there will be no quarter for anyone who does.[38]

This safeguarded the Theatre's reputation, but what was to be done for its artistic development was less clear. Kachalov's company returned to Moscow in May 1922. In July the Art Theatre ended the season with a production created by the Music Studio of Offenbach's *La Péricole* and, just as the theatre scene in Moscow was beginning to flourish and bear fruit, started preparing for its departure for an extended foreign tour, rehearsing Alexey Tolstoy's *Tsar Fyodor*, with which it had opened its doors in 1898, and the plays of Chekhov. New casts were found for old productions.

In the autumn of 1922, the Soviet Government agreed to send off the 'First Group of the Moscow Art Theatre', headed by Stanislavsky, on a tour of Europe and America which was to last for two years. In effect they left without having resolved the major problem of whether they could exist in Moscow as a Soviet theatre.[39] They left Studio productions behind them on the Art Theatre stage, and sailed the ocean not so much in search of success and the high life as to discover once and for all whether the Theatre could survive in the changed historical circumstances. 'I am leaving with the firm intention of returning to Moscow either "with a trophy, or as a trophy",' K.S. wrote on the eve of their departure. 'Either we shall succeed in pulling the First Group together and be able to go on, or we shall fail, in which case it will be time to call it a day.'[40]

For all its tremendous external success the Art Theatre's foreign tour did little to resolve the problem of the Theatre's future. More than that, it was while they were abroad that Stanislavsky's last illusions were dissipated, and he recognised how essential it was to institute a radical reconstruction of the whole enterprise. The new success of such old chestnuts as *Tsar Fyodor*, *The Brothers Karamazov*, and even of Chekhov, only upset and wearied Stanislavsky. He wrote from his flower-filled luxury suite in a Berlin Hotel to Nemirovich-Danchenko,

It would be absurd to be proud and happy that *Fyodor* and Chekhov are going down well. Acting the scene where Vershinin takes his farewell of Masha in *Three Sisters* my mind is confused. After what we have been through it is quite impossible to be moved that an officer is having to leave and his lady is having to stay behind. I am not enjoying Chekhov. On the contrary, I would prefer not to be acting in his plays . . . It is impossible to carry on in the same old way, but we simply lack the actors needed to change to the new.[41]

Six months later Stanislavsky was writing a confessional letter from New York which, even allowing for his well-known penchant for exaggerating and dramatising a situation, deserves to be regarded seriously.

We must reconcile ourselves to the thought that the Art Theatre has ceased to exist. I think you realised this earlier than I. All these years I have been allowing myself to hope, and trying to rescue something from the musty remnants. During this extended tour I have come to see everything and everybody in their true light. None of us has any underlying *belief*, *idea*, or great *aim*, and without that no intellectually challenging project is possible.[42]

The intellectually challenging theatre was in Moscow, with Meyerhold and Tairov, and in the Art Theatre's Studios. Left behind in Moscow, an acutely anxious Nemirovich-Danchenko was keeping a close watch on the volatile theatrical scene in which the Art Theatre would shortly have to find a place. 'A new play (by a Russian author) in Meyerhold's theatre is being well received . . . There is a new play by a new Russian author at the Maly Theatre too. These authors somehow don't seem to lodge in the memory for the moment, which is why I can't give you their names.'[43]

The play by a new Russian author at Meyerhold's theatre was Alexey Fayko's

Lake Lulle. New Soviet dramatists and prose writers were appearing with whom Nemirovich-Danchenko had no contacts and of whom he knew nothing. His own ideas for a new repertoire so far amounted to a single title, Jules Romains's *Cromedeyre-le-Vieil.*

By spring 1924, when Bulgakov had virtually finished *The White Guard,* the Director of the Art Theatre was literally at his wits' end trying to find a way forward into the coming year. What would the Art Theatre be like in the future? 'This question, this *memento mori,* is becoming ever more pressing, acute and terrifying. What plays should we put on? Who should act in them? How should they act in them?'[44]

Nemirovich-Danchenko was keeping a close watch on theatrical Moscow, but from a very different angle from that of the satirist on *The Hooter.* He tried to work out what Meyerhold was doing right, and if the Maly Theatre reminded him of 'a stroll at evening through a graveyard', he drew little comfort from that. Quite the reverse. It only served to remind him all the more painfully of his own problems, mainly of repertoire.

It's no good even thinking about *Uncle Vanya. Three Sisters* would be a joke both in terms of the content and of the *age* of the actors and actresses. *The Cherry Orchard* would be banned, or rather they would ban the lamenting of the estates of the gentry, and the play can't be staged from a different 'Hello, new life!' angle.

Ivanov is so out of sympathy with an optimistic age as to be incomprehensible . . . .[45]

Nemirovich-Danchenko had an ideological bent which the optimistic new age brought to the fore. He had what Inna Solovyova described as the ability to 'discover a new age as he might a new play', and he understood the urgent necessity of decisive and well-judged action if the Theatre was to be saved. That action he took in the spring and summer of 1924, shortly before the return of the Art Theatre's 'old stagers'.

Vested with dictatorial powers, he tackled head-on what had been one of the Theatre's main ongoing problems since the revolution: what to do about the Studios. In the process he decided the future direction of the Art Theatre itself.

We know at this time Stanislavsky was feeling that while he had been abroad the Studios, like the daughters of King Lear, had betrayed him. He gave the name of one of Shakespeare's heroines to each of them, and it has to be said that the tapestry of Shakespeare's plot began to be picked out on the canvas of reality. Goneril was the First Studio, of which Stanislavsky had had the highest hopes. In the summer of 1924 it attained independent status under the title of Moscow Art Academic Theatre II and went its own way under the artistic direction of

Mikhail Chekhov. In the autumn it presented *Hamlet*, a new, twentieth-century Hamlet in a leather jacket, riven by the contradictions of the age. 'Chekhov stands before the spectator and tells him about someone who has lived through our days.'[46]

After the death of its director Yevgeny Vakhtangov the Third Studio, Regan by Stanislavsky's nomenclature, tried to nestle under Meyerhold's wing, but ultimately it too declared independence and became a new theatre free of its parent's tutelage.

As in *King Lear* only Cordelia, the Second Studio, the least like her father, the least prominent and striking of the daughters, stayed true to her origins. In a letter of 10 July 1924 'King Lear' approved Nemirovich-Danchenko's plan to cut off the First and Third Studios. His only reservation was that he doubted whether much good would come of merging with the Second.

Cordelia, the Second Studio, should be incorporated. They are very sweet, and there is something good there, but, but, and again, but . . . Can the stallion lie with the tremulous doe? From this distance I cannot imagine what they are like now after their orgy of futurism.[47]

The 'orgy of futurism' to which Stanislavsky refers was presumably Schiller's *Die Räuber* which Boris Vershilov had staged in the style of Meyerhold. It was the style of the times, and affected the Second Studio no less than it did Goneril and Regan. To cut a long story short, the company of the main Moscow Art Theatre was augmented in the autumn of 1924 by the arrival of Nikolai Khmelyov, Ilya Sudakov, Vera Sokolova, Mikhail Yanshin, Mark Prudkin, Victor Stanitsyn, Anastasia Zueva, Anna Tarasova, Olga Androvskaya and Vsevolod Verbitsky. One further step remained . . .

Just at the moment when the theatre companies of Moscow were becoming aware of new opportunities and beginning to spread their wings, Bulgakov was still trying to find a means of survival. In February as the Vakhtangov company was giving the dress rehearsal of *Princess Turandot*, Bulgakov was noting in his diary, 'This is the worst period in my whole life. My wife and I are starving. I have been running all over Moscow. There is no work for me. My felt boots have disintegrated.'[48]

Bulgakov's mother died of typhus in Kiev on 1 February 1922. In January and March he received news for the first time of two brothers who had vanished in the chaos of the civil war. These painful events in his life finally jolted him into beginning work on his novel about the great battles in Kiev, an orphaned family, and their lost home.

Bulgakov's story *The Red Crown* appeared in the literary supplement of the newspaper *On the Eve* on 22 October 1922, a few days after the Art Theatre company had given the last of their performances in Germany. The story is narrated in the first person by someone who is mentally ill and who decides to shoulder the responsibility for all the evil in history, for his brother sent to his death in the White Guard, for a worker, his cheek smeared with soot, hanged in Berdyansk. The burden of guilt crushes the hero who loses his mind. Every day in the twilight, 'at the most terrible and portentous of the day's twenty-four hours', his younger brother appears to him, his head crowned in red, and always repeats the same thing: 'I cannot leave my squadron.'

The phrase is a recurrent motif which comes to stand for the irresistible course of historic destiny. Against the encircling madness, there rises in the shattered memory of the sick man an opposite world of home, culture, and comfort, conveyed in images familiar to us from Bulgakov's later works: '. . . the piano was open, and the score of *Faust* was on it . . . He was playing the piano, golden rays dappled the room, and his voice was alive with laughter.'

This story is a distillation of the whole emotional and plot outline not only of the *The White Guard*, but of two plays Bulgakov was yet to write, *Days of the Turbins* and *Flight*.

In 1927 Lidia Ginzburg, a young literary scholar, noted in her diary her impression that Anna Akhmatova was 'quite clearly assuming responsibility for the age, for the memory of those who have died, and the repute of the living'. She notes at the same time that some might find such exalted aspirations irritating, but that this is 'a matter of taste'.[49]

In all likelihood some such estimate of the importance of his writing is a necessary attribute of any major writer. Bulgakov was later to acknowledge that *The White Guard* had been born only after great efforts to overcome bias towards the Reds or the Whites, and to follow in the tradition of *War and Peace* in tracing the history of a cultivated family from the nobility which found itself thrust into the camp of the White Guards through the workings of a relentless historical fate.[50] Bulgakov's more sensitive contemporaries had a due recognition and appreciation of what he was attempting. It was less any formal influence than the sheer scale and ambition of the project which reminded Maximilian Voloshin of the literary debuts of Tolstoy and Dostoevsky after reading the first two parts of the novel published in the magazine *Rossiya*.

Equal ambitiousness was seen in the satirical prose of *The Diaboliad*. 'Bulgakov's aim is nothing less than to become the satirist of our age,' the critic of *The Book Pedlar* (*Knigonosha*) revealed with evident amazement in 1925.

Bulgakov's novel was not, of course, created in a literary vacuum. 'Responsibility for the age, for the memory of those who have died, and the repute of the living' was something assumed by many writers born of the revolution or who found it an unparalleled source of creative energy. Contemporary with Bulgakov's novel are the first published writings of such authors who subsequently became major figures as Vsevolod Ivanov, Leonid Leonov, Andrey Platonov, Alexander Fadeev, Konstantin Fedin, Mikhail Zoshchenko, Yury Olesha and Valentin Kataev. Other contemporary works were Boris Pilnyak's *The Naked Year*, Alexey Tolstoy's *Sisters*, and Isaac Babel's *Red Cavalry*. Ilya Ehrenburg produced book after book. Bulgakov's novella *The Diaboliad* and Alexander Serafimovich's *The Iron Flood* were published between the covers of one and the same almanac. It was when Bulgakov's work on *The White Guard* was at its height that Viktor Shklovsky's *A Sentimental Journey. Memoirs, 1918–23* appeared.

By all accounts Bulgakov studied Shklovsky's memoirs closely and appreciatively. In *Sentimental Journey* Shklovsky tells of the events in Kiev, how the City went to its doom, and how the vehicles which were to have defended it were sugared and put out of action. He builds up a complex literary personality for the author of his memoirs, weaving it into the artistic fabric of the novel and trying to place his own biography in its historical context. The author is characterised as someone capable of accepting anything. 'I can fit myself into any boot or shoe.' The biography of a member of the intelligentsia during the civil war cannot be gathered into a coherent confession: it simply disintegrates.

The destiny of the intelligentsia was the destiny of Dushechka. At one moment I was running over a ploughed field into the attack for Russia; at another I was fighting with the Socialist Revolutionaries against the Bolsheviks; at another again, in deference to some will which was always external to me, I was battling with Wrangel on the Dnieper or arresting volunteers in Kiev.[51]

Early in 1922 Osip Mandelshtam gave an exposition of the difficulties facing biography in his article 'The End of the Novel'. 'The measure in the composing of a novel is a human biography, but nowadays people are ejected from their own biographies like balls from the pockets on a billiards table.'

Eight years later, in a wholly changed historical situation, Bulgakov's junior colleague on *The Hooter*, Yury Olesha, was to enter a similar thought in *Chukokkala*:

The main thing now is that *belles lettres* are doomed. It is a disgrace to be writing fiction. We thirty-year-old representatives of the intelligentsia should be writing only about ourselves. Confessions, that's what is needed, not novels.[52]

Bulgakov was thirty years old when he began writing *The White Guard* in the form of 'a private life in history', using his own biography to understand and elaborate the most important suprapersonal cataclysms of the times. Bulgakov was incapable of being a Dushechka. He had no desire to 'fit himself into any boot or shoe'. His book is constructed on his wish to pick up the pieces and make sense of one man's shattered biography, and restore it not only to its position as the compositional measure of the novel but indeed as the measure of life itself. 'I shall finish the novel, and make so bold as to assure you that it will cause a stir in heaven.'

In the event not only did it not cause a stir in heaven, but it was prevented from having any great effect on contemporary literature or social consciousness at all, since the magazine in which it was being published folded. Bulgakov had subsequently to give the third part to the Art Theatre's actors in typescript.

'I regard my novel as a failure, although I took the writing of it very seriously,' Pavel Popov records Bulgakov as saying several years later.[53] The trouble was not merely that it was not printed in full: in its very conception there lurked an irreconcilable contradiction rooted in the historical situation. Bulgakov presented it to his reader in intensely lyrical digressions of a directness and naivety reminiscent of the digressions in Gogol's *Dead Souls*.

Will anybody redeem the blood that [Petlyura] shed?
    No. No one.
    The snow would just melt, the green Ukrainian grass would grow again and weave its carpet over the earth . . . Luxuriant shoots would sprout . . . The air would shimmer with heat above the fields and no more traces of blood would remain. Blood is cheap on those red fields and no one would redeem it.
    No one. (p. 290)

Drawing the proceedings to an end, Bulgakov invited mankind in the final paragraph of *The White Guard* to raise its eyes to the stars and understand from a loftier viewpoint how senseless enmity and hatred are.

Everything passes away – suffering, pain, blood, hunger and pestilence. The sword will pass away too, but the stars will still remain when the shadows of our presence and our deeds have vanished from the earth. There is no man who does not know that. Why, then, will we not turn our eyes towards the stars? Why? (p. 297)

The question with which he ended his book went unheard. Nobody was able even to read it.

On 19 January 1925 Bulgakov began drafting a play from the material of his still only partially published novel. He had no commission from any theatre, and began work on his own initiative. The problems he had given living form to in prose had now to be embodied in dramatic form, objective and separate from the author.

On 3 April 1925 Bulgakov received a pencilled note on the headed notepaper of the Moscow Art Theatre's Second Studio from the director Boris Vershilov. It contained an intriguing request to Bulgakov to come in to the Theatre to talk about 'a number of matters' which might be 'of interest' to both Theatre and author.[54] Needless to say, the matter discussed at the now demolished building at 22 Tverskoy Street was the proposal that Bulgakov should adapt *The White Guard* for the stage. With the first drafts of the play already written, he took little persuading.

In the summer of 1925 the Moscow Art Theatre, rejuvenated by the influx of the Second Studio company and a number of actors graduated from the Third Studio's drama school, embarked on a tour of the Soviet Union. In Tiflis, Baku, Rostov-on-Don, Odessa, Kharkov and Kiev the older generation and the younger generation were to get the measure of each other by working together, find a common language and prepare for the first season of the new Art Theatre. On 30 June Konstantin Stanislavsky marked the ending of the tour by inscribing a group photograph of the participants in the spirit of the times, 'Actors of all MAAT Theatres and Studios – unite!'[55]

While the Art Theatre's actors were uniting on tour, the Theatre's brains in Moscow were working flat out. A new literary director, the brilliant theatre historian and critic Pavel Markov, was considering every possible approach to renewal of the repertoire. He was under pressure. From Sverdlovsk, where the former Second Studio was currently staging its productions, Ilya Sudakov reminded him that the young actors needed 'two plays at the least' by the beginning of the coming season.[56] Faced with resolving an equation with multiple variables, Markov made a vitally important choice. He decided to back *The White Guard*. At the end of May he wrote to Bulgakov urging him to deliver the promised play as soon as possible. Bulgakov replied with a postcard from Voloshin's dacha in Koktebel. 'I am writing the play of *The White Guard*. It will be completed by the beginning of August.'[57]

At the gathering of the entire company which took place on 15 August 1925, Bulgakov, ever irreproachably exact in fulfilling his obligations, presented his play, *The White Guard*. It ran to five acts, which further broke down into sixteen scenes. It was the moment when the lifeline of a great Theatre crossed with that of its new Author.

2

The Magical Little Room

Prologue

A writer is not like other mortals. His romance with the theatre begins not when someone takes his coat at the cloakroom, but when he gets his complimentary tickets. At all events, when Bulgakov was compiling a scrapbook on the production history of *The Days of the Turbins* he gave pride of place to a slip addressed to Ivan Gedike, administrator of the Little Stage, requesting him to issue two free tickets to the author of *The White Guard*. In his later writings Bulgakov speaks of his first impressions of the Art Theatre, the Studio's performances of Calderón's *Woman is a Riddle* and Dmitry Smolin's *The Empress Elizabeth* as nothing less than induction into a world of magic and mystery. The portrayal of the golden horse and *The Favourite* in *Black Snow* is a recollection of these not particularly distinguished productions transformed and magnified a hundredfold by memory and nostalgia.

On 26 May 1925, almost as soon as they had made each other's acquaintance, Vershilov was writing to Bulgakov about his new play as if everything were settled. 'How is our play *The White Guard* coming along? I am still quite bowled over by your novel, and can't wait to work on your writing. I calculate you must already have completed the first act of "our" play.'[1]

If it had been this extremely gentlemanly producer who invited Bulgakov into the Theatre, it was not he who was to work on his writing. The end of August sees the entry into our documentary history of Bulgakov's romance with the Theatre of perhaps its most important character, Ilya Sudakov. Entry is perhaps not quite the word. Rather Sudakov burst in, instantly sizing up the situation and taking matters energetically in hand. In late August and early September he sent Bulgakov several short notes summoning him to Leontiev Lane to see Stanislavsky and read the play. In the first note Sudakov managed to get

Bulgakov's patronymic wrong. In the second his style of addressing Bulgakov was guaranteed to rub him up the wrong way. Bulgakov preserved Sudakov's missives in his scrapbook. 'Tomorrow, Sunday, at 3.00 p.m. *you are* to read the play to K.S. Stanislavsky at his flat at 6 Leontiev Lane,' he was instructed.[2] Bulgakov underlined the words *you are* in red pencil and awarded them an exclamation mark.

In the absence of documentary evidence we have no way of knowing whether this reading took place or not. There is a play-reading episode in *Black Snow*, where Aunt Nastasya Ivanovna takes fright at the very thought of writing a play, let alone one about the present day. ('We don't want to attack the government.') This mythologised reading, cut in two halves by Ludmilla Pryakhina and finally wrecked by a fat neurotic tabby cat, was a brilliant composite which drew on the atmosphere at the rehearsals of *Molière* much more than on Bulgakov's memories of the early days of work on *The White Guard*. Be that as it may, there is no doubt that in September 1925 Stanislavsky was indeed cool towards this brainchild of the Studio and Markov. Many years afterwards the latter was to write that Stanislavsky was 'rather unsure about the play itself',[3] and in conversation with the present author Markov passed on a much more abrupt remark by Stanislavsky which does not square at all with the account in *Black Snow*. 'What would we want to go staging this Soviet *agitprop* for?' he asked his literary director.

Meanwhile the Theatre was in the throes of the greatest revamping of its internal structures since its foundation. At the start of the new season in September 1925 the administrative side of the Art Theatre was given a novel 'parliamentary' structure, with a Council, its 'upper chamber', consisting of Stanislavsky, Leonidov, Kachalov, Moskvin and Luzhsky. The 'lower chamber' was the Collegium for Artistic Affairs and Repertoire under the chairmanship of Pavel Markov. The young people in charge of this side of things initially included Ilya Sudakov, Boris Vershilov, Nikolai Gorchakov, Yury Zavadsky, Yevgeny Kaluzhsky, Mark Prudkin, and Nikolai Batalov, although the composition changed subsequently. This Lower Chamber had quite extensive powers in matters of repertoire and artistic policy, and it was hoped that it would contribute to unifying the Theatre on a new basis. The first announcement of its existence mentions that it had 'embarked upon a reworking of Bulgakov's *The White Guard*, which will be the Theatre's first major contemporary play since *The Pugachev Uprising*'.[4]

On 5 October, after the Lower Chamber had met, Sudakov informed Bulgakov that:

1) The producers of *The White Guard* have been appointed. These are B. I. Vershilov and myself; 2) We have completed the casting, as will be confirmed tomorrow; 3) A. V. Lunacharsky has informed V. V. Luzhsky after reading three acts of the play that he finds it excellent and sees no obstacles to its being staged. I should be grateful if you would come to see me and B. I. Vershilov at the Theatre tomorrow at 3.30 p.m. I should like to re-read the novel *The White Guard*. Could you kindly bring a copy with you if you have one. *The White Guard* will go into rehearsal forthwith, as soon as the actors' scripts have been typed up. The date for opening is March 1926 on the Art Theatre's Principal Stage.[5]

Everything in Sudakov's letter turned out to be overstated. No decision had been taken on whether to use the Principal Stage, and the date for the opening night had yet to be agreed by the Council. Not only had Lunacharsky, the People's Commissar of Enlightenment, not found the play excellent, he had felt obliged to write an official letter to Vasily Luzhsky which initiated a further convoluted sub-plot wholly in character for the saga of Bulgakov's romance with the Art Theatre.

I have carefully re-read the play *The White Guard*. I find nothing impermissible in it from the political angle, but cannot but express to you my personal opinion. I consider Bulgakov very talented, but this play of his is extremely poor, with the exception of the tolerably lively scene where the Hetman is taken away. All the rest is either military fuss or else exceptionally commonplace, unimaginative, and uninteresting scenes of the way of life of the bourgeoisie which we can well do without. All things considered, there is not a single typical character or interesting situation. As for the ending it positively makes one bridle, not only at its vagueness but also at its total lack of effect.[6]

Clearly Lunacharsky's review, added to the generally cool attitude of Stanislavsky and the senior members of the Theatre, who saw little for themselves in the 'junior members' play', left Bulgakov in a parlous situation. It was not long before things started moving against him. Just one day after Lunacharsky's letter and eight days after Sudakov's sunny epistle, on 14 October 1925, there was a meeting of the Collegium for Artistic Affairs and Repertoire. The second item in the minutes reads:

Considered: Production of the play *The White Guard*
    Resolved: To note that prior to production on the Principal Stage the play will require radical revision. The play can be produced on the Little Stage after relatively minor revisions.[7]

That is the way the theatre works. So many people are involved in the gestation of a play, so many interests and considerations are brought into play, that the playwright is bound to feel constantly under attack from all sides. Bulgakov was present at the meeting. The following day he replied in writing to Vasily Luzhsky, putting his whole future as a dramatist, which was just beginning to show signs of promise, on the line.

Dear Vasily Vasilievich,

Yesterday's meeting, which I had the honour of attending, made it clear to me that the situation surrounding my play is complex. There was talk of producing it on the Little Stage, of putting off the production until next season, and finally of radically reworking the play to the extent of virtually writing a new play.

While entirely willing to accept certain improvements in the course of working on the play jointly with the producers, I feel unable to write a new play.

The thoroughgoing and blunt criticism at yesterday's meeting (which I welcome) made me considerably lower my estimate of the play, but not to the extent of persuading me that it should be produced on the Little Stage.

Finally, the question of which season. The only answer acceptable to me is: this season, not next.

For this reason I must ask you, Vasily Vasilievich, to raise the following question with the Board of Management as a matter of urgency and give me an unambiguous reply:

Is Moscow Art Theatre I prepared to include the following non-negotiable points in the contract relating to the play:

1. Production only on the Principal Stage.
2. In the present season (March 1926).

If these conditions are unacceptable to the Theatre, I must ask to be allowed to consider a negative response as indicating that my play *The White Guard* may be freely offered elsewhere.[8]

It is not every day a beginning dramatist delivers an ultimatum to a renowned theatre, and a theatre which, moreover, has just received a review like the one from People's Commissar Lunacharsky. One might have supposed that the fate of *The White Guard* was sealed, and that even the problem of letting the author down gently had been resolved by the author himself.

One would have been wrong. Among the Theatre's conflicting interests the decisive factor was to prove the junior members' determination to have their say about the times they lived in.

On 16 October an emergency meeting of the Collegium was called, Luzhsky reporting on Bulgakov's ultimatum. The Lower Chamber effectively conceded all his demands, resolved to start work on the play without delay, and was unable only to guarantee that it would be staged in the current season.

On 21 October the casting was approved, with Sudakov proposed for the role of Alexey Turbin, Livanov as Nikolka and Kedrov as Malyshev. In the event they got it right only with Prudkin, Dobronravov, and Sokolova, who did eventually act the roles allocated at this point.

On 31 October Bulgakov read his play to the company. The 'senior members' were greatly taken by the play, but put Bulgakov on the back burner for three months because there were no roles in it for them. *The White Guard* was farmed out to the junior members as, in Vasily Luzhsky's phrase, 'an experimental production'.

Mark Prudkin recalls that at the reading 'Bulgakov was terribly nervous and smoked incessantly. Afterwards Kolya Khmelyov and I went up to him and told him we would love to act in his play, to which he replied edgily, "That is not within my gift." '9

'That' depended on many factors. Stanislavsky had not only the junior members to consider, but also the senior members who had, after all, spent their entire working lives alongside him in the Theatre. Nemirovich-Danchenko had just gone off with the Musical Studio for a tour of Europe and America. The new season began in an atmosphere of general unease, with a presentiment that some major change of direction was imminent. Opinions were divided on what might precipitate this. Nobody suspected *The White Guard*.

All around the Art Theatre the theatrical life of Moscow was reaching dizzying heights. The autumn of 1925 and early 1926 was damned as 'Thermidor in the theatre' by Vladimir Blyum. The chief left-wing critic was taken aback to learn of Stanislavsky's open admiration for the Meyerhold production of Nikolai Erdman's *The Mandate*, and by Meyerhold's welcoming of the Art Theatre production of Alexander Ostrovsky's *The Ardent Heart*.

The first night of Ostrovsky's play took place on 22 January 1926 and was the Art Theatre's first real success for many years. The left-wing critics, however, saw things in their own way. Mikhail Zagorsky considered the production to have 'set the theatre back whole decades'. Later, one of the notorious cohort of proletarian zealots concluded his diatribe with a warning: 'We shall be waiting for *The White Guard*, which will finally decide the fate of this theatre in the age of our revolution.'10

The play which was to bear so momentous a responsibility was in the meantime undergoing radical reconstruction, quite without the involvement of the Council.

The success of *The Ardent Heart* revived the Art Theatre's spirits. Immediately following the first night a joint session of the Council and the Collegium was convened, and the decision was taken to start work on *The White Guard* without delay. How Markov and Sudakov got the resolution passed we have no way of knowing. We can only take the word of Maxudov, the hero of *Black Snow*, who supposed 'it was arranged by Panin and Strizh, but how they did it, God only knows, because it was a super-human achievement. In fact – it was a miracle.' (p. 146)

Sudakov, party to the miracle, informed Bulgakov of the decision on 26 January, a hint of suppressed glee breaking through in the phrase he underlined:

Dear Mikhail Afanasievich!

Further to today's resolution of the joint session of both the Theatre's bodies regarding immediate commencement of rehearsals of *The White Guard*, I should be grateful if you would come to the Theatre tomorrow at 12 noon. [. . .] Rehearsals will begin the day after tomorrow at a *revolutionary pace*.[11]

This time Sudakov's letter and his emphasis contained not a single exaggeration.

The play was handed to the junior members. This was their big chance, their moment of destiny, their hour of glory. These were the terms in which they later recalled the atmosphere at rehearsals, which Sudakov really did conduct at a revolutionary pace.

'We were elated by the marvellous opportunity the senior members had given us. We rehearsed uninterruptedly, without rest, in a very special mood of friendship, trust, love, and mutual encouragement the like of which we were never to know again.' Thus did Mark Prudkin recall those events of the winter and spring of 1926 in conversation fifty-seven years on.

On 29 January 1926 Bulgakov read the new version of his play to the new cast. A drama had been wrung from the earlier unwieldy adaptation of a novel which now worked as theatre. The creating of this play was of tremendous importance for Bulgakov's growth into an Author of the Theatre, and a tremendously important step too in the preparing of a production which would indeed finally decide the fate of the Theatre in the age of the revolution.

An Author of the Theatre

Bulgakov so well describes the transmutation of prose into drama in *Black Snow* that no contemporary student of artistic space can afford to ignore it. Let us recall Maxudov's description of the 'magical little room' he began to play with for his own pleasure:

In the evenings I began to feel that something coloured was emerging from the white pages. After staring at it and screwing up my eyes I was convinced that it was a picture – and what's more a picture that was not flat but three-dimensional like a box. Through the lines on the paper I could see a light burning and inside the box those same characters in the novel were moving about. It was a delightful game [. . .] After a while noises began coming from the room inside the book. I could distinctly hear the sounds of a piano. [. . .] I used to catch the yearning strains of an accordion through the storm [. . .] And I could see sharp swords, hear them as they whistled through the air with a blood-curdling sound.

There – there was a man, panting as he ran. Through the tobacco smoke I followed him as he went and by straining my eyes I could see that he was being chased . . . There was a shot . . . with a groan he fell headlong. (p. 51)

After that all that is required is to learn to note down what is seen in the 'magical room'. The descriptive technique could not be simpler:

What I saw, I wrote down; what I didn't see, I left out. There was the scene: the lights came on and lit it up in bright colours. Did it please me? Extremely. So I'll write that down – Scene One. It's evening, the lamp is burning; it has a fringed shade. Music lies open on the grand piano. Someone is playing *Faust*. Suddenly *Faust* stops and a guitar starts playing. Who is playing it? Here he comes, with the guitar in his hands. I hear him start singing. So I write: 'Starts to sing'. (p. 52)

We need have no doubt that Bulgakov's description of Maxudov's anguish as he struggles to fit his novel into the compass of a play has a solidly autobiographical basis. With a watch in his hands, counting the minutes, the newly fledged author establishes that a straightforward reading of his play takes three hours. Unfortunately the actual theatre is not straightforward. The playwright recalls with horror that theatres have intervals and performances have pauses in the action.

For instance, the actress is standing, crying and arranging some flowers in a vase. She has nothing to say, yet time is flying all the same. Obviously, muttering the dialogue to oneself at home is one thing and speaking it on stage is quite another. (p. 75)

Maxudov goes on to describe the technicalities of restructuring his novel into a play, the description largely coinciding with Bulgakov's experiences in reality. Maxudov first cuts out a scene, but that does not go far enough.

Something else had to be thrown out of the play – but what? It all seemed to me equally vital and I felt, too, that as soon as I condemned some part of it to extinction, the whole laboriously constructed edifice would start to totter. I dreamed of ceilings collapsing and balconies disintegrating and those dreams were prophetic.

Then I removed one of the characters. As a result one scene became lopsided and finally it had to go. There were now eleven scenes. (p. 75)

By and large theatre history is here coinciding with fiction, but with one extremely important difference. Accommodating themselves to the exigencies of stage time or, as Bulgakov was to say at a debate after the first performance, making sure the audience were in time for the last tram, was the least of the editors' worries. Their chief problem was what to present to the audience. The endless amending of the text, which underwent no fewer than seven redactions according to Markov, was necessitated by the need to work out a way of making *The White Guard* fit into the exigencies of the historical times.

Three of these versions survive.[12]

The first, 'untheatrical' version which Bulgakov produced in the summer of 1925 has not been adequately understood or appreciated. This play, which runs to sixteen scenes, sets down all the most important features. Bulgakov's future as a playwright is clearly mapped out here, in much the way that all of the later Chekhov is to be discovered in his first, immensely long and equally 'untheatrical' play, staged nowadays under the title of *Platonov*. In this first version of *The White Guard* Bulgakov's 'handwriting' comes through, that 'bloom' of an author that Nemirovich-Danchenko liked to talk of.

As Bulgakov and the Theatre resolutely restructured the play, tearing out everything superfluous, subordinating casual irregularity to strict rules and canonicity, they occasionally destroyed that uniquely individual bloom in the process.

With hindsight we can easily see the threads running from the first version of *The White Guard* to Bulgakov's later works. Many directors turn to it nowadays in persistent efforts to restore *The Days of the Turbins* to its original state. No one has yet succeeded in this endeavour, and there is no reason to suppose they ever will, because what exists under one umbrella is not so much different versions of a play as entirely separate literary works. Where they are crucially dissimilar is in Bulgakov's having tried in the first version to retain the main character of his novel, Doctor Alexey Turbin.

The idea of 'removing one of the characters' was Sudakov's. Removing Alexey Turbin had crucial consequences. Along with the hero they removed his lyrical understanding of history. They banished the blurred, vague, perhaps rather irresolute but nonetheless very important uncertainty around which the atmosphere of the drama was built up. Colonel Alexey Turbin inherited some of his predecessor's phrases and even monologues, but he was a different person, a different breed, in a different play.

Alexey Turbin the doctor was like an umbilical cord linking the stage adaptation with the novel. It was this umbilical cord that Bulgakov and the producers cut as they struggled their way through to a new, theatrical, concept.

In the first version Bulgakov had yet to discover the secret of this kind of thinking. On the contrary, that play testifies to his strenuous efforts to retain and objectify the novel's underlying themes. To take an example, at the beginning of the play there is an attempt to condense the novel's theme of contrasting historical reality with the insights and prophecies of 'great literature'. The following dialogue on the subject between Turbin and Myshlaevsky makes the point.

Alexey. But why were you there, for God's sake? Surely Petlyura can't be at Red Tavern?
Myshlaevsky. Have you ever read Dostoevsky?
Alexey. I'm reading him right now. That is *The Possessed* lying there. I think he's amazing.
Nikolka. A great writer of the land of Russia.
Myshlaevsky. Quite so. And one I would cheerfully hang.
Alexey. What has he done to deserve such a fate, may I enquire?
Myshlaevsky. He's written all that tosh about the Russian people embodying God's will,
   the sower, guardian, ploughman and . . . but actually that was Apukhtin.
Alexey. Actually that was Nekrasov, you philistine.
Myshlaevsky (yawning). Then I would hang Nekrasov.[13]

Interspersed in the first version with the scenes in the Turbins' apartment were episodes in the downstairs apartment where Wanda and Vasilisa lived. Bulgakov was long reluctant to part with this purely novelistic device, but even while distancing his heroes from the philistine world, he sought purely theatrical devices to substitute in the Turbin scenes for the deprecating and ironical commentary of the narrator in the novel. In the third act, which develops the major theme of how people can be tricked by history, Alexey rhetorically extols the simple Russian peasant who would never have succumbed to 'the Moscow sickness'. Immediately, in the midst of that noisy, drunken, despairing gathering we again hear the motif of Dostoevsky and the Russian cultural tradition, prophesying, foreseeing, predicting, but for all that failing to prepare its sons for what was to come. It is for this 'fraud' that Myshlaevsky would hang the author of *The Possessed*.

Alexey. Captain, you understand nothing. Do you know who Dostoevsky was?
Myshlaevsky. A highly suspect individual. [. . .]
Alexey. He was a prophet! He foresaw everything that would happen. Look. See it lying
   there – *The Possessed*. I was reading it just before you arrived. Oh, if only we could all
   have foreseen all this earlier!

After this in the first, as indeed in the final version, the Captain begins shooting at imaginary commissars in drunken bravado. Everybody sings the national anthem 'God save the Tsar', and the action is again interrupted by a scene with Vasilisa which breaks the mood of the act.

With the musical tenacity of a composer Bulgakov introduces a variation on the theme of *The Possessed* in the concluding scene of his oversized Act One. This introduces the most bitter and anguished theme of both novel and play, the consciousness that 'the Russian people is not with us, but against us'. Simultaneously he condenses into a single short dialogue the entire range of ideological clichés and intellectual stereotypes by which the intelligentsia tries to use its book-learning to make sense of what is occurring around it.

Myshlaevsky. We ought to horse-whip the blackguards, Alyosha. [This refers to the Russian people.]
Alexey. Dostoevsky saw that too and said, Russia is a penurious land of wooden huts, and honour is to a Russian but a needless burden.
Shervinsky. Only one thing works in Rus. It has been rightly said: Russia defers only to the Orthodox faith and the Tsar!
Nikolka. Right! A week ago, gentlemen, I went to the theatre to see *Paul the First*, and when the actor said those words I couldn't keep quiet and shouted out, 'Quite right!' [. . .] And do you know what? Everyone clapped. All except some swine in the gallery who yelled, 'Idiot!'. [. . .]
Studzinsky. Damned Yids.

At the end of his first act Bulgakov produced a highly fraught atmosphere among people whose ideals have led them nowhere, and whose pitiful, distraught bravado testifies to their sense of losing their place in history. He concludes the act with Yelena and Shervinsky kissing, and Nikolka's appearing and being appalled by the improper spectacle. As yet there has been no hint of Lariosik. Bulgakov adheres closely and consistently to the plot line of the novel, even as he tries to find theatrical means for communicating the novel's powerful lyricism in the play.

To do this he makes extensive use of dreams in the first version of the play. These are important in the novel, and indeed in all Bulgakov's later writings. Here too the first version anticipates the later dramas, perhaps nowhere so evidently as in the first scene of Act Two (of which nothing remains in the canonical text).

Alexey Turbin's dream, briefly mentioned in the novel, is developed into a major scene. Nightmare appears to Alexey, who has fallen asleep over Dostoevsky's novel. 'His face is wrinkled and he is bald. He wears an 1870s morning coat, baggy check pants and boots with yellow tops.' Turbin's dialogue with Nightmare parodies Ivan Karamazov's conversation with the Devil, and there was probably a further allusion to the famous nightmare scene in the Art Theatre's production of *The Brothers Karamazov* in which Kachalov played the parts of both Ivan and the Devil.

In Bulgakov's play Nightmare displays a freedom which is the prerogative of a character in a dream. He sings Nikolka's songs, fills the stage with the sound of a guitar and finally 'leaps on to Alexey's chest and throttles him'. He makes no attempt to conceal his literary origins: 'I bring you greetings from Fyodor Dostoevsky . . .'

We are witnessing the first, tentative confrontation in Bulgakov's writing between the power of Evil, which knows the complexity of life and is itself a part of the chaos it so loves, and pedantically precise human reason which cannot abide chaos and does its utmost to find a neat, rational explanation and a proper place for everything.

Some years later Ivan Bezdomny in *The Master and Margarita* tries to make sense of the chain of events anticipated by Woland and does his best to find a connection between Anna who spilt the Lenten sunflower-seed oil and Pontius Pilate.

In the first version of *The White Guard* Alexey tries to think logically and rationally even in his dreams, and to drive from his mind the possibility that delirium might be real, or more precisely that reality might be a delirium beyond the reach of reason.

Alexey. Hence, hence, Gansilezy – what nonsense. There is no such word. And you do not exist. [. . .]
Nightmare. You are mistaken, doctor. I am not a dream. I am absolutely real, and anyway who can say what is a dream? Eh?

In order to demonstrate his power Nightmare goes on to predict the future much as Woland will later foretell Berlioz's future at Patriarch's Ponds.

Alexey. What? What?
Nightmare. Bad, bad things. (*Shouts in a muffled voice.*) Doctor, hurry up. Get your epaulettes off.

Traditional ways of thinking cannot cope with such a monstrous overload. Beginnings and endings are unrelated. No sense can be made of anything.

Alexey. Go away, I feel dreadful . . . You are a nightmare. The worst of it is, your boots have turned over boot tops. Brrr. How disgusting. You never see tops like that when you're awake.

Nightmare. What do you mean? Of course you do if, for instance, there is no leather in Zhitomir.

We need not detail here all the good things which will spring from this dialogue in Bulgakov's later writing.

Alexey sees the lack of leather in Zhitomir and the unexpected appearance of Colonel Bolbotun's disagreeable countenance on the fireplace tiles at Night- mare's command as the product of jangled nerves, a madness, a discord which must be put a stop to. The absurdity and disorder of what is taking place challenge traditional ways of thinking, with their received veneration for 'the reasonable, the good, and eternal'. 'I know perfectly well that I am asleep and that my nerves are on edge. Get out, or I'll shoot. All this is a myth, a myth,' Alexey shouts at his elusive enemy.

That word 'myth' belongs not only to Turbin but also to Bulgakov. It is used in the novel to characterise and disparage a life without logic, in which the natural and, it had seemed, eternal foundation of good and reason had been under- mined. At this point the lines of the novel and play converge, even as Bulgakov achieves a new insight which was to enable him to link Anna's spilling the Lenten sunflower-seed oil with Pontius Pilate's sending a prophet to execution in ancient times.

At this high point in the prophetic dream Bulgakov, with a boldness unusual in a stage adaptation, suddenly offers the theatre a device for throwing open the Turbins' apartment to the raw elements which know only the law of brute force. Nightmare shows the sleeping Turbin what Petlyura's reign means, 'a revolt, senseless and pitiless' which relishes human humiliation, where a man is trampled underfoot and crushed, has his innards torn from him and his soul defiled.

Nightmare. Oh, it's a myth, is it? I'll show you the kind of myth it is. (*Whistles ear-splittingly.*)
The walls of the Turbins' flat vanish. A barrel, a chest and a table rise from beneath the floor. A deserted room with broken windows and a sign reading 'Headquarters 1st Cavalry Division' in Ukrainian emerges from the darkness. A hurricane lamp by the door. Alexey vanishes. Colonel Bolbotun is on stage, fearsome, pockmarked, in a greatcoat and tall Astrakhan hat with a red ribbon.

This is no ordinary stage direction detailing a scene change, but a sudden burst of theatrical and dramatic imagination which blows traditional ideas of stage adaptation clean out of the water. This is a quintessential Bulgakov stage direction, a Bulgakov scene change, the Bulgakov way of seeing things. This is the Bulgakov 'bloom' which it was for the junior members of the Art Theatre to respect.

They failed to do so. The dialogue between Doctor Turbin and Nightmare, Doctor Turbin himself, and the 'hellish glow' bathing the Petlyura scene were all cut as the collaborative work progressed. There is a simple explanation for this. The burst of originality here, giving birth as it did to a new form, was an isolated event and something quite outside the structures congenial to the Theatre towards which Bulgakov's tutors in stagecraft, Sudakov and Markov, were coaxing him. They took their bearings for the new play from Chekhovian drama.

Let us, however, not run ahead of ourselves or jump to conclusions, but persevere through this first version of the play to the very end, with all its incongruities, its 'untheatrical elements' and bursts of originality whose significance can be appreciated only in retrospect.

After the Petlyura scenes with their hideously cruel and violent degradation of a man, Bulgakov returns us to the dissolving dream of Alexey Turbin. Nightmare is no longer there, the unbounded space is again reduced to the dimensions of the Turbins' flat. The visionary dream ends on a note profoundly Bulgakovian, with a cry of despair from a man compelled to watch the deriding and killing of an innocent victim while he, a doctor, can do nothing to help.

Alexey (in his dream). Help! Help! . . . Quick! We've got to help. Look, he may still be alive . . .

This lyrical leitmotif, which first appears in *The Red Crown* and then recurs in all Bulgakov's principal works, was also to disappear in the course of rehearsals. Such tender-heartedness was seen as something to be overcome. A more objective viewpoint was required.

The first three acts of the first version, which culminate in the overrunning of the High School and the triumphant ascent of Bolbotun, basically keep to the course of events we find in the novel and revolve round a passive hero. In this first version we already find virtually all the scenes and characters present in the final play: Yelena, Nikolka, Shervinsky, Myshlaevsky, all those who, without thinking about it particularly, live by the precepts of their ancestors, in accordance with tradition, by the rules of their family or the Army. The substance of the future play was all there, but it had not yet assumed dramatic form.

It had not assumed dramatic form because there was no active hero involved in the making of history. The drama lacked a mainspring. It fell apart. The images in the 'magical room' were faint and dim. In the last two acts Bulgakov tried to find a way out of the Turbins' 'badger sett' life along the same lyrical lines as in the novel, if without the direct voice of the narrator.

At the beginning of Act Four the hapless poet Larion Surzhansky appeared, an 'Illarionushka' type who struck readers of this first version as defiantly traditional. We know that neither Bulgakov nor the Art Theatre were in the least averse to traditionalism and, playing a long game, they were to turn this peripheral figure into one of the principal characters at the next stage in their work. In the first version, however, Lariosik appears in boots with the nightmarish yellow tops. Bulgakov, employing one of his favourite techniques of linking concepts remote from one another, uses the first sentence uttered by the cousin from Zhitomir to give a purely practical explanation of the mystical coincidence. 'Mother ordered the boots for me, and there was a shortage of black leather so we had to have the tops yellow. There is no leather in Zhitomir.'

Thus does Nightmare's puzzling costume recur.

Larion enters with a birdcage in his hand and promptly starts blurting out the story of how his wife was unfaithful to him on the divan where he read Pushkin's poetry to her 'at the beginning of our life together'. The Turbins, having come through the horrors of the Petlyura regime, see Larion as a precious relic from the times of legend.

Nikolka. Do you always live with a bird like that?
Larion. Always. Do you know, I am just a little afraid of people, and I've got used to birds. Birds are man's best friend. Birds never do anyone any harm.

What can a bird-brain do for his country? How should someone with such a delightful canary-based philosophy live his life?

Bulgakov sits the entire company of his characters down to play a game of whist. 'The time will fairly fly,' Myshlaevsky explains. In the course of the game Lariosik expatiates on the horrors of the civil war and how peaceful it is in the Turbins' home. He informs Yelena that she 'spreads a kind of inner light, a warm feeling around her'. Nikolka is awarded an equally agreeable Zhitomir compliment: 'You have an honest face.' The card game, bird-brained Lariosik, the whiling away of time with a familiar ritual taken from a life which no longer exists are depicted with a deceptive irony. Behind Bulgakov's irony there is despair, uncertainty, a sense of destitution.

It is unclear how life is to be lived in the impending new age, not in any metaphysical sense but in a literal, physical sense. The streets are empty after the last of Petlyura's transports have left: Red Army units will enter the city at any moment. The Turbins sit it out behind their cream blinds. Bulgakov delays the crucial moment. Like a skilled film director he again interrupts the Turbins' story, slotting in an episode from the apartment downstairs. He depicts the final robbing of Vasilisa with contemptuous and somehow jubilant wit. The robbery takes place to the parodistic accompaniment of an opera on the gramophone, first a deafening rendering of 'Whither, whither art thou gone?' then 'Shall I fall, by arrow slain?' One of the three burglars eyes Wanda, the houseowner's wife, and berates the distraught engineer, 'What sort of a state is your wife in that honest folk don't even fancy her!'

After the Vasilisa episode Bulgakov begins his final act with a significant stage direction: 'The Turbins' apartment is brightly lit. A decorated Christmas tree. An inscription in Indian ink above the fireplace reads "Welkum 2 Kiev, Komraids".' The Christmas tree, the light flooding the flat, and the inscription above the fireplace all tell the same story. This is a time of waiting, the eve of something momentous, a turning-point, but for all that they express defiance of what is taking place beyond the cream blinds. The welcome is expressed in a style which will have to be acquired, the inscription reminiscent of the order which Nikolka penned in the novel on behalf of 'Abraham Goldblatt, Ladies, Gentlemen's and Women's Tailor. Commissar, Podol District Committee'.

To parody a style is not difficult, but to live in a parody is impossible. At this moment of historic change Bulgakov attempts to put his characters back in their usual places. The doctor is sitting at the writing desk in his study being busy. Yelena and Shervinsky are 'making music'. Nikolka's attempt to tell his sister the Bolsheviks are entering the city and that even the bourgeois are rejoicing is stopped with, 'What's the hurry. Leave her be!' Shervinsky, who has succeeded in acquiring a 'threadbare, politically neutral overcoat', is preparing for an opera first night and testing his voice. 'Who cares who's in power!'

Was it all just going to be a matter of business as before?

Certainly that was how the final act was viewed, the play's 'full circle' structure being seen as reflecting an un-Soviet approach on Bulgakov's part. There was going to be a good deal of agonising in the Theatre in the months ahead. One version followed another as they tried to change the final scene to make it less ambiguous.

In the autumn of 1926 the spotlight in the final scene was focused on Captain Myshlaevsky, who declared his readiness to serve in the Red Army. In the first version the central character was Doctor Alexey Turbin who was recovering from a wound and had returned to his proper profession. The question of what the future held was posed in the first version in a naively straightforward way:

Nikolka. What will happen to us now, Alexey? We really need to talk about it. I just can't imagine. We sat it out in our apartment while Petlyura was around, but what now? Tomorrow it's Sovdepia.

The last scene of the play was almost completely taken up by a family meeting improvised in the new Soviet style. Alexey is elected Chairman, Lariosik Secretary. Yelena and Shervinsky are absent, 'rehearsing' as the Doctor wryly remarks. The meeting gives a concentrated run-down of what people like the Turbins anticipated the future might bring, much like the survey of attitudes towards the past provided in the first act.

Alexey. Right. We have two items on the agenda. [. . .] The floor is given for a point of information to former Captain Alexander Studzinsky.
Nikolka. Just like the Bolsheviks. It really is! (*Takes his guitar*) [. . .] Exemplary order. Everybody imbued with politically conscious discipline . . .

There follows a succession of proposals and counter-proposals all along much the same lines.

Nikolka proposes 'We should all emigrate. There!'

Studzinsky, supporting the impetuous cadet, adds 'How can we stay here? When they can't even bear the words "White Guard"? [. . .] Perhaps we really should, while there is still time to get out and follow Petlyura's lot?'

Myshlaevsky. Where to?
Studzinsky. Abroad.
Myshlaevsky. And then, after we are abroad, what next?

Nikolka interrupts this highly germane question with his guitar, and then Captain Myshlaevsky asks to speak. 'May I?' 'Certainly, Comrade.'

Myshlaevsky, newly christened as a comrade, announces a change in his position. He has been fighting since 1914 and has no wish to fight any more, not for anybody. He makes a V-sign at the audience, at which the well-bred doctor asks him 'from the Chair' to refrain from making V-signs and other non-verbal communication. Myshlaevsky it is who, despite his limited vocabulary, articulates the word on which the play's finale hangs. That word is 'Fatherland'. Studzinsky, professionally obligated to be indignant, demands to know what kind of Fatherland there can still be when 'Russia is finished'. In return Doctor Turbin uses his position as Chairman to pronounce a monologue about Russia which draws together the highest level of insight the characters in Bulgakov's first version of his play are capable of attaining:

Alexey. I tell you what . . . Myshlaevsky is right. The captain mentioned Russia just now, and says it doesn't exist any more. Do you see this . . . What is it?

Nikolka. A card table.

Alexey. Perfectly correct, and it is always a card table, whatever you do with it. You can turn it upside down, you can knock it over, you can stick money under it like that idiot Vasilisa, but it will still be a card table. What's more, the time will come when it will be back in its proper position, because lying on the floor with its legs in the air is not what it's there for . . .

This organic conception of history always returning, like the card table, to its proper position, and of a Russia always equal to herself, was less than totally convincing. It struck those in the Communist Party who had undertaken to re-make Russia as defiant. 'Turn Russia upside down, and the hour will come when she will right herself. Anything may happen. Let them come pouring in. Let them flood her and try to change everything. They will not change Russia. Russia will always be Russia.'

The years separating Bulgakov from the date of this scene had shown otherwise, but Turbin's less than adequate crystal-ball gazing, unqualified in the play by authorial comment, could be used against Bulgakov. People were just as unwilling in the new Russia as in the old to distinguish an author from his characters. Writing 'only what you see, and not writing what you don't see' was going to necessitate a major restructuring of the play, not merely in terms of the text, but at the deepest level of how it would function on the stage.

Doctor Alexey Turbin was to disappear. No trace would remain of the theme of Russia as a self-righting card table. The playwright and the Theatre would between them change the perspective and shift many accents, but one theme in the Doctor's final monologue would remain and be made if anything more prominent: the theme of Russia, one's country which must not be abandoned no matter what might be taking place within its borders. This did not only grow out of the Turbins' predicament: right through to the end of the 1920s it was a major element in Bulgakov's thinking both as a writer and on a personal level. It was something he professed at the most critical moments of his writing career and in this respect at least he could justifiably be identified with his hero.

Anna Akhmatova cast a similar sentiment in bronze with her lines:

> I heard a voice. It seemed consoling.
> It said, 'Go from hence, leave this obscure
> And sinful land. Leave Russia for ever.
> But impassively and calmly
> I covered my ears with my hands
> That this unworthy talk should not
> Contaminate my sorrowing spirit.

Doctor Turbin expresses the same thought in a more mundane fashion, as befits a fairly ordinary member of the Russian intelligentsia. He repeats, as if intoning a spell, 'I will not emigrate, I will not, I will not!'

Captain Myshlaevsky puts it in even more basic terms: 'They'll shit on you wherever you go, from Paris to Singapore . . .', his soldierly maxim anticipating the plot of *Flight*.

Geographical displacement resolves nothing because the question remains, 'And then, when we are abroad, what next?' This is probably why Bulgakov gives that great intellectual Captain Myshlaevsky the honour of bringing the meeting to a close with lines of self-incrimination which Mr Punch might envy: 'Comrade Audience, this is the end of the White Guard. Captain Myshlaevsky, a non-member of the Communist Party, leaves the stage. I've drawn straight spades.'

Bulgakov accompanies this blatant violation of the principle of the fourth wall with the stage direction, 'The stage suddenly goes dark'. Only crippled Nikolka is left illuminated by the footlights singing a cadet song, and on this song the production fades out.

Such, then, was the verbose but prophetic play which Bulgakov carved from his novel. He threw his prose into the crucible of the theatre and brought the Art Theatre not a play but molten lava which it still remained to pour into some kind of mould. The junior members of the Art Theatre had no specifically Bulgakovian mould at their disposal. The model Sudakov knew was the tried and trusted form of classical Chekhovian drama, and into this mould the Theatre and its playwright duly poured *The White Guard*. Much would not fit and had to be abandoned. Inevitably there was a price to pay. What was rejected as superfluous was what was specific to Bulgakov. Bulgakov was trying to find his feet and the Art Theatre was trying to understand its new playwright. It was no idyll, but a heated artistic confrontation into whose niceties nobody cared to delve later on. The play was a staggering success, but its author went unmentioned in accounts of that success for several decades. During those years virtually nobody working in the Theatre's archive requested a folder headed '*The White Guard*, a play in five acts (Library of the Repertoire Section, Item 832)'.

Having read 'Item 832', with which Bulgakov's romance with the Art Theatre began, we can truly repeat, 'Manuscripts do not burn'.

In Search of a Hero

The play the Art Theatre began rehearsing at the end of January consisted of twelve scenes. That is, it was what is now traditionally considered the second version. This new version was rehearsed with constant amendments and alterations until 25 June 1926, which was the end of the season, when a dress rehearsal of *The White Guard* was held.[14]

The distinctive feature of the second version is the appearance as the play's hero of Colonel Alexey Turbin. His arrival necessitated a complete restructuring of every aspect of the plot on every level, structural, semantic and plot. A passive hero was replaced by a hero who was an ideologue. The meditative intellectual was replaced by a man whose temperament was literally heroic. Alexey Vasilievich Turbin, a man in a position to make choices, freely exercised his volition, took full responsibility for his actions, and paid for his choice with his life.

Turbin's death in the High School became the play's climax and its moment of catharsis. It raised *The White Guard* to a plane both Theatre and playwright needed as they groped their way towards a full awareness of the complex relationship between the intelligentsia and the revolution. Acquiring a hero raised the play to new heights, giving it a fulcrum for the action to revolve round and developing a sorely needed dynamism. Bulgakov's private game of 'magical rooms' became a public, socially significant play addressed to a country which had suffered the ravages of civil war.

A new, specifically dramatic theme was added to the themes in the novel, that of an intellectual, a bearer of the country's culture, resolved to defend what he believed in to the last.

Underpinning the collaboration between Bulgakov and the Art Theatre was a determination to drive home the senselessness of this bloodshed, and to restore an unchallengeable belief in the sanctity of human life.

Some years after the play premièred Sudakov recalled, 'Bulgakov was perfectly willing to change everything, subject of course to observing the truth of art. The least prompting on our part produced brilliant and wholly unexpected ideas quite independently of us, and resulted in complete scenes being magnificently rewritten.'[15]

The rewritten scenes were necessitated by the arrival of Colonel Turbin in place of Doctor Turbin. A second factor was the expanding and deepening of the role of Lariosik, who now appeared at the very beginning of the play. The appearance of Lariosik considerably strengthened the Chekhovian atmosphere of the scenes described in the rehearsal sheets as taking place 'in the Turbins' apartment'.

In the second version Bulgakov cut the references to Dostoevsky's *The Possessed* and the prophecies contained in 'the best books in the world'. Nightmare in his baggy check trousers and 1870s morning coat also disappeared, and the atmosphere of fear, doom and foreboding was dissipated.

Ultimately even Bulgakov's much-loved game of whist was excised, although he managed to defend it right through to the middle of March. The novel's layer of literary allusions, and the way literature affected the everyday and the domestic, people's behaviour and ideas, were all given three-dimensional form on stage in the figure of Lariosik, the hapless poet from Zhitomir. He seemed to be an incarnation patched together out of a dictionary of quotations from Russian literature.

Lariosik, making his way to Kiev 'across the waves of civil war' with a collection of works by Chekhov wrapped in his only shirt was a generalised token of the previous life of the Turbins and the attitudes of an earlier time. Lariosik became the theatrical 'equivalent' of this theme, which the novel had developed in such a complex and delicate way. It is a truly striking example of the switch from fictional to dramatic thinking.

It is also worth noting the switch from Dostoevsky, who had still retained pride of place in the first version of the play, to Chekhov who was so integral a part of the Art Theatre's tradition. It was a complex change, with the legacy of Chekhov representing the apogee and recent past of Russian culture, the Moscow Art Theatre as it had been, a particular type of drama and a particular way of understanding and exonerating the human race.

Bulgakov displayed a rare sensitivity to the kind of theatre and the kind of stage his beloved characters were going to be living on. He introduced the Chekhov 'gene' into the composition of the play with a delicate irony and just that degree of historical distancing which the new Art Theatre needed. The thunder of the six-inch gun batteries against which Lariosik pronounced the classic Chekhov quotation, 'We shall rest, we shall rest,' was the culmination and resolution of the Chekhov theme. It was like a parting token of respect to Chekhov from the new Theatre and its new Author, both of them called upon to find an answer to the predicament of the intelligentsia in new historical circumstances.

The critics of the time saw no such subtlety in the way the Chekhov tradition was treated. The general opinion was to be that both playwright and Theatre were simply plagiarising Chekhov. Vladimir Mayakovsky joked that the Theatre merely demonstrated 'an endless succession of Auntie Manyas having it off with Uncle Vanyas'. This, however, was still far in the future, almost six months distant. In the spring of 1926, meanwhile, ceaseless rehearsals were in progress at which the scenes in the Turbins' apartment were being jointed together to produce the sense of home and family which was to be such a striking feature of the production. In the rehearsal diary Batalov, never one to waste words, several times comments on the nature of the collaboration:

All the cast were talking about the giving circumstances, [evidently our La Grange meant what the Art Theatre termed 'given circumstances'], their own relationships with other characters, and fantasising towards creating a vivid realisation. Everyone was remembering 1918.[16]

Unfortunately, Batalov tells us little about Bulgakov's contribution in the rehearsals, his anecdotes and acted demonstrations which the cast reminisced about endlessly in later years, and about which Stanislavsky wrote to his 'Red Director' Mikhail Heitz in 1930:

We set great store by Bulgakov. He may yet develop into a producer. He is not only a writer, but an actor too. I am judging by the way he demonstrated things at rehearsals of *The Turbins*. Really he was the director, or at least it was he who put in those sparkling highlights which made the production a success.[17]

Stanislavsky may have been exaggerating the importance of Bulgakov's contribution to directing the play because of his dislike of Sudakov, but there can be no doubt that he greatly facilitated the creation of a historically authentic atmosphere in the Turbin scenes, and added many other touches to the production.

The creative verve of the young performers communicated itself to Bulgakov, firing his imagination, and revealing great reserves of a fresh talent for theatre which he probably never suspected in himself. Bulgakov blossomed in the theatre air; he was set ablaze by the acting of the cast, and himself became an actor and director. It was the reaction of any real playwright who produces not words for a play but a particular kind of deeply intuited and understood life hidden within a script.

Leonid Leonov, Bulgakov's immediate successor at the Art Theatre, was pressed into service during rehearsals of *Untilovsk*. The actors so exhausted him with their questioning that he exclaimed in exasperation, 'These are not actors: they are investigating magistrates!'

It was just this meticulous workmanship that Bulgakov appreciated and which set him alight. Nothing less than real life was to be recreated on the stage. That was the only standard for an Art Theatre production. It was this knowledge of the reality of the period that Bulgakov conveyed to the actors, putting something of his creative self into every role, scene and twist of the plot.

The life of the recent past was recreated on the basis of memories common both to Bulgakov and to the Theatre, with all those homely details and trivia so beloved of the Art Theatre. Batalov, for example, noted down the director's strict injunction that at rehearsal the final supper in the Turbins' house should be appropriately served: 'The table is to be set for seven diners. . . Expensive settings, silver, china'.[18] Ethnographical exactitude was demanded in the kit of Yanshin's Lariosik as a relative who had managed to travel from Zhitomir to Kiev in 1918.

In 1937 when the Art Theatre took *Anna Karenina* to Paris on tour, Mstislav Dobuzhinsky was among the members of the audience. He noticed a number of inaccuracies in the period setting, and offered his services as an old friend to put things right. 'I was told "These are minor details which an audience is not going to notice." '[19] It was an answer which seemed, to an artist brought up in the old Art Theatre, to signal disaster.

In *The Days of the Turbins* there were no 'minor details' of no consequence. The reconstruction of a vanished way of life proceeded with a meticulousness which suggested it had disappeared not eight years before but eight hundred. Creating the atmosphere of a family home was virtually the top artistic priority.

No less important was complete historical authenticity in scenes set in the world surrounding the Turbins. The scene at the headquarters of the Hetman or Petlyura's troops, the episodes at Vasilisa's or the climactic scene at the High School demanded the same gift for observation and exact memory for detail as the life behind the cream blinds. This was an area where the art of a theatre brought up on the plays of Chekhov was of no assistance, an area of experience Chekhov had known nothing of. In the episodes in the Turbins' apartment Bulgakov had only to drop a hint for the scene to come alive: 'Play this scene [Shervinsky's declaration of love to Yelena] the way Stanislavsky played Astrov's in *Uncle Vanya*.' But Chekhov's plays offered no insights into how to act the robbing of the shoemaker; how the Cossack Lieutenant Galanba would crow over a Jew; how, for example, he would say the lines 'He's got his mother here, his kids in town. He's taking over the whole bloody world.'

The insights on how Petlyura's men would rob the shoemaker, or how Bolbotun should wear the red ribbon in his hat, came from Bulgakov. He acted out the entire High School scene for each actor in turn, stimulating their creative ideas by the precision of the historical *mise-en-scène*. When the Art Theatre first went with the play to Kiev in 1936 Bulgakov took the actors to what had been the High School and, Prudkin recalls, acted out the scene on the steps of the grand staircase in its original 1918 setting, again for each of the characters in turn.

Historical authenticity was essential to the achieving of historical truth, which was what both Theatre and playwright were principally aiming for.

A new feature in the second version is the introduction of four episodes set in Wanda and Vasilisa's ground floor apartment. Anastasia Zueva and Mikhail

Tarkhanov rehearsed the scenes for several months, running through them with Stanislavsky, and they were an important structural part of the play right through to the finale, when the robbed houseowner and his wife whom 'honest folk don't even fancy', took refuge with the Turbins and waited with them in the shelter of the Christmas tree for the new times to descend on them.

Zueva and Tarkhanov must have made a remarkable couple. At all events a full thirty years later Boris Vershilov was to recall these scenes in a letter to Yelena Bulgakova with a sense of irreparable loss. 'I shall always hope that Vasilisa and Wanda will be brought back some day, and that the First, Second and Third Robbers will again take the stage. [. . .] Future directors will surely restore these amazing pages from this version of *The White Guard*.'[20]

Bulgakov did not let Vasilisa and Wanda go until late April, but then did away with the entire sub-plot. This naturally necessitated devising new transitions within the Turbin scenes, and restoring their balance with other episodes. Before showing Stanislavsky a run-through with the full cast, Sudakov paid most attention to the High School and Petlyura scenes. The latter had a large and elaborately constructed crowd scene.

The twenty-sixth of March was a momentous day in the production history of *The Days of the Turbins*. This was the day on which Bulgakov and Sudakov ran through two acts of the play for Stanislavsky, including the first scene in the school. Just how important the impression the junior members made on Stanislavsky was for the future of their production hardly needs to be stressed. Let us just add Pavel Markov's reminiscence that 'a very short time indeed before the run-through we were dismayed to hear Stanislavsky say, "What are you thinking of? You've cast some nonentity called Khmelyov in the principal role!" '[21]

In all probability Stanislavsky was in much the same mood when he arrived at one o'clock in the afternoon at the Comic Opera Theatre. Here all those involved in the production had been assembled since morning 'sitting round a table remembering what we had developed, concentrating our attention, and going through every scene mindful of the "through line of action".' Batalov duly recorded in the rehearsal diary a situation familiar to any man or woman of the theatre. '. . . the performers were in buoyant mood, but feeling far from confident. Raging butterflies in every stomach, but calm on the surface.'[22] The Art Theatre's registrar proceeds to note the outcome with a solemnity befitting a chronicler:

When Konstantin Sergeevich had seen the two acts of the play, he said it was coming along nicely. He very much liked the High School and Petlyura scenes. He praised certain members of the cast, and said he considered the work done had been correct, successful, and necessary.[23]

Markov gives an altogether more vivid and informative account:

The cast approached this crucial examination in a mood of manful and joyous abandon. Bulgakov sat it out behind a mask of humour and scepticism intended to conceal the acute anxiety of a novitiate playwright. As always, Stanislavsky's face reflected every last subtle nuance of the performance. Those present kept their eyes on him almost more than on the performance.

Stanislavsky was an exceptionally responsive spectator. He laughed and cried openly at the run-through of *The Turbins*. He followed the action closely, biting his hand as he always did, throwing down his pince-nez and wiping the tears away with his handkerchief. In short, he empathised with the performance deeply. [. . .] At the end of the run-through, he harumphed and pronounced his catch phrase, 'Well now, you could put it on tomorrow', which usually signalled the beginning of a lengthy period of his personal involvement.[24]

This was more than an internal victory within the Art Theatre, and more than a victory for the younger actors. For Stanislavsky himself it was a victory of genius over a dearly loved prejudice, which held that the real Art Theatre was finished. It was a victory over his own grave mistake in supposing that the old guard were playing out the last act of the Art Theatre's story. It was a victory over the belief that only with their involvement could life in post-revolutionary Russia be captured with the compelling artistry which alone entitled his Theatre to be heard in the contemporary world.

This was a decisive moment. Indeed it was a breakthrough for the Art Theatre, with the searing truth about the times people had recently lived through and suffered pouring out on to its stage. If we were to extend Stanislavsky's own metaphor we could say that Lear was beginning to see the faces of those around him, and to realise and recognise that here was an opportunity for his Theatre to begin life again. Its reuniting with its 'daughters', the Studios, had been far from fruitless.

Needless to say this was not the end of friction between the generations in the Art Theatre. That story still had some way to run.

But to return to 26 March. For once Stanislavsky did not join in the production or start altering it at this stage, although he did add touches to some of the most important scenes. This was a production by his Theatre, but it was not his style.

The director of the production was Ilya Sudakov.

We must not exaggerate the personal chemistry between Sudakov and Bulgakov. In many respects they were complete opposites. Sudakov was the son of a bailiff. He had failed to complete his studies at a seminary in Penza, and had been brought up on the radical literary critic Dmitry Pisarev, whom he considered a tremendous authority who had crushed 'idiotic belief in God like the serpent of evil'.[25] Sudakov's roots and his experience of life made him the antithesis of Bulgakov, but this was a case of a project making strange bedfellows. As the production progressed there was a meeting of opposites, a striking synergy; and Sudakov had the wits not to let the main chance slip through his fingers when he had it in his grasp.

That successful run-through in the presence of Stanislavsky inspired the cast with new faith, and on 11 April the Collegium for Artistic Matters and Repertoire took the important decision to set back rehearsals of *Prometheus* and move them out to the foyer, letting *The White Guard* have the Principal Stage in order to be ready for public performance by 1 June.

This was the practical fruit of the victory won at the Comic Opera Theatre. Aeschylus yielded to Bulgakov.

The entry in the rehearsal diary for 15 April details the sound effects and background noises for the production, which Sudakov was faithfully creating in the best Art Theatre tradition. Musical instruments and various machines were assembled after painstaking thought to reproduce a snow storm, a blizzard, a raging tempest, 'chimes and accordions were tried out', and the entire complement of the Musical Studio was invited in to devise and write down the play's acoustical accompaniment in music manuscript books.[26] In 1962 Ilya Sudakov wrote his memoirs under the title, *A Parting Glance at My Life of Toil and Struggle*. Although he gets some dates and facts wrong, he recollects this work on the 'scoring' of the production accurately and in detail. Sudakov's memoirs enable us to piece together the larger overall picture from the diary's brief entries. 'Procure two sirens'; 'procure two metres of repp for wind'; make 'two sets of thundering surf', etc. Sudakov recalled:

The kernel of the play was a storm, a hurricane and people who had lost their way. I portrayed 'Wind, wind over all God's earth' using musical sounds. I got all the wind machines going. Izrailevsky, the musical director, added violins which wailed and moaned like telegraph wires in the wind. Izrailevsky helped me enormously with the prelude of musical and background sound effects with which we began the Petlyura scene in Act Two. The wind howled, the wires moaned, and from start to finish of that lengthy scene Vanya Kudryavtsev was to be heard spiritedly singing the unforgettable 'Hey, little apple! Where are you rolling!' in his high tenor voice.[27]

Sudakov recalled the abrupt transition from the clean, cosy apartment of the Turbins, 'whom the spectator had already come to love as people of refined taste and representatives of civilised and humane values, to these wild, rabid, pseudo-revolutionary enemies' as one of his greatest achievements as a producer.

Bulgakov meanwhile was elaborating his own musical commentaries within each scene. A musical intonation was always integral to his sense of a scene and the way he envisaged it, and the second version gives us an idea of how he felt his way towards this aspect of his poetics. The songs Nikolka sings, from the bawdy to the *Lay of Oleg the Seer*, Shervinsky's Epithalamion from the opera *Nero*, 'God save the Tsar', Vertinsky's romances, the song written to Pushkin's lines 'The blizzard blinds the sky with darkness' which accompanies the destruction of the High School, the delicate minuet by Boccherini which begins the play, and the strains of 'The Internationale' with which it ends: all this polyphonic richness was discovered during the rehearsals in the spring and written into the second version.

The musical commentary is never a mere accompaniment, never mere atmospherics. It abruptly breaks into particular scenes, forcing the inner meaning on the audience. The main trends of genre in the play, tragic, lyrical or comic, are signalled and introduced by musical modulations. It was in these modulations and the slipping between genres that the as yet untitled production began to come to life.

The title might hardly have seemed a problem. There was a novel called *The White Guard*, and a play of the same name which everyone in the Theatre was accustomed to. While the production was merely a bit of 'experimental' fun for the younger actors nobody worried about the title, but immediately the production began to become a reality the problem could no longer be ignored. Let us turn to the first document in what was to become something of a drama in its own right. On 29 April the Collegium for Artistic Matters and Repertoire resolved:

Having due regard to the fact that the title of M. A. Bulgakov's play *The White Guard* has very serious connotations and to the difficulties which may be anticipated in the production's passage [through the censorship] . . . the Collegium considers it essential that some alternative title be found for the play *The White Guard*.[28]

Appended to the minute are the comments of members of the Art Theatre's Council: 'Absolutely!' (Vasily Luzhsky); then, in the large, flowing, indeed billowing hand of Leonid Leonidov, 'I really must insist that "The White Guard" be replaced with a different title.' Below is Vasily Kachalov's ever laconic 'Agree', and at the bottom of the minute is Stanislavsky's unequivocal conclusion: 'The title must certainly be changed from *The White Guard*.

Furthermore, the Hetman must not in any way be identified as Skoropadsky. What is relevant is not Skoropadsky, but the fact of a usurper.'[29]

Rehearsals continued at full speed, but for the time being without a title. On 13 May the Lower Chamber discussed four possibilities suggested by Bulgakov: *White December*, *1918*, *The Fall of a City*, *The White Storm*. None of these was acceptable either to the Collegium or to the members of the Council. Vasily Luzhsky tried inventively to reconcile Leonidov's proposed *Before the End* with Bulgakov's suggestions and ended up, perhaps predictably, with some choice pearls: 'How about, "A Storm – an End"? Or perhaps, from the saying, "The Bitter End"? [. . .] Or "Ending Storm"? "Stormy End"?'

Leonidov states his position in a flowing hand, the line trailing downwards as if bent, 'The title I favour out of all of these is *Before the End*.'

Kachalov added, 'I agree.'

Stanislavsky did not like *Before the End* 'from the literary and aesthetic point of view. It suggests a mediocre play by the likes of Shpazhinsky or Gnedich, but I can't think of anything better.' Stanislavsky was sure that any of Bulgakov's titles would doom the play. 'I would avoid the word "White". They will only accept it in a combination such as "The End of the Whites", which is not an acceptable title. As I can't think of anything better, I recommend calling it *Before the End*. I think this will make them take a different view of the play from the very first act.'[30]

Bulgakov stuck to his guns. 'Stormy End' must have made him shudder. On 19 May the Collegium instructed Bulgakov, Markov and Sudakov to 'advise of the play's new title within seventy-two hours'.[31] They reached deadlock. Worse, the nearer the preview came the more radical were the suggestions regarding the play itself. Somebody thought the Petlyura scene should be removed and the play reduced from four to three acts. At this point Bulgakov once more dug in his heels and became loudly intractable. On 4 July he erupted with an angry and categorical ultimatum:

To the Council and Directors of the Moscow Art Theatre.

I have the honour hereby to advise you that I cannot agree to removal of the Petlyura scene from my play *The White Guard*.

Motivation: the Petlyura scene is an organic part of the play.

I further do not agree that the title of the play should be changed to 'Before the End'.

Neither do I agree that this four-act play should be turned into a three-act play.

I am prepared to discuss a title other than *The White Guard* with the Theatre Council.

In the event that the Theatre should be unable to agree the substance of this letter, I must ask that *The White Guard* be removed from production forthwith . . .[32]

'The honour hereby to advise you . . .' The ultimatum was couched in the icy politeness of an author who had expended an enormous amount of hard work, had actually seen his production and was fully aware of its possibilities. This was the tone not of some hack employed to adapt a novel for the stage but of a fully-fledged dramatist, and one moreover who had in the interim been to the dress rehearsal of his *Madame Zoyka* at the Vakhtangov Studio. Bulgakov was asserting himself not as the writer of a play script but as an Author of the Theatre, who worked in partnership with the Moscow Art Theatre to create his own theatre, and who shaped its destiny as much as he shaped his own.

Luzhsky's reply survives in the archive, calming, reassuring, defusing the situation. 'Goodness me, who on earth has upset you so, our own dear Moscow Art Mikhail Afanasievich . . .'[33]

Moscow Art Bulgakov stood his ground, and the title stayed the same. Rehearsals continued at full tilt, and Stanislavsky involved himself in them personally. It has long been known that Stanislavsky conducted several rehearsals in autumn 1926, immediately before the first night, but from the diary of Pavel Podobed, an actor and member of the Theatre's Board, we learn that Stanislavsky was already actively rehearsing the play in June; not only the scenes in the Turbins' apartment, but also the Petlyura scene. There were rehearsals on 19, 20, 22 June, and on 24 June the first closed dress rehearsal took place with choir, orchestra, and full sets. Podobed tells us how it went, in the presence of Vladimir Blyum and Alexander Orlinsky, two of the most aggressive left-wingers in the theatre world of those years.

Podobed's entry reads: 'Mood after the performance: delighted as regards the young actors' acting, and extremely sour and tense regarding the impression made on the visitors . . . Supposedly overheard in their box saying, "Well, maybe in five years' time or so".' Podobed goes on to give an important insight into Stanislavsky's attitude to the production's possible fate: 'K.S. says, if they do we should close the Theatre [. . .] What are they playing at! *The White Guard* unacceptable, *Othello* unacceptable.'[34] (The left-wing theatre critics were also conducting a campaign against Shakespeare at the time for propounding 'idiotic patriarchal values'.)

Podobed's unpublished diary entry is borne out by a published note by Ivan Kudryavtsev:

For the first time ever K.S. said nothing when we came out from the stage to hear his comments. He just sat there, looked at us lovingly, and left. The next day he met me by the doors of the Theatre: 'For heaven's sake, what are they playing at! They've censored your Nikolka, censored him . . .'[35]

Stanislavsky was on his way into the Theatre, so in all probability he did not yet know the outcome of that morning's meeting of the government's Main Repertoire Committee. It was a Friday and the last day of the theatre season. Not, happily, Friday the thirteenth.

We have two accounts of what transpired on 25 June and, at least on the surface, they conflict. An excerpt from the minutes of that meeting is glued in Bulgakov's scrapbook of the production history of *The Days of the Turbins*. Even before the meeting began, Chekina, an editor, 'advised the representatives of the MAAT of the view of the Head of the Theatre Section Comrade Blyum that *The White Guard* was an outright apologia for the White Guardist cause, and right through from the scene in the High School to the death of Alexey inclusive was entirely unacceptable and it certainly could not be passed in the manner the Theatre was staging it in'.[36]

The Art Theatre representatives were Markov, Sudakov and Luzhsky. They were past masters at defending the Theatre, and knew when a flanking manoeuvre might prove more effective than frontal attack. They made no attempt to argue directly with Chekina. Indeed they stated, as is noted in the minutes, that 'after the preview dress rehearsal they had themselves realised that an unpleasant impression had been created, but that this production, which was the work of the Theatre's younger actors, was very dear to them, and they were prepared to amend the staging'.[37]

With the preliminary discussion over, Orlinsky and Richard Pelshe arrived for the meeting.

For the first time in the documented history of *The Days of the Turbins* Orlinsky set out, at his superior's request, the objections to the play. These were essentially:

The scene in the High School should not be presented in such a way as to present White Guardists as heroic but so as to discredit the entire White Guard movement.

The mutual relations of the White Guardists with other social groupings should be brought out, at the very least with their domestic servants, porters, etc.

Some of the White Guardists or 'gentlemen of the nobility' or bourgeois should be shown joining in the Petlyura atrocities.

To approve the statement made by Director Comrade Sudakov about the part in the first version, not subsequently included in the play, in which Nikolka, the youngest person, could be the vehicle for a shift in sympathies towards the Bolsheviks . . .[38]

That was the sum total of Orlinsky's ideas. After the première he was to use them to berate the Theatre and Bulgakov in newspaper and magazine reviews and at innumerable meetings and 'tribunals on *The White Guard*'. In February

1927 Bulgakov tried at one such debate to answer his opponent point by point, not overlooking his advice about the domestic servants. Fortunately he was not at the meeting of 25 June. The Art Theatre representatives made no attempt to argue against Orlinsky and Blyum, behaving instead like the three wily muzhiks in Tolstoy's *The Fruits of Enlightenment*. When Pelshe asked whether the Theatre accepted Orlinsky's suggested corrections and wondered whether they were not perhaps oppressive, the Theatre's representatives replied that of course they accepted the 'corrections required and would willingly rework the play, and a new preview would take place in the second half of September'.[39]

This was agreed. The reader unfamiliar with the situation in the theatre in 1926 might see this discussion as naive or indeed offensive to both Bulgakov and the Art Theatre, whose good faith was clear to see. Back at the Theatre, however, the discussion was seen in quite a different light. Our second source, again Podobed's diary, throws an unexpected light on that extract from the minutes.

On 26 June at three in the afternoon both Chambers of the Art Theatre parliament gathered for a final session before dispersing for the summer break. Markov, Luzhsky and Sudakov reported on the previous day's meeting. Despite Podobed's abominable handwriting we can decipher a number of highly pertinent sentences in his diary entry:

Outright victory at the Main Repertoire Committee [. . .] Orlinsky spoke first. He characterised the production as White Guardist. This was rebutted by the Committee chairman, Pelshe. 'A theatre which has staged such productions in the past season as *The Pugachev Affair*, *Nicholas the First and the Decembrists*, and *Merchants of Glory* cannot be even remotely suspected of mounting a White Guardist production.' [. . .] He even said MAAT's productions had been the highlight of the theatre season and highly significant. The past season's productions were putting MAAT in the forefront of the world's theatres. [. . .] Sudakov and Markov defended the production very warmly and courageously and now they are the heroes of the hour. Praise was heaped on the Theatre at the meeting, and Pelshe gave a very strong defence which has the force of an order to his subordinates.

At this point several words are totally illegible, and then we read, fairly clearly, 'News of how the meeting had turned out produced jubilation at the Theatre. [. . .] K.S. to the younger actors: Don't get too big for your boots. You'll be saying you don't need the old stagers any more.'[40]

Quite clearly the 'heroes of the hour' gave a rather slanted account of events, but it is equally clear that the excerpt from the minutes was also selective. There was real hope in the fact that the dress rehearsal on 24 June had been attended by people whose opinion, as the Theatre well understood, would be decisive. On 2 July 1926 Khmelyov wrote to Kudryavtsev, by then already on holiday in the country, to give him 'the latest about *The White Guard*'.

> Luzhsky, Markov and Sudakov have been to see the Repertoire Committee. After lengthy altercations the Committee agreed to let WG go ahead. The first two scenes are unchanged, except for the word 'Trotsky'. In the High School they are considering dropping the appearance of Petlyura's men and giving me a few extra lines [. . .]
>
> The first scene of Act Three (news of Alexey's death) got up the Committee's nose but found support with Higher Authority, so what will happen there, and also with the ending, nobody knows. At all events the Government says everything is acceptable as it stands except for the end of the High School and the Petlyura scene, which they want to cut entirely. The general view is that this is an acting masterpiece, and it would be a crime not to let a production of this stature proceed.[41]

Khmelyov's letter makes it clear why the Theatre saw the opportunity of a preview in September as unconditional victory.

Thus a historic season drew to its close. It had seen the staging of Ostrovsky's *The Ardent Heart. The Marriage of Figaro* had made major progress in rehearsal, and Bulgakov's play had been seen through to dress rehearsal stage. On the last day of the season Stanislavsky gave an address to all members of the Art Theatre, in which he called the season a 'second Pushkino', comparing it with the year in which the Art Theatre began.[42] He could bestow no higher praise.

Luzhsky as Acting Director was moved to issue a special circular that very day 'To all 380 at MAAT'. Reviewing the past season he mentioned the 'quite exceptional artistic success of the new experimental production' and, full of pride at the revival of the Theatre of which he was a founder member, ended his address with what sounded like a toast: 'Allow me, as a member of the cast of our latest general production, to say to all of you, Bravo!'[43]

Events were to show that it was early days to lapse into rhetoric perhaps better suited to Lariosik. The summer break, which lasted until 24 August, was only a breathing space before the last and severest test of all.

The First Night

Bulgakov spent the summer at Kryukovo near Moscow. It was a busman's holiday, his cares at the Art Theatre merely being replaced by problems at the Vakhtangov Studio. One project ran into the other and everything became very confused. On 11 August he wrote to Alexey Popov:

I certainly am exhausted. In May I had all sorts of surprises, not related to the theatre, and in May there was all the rushing around with *Guard* at Art Theatre I . . . In June I was constantly taken up with silly, trivial work because none of the plays is actually producing any income yet, and in July there was the correcting of *Madame Zoyka*. Come August I find I've got the whole lot to deal with at once.[44]

The surprises in May which were 'not related to the theatre' were a search at Bulgakov's flat on 7 May 1926 during which his novella *Heart of a Dog* and personal diaries were confiscated.

Heart of a Dog had already been read to the Art Theatre and agreement even reached that Bulgakov would dramatise it. Needless to say, after the May surprises the agreement fell through.

In August Bulgakov suffered the first indications that fame was about to be his. These were not at all what might have been hoped for. He began to recognise, as Molière would in his future novella, that fame 'primarily consists of your being subjected to unbridled abuse at every turn'. The first of the abuse was inadvertently prompted by the Art Theatre's sending out its list of forthcoming performances to subscribers in the summer. Here the plays of Aeschylus, Beaumarchais, Shakespeare, Sukhovo-Kobylin and . . . Bulgakov were listed in succession. This caused apoplexy in some quarters. On 9 August 1926 a certain V. Chernoyarov wrote a riposte in *New Theatre-Goer* under the title 'An International Team'. Within his highly noticeable limitations, Chernoyarov did his best to deride the notion that a modern writer could be placed alongside classics.

Bulgakov stored this gratuitous rudeness away for future reference, subsequently immortalising it in *Black Snow* where Chernoyarov is given the merited pseudonym of Volkodav (Wolfhound). The article was published in the summer and nobody paid any attention to it, aside from a few fellow members of the 'Disgusted of Krasnaya Presnya' brigade, who were considerably heartened.

On 24 August the Theatre returned from the summer break, on which day there is an entry in the rehearsal diary: 'Meeting on the play. Konstantin Sergeevich, V. V. Luzhsky, M. A. Bulgakov, I. A. Sudakov, and P. A. Markov.'[45] In the rehearsal sheets and the diary the play is now called *The Turbin Family*, and a resolution of the Collegium gives a final proposal for the playbill: *The Days of the Turbins (The White Guard)*. The protracted controversy brought forth a title combining a family chronicle with a historical chronicle, which corresponded exactly to the spirit of the production.

The change of title was accompanied by major changes in the text. The High School scene was rehearsed on 25 and 26 August, and Bulgakov supplied a text 'to an outline approved by Stanislavsky' for the occasion.[46] Sudakov describes in his memoirs how he persuaded Bulgakov to rewrite Alexey Turbin's speech to the cadets, the main thrust of which is expressed in the words 'The White cause in the Ukraine is finished. And it's finished in Rostov-on-Don, finished everywhere!' (p. 62) 'At my request Bulgakov also rewrote the finale of the play. [. . .] I persuaded him to add the following lines for Captain Myshlaevsky: "Let them mobilize me [into the Red Army]. At least I'll know that I'm serving in a Russian army."' (p. 85)

As we can see, Turbin's role was developed in accordance with an outline devised on 25 June. In accordance with the same plan the function of Myshlaevsky was revised and it was he, not Nikolka, who was given the theme of 'the shift in sympathies towards the Bolsheviks'.

Whatever one may think of Sudakov's co-authorship, it has to be said that Bulgakov accepted these changes without being pressured by ultimatums. It was he who actually wrote them in. Between them Bulgakov and the Art Theatre really did sharpen up and improve certain aspects of the script, but in other places they simply gave way to the demands of Blyum and Orlinsky. In the school Alexey Turbin was only spelling out what every member of the audience already knew anyway. 'They want Alexey Turbin to recognise,' Khmelyov wrote in the letter to Kudryavtsev quoted above, 'that something catastrophic has happened and there is no way out, that the White cause is doomed, as is the old order as a whole, and that something new and unknown is coming which everyone should strive towards.'[47] Khmelyov's Turbin was thus obliged to start explaining things which drama critic Blyum and director Sudakov regarded as self-evident, but which certainly would not have been self-evident to a regular White officer in December 1918. 'They'll make you fight against your own people. And when the Russian people fights back and splits your heads open, those generals will run away abroad . . .' (p. 61) A real Colonel Turbin could never have said anything of the sort, any more than he could have told the cadets in the High School scene 'I know that things in Rostov are exactly the same as in Kiev . . . Artillery regiments without any shells to fire, cadets without boots to wear, and the staff officers sitting around in cafés.' (p. 61)

This patching up of the script took place actually during rehearsals, and was not even always done by Bulgakov. On 7 February 1927 Pavel Markov was to explain at a debate on *The Days of the Turbins* and *Lyubov' Yarovaya* that Bulgakov could not be held responsible for several oddities in the final act, since it had been written 'by at least fifteen different people'.[48]

There is no disputing the fact that the end result of these collective endeavours was a worse play than the one they started with. Bulgakov's drama about the collapse of the White cause was vulgarised to make it fit a primitive stereotype. At the debate Markov explained, '. . . in my view [the fourth act] should have been made much more terrible, pessimistic and sombre, but that was out of the question given the constraints within which we were working when producing the play'.

The 're-education' of Myshlaevsky was dictated by the same constraints, and also collectively elaborated. This marked a more serious change in the play's direction, but did in fact fit in credibly with the character as Dobronravov had been developing it. The Captain, representing Russian patriotism, and with his existing diatribes against the generals, could take the additions to the script on board without suffering damage. Dobronravov had in any case been developing him as a character who lived by his own lights.

Bulgakov was mastering the dramatist's ancient craft of cutting and pasting. In his history of the life of Molière, he agreed with the author of *Tartuffe* who 'justly averred that . . . no amount of alterations to a work can change its basic meaning by so much as one iota'. In this connection the narrator recalls the parable of the lizard which is prepared to lose its tail because 'any lizard knows it is better to live without a tail than to lose your life'. In the same place Bulgakov relates with evident professional insight how 'Molière broke off not his tail but the beginning of his play, cutting out an introductory scene, and in addition going through the other parts of the play also, spoiling them as far as circumstance allowed. The first scene was essential and removing it detracted from the play's quality, but changed nothing in the basic point on which it hinged.'

Such apparent faint-heartedness on the part of a dramatist might seem cause for a wry smile, or even embarrassment; but let us take the advice of Molière's biographer and refrain from casting stones at him or, come to that, his successor. Our restraint is all the more merited since Bulgakov really did manage to revise his entire play without changing the point on which it hinged in the least. The false hindsight brought to the monologue Turbin delivers shortly before his death does not detract from his stature. The main thrust of the monologue survives, which is that Alexey Turbin refuses to send people to their deaths even when his principles and ideals are facing destruction. Human life means more to him than principles, more, indeed, than the White cause itself.

Bulgakov expanded the monologue and introduced an element of political commentary into it, enlarging its frame of reference as it were. The crux of the scene remained, however, just where it always was: in his last memorable words.

And I, Alexey Turbin, an officer of the Regular Army who fought through the entire war against the Germans, as Captains Studzinsky and Myshlaevsky here can witness, I take all my actions on my own conscience and responsibility – everything. I am warning you, and because I love you, I'm sending you all home. That is all I have to say. (p. 62)

The texts of the many different versions of Act Four have not survived. As always in the theatre, no one had time to think about history in the midst of the feverish preparations for the first night. Discarded scripts instantly disappeared without trace. By some miracle an intermediate version of the final act is to be found in the Art Theatre Museum from which we can see the direction things were moving in and the search for the final semantic boundaries of the play. The 'point', however, of Act Four, with its Christmas Eve setting, its anxious expectation of change, and the sense of one epoch ending as another begins, was left firmly in place by both Theatre and playwright.

The foundations on which the Turbins' future life would have to be based and the choices open to them were behind the changes to Act Four. The theme of assuming a disguise, changing one's style of dress, adapting to new regimes had been stated in the First Act. At its most extreme it is expressed in Talberg's return from Berlin just in time for his wife's marriage to Shervinsky. 'I have decided to return,' he announces, 'and collaborate with the Soviet authorities. We must change our political landmarks. It's as simple as that.'

Lack of a principled historical perspective may be natural to a Talberg or to an irresponsible songster like Shervinsky, who is untroubled by the least awareness of historical choice. The characters Bulgakov admires live by different lights. All the versions uncompromisingly bring out this stratification within the Turbins' home, with the very different demands different individuals make of history. Even the dim-witted Studzinsky finds himself located within the charged field of choice. He is quite prepared to follow the example of Shervinsky, who has hired a 'politically neutral overcoat' from the porter. He changes into civilian clothes and is all for joining Petlyura's unruly forces. A dialogue between him and Myshlaevsky, which did not survive beyond the draft, tells us a great deal about the way Bulgakov's ideas were moving, and not only with reference to *The Days of the Turbins*.

Studzinsky. Coming. (*Fetches a piece of paper. To Myshlaevsky*.) Here.
Myshlaevsky (reads). I see . . . hmm . . . Borisovich . . . You don't think Bronislavovich would be prettier?
Studzinsky. You never stop.
Myshlaevsky. What do you mean! I couldn't be more serious. Studzenko . . . What sort of a name is that! Who's going to take you for a Studzenko with an accent like yours? Just talking to you makes me feel I'm sipping café à la Varsovienne . . .

The Captain responds to Studzinsky's proposal to join up with Petlyura's forces with an argument which clearly has Bulgakov's approval. 'I see. *Merci*. Follow the baggage trains of that rabble . . . Myshlaenko . . . No, actually I think I'll remain Myshlaevsky.'

This motif of stoicism was to be carried through to *Flight*, where Khludov was to raise the concept of a kind of honour and arrogant pride in one's place in history to the level of tragedy.

Khludov. I'm going back to Russia too, I may even go tonight. There's a steamer leaving tonight for Odessa.
Serafima. Are you going back secretly, under a false name?
Khludov. Under my own name. I shall turn up and say: I've arrived – I'm Khludov.
Serafima. But you'll be shot out of hand!
Khludov. Instantly. (p. 223)

Different versions of a finale for *The Turbins* were discarded like different possible destinies. Man's place in history had to be decided naturally and with integrity.

Bulgakov was to find his own way of asserting this theme and resolving it in the final version of Act Four in September. It was a musical rather than a textual solution. His favourite plot and compositional device was to repeat a particular motif in a new context, and in Act Four of *The Turbins* he deploys it to perfection.

Let us recall the second scene in the Turbins' apartment. The whole family is gathered and a last desperate 'feast in time of plague' begins. When they are forced to recognise that battle must be joined but that nobody knows on whose behalf, that there is not even anything they can drink a toast to any more, they sing 'God save the Tsar'. It merges with the popular soldier's ballad 'The Lay of Oleg the Seer', a march composed during the First World War which particularly appealed to the Bulgakovs. Lariosik begins singing, and the others join in: 'So let the music play the march of victory. The enemy is running away, away, away. And for the . . .'. Lariosik blurts out 'Tsar!', but none of the others support him. They omit the words 'And for the Tsar, the pride of Russia's history', and finish off the song, 'Let's raise the mighty cry: Hurrah! Hurrah! Hurrah!'[49] Immediately after the singing of the national anthem, minus the Tsar, Nikolka begins singing: 'Towards him there comes from the forest's dark shades', and the others take up the soul-searing lines of Pushkin's poem. Thus Bulgakov states the 'thesis', and sets the mood in which the Turbins anticipate their lot.

In Act Four Bulgakov gives a mirror image of this scene. In Act One, Scene

Two Nikolka capped the singing of the others. Here, now crippled, it is he who begins, combining the Pushkin ballad with a parody of the national anthem:

> 'Oh, tell me magician, beloved of the gods,
> What fate is in store for me lying?
> How soon in the fight 'gainst impossible odds
> Shall foemen rejoice at my dying?
> No, let the music play the march of victory,
> The enemy is running away, away, away!' (p. 106)

It was during rehearsals that someone had the idea that Myshlaevsky should suggest substituting 'the Council of People's Commissars . . .' for 'the Tsar', and as in Act One all except Studzinsky join in the refrain, 'Let's raise the mighty cry: Hurrah! Hurrah! Hurrah!' (p. 103)

Studzinsky is outraged, Lariosik delighted. Yelena and Shervinsky are preparing to be married. The decorations twinkle on the Christmas tree. It is Nikolka who pulls the carpet from under their high spirits, revealing the grim reality by singing,

> 'Towards him there comes from the forest's dark shades,
> Divinely inspired, the magician . . .' (p. 104)

The sense of waiting is unaltered, the sense of trepidation is unaltered; the meaning of Pushkin's ballad is unaltered. Bulgakov draws the theme to its conclusion with the prophecy of Pushkin's magus, without in any way having betrayed his own 'free and truthful voice'. The whole structure of the drama takes its cue from the objective truth of Pushkin.

Such were the end results of the revising of the play. The lizard was still alive, and the production was still in contention.

As Bulgakov dictated the final text it was typed by Olga Bokshanskaya, the secretary of Nemirovich-Danchenko and sister of Bulgakov's future wife, Yelena Sergeevna. Olga was already an important figure in the Theatre, and was to become ever more indispensable with the passage of time. She had a talent for shrewdly taking in the situation in the Theatre and summarising its essentials very succinctly. In 1931 Bulgakov received a letter from her, posted in Leningrad where the Theatre was on tour, and described it as 'a real theatre letter. Everything is crystal clear.'[50]

In September 1926 Bokshanskaya sent similar 'real theatre letters' to Nemirovich-Danchenko in America. She reported to her boss religiously, missing nothing; and her letters survive. They give a trustworthy account of the last three weeks before the first night of The Turbins.

On 3 September she reports that 'the Management' have been chivvying her for the best part of a week to 'get back to doing her own work instead of writing with Bulgakov'.[51]

On 10 September she tells Nemirovich-Danchenko that the play's title has been changed and work on the text completed. 'Bulgakov has delivered the revised script, which is in rehearsal and will be staged as amended. Whether the amendments will be accepted is anybody's guess.'[52]

The first public dress rehearsal was scheduled for Friday 17 September. Worker correspondents from the press were invited, as were representatives of the Main Repertoire Committee, and the Art Theatre's own Studio actors 'except for MAAT II and the Third Studio, who treat our rehearsals as if they were a finished production'.[53]

These of course are Stanislavsky's words and instructions. Immediately before the dress rehearsal he himself was conducting rehearsals, attending to every detail, and requesting that complimentary tickets should be given 'only to your very closest relatives, and under no circumstances to actors from other theatres or individuals professionally involved in the arts or the press'.

The previous March, on the day before their run-through for Stanislavsky in the Comic Opera Theatre, the cast had gone through the entire play bearing the through line of the action in mind as Stanislavsky had taught them, and had been greatly agitated by the important examination they were about to take.

Now it was Stanislavsky's turn to be agitated. The day before the dress rehearsal he assembled the cast to 'establish the place of each psychological factor in the stream of the play' and finalise the staging.[54] This time it was he who had an examination to pass.

This Friday the seventeenth was, alas, to prove unlucky. Stanislavsky wasn't at the dress rehearsal because he was acting Astrov in *Uncle Vanya* that evening at the opening night of the Little Stage. Luzhsky missed the discussion because he was playing Serebryakov.

Olga Bokshanskaya gives us a full account of what happened.

The rehearsal went swimmingly and was a great success. Some members of the audience were reduced to tears. Khmelyov and Kudryavtsev really do play the Turbins very movingly. Immediately after the rehearsal the members of the Repertoire Committee (Pelshe was not there, but Blyum was) and the worker correspondents held a meeting in our Board Room.[55]

She goes on to convey Blyum's decision, which he announced

to Sudakov and the others, that as it stood the play could not go on the playbill. Sudakov said, 'Come now, is it a matter of making a few corrections, or completely restructuring the production?' He received the reply that it was indeed a matter of completely restructuring and remaking the play. This conclusion to the rehearsal naturally upset everybody . . .[56]

That highly theatrical ellipsis was doubtless inserted by Bokshanskaya to give her addressee a Chekhovian pause in which himself to experience what had occurred at Art Theatre Passage.

Blyum, of course, had no power to decide anything and it was in any case perfectly clear well in advance what his point of view would be. Vladimir Blyum wrote his vitriolic pieces against the Art Theatre under the poetic pseudonym of 'Sadko', and persecuted the Art Theatre and all its works as a matter of principle. After the first night he was to fall upon the Theatre and its Author with such fury that Verbitsky, who played Talberg, was moved to contribute a note to Bulgakov's scrap-book:

> In vain the cries of 'Author! . . .', 'Bravo! . . .'
> Bulgakov will not emerge from the gloom
> While he serves as a matador's blood-red cloak
> To that raging bull, Vladimir Blyum![57]

It only remained to appeal to those who did decide such matters. Anatoly Lunacharsky, Commissar of Enlightenment, was duly advised of the outcome of the rehearsal.

That evening Anat. Lunacharsky tried to phone Vasily [Luzhsky] but only managed to speak to Markov. It is not only the Art Theatre that has been full of rumours and gossip. All of theatrical Moscow is buzzing. The Theatre and individual actors have been bombarded with phone calls from people eager to know what is likely to happen. [. . .] We are expecting to hear something definite in the course of today.[58]

Olga Bokshanskaya's letter of 18 September 1926 gives an important insight into Lunacharsky's position. 'Anat. Lunacharsky wants us to give a rehearsal for him and the entire Collegium of the Commissariat, as well as for the authorities, who are taking a great interest in the production.'[59]

The new preview was scheduled for 23 September, which necessitated the extraordinary step of cancelling an evening performance. The audience at the preview were not the kind of people who could be expected to turn up to a theatre performance during the day.

Luzhsky noted in his diary that day, 'A meeting, to discuss what to do if they decide to ban *Days of the Turbins*, who should speak and what they should say. The speakers will be K.S., Markov, Sudakov, and Yustinov.'[60] The latter was the Theatre's financial director, and it would doubtless have been his job to paint a picture of the Theatre's dire financial plight if 'they' should decide on a ban.

The day before the preview we find the actors rehearsing 'the script of Act Two, with cuts and alterations', and on the morning of the performance the Petlyura scene had the episode with the baiting of the Jew, acted by Joseph Raevsky, removed from it. At the same time Sudakov devised a necessary apotheosis: 'Instead of singing "The Internationale" diminuendo it will be sung crescendo.'[61]

On 22 September Stanislavsky addressed his company like a commander addressing his troops before a crucial battle.

Serious considerations oblige me to categorically forbid actors and staff of the Theatre who are not involved in the performance of *The Days of the Turbins* on 23 September from being present among the audience in the auditorium, foyer or corridors during the play or the intervals.[62]

The Art Theatre's preview turned into an event of importance for the whole Russian theatre. On 21 September Vsevolod Meyerhold was moved to write to Stanislavsky, who was not very experienced in these matters, advising him whom to invite to the preview. He listed old Bolsheviks, appended an address list, and even told Stanislavsky that 'all the individuals listed' had already been apprised of what was afoot.[63]

The entry in the rehearsal diary for 23 September 1926 states tersely:

Full dress rehearsal with audience. Representatives of [the Government of] the USSR, press, and Main Repertoire Committee, Konstantin Stanislavsky, the Art Theatre Council and Producers' Committee. Whether the play proceeds or not will be decided after today's performance.[64]

Olga Bokshanskaya's letter of 30 September fleshes out that formal entry with an eyewitness account of this major event.

I wrote to you last time about the proposed public preview of the play. This took place on the 23rd. A batch of tickets were sent to the Government and the remainder to the Moscow Committee of the Communist Party for distribution to various organisations. The Theatre received an allocation of 100 tickets for distribution to friends, the old stagers and their families. The closed nature of the performance only served to further heighten interest and speculation about it. The Theatre was packed. Absolutely everybody who had been sent tickets turned up. From the first interval there was heated discussion of the play going on in all the corridors and the foyer. [. . .] The performance was very well received with many outbursts of clapping in mid-act, especially for Yanshin who really does play the student Lariosik splendidly. Prudkin's interpretation of Shervinsky has gone down extremely well at both rehearsals. [. . .]

All the talk during the intervals centred on the play and the acting. The play provoked arguments, some amazingly heated.

There was no disagreement as regards the acting. Absolutely everybody leaving the auditorium was saying first and foremost, 'What brilliant acting, though. Brilliant!'

There were so many famous and familiar faces in the audience, and they expressed their views on the play so ardently, that now at one spot in the foyer now at another, or somewhere in the corridor, listeners would group. [. . .] Someone called them 'lightning political meetings' . . . There was supposed to be a joint meeting of the Collegium of Narkompros and the Repertoire Committee after the performance to decide finally whether to allow the play to be staged, but it never took place. Everyone just wanted to get home because it was late and they were tired. We did try to insist, because the Commissar made his support for the play very clear indeed . . .[65]

On 25 September an official announcement was made in *Our Newspaper* that *The Days of the Turbins* had been passed for performance. One further rehearsal was held before an audience on 2 October, with final changes to the script.

The first night was on 5 October 1926. Vasily Luzhsky noted in his diary, 'No ructions yesterday at the first night of *The Turbins* . . . A full house. By today's standards the audience was sophisticated and restrained. A major success . . .'[66]

Luzhsky very much liked including a weather report in his diary. On 29 September he noted, 'Cold. Sunny, but cold.' On 30 September he volunteered the same straightforward meteorological observation, 'Sunny, but cold!'

As luck would have it we are not told what the weather was like on the sunniest day of Bulgakov's romance with the Theatre. On Wednesday 6 October, however, we learn it was 'Cold and grey. Snow.'[67]

The celebrations were over. It was time to return to the workaday world. Anna Akhmatova had seen 1917 as the year when the twentieth century began, not by the calendar but in earnest. *The Days of the Turbins* emerges now from our calendar-based account into the real and turbulent world of theatre history.

3

Finding a Home

Stephenson's Steam Engine

In his scrapbook on *The Days of the Turbins* Bulgakov preserved a page from a tear-off calendar for 5 October 1926. It bears an illustration of the first steam engine built by George Stephenson in 1829. The idea behind Bulgakov's bold and unexpected conceit was to become clearer with the passing of time. Stephenson's great invention did not meet with unanimous approbation from his contemporaries. There were some who had no faith in steam, and put their trust literally in horse-power. There were envious rival engineers who 'mounted a veritable campaign of persecution against Stephenson' in Parliament. A historian of those times tells us there was even one aristocratic landowner who gave orders to 'shoot at the surveyors if they should set foot on his land'. The advantages and usefulness of the new means of locomotion were, however, so evident that pig-headed men and guiltless horses alike were obliged to move aside and make way for it.

The destiny of the discovery which Bulgakov and the Moscow Art Theatre had made with *The Days of the Turbins* was to prove immeasurably less straightforward. Decades were to pass before the usefulness and importance of the first Art Theatre performance to address the revolutionary present day were recognised. Today they seem self-evident, but there is a history here which merits examination.

In 1930 a certain exceptionally diligent journalist calculated that the reviews of *The Days of the Turbins* came in total to some 200,000 words. Sadly, the whole lot together cannot compensate us today for the lack of a straightforward eyewitness account of the performance. In the heat of battle nobody bothered to create a pen portrait of it. The image of this legendary production lived on in the memories of several generations of theatregoers, of the actors themselves, and in the diaries of trustworthy admirers of the Art Theatre. One such is Police Constable Alexey Gavrilov who was on duty at *The Days of the Turbins*, saw the play dozens of times, and noted down many things which would have been noted by the theatre critics if they had been doing their job.

But there are difficulties of a different order. An Art Theatre production was born into an established system of stagecraft, with the result that there was nothing resembling a written director's score. The *mise-en-scène* was fairly free, and tailored to what suited the actors and their creative needs. In effect *The Days of the Turbins* was a workshop-style performance whose overriding aim was to create on stage the figure of a live human being, unencumbered by the loud propaganda or otherwise stereotyped value judgements which were a feature of the time.

It is sometimes possible virtually to sight-read a production constructed within the conventions of stylised theatre. The overall design is clear, and the pulse can be clearly felt. The musical score of *The Days of the Turbins* was a matter of its protagonists' irregular breathing, nuances of intonation and changes of topic, trepidation and breaks in mood which exerted a magnetic field but which did not at all lend themselves to being reconstituted in words. The historian can only note the presence of a first aid team in the auditorium for the first year after the première. Hysteria and fainting were not uncommon, necessitating, as PC Gavrilov notes, the removal of members of the audience during the performance. The death of Alexey Turbin or the bringing on stage of the wounded Nikolka were experienced by members of the audience, who had been conditioned by the Art Theatre to identify emotionally with the reality of theatrical action, as an agonising reality which the Russian intelligentsia had suffered only yesterday.

Of course, the audience was far from homogeneous, just as the controversy surrounding the production was a mixed bag. One of the first articles written against *The Turbins* conveys the emotional atmosphere in October 1926: 'Concrete results: at the Art Theatre preview one tear-stained citizen bawled "Thank you", and at the debate in the House of the Press a deeply affected female citizen shrieked, "All men are brothers." '[1]

For all the author's contempt for his fellow 'citizens', he has left us valuable evidence and a direct insight into the production's impact, which was one of humanity pure and simple.

The production was largely posited on negatives, recognisable only within the context of the period. The aesthetics of negation were evident from the outset in the design of the settings. In an age when the constructivist stage set ruled supreme, Nikolai Ulyanov put an entirely traditional three-walled set on the stage of the Moscow Art Theatre. When the curtain rose the audience discovered the spacious dining room of a professor's house in Kiev, with a fireplace, mahogany furniture and a dazzling bronze chandelier. The whole homely atmosphere was reproduced in a Chekhovian idiom, from the cream curtains in the windows to the soothing silver-blue wallpaper and the austere and precise lines of the slightly sloping room. This signalled the production's loyalty to tradition and its lineage. 'The heavy, ponderous fourth-wall naturalism of a quarter of a century ago,' as Emmanuil Beskin wrote acidly.[2]

Everything about the house seemed to hark back a quarter of a century, with the clock stolidly chiming and playing a genteel minuet by Boccherini. The tablecloth was as dazzlingly white and starched as ever and there were flowers on the piano. The house's air of domesticity was not traditional: it was glaringly traditional. 'Everything was done to make it easier to see a human face,' Pavel Markov was to specify with his usual precision in 1937.[3]

Real life invaded the Turbins' home with a sudden power cut and a darkness in which the candle flames flickered uncertainly, the shadows on the walls merging and parting. It encroached on them as the howling of the wind, the thunder of distant guns, and the wailing of wires. History could be sensed disrupting the rhythm of the Turbins' life; it was a heaviness in the fervent dark eyes of Alexey Turbin; it broke through in the wild, despairing cadet songs of Nikolka, and finally became tangible as the Turbins' apartment disappeared and was replaced by the headquarters of Petlyura's division or the steps of the main staircase in the High School, with the restive cadets scattered over it. The production began on a Chekhovian note with authentically Chekhovian atmosphere, but abruptly moved on to a challenging new departure for the Art Theatre, recreating on its stage a life which brought those on the stage very close to those in the auditorium.

The thing that riveted the audience's attention was the figure of Alexey Turbin as interpreted by Nikolai Khmelyov. The actor Khmelyov completed a lengthy questionnaire on the art of the theatre in 1929 in which he detailed a number of factors which are important for an understanding of Turbin. 'For *Days of the Turbins* I read a great deal of Dostoevsky and Chekhov. Taken together they became Bulgakov.'[4] This throws into relief how closely Turbin's inner life is linked with the wider question of Russian cultural awareness. Khmelyov goes on to offer a further important insight into the character: 'Alexey Turbin already bears this universal element within himself. Indeed, there is nothing specifically individual in him.'[5]

It was just this universality in Turbin that drew the sharpest criticism. The very possibility of approaching Colonel Alexey Turbin on a psychological or historical level still seemed wholly out of order. The critics' attention focused much more on the heroic officer's epaulettes than on his smouldering eyes. This was only natural. A mere six years separated them from the taking of the Isthmus of Perekop. Summarising the controversy in his *Twilight of a Theatre*, a book written against the Art Theatre which caused a great stir at the time, Vladimir Pavlov articulated what it was in the production that gave the greatest offence. '*The Days of the Turbins* as presented by MAAT,' he wrote, '. . . left no possible doubt that it was written from the old standpoint of the Russian intelligentsia.'[6]

About this time one of Pavlov's fellow-critics had christened him 'the most short-sighted sharp-shooter in the USSR'. In this instance, however, Pavlov was on to something important, even if his criticism was well off target. He had failed to notice that the inner logic of the production shattered and overturned the 'old standpoint of the Russian intelligentsia', demonstrating its manifest inadequacy in the new historical conditions. There was a wry smile playing on the lips of the production's creators as they presented Lariosik's dream of peace, formulated in a quotation from Chekhov, his liberal understanding of personality ('Yelena . . . deserves happiness because she is a remarkable woman' p. 90), and the whole complex of intelligentsia attitudes. Their concern was to examine how the old concepts and ideas meshed with harsh reality and a new understanding of things.

The predominant image in the Turbin scenes was that of the doomed home. The sense of a pleasant place to live, house and home, collided with the sense of a deadly, untamed space outside, from which the frost-bitten Myshlaevsky emerged and into which the Turbins departed. The notions of brother, wife, friend and family were subjected to monstrous trials. The meaning of the production became evident as it focused increasingly on the man and the human.

If Nikolai Khmelyov was the bearer of the tragic theme of *The Days of the Turbins*, Vera Sokolova carried its lyrical theme. The sense of home, domestic cosiness and security came together in this unattractive, irresistible Russian officer's wife. She radiated a sunny, self-possessed calmness.

The Art Theatre's new production was clearly related to its earlier productions of Chekhov. Here was the same interweaving of the profoundly dramatic and the profoundly comic in the depiction of the life of the intelligentsia. Here was the same sense of compassion for the human race, derived from a more general insight into the inescapable drama of human life itself. Here were the pervasive humour, the love of everyday detail, and much else besides. The tell-tale signs of relatedness quite blinded the critics to the major signs that both Bulgakov and the Art Theatre were reacting against the Chekhovian canon. 'This is much the same way that play for White officers,

Three Sisters, was staged.' 'Bulgakov cramps *The Turbins* within the strict framework of a play after the manner of Chekhov.' 'The intimate scenes of *The Turbins* are made to Chekhov's recipe.' 'I ask you, are not the soulful cadets in *Days of the Turbins* in direct line of descent from Trofimov and Anya?'[7] Such were the commonplaces of contemporary criticism, and that despite the fact that at crucial moments the production, following the lead of the play, took polemical issue with Chekhov's way of writing and a number of themes absolutely basic to Chekhov. The decisive parting of the ways came in the evaluating of the historical choice the play's heroes were forced to make.

It is generally accepted that the intelligentsia in Chekhov's dramas profess a 'mass Hamletism'.[8] They dream of definitive acts which will change their lives, but do not actually get round to performing them. Events, actions and individual deeds are not definitive, nor have they any particular priority in Chekhov's world. On the contrary, the typical world view in Chekhov and the Art Theatre as it sought to interpret him saw life as an unchanging stream, where an ongoing inactivity and uneventful humdrum existence were the norm rather than the exception. It is left to those on the periphery or beyond the pale in Chekhov's plays to break an orchard up into plots for letting, move to Moscow, or indeed get round at all to 'doing something'. An actual event or action is most often, in Naum Berkovsky's words, a cause for celebration for the baser forces in life. The less individual, the more vulgar and unoriginal a person is, the more surely will he be allotted an active role in Chekhov's dramas.[9]

Bulgakov's formative years as a writer fell in a period when the Chekhovian tradition had been trivialised. Much has been written of how Chekhov's dramas depict the world as 'tragically humdrum', constraining human impulses and hopes, and clipping the wings of dreams and aspirations. It prevents events from developing and deeds from being accomplished. It snuffs out desires, and bogs down the progress of the dialogue, disrupting its rhythms, making it tail off into pauses and a melancholy from which there is no escaping. This perception of life called for a particular mode of play-writing, tellingly characterised by Boris Pasternak in a letter of the late 1950s.

As for Chekhov's technique as a playwright, the originality, principal merit and ornament of his plays is the way he sets his people in the landscape. He does it using the same expressions as one would for describing trees and clouds. As a playwright he was against throwing social and humanist ideas around in the dialogue, which is not written to accord with the logic, interests, emotions, and personalities of his characters. Their speeches and lines are taken or plucked out of space, from the air in which they were spoken. They are like the dots and dashes someone uses to draw a forest or meadow.

Pasternak then comes to an important conclusion:

This precisely is how the dialogue achieves true simultaneity and corresponds to the theme of the play. It incorporates the theme of life in the broadest sense of the word, that vast inhabited form, with all its symmetries and asymmetries, proportions and disproportions; life as the hidden, mysterious principle of all being.[10]

Nothing could be more remote than this penetrating characterisation from describing the playwriting technique of Bulgakov, even though 'the theme of life' is an equally central concern of the author of *Flight*. The difference between the two playwrights shows up most irrefutably in the way they treat that most fundamental theme of 'the home'. For Chekhov's heroes home, more often than not, is menacing, enclosed, a place which confines, ties down and domesticates people, giving them no room to move. Home is in opposition to the garden, the park, the orchard. It is not associated with childhood dreams and hopes, and is not felt to be the living, breathing entity it is in, for instance, *The White Guard*. The bookshelf with the accumulated wisdom of a century prompts only Gaev's liberal chatter. Of the fragrance of books which smell of old chocolate there is never a trace.

Home is a place inimical to man. In *Uncle Vanya* Voinitsky and Sonya have disfigured their lives because of the wretched estate. In *Three Sisters* the Prozorovs' home is easily taken over by Natasha, and nobody is all that bothered to defend it. In *The Cherry Orchard* a sick old man is boarded up within the walls of an abandoned dwelling, an astonishing fact which Stanislavsky simply could not square with Chekhov's insistence that the play was 'a comedy, almost a farce'.

On all these levels Bulgakov's aesthetic sense of the world about him is diametrically opposed to Chekhov's. His prose and plays brought back a taste for eventfulness, occurrences which 'follow on in a sparkling and orderly succession'. The Art Theatre's junior actors had to come to terms with open inventiveness and imaginativeness, undisguised theatricality, dialogue with a deceptively light rhythm, characters virtually all of whom are endowed with sophistication and wit, and finally a different sense of reality, a different attitude towards the everyday than Chekhov's.

Not only is the humdrum not tragic for Bulgakov's characters, it is actually a kind of norm towards which one can only strive, an ideal life which has been lost irretrievably. Peace and quiet, home and hearth, cream-coloured curtains and a bronze lamp with its shade, antique clocks, and 'the finest bookshelves in the world . . . with their Natasha Rostovs and their Captain's Daughters . . . all seven of those crammed, dusty rooms in which the young Turbins had been raised'. All of this a mother bequeathed to her children, along with her dying wish that they should be kind to one another. But 'the walls would fall away . . . the light in the bronze lamp would go out and the Captain's Daughter would be burned in the stove. And though the mother said to her children "Go on living", their lot would be to suffer and die.' (*WG*, pp. 11–12)

Much, not only in *The Turbins*, but in Bulgakov's other work as well, was to be founded on this junking of ideals, and this inner opposition to the themes and motifs of Chekhov. Bulgakov's choice of surname for the contemporary poet in *The Master and Margarita*, Bezdomny, 'Homeless', was far from random. It is one of the most significant names in the semantic structure of the novel and compares with such surnames and pseudonyms of actual writers of the time as Bedny ('Poor'); Vesyoly ('Jolly'); Golodny ('Hungry'); Besposhchadny ('Merciless') and Bezymensky ('Nameless'). The transformation of Ivan Bezdomny in the novel's finale into Ivan Nikolaevich Ponyryov, Professor of History, is a symbolic restoration of memory, name, and home, without which culture is impossible.

This is not, of course, to say that we shall not find in Bulgakov's writing, in his own orchestration, characters condemned merely to mark time in history, the theme of bearing one's cross patiently, or of the need to believe against all the odds. In *The White Guard* the narrator directly exhorts his characters in 'Chekhovian' terms: 'Never, never take the shade off a lamp. A lampshade is something sacred. Never scuttle away like a rat from danger into the unknown. Read or doze beside your lampshade; let the storm howl outside and wait until they come for you.' (p. 29)

Bulgakov's beloved heroes do not, however, doze beside the lampshade or wait to see what fate has in store for them. They rush out to meet it, renouncing Hamletism, and going out, armed, in defence of their hearth and their tranquillity. An impulsion so diametrically opposed to that of Chekhov naturally entails a different approach to the construction of dialogue, altering the relationship between the script and the underwater currents. It colours the words of the characters in a particular way. 'That's enough sentimentality. We've been sentimental the whole of our lives. Enough!' Historical events suck the Turbins up like a tornado drawing them into its flight, shattering biographies, scattering a family, and placing them in direct dependence on the impersonal forces of history, that movement of the masses which, as Alexander Blok was to say, alone determines the character of a century.

In the novel, for all the spectral quality of the world inhabited by the old, 'Chekhovian' intelligentsia, the conviction remained that all the rest was chaos and void. As the play was performed, the implication was that the downfall of one world would see the rise of another. It is not that all of life is chaotic and all reality deranged. This led to the insertion of an important line, endorsed by Bulgakov's conscience, which Myshlaevsky was given in the play's final version: 'She won't be the old Russia, but a new one.' (p. 85)

After the first night of *The Days of the Turbins* Bulgakov received a letter signed with the name of one of his characters, Victor Myshlaevsky. This document, interesting in both social and psychological terms, survives in his archive.

Having remained in Kiev until the arrival of the Reds I was mobilised and entered the service of the new authorities, not under compulsion but at the dictate of my conscience. I was even able to really put my heart into fighting the Poles. It seemed to me at that time that only the Bolsheviks, strong because of the people's faith in them, had the power to bring Russia happiness and prosperity. They would raise Russians out of their general philistinism and shifty religiosity and make strong, decent, honest citizens of them. The Bolsheviks really seemed to have everything sewn up. They really knew what they were doing. I saw everything in such a rosy light I got a bit rosy myself and all but joined the Communist Party. I was saved by my past and by belonging to the nobility and the officer corps. But then the honeymoon period of the revolution passed, to be followed by the New Economic Policy and the Kronshtadt Uprising. For me, as for many others, the intoxication wore off and the rose-tinted spectacles took on a darker hue . . .

There were mass meetings under the vigilant and inquisitorial eye of the local Party Committee, resolutions passed and demonstrations mounted under duress. Semi-literate boss men who looked like Votyak totems and breathed heavily over every typist. No understanding of how to do anything, but a dogmatic opinion, formulated on the hoof, about everything. The Young Communist League with its zealous spying campaigns. Delegations of workers. Illustrious foreigners looking like the general who gatecrashed a wedding. And endless lies . . . And what of the leaders? They were either small men clinging to power and luxury the like of which they had never known, or crazed fanatics who thought they could demolish brick walls with their heads. But what of the idea itself? Not a bad idea, to be fair. Tolerably coherent, but totally unrealisable in practice. Just like the teaching of Christ, really, except that Christianity is a good deal more readily comprehensible, as well as being considerably less disgusting . . .

So there we have it. Here I am now, like the greedy old woman in the folk tale left standing beside her broken trough. Not materially, of course. I am a soldier even now . . . nothing to complain of there. I get by. But it's a lousy life when you have nothing you can believe in. Having nothing to believe in and nothing to love is, after all, the privilege of the generation of orphans which is going to take our place.[11]

Marietta Chudakova published this letter in 1988, in the third of the *Tynyanov Miscellanies*. What an insight it gives us into what the future held for Bulgakov's heroes, and the resonance the Art Theatre's play had in the Russia of the second half of the 1920s.

Bulgakov distanced the final act from Alexey's death by two months, and had the Turbins gather in a well-lit apartment, round an intentionally symbolic Christmas tree. The return to this close circle of friends, gathered in the same comforting place, called forth a barrage of indignation from the critics. Anatoly Lunacharsky wrote that moving the action back to the Turbins' home after the scene at the High School 'kills any credibility the intelligentsia might have had left'. Another critic was driven to complete despair by the playwright's '*gaucherie* and lack of *nous*', adding that in all of world drama you would be hard pressed to find a more pathetically ineffective final act than that of *The Days of the Turbins*.[12]

What so perplexed the critics was precisely the theme of this indestructible routine, life returning to normal. It was being given back to people who, by all accounts, should no longer be in existence. Bulgakov explained to Popov, 'I have set the events of the last act on the Feast of the Baptism of Christ, that is 19 January 1919. Shervinsky sang on 9 November. I stretched the time sequence deliberately. I had to have the Christmas tree in the last act.'[13] Bulgakov needed the Christmas tree as a symbol of eternity, of renewal of life, of the nativity. What was paramount in the mood of the last scene was the sense of life reborn from the ashes, and the instinct to go on living. This was the instinct breaking through in Yelena as she came back to life, the instinct behind the banal but eternal love talk pitted against the shooting and destruction. It broke through in the embittered heart of Myshlaevsky as he prepared to serve the new Russia. It shone in the eyes of crippled Nikolka, humming Pushkin's lines about the prophecy to Oleg. The spirit of the 1918 carnival in Kiev lived again as Shervinsky made his grand entrance, arriving at the house in an old, dirty coat, outrageous hat and dark glasses, only to throw off his ragged disguise and stand before them in immaculate evening dress. And then, as if in one of the old vaudevilles, the deceived husband returned, to be laughed out of court by the entire household. Shervinsky, played by Prudkin, seized the portrait of Talberg which stood by the fireplace, broke the frame with a great crash, and rapturously destroyed the portrait itself.

Bulgakov's heroes looked to the future with hope. Orderly human existence was being reborn. The lights twinkled on the Christmas tree, the amorous Lariosik declaimed poetry, and everybody sat together at the table drinking toasts and mindful that, in the end, life is but a dream. As far as the left-wing critics were concerned all this only demonstrated the hopelessly bourgeois mentality of both Theatre and playwright. In fact, however, it meant only that life in peace-time was regaining its rights. This was the meaning of the most 'pathetically ineffective' act in all of world drama. The final scene was played with people who had survived the civil war and were prepared to start living a new life.

In 1929 those opposed to *The Days of the Turbins* succeeded in having it removed from the Art Theatre's repertoire for three years. In February 1932, after many events which we have yet to relate, the play was restored on the personal orders of Stalin. Bulgakov's description of the revived production to Popov makes crystal clear why *The Days of the Turbins* was considered the equivalent for the Art Theatre's second generation of Chekhov's *The Seagull* for its first generation.

I was not in the audience. I was behind the scenes, where the actors were so nervous they passed it on to me. I began moving from one place to another, with an odd feeling that I ought to have something in my hands. Bells were ringing all over the place. At one minute the arc lights would be blazing, and the next it was as dark as if you were down a mineshaft, and the stage-hands were switching their torches on. We seemed to be galloping through the performance at dizzying speed. Petlyura's henchmen had no sooner finished their mournful singing when there was a blaze of light and from the semi-darkness I saw Toporkov running out on to the wooden staircase, panting and panting . . . He filled his lungs with air and couldn't bear to breathe out . . . A shade from 1918 was standing there, totally done in from running up and down the stairs in the school, and trying to unbutton his greatcoat collar with hands which had lost all their strength. Then the shade came suddenly back to life, hid its fur hat, whipped out its revolver and again disappeared somewhere in the school. (Toporkov acts Myshlaevsky superbly.) The actors were so agitated they turned pale beneath their make-up, their bodies bathed in sweat, and their eyes haunted, alert, and questioning.

When Petlyura's men were hunting Nikolka in wild excitement the stage assistant fired the shot right beside my ear and brought me back to my senses instantly.

Suddenly there was any amount of room on the revolving stage, a piano appeared, and a boy baritone began to sing the Epithalamion.[14]

In autumn 1926, however, the atmosphere had been different. After the first performance, in accordance with tradition, the actors had joshed Bulgakov showing him how much they loved him, and affectionately inscribing photographs and programmes to him. Vsevolod Verbitsky had written, 'If I had my own theatre I would turn it into a Temple of Bulgakov.' Mark Prudkin wrote no less touchingly, 'Working on *The Turbins* has been as unforgettable as first love.'[15]

The play was performed virtually every other day. The actors awoke to find themselves famous. The Theatre rang to one-liners and catchphrases from the play. If someone left early, people would say, 'Leaving all of us to our fate, I suppose?' If the Head of the Administrative Section, Fyodor Mikhalsky, was taking a rest in his study, insistent callers would be held at bay with 'The Hetman has retired for the night'. These theatrical touches were duly noted in his diary by our ally Alexey Gavrilov, the love-sick duty policeman and first chronicler of a production which was to become a legend.

The 'Tribunal on *The White Guard*

Anna Akhmatova is said to have protested against scholars quoting what the enemies of Pushkin said because it ensured them a place in history. Pushkin did not die, she evidently felt, only to have his foes' portraits hung on the walls. It is a point of view not to be lightly dismissed, and one which is relevant to our researches at this point, because we have now to turn to the controversy which broke around *The Turbins*. A few shrapnel fragments have already lodged in our book.

The Lenin Library preserves in its archive section a bulging scrapbook into which for many years Bulgakov meticulously pasted the articles written about him in the newspapers and magazines of the 1920s. More than half a century has passed, and today the scrapbook is looking its age. The newspaper cuttings are yellowed and brittle, and some crumble at the least touch. As you plough through the album you can't but wonder whether Akhmatova was right, and whether it is a mistake to rake over old embers. Is it really necessary to make the descent into this spent and dated avalanche of sincere, incredibly blind, peculiar and furious viciousness which engulfed the dramatist and the Art Theatre's play even before the official first night? I think we must. It was after all Bulgakov, who took his literary career very seriously, who chose to keep this scrapbook. The insights cost him too dearly for us to leave the book in the care of the archivists, who long ago ceased issuing it, marking it 'Restricted Access' on the grounds of its fragility.

Even a glance through the endless newspaper cuttings and Bulgakov's underlinings enables us to see through his own eyes the points which most took him aback, giving us a feel for the passionate convictions of the time, something we have no other way of discovering.

For all its exaggerations and extremes, the controversy over *The Days of the Turbins* reflects the underlying process by which the Russian theatre made its peace with the revolution. Here, if ever, we have to adopt the judicious thinking of the historian, to be willing to hear out every side. We need to be able to understand the logic of the debate, and what the reasons were, historical, psychological and aesthetic, which made it inevitable. We need also to recognise that the forces ranged against Bulgakov and the Moscow Art Theatre were not a monolith composed of RAPP (the Russian Association of Proletarian Writers) and 'the Left', but a decidedly motley crew who were at daggers drawn among themselves.

Among those who took Bulgakov and the Art Theatre to task was Mayakovsky. In his *Hamburg Score* Viktor Shklovsky awarded Bulgakov the status of a circus clown who fills in while the scenery is changed. Alexander Voronsky, no friend of the Left, also found much he could not accept, and there was sharp criticism of the production from the theatre directors Vsevolod Meyerhold and Alexander Tairov. Bulgakov's enemies, then, argued no less furiously amongst themselves than they did against him, which further complicates a picture of the battles in literature and the theatre in the second half of the 1920s which, heaven knows, is chaotic enough already. Some idea of the situation can be gained from the poet Ivan Molchanov's report to Maxim Gorky that Bulgakov's *Flight* had been banned by RAPP solely because it had been praised by Gorky.[16]

If Leopold Averbakh's rhetoric was bureaucratic demagogy, Andrey Bezymensky's condemnation of the Art Theatre was a sincere protest in the name of a brother who had died in the fighting in the Crimea. Envy of a fellow playwright's success even prompted Vladimir Bill-Belotserkovsky to write to Stalin demanding that *The Days of the Turbins* should be banned, and was matched by a savage onslaught from V. Kirshon. Recognising the advantages of factional solidarity and group discipline the Leftist critics had earlier shelved their own disagreements, and now in the late 1920s they launched a no-holds-barred campaign for the total annihilation of their literary opponents. Kirshon deliberately linked the battle against Bulgakov's plays with problematical developments in the countryside. 'In the countryside we have not only the rich kulaks to contend with but also those who pander to them. In just the same way, in art, we have to confront not only the Bulgakovs, [. . .] but those who pander to his like.'[17]

Among those pandering to the Bulgakovs and their like were, it transpired, Gorky, Stanislavsky, and even Alexey Sviersky, Head of the Main Committee for the Arts, established in 1928 as the state body overseeing theatre policy. It had been set up following a famous conference at the Agitprop Section of the Communist Party's Central Committee where 'guidelines for the development of the theatre' had been formulated. The different schools, tendencies and groups had stated their positions, their attitude towards *The Days of the Turbins* being virtually the main thing they all disagreed about. The conference took place in May 1927, but emotions had been fuelled by discussions which had been taking place over the preceding six months, and it is to these we now turn.

On 2 October 1926 *Evening Moscow* reported a lecture A. V. Lunacharsky had given at the Communist Academy in which he said, 'The play *The White Guard* is not ideologically sound, and in places it is politically incorrect. Permission has nevertheless been given for it to be staged because the Soviet public will judge it as it deserves.'[18] A few days later, coinciding with the production's first night, *Our Newspaper* gave a fuller account of the Commissar's speech. 'The presentation of this play on the stage of the Moscow Art Theatre is of course a thorny

matter . . . but substantial financial resources and creative endeavour had been
invested in it, and banning it would have radically undermined the Theatre.'
According to the report, Lunacharsky did not consider Bulgakov to represent
any real danger since 'our stomach is now strong enough to digest even strong
meat'. The same report contained objections to the Commissar's speech made
by Orlinsky, who characterised the play and the Art Theatre's production of it as
'a political demonstration in which Bulgakov exchanges winks and nudges with
the remnants of the White cause'.[19]

Orlinsky's objections put Lunacharsky in an extremely awkward and ambiguous position, the more so since 'almost all the other speakers supported
Orlinsky'. Only Mayakovsky commented that 'This squeak from Bulgakov poses
no threat.' There were to be later developments, but for the moment let us note
only that Mayakovsky believed the production to be wholly consonant with the
Art Theatre's first principles. 'The White Guard is a perfectly logical conclusion.
They started off with Auntie Manya and Uncle Vanya and they've fetched up
with The White Guard. [. . .] Take Stanislavsky's notorious book My Life in Art,
that obligatory bed-time read for epicures. It's all just the same old White
Guard.'[20]

In the same issue of New Theatre-Goer that reported Mayakovsky's theatrical
speculations, Osaf Litovsky made what is apparently the first reference to 'the
cult of Bulgakovism'.

On 8 October Orlinsky took the baton from Litovsky with an article headed
'The Civil War on the Stage of the Art Theatre'. It was a more concentrated
version of the indictment of the Theatre and Bulgakov which, we recall, Orlinsky
had made earlier. The argument now ran that 'there is a policy of strictly
insulating the White Guards in socio-class terms. The family of a major military
figure, and all the commanders and officers, live, fight, dine, die and get married
without the presence of a single batman, or any servants, and without any contact
whatsoever with people from other classes or social groupings.'[21]

Referring in passing to the 'outstanding performances by the actors', Orlinsky
made no further mention of them and trumpeted a threatening call to 'rebuff the
cult of Bulgakovism'. (In The Master and Margarita a contamination of Litovsky
and Orlinsky spawns the critic Latunsky with his slogan 'Let us strike hard at the
cult of Pilatism'.) The call to arms came too late. Battle had already been joined.
On 5 October, the very day of the première, Bezymensky's open letter to the Art
Theatre appeared in Komsomolskaya pravda, and there was also an article by
Blyum, who was to become principal tenor in the anti-Bulgakov chorus. He
raises the accusations to the level of political denunciation, revealing that 'this
shifty play conceals not only the fact that the Turbins have servants and batmen,

but also an apologia for chauvinism', since the Petlyura bands were 'petty bourgeois, but nonetheless revolutionary', and he therefore considers them preferable to the heroics of the White Guard who were 'the embryo of Russian Fascism'.[22]

Orlinsky wrote with restraint in the pages of *Pravda*, while Blyum fired one article after another from small-calibre theatre publications like the booklet *Programmes of the State Academic Theatres* or *New Theatre-Goer* which, incidentally, was edited by none other than Orlinsky. On their home ground the Leftists did not pull their punches, and showed who they were really gunning for. Bulgakov and the Moscow Art Theatre's production of his play were not by any means their primary target. In the October issue of *New Theatre-Goer*, declaring that 'MAAT is falling into a puddle along with that roué Bulgakov', Orlinsky immediately went on to blame the entire incident directly on Lunacharsky and his policy towards the theatre. 'We may need Ostrovsky, but that does not at all mean we need an Ostrovsky like Bulgakov.'[23] The unambiguous allusion was to Lunacharsky's famous call to Soviet playwrights to go 'Back to Ostrovsky!' In the next issue but one the same magazine is characterising the Commissar's stance as an 'opportunistic fall from grace' and proclaiming that 'the contradictory development of the contemporary Soviet theatre is proceeding along the line of, on the one hand, the production of *The White Guard* and, on the other, of Bill-Belotserkovsky's *Storm*. The struggle between these irreconcilable tendencies has reached the point of no return.'[24]

Finding himself under pressure from several directions, Lunacharsky began shifting his position and tightening up his judgements. In a period of a few days he published a series of articles in the newspapers of Moscow and Leningrad in which he gave a detailed assessment of the play's first night. He had quite a few harsh things to say about the play itself, which Bulgakov found deeply wounding. The Commissar of Enlightenment did, however, defend the production's right to exist on the grounds that it would provoke controversy and 'move the theatre into the arena of political struggle'. It was a clear policy decision, and one which Lunacharsky was trying to maintain under pressures which became more acute every day.

On 11 October a debate titled 'A Tribunal on *The White Guard*' took place before a packed audience in the Press Club. This is how it was reported in the press.

The signal for battle to commence was given by Comrade Litovsky. [. . .] And the trial began! A veritable bath-house lashing! The main bath-house attendants were the ubiquitous Orlinsky, Podgaetsky, the author of Meyerhold's *D. E. Trust*, and the Press

Club's resident orator Levidov. And still they came! Almost all of them arrived fully equipped for battle, armed to the teeth with quotations short and long. [. . .] Only occasionally did the odd plea for clemency for the theatre and its actors manage to break through.

The report contains one remarkable detail: 'The Art Theatre actors sat in silence. They refused demands from the audience to speak, claiming they "had not been authorised, and Stanislavsky is ill and unable to attend". Nevertheless, the debate gave them a good and undoubtedly instructive lesson in political literacy.'[25] Another report of the 'tribunal' mentions the 'deeply affected female citizen' who 'shrieked "All men are brothers." '

The fact that there was the 'odd plea for clemency', no less than the reference to the uninhibited lady citizen, is worth noting. Among the few to speak up for the defence was Lidia Seyfullina who 'attempted to present the author of *The Days of the Turbins* as "someone who had honestly undertaken to describe the enemy without misrepresentation".'[26] One other plea broke through in *Komsomolskaya pravda*, if only in December, this time from Nikolai Rukavishnikov who declared that the criticism of *The Days of the Turbins* was misplaced and

Bezymensky with his letter to the Art Theatre is downright comical. Plays of this kind would have been wholly inappropriate five or six years ago, but the critics seem to be forgetting that it is being staged on the threshold of the tenth anniversary of the October revolution. It is perfectly safe to show an audience real people. They have had more than enough of the shaggy-haired priests of the *agitka* plays and fat-bellied capitalists in top hats.[27]

Even before that Adrian Piotrovsky had written in his article 'The Art Theatre's Young Actors', published in *The Red Paper*, that the much abused production was evidence of

the growth of the Main Theatre and its continuing development, direct and unmediated, under the established leadership of Stanislavsky. Moreover this young company has shown outstanding talent and an excellent style which is wholly of the Art Theatre, yet at the same time fresh, strong, and vital. *The Days of the Turbins* has propelled the Little Stage of MAAT I into the ranks of the finest young companies in Moscow. In terms of their exceptionally delicate, but also nimble-footed and varied manner, their incomparable ensemble acting and their exceptionally professional attitude, this company may be said even now to have no rivals.[28]

This kind of criticism of the artistic aspects of the production seemed so out of place that it simply went unnoticed.

On 12 October a new and strident soloist made himself heard in the chorus of voices raised against *The Turbins*. Emmanuil Beskin titled his attack 'The Cream-Coloured Blinds', providing as it were a more material and tangible target. On the same day an account was published of a speech by Alexander Tairov in which he took MAAT to task in the name of the 'truly revolutionary theatre of our days'. The famous director 'pointed out the philistine character of the dramatic devices Bulgakov employed in *The White Guard*. Another report made Tairov's speech seem even more categorical. '*The White Guard* is counter-revolutionary not because of its politically saccharine attitude towards our class enemies, but because of the specific, vulgar taste it leaves behind in the manner of Chekhov.'[29] Vsevolod Meyerhold, who in the summer of 1927 was to press Bulgakov to let him have a new play for his own theatre, publicly stated in 1926 that *The Days of the Turbins* should have been staged not by the Art Theatre but by him, because he 'would have staged the play in the way the Soviet public rather than Bulgakov required'.[30] Bulgakov awarded Meyerhold's suggestion a triple exclamation mark.

On 14 October Andrey Bezymensky's letter, which we have already referred to, was published in *Komsomolskaya pravda*. It attempted to drive a wedge between Bulgakov and the Art Theatre, the first of many such attempts, culminating in Stalin's formulation that the author was in no wise 'to answer' for his play's success. At this stage the idea had no powerful protagonists. The Leftists tried their utmost to sway the Theatre, or to sow dissension between the Theatre and its Author from within. The correspondent of *The Workers' Newspaper*, for example, started his report with the intelligence that 'several of the Art Theatre actors in *The Days of the Turbins* (*The White Guard*) have stated that they are fully aware of its falseness and political harmfulness' and that they were 'in complete agreement with the harsh criticisms levelled at it'.[31] A few days later the same newspaper could not wait to convey to its readers the joyful tidings that *The Days of the Turbins* was, supposedly, already playing to less than full houses.

These naive tricks and pinpricks, dramatised 'tribunals', and open letters did in the end have an effect. For the first time since the revolution the Art Theatre found itself the centre of attention of the theatregoing public of Moscow. It became impossible to obtain tickets for the play. At the close of the season *Evening Moscow*'s satirist summarised in verse the results of the critics' efforts in this first phase of the production history of *The Days of the Turbins*:

> To MAAT this year there came a mighty flood
> Of people seeking tickets, spilling blood.
> Not turbines were the source of their propulsion:

> *The Turbins* were the cause of their compulsion.
> What sucked them in, you ask, when sources say
> That truth to tell it's not that good a play?
> Publicity! With all the nitty gritty
> Provided by the Repertoire Committee.[32]

In November and December the storm around *The Turbins* subsided somewhat, but the opening of Bulgakov's *Madame Zoyka* at the Vakhtangov Theatre was grist to the reviewers' mill. 'Bulgakov Sets about the New Economic Policy', 'Madame Zoyka's New Cleaner' shouted their eye-catching headings.[33] The first night of Konstantin Trenyov's *Lyubov Yarovaya* at the Maly Theatre was the signal for a renewal of the campaign against the Art Theatre.

The director of Trenyov's play, Lev Prozorovsky, learned from the fate of *The Days of the Turbins*. He quarrelled with the playwright at the outset by insisting on removing the figure of Lieutenant Dremin, an honest and decent man for whom the defeat of the White cause was a tragedy and who finally committed suicide. Trenyov felt that without Dremin the play would degenerate from a realistic depiction of the White movement into caricature. The director's sole concern, however, was to avoid any possibility of being compared to *The White Guard*. Trenyov did cut his hero out, although, as his biographer was to write many years later, 'being a fellow-traveller at this time, Trenyov failed to understand' the necessity for this surgery.[34]

It would be a mistake to imagine that the critics were uninfluential. The 'Leftyrevs', as Lunacharsky ironically dubbed the Leftist theatre reviewers, elaborated a system of ideas about theatre art which was uniquely their own, rather as the members of RAPP did in literature. Theatre historians are familiar enough with the huge amount of activity they put into newspaper and magazine publications and the personal passion they brought to the battle in literature and the theatre. This was often potentiated by their aesthetic illiteracy, political opportunism, readiness to cut down those who would not submit, and lust for power over literature. Another weapon was their application of the terminology used in the debates going on within the Communist Party to arguments in the cultural field, which indeed explains the provenance of the notions of 'Left' and 'Right' in the theatre. It is worth emphasising, however, that the Leftists made use of a very idiosyncratic sociology of art. Their primary concern was to seek out the artist's 'class psycho-ideology', which they believed was concealed in any work of art. This psycho-ideology was the dominant criterion which subsumed or excluded all others, such as genuine aesthetic judgement. Needless to say, for a tragic hero to turn up in Bulgakov's play, with the possibility of another tragic hero making his appearance in the work of the fellow-traveller Trenyov, was seen as an extremely serious violation of the current aesthetic norm. The Leftists' dogged search for inherent class bias left them quite unable to agree on how to treat the cultural heritage of the past, let alone how to interpret those aspects of post-revolutionary art linked with or evolved from it. The system of values adopted by the reviewers on RAPP's *On Guard* magazine and the Leftyrevs denied the Turbins and their Chekhovian predecessors any aesthetic right to a tragic incarnation. As Litovsky put it,

The White Guard is *The Cherry Orchard* of the White movement. What possible interest can there be for a Soviet audience in the sufferings of the landlord Ranevskaya as her cherry orchard is pitilessly cut down? What possible interest can there be in the sufferings of the émigrés, external or internal, at the untimely demise of the White movement? None whatsoever. We have no need of this.[35]

To tell the truth, their system had no need of art itself, if by that we understand spiritual productions addressing basic questions of the social significance, dignity and very existence of human beings. The eternal conundrums held no terrors for the Leftists. Talent, as a deeply personal experiencing of the world, was something they had no time for. The philosophical pedigree of their disregard and even hatred of talent went back to egalitarian barrack-room communism, whose features were familiar to the founding father of their doctrine. Marx's hypothetical definitions were to be fully realised in history when he wrote that this kind of communism was 'an abstract negation of the entire world of culture and civilisation', an urge 'to destroy *all* that which on a *private property* basis cannot be the property of all; it seeks to forcibly disengage itself from talent'; and further, 'this communism, which at every turn denies the *individuality* of man', affirms a 'universal *envy* which constitutes itself into power'.[36]

The Leftists liked to proclaim that they were acting in the name of the Party and 'the entire Soviet public'. In fact, however, the Party line expounded in 'On the Policy of the Party in the Field of Belles-Lettres', a 1925 resolution of the Party's Central Committee, was directed in letter and in spirit not at inciting hostility towards the fellow-travellers, but at 'peaceful organisational work'. 'The overall objective here,' it stated, 'must be a tactful and caring attitude towards the fellow-travellers such as to provide all the conditions necessary for their coming round as rapidly as possible to support for communist ideology.' The same resolution, which largely reflected the views of Nikolai Bukharin, also stated that critics should 'resolutely eschew any pretentious, semi-literate and smug communist conceit', and not write as if they were issuing 'literary orders'.[37]

It was this considered line in culture that Lunacharsky was trying to implement, and it was entirely predictable that their campaign against the Art Theatre would bring the Leftists into conflict, and irreconcilable conflict at that, in just this area. The People's Commissar of Enlightenment might see art as an important means of exerting social and class influence, but he did not see its significance solely in such utilitarian terms. Lunacharsky understood art as something which proceeded from the organic, natural flowering of the culture of a particular class on a cultural soil naturally ready for it. Those were the words he used in explaining his position at the Party conference on questions of theatre policy. Pouring cold water on the ardour of the Furious Zealots, he warned that 'while the soil is not producing flowers it is quite pointless to tie paper flowers to bare branches'.[38] Conscious of his historic responsibility, Lunacharsky did his best to prevent any one literary or theatre faction from seizing a dominant position in the administration of the arts. His policy towards the theatre provoked not only intellectual hostility from the Leftists but considerable personal animosity as well. They interpreted the catholicity of his tastes, his passion for the multi-faceted culture of the past, his artistic flair, even the fact that he was reasonably well-educated, in terms of their 'class psycho-ideology', and found them indicative of a member of the Russian intelligentsia who carried within himself the poison of the old world. Boris Alpers is knowledgeable about the mood in the theatre world in this period, and recalls that in the original version of *Storm* Bill-Belotserkovsky who, like his hero Bratishka, had a deep-seated 'mistrust of culture and those who bear it', represented Lunacharsky as 'the director of a local Department of Popular Enlightenment. [. . .] In the finale of the play he was sentenced at Bratishka's insistence to execution by firing squad for moral turpitude. In the original version this character was transparently named Charsky'.[39]

The Art Theatre controversy was part of the wider question of the future of Russian culture within the permitted parameters of the revolution. If we turn again to the situation in the aftermath of the Maly Theatre's production of *Lyubov Yarovaya*, we note that Lunacharsky welcomed the production and saw it and *The Days of the Turbins* in a favourable light as indicating a general moving on the part of the academic theatres towards 'modern' concerns. He elaborated on this in his article 'Two Plays', published in the Tiflis newspaper *Dawn in the East*.

The theatre is at its best, of course, when it manages to give a play the most perfect and sharply focused expression possible. This is what MAAT I achieved when, perhaps for the first time ever, it had all Moscow talking excitedly about a theatre production, not, indeed, in terms of the performance, but as a slice of life. [. . .] For those of us who would like to see the theatre as a reflector of life which organises human awareness . . . the very intensity of the public interest which *The Days of the Turbins* whipped up was a heartening phenomenon.

The newspaper's editors, who knew the real state of affairs in the theatre in Moscow, felt obliged to append a note to the effect that they did not wholly share his point of view, 'in particular in respect of his view of *The Days of the Turbins*'.[40]

For the Leftists there were no points of contact between *The Turbins* and *Lyubov Yarovaya*. They were on the look-out for an opportunity to fan the flames of conflict, and found one at a debate in the Meyerhold Theatre. This debate was to provide one of the most dramatic moments in the history of Bulgakov and the theatre, if only because it was here that the antagonists met for the first time face to face. Bulgakov thought it no part of a writer's duty to answer critics. Up until this moment he had made no public appearances or statements regarding his attitude to what was going on. Back in 1922 he had written in his article on Slyozkin that literary criticism was 'the equivalent of the plagues of Egypt for Russian writers', and endured his share of the 'plague' with the utmost composure he could muster.[41] On 7 February 1927, however, he could stand it no longer. Perhaps Bulgakov wanted 'to look his tormentor straight in the eyes', as he was to put it several years later when one of his contemporaries was attacking *Molière*.[42] Stylishly dressed and sporting the famous starched shirt-front, he arrived at the packed auditorium of the Meyerhold Theatre in the company of Pavel Markov and several of the Art Theatre actors. Lunacharsky opened the debate, reiterating his own stance. 'I do not in the least regret that *Days of the Turbins* was passed for performance. It has served a useful purpose. It was the first political play on our horizon to raise serious, socio-political matters.'[43] Lunacharsky went on to refute allegations that the spirit of the production was that of the émigré 'Change of Landmarks' movement, while pointing out the real significance of that movement as an 'enormously important factor for a very large section of our intelligentsia'.[44]

Do you really suppose that we are not aware that the vast majority of the academic community adhere to the Change of Landmarks philosophy? I am not persuaded when I see a liberal perform three somersaults and turn into a communist. I feel I am merely watching a rather questionable trick. Sometimes this results from a genuine impulse, but sometimes it is just a chameleon changing colour. What we really need is precisely a changing of landmarks, when people come over to us, mindful of history, even wistfully looking to the past.[45]

Lunacharsky's somersaulting intellectuals may have come to Bulgakov's mind in March 1930 when he was explaining his situation in a document which was of critical importance for him. He described any attempt to renounce his views on literature without more ado as 'a clumsy and indeed naive political curvet' which could only discredit him in the eyes of the Soviet government.[46] In February 1927, however, Bulgakov did not touch on such weighty matters. His task was to rebut Orlinsky who had been belabouring him for the *n*th time for his 'craven fear of the masses', and for having 'dropped the batman, and hidden the workers and peasants away'. Orlinsky even made much of the changing of the play's title, and included it as a point in his closing indictment. Bulgakov answered each point in turn, spicing his speech with that 'magnificent contempt' which Akhmatova was to pick out as the distinguishing feature of his personality in a poem dedicated to Bulgakov after his death. Here are the salient excerpts from his unique speech.

I have no wish to enter into discussions, and shall not presume on your attention for very long, but there is one thing of which I should like to persuade Comrade Orlinsky. For several months now, more precisely since 5 October 1926, a day I remember very well because it was the first night of *The Days of the Turbins*, this man, this individual has been arousing in me . . . a strong desire to meet him and to tell him one simple but important thing. That is that if you are a critic, if you are analysing a piece, you may say and write whatever you please, apart from things you know full well to be untrue or things of which you have absolutely no knowledge.[47]

Having dealt with the matter of the play's change of title, Bulgakov went on to the question of the 'missing batman, workers and peasants'.

I shall deal with all three. First the batman. I, the author of *The Days of the Turbins*, having resided in Kiev during the period of the Hetman's and Petlyura's rule, having observed White Guardists in Kiev from the inside, from behind the cream curtains, categorically affirm that it was impossible to get a batman in Kiev at that time for love or money. (*Laughter, applause.*)[48]

We shall omit Bulgakov's development of this theme and pass on to the two other points in the indictment.

On the question of servants. By October I was seething, and not without Mr Orlinsky's involvement. The producer kept saying, 'You've got to have servants'. I kept saying, 'For heaven's sake, there's no room for them. I have been an accomplice as great chunks of my play have been hewn off to make it fit on to the stage and because the trams only run until midnight.' Finally, absolutely furious, I wrote in: 'Where's Anyuta?' 'Anyuta has gone off to the country.' I should make it clear that I am not inventing this. I have a copy of the play, and this phrase about the servants appears in it. Personally I consider it a matter of major historical importance.

Finally, the workers and peasants. Personally I have observed and am familiar with a different milieu and different tastes. In Kiev in that terrible year of 1919 I witnessed a wholly unique situation which it is quite impossible to convey and of which, I suspect, Muscovites know little and Mr Orlinsky nothing whatsoever. It is precisely the flavour of that period which has apparently passed him by, a flavour which consisted of the following. If you were sitting surrounded by the Skoropadsky regime, by officers and intelligentsia refugees, the situation regarding the Bolsheviks was obvious. They were a dreaded force advancing on Kiev from the north, and one which was to unseat the Skoropadsky regime . . . What was needed in the play was the portrayal of two forces only: Petlyura's bands and the White Guard forces who were relying on Skoropadsky. Nothing else. For this reason when . . . some people see Petlyura's bands as Bolsheviks in disguise I can state in all conscience and wholly without guile that I would have had no difficulty in portraying the Bolsheviks and the confrontation with them just as well, but in so doing I would have ruined the play . . .[49]

Bulgakov's speech was reported in the press as follows:

Now it was time for the treat of the evening. The author of *The Days of the Turbins* took the floor, Mikhail Bulgakov who has declined for so long to make any public pronouncements about his play. Alas, the audience was in for a disappointment. Bulgakov tried to fob off his critics with jokes but failed dismally.[50]

Nobody bothered to report Pavel Markov's contribution to the debate. He was wholly in earnest and indeed tried very seriously, and just a little bitterly, to speak up for the play and the production. 'It had what matters more than anything else for the Art Theatre, and that is the revelation of the moral destiny of a man and, through that, the revelation of an era and its events'. He continued no less to the point:

We realised in the end that there was nothing in all that criticism beyond simple malice. Was the fact that we had found our approach to this human being and through his destiny to that period as a whole really so little? Was the fact that here was an actor who had been trained until he could convey the innermost tremor of a human being really so little?

'With this production,' Markov concluded, in all probability with Stanislavsky's backing, 'the Art Theatre accepted a re-alignment of its thinking, and took a step so major that it is never likely to forget it.'[51]

Markov's speech was like a red rag to a bull, and even led to attempts to introduce the concept of a cult of Markovism to parallel the cult of Bulgakovism. At the May conference at the Agitprop Section of the Central Committee the Leftists accused him of being one of those chiefly responsible for *The Days of the Turbins*, and even demanded that he should be debarred from writing for *Pravda*. We have already mentioned that this conference played an important part in the way the Soviet theatre developed in the 1920s and in Lunacharsky's battle against the Left. The Commissar's opponents presented a united front, and Lunacharsky was obliged to retreat to a purely defensive position under the hail of political accusations which were thrown at him. One of the trumps in the prosecution's hand was his support for *The Days of the Turbins* at the Art Theatre.

Most importantly, the Left rejected from the outset Lunacharsky's understanding of art as something natural and organic which required reasoned leadership rather that the big stick and the *knout*. Lunacharsky's talk of artists coming over to the Party 'mindful of history, even wistfully looking to the past' struck them as outrageously woolly. 'You are not going to get far with natural flowering and especially not from this lot. You need a midwife,' Boris Vaks suggested pointedly. Lunacharsky parried with a quote from Marx about ignorant midwives who tried to deliver the baby in the seventh month. Vladimir Pletnyov was even more categorical than Vaks. 'We shall wage class warfare and, yes, why mince words, civil war in the theatre.'[52]

For people who thought like that Stanislavsky was still an 'ideologue of the merchant class'. 'He has recognised us *de jure*, but not *de facto*,' one speaker concluded. Another bemoaned the fact that 'Of course we can't remove Nemirovich-Danchenko at the same time.'

The Leftists, however, also ran into stiff resistance. Lunacharsky talked of 'yapping little monsieurs' and 'MAAT-baiting', a worrying, indeed dangerous infection in the theatre. The atmosphere became extremely heated. Vladimir Blyum's speech was constantly interrupted by heckling. 'Sadko' complained, 'You treat an apolitical figure like Stanislavsky with such piety. How come you don't want to hear out a Bolshevik?' The conference declined to hear out Blyum, but after him came Leopold Averbakh and Pavel Novitsky, Pyotr Kerzhentsev, I. Mandelshtam, a force to be reckoned with at that time in the Moscow Party Committee, and others who were much more skilful fighters. They pressed home the attack on Lunacharsky and his policy on developing a Soviet theatre. The general drift of the speeches was unmistakable: a fight to the finish with all who at that time were classified as fellow-travellers. ' "Smash them first and win them over afterwards." "Why waste time arguing?" Or to put it more simply "Let us at 'em!" ' as Lunacharsky summarised his opponents' slogans in his concluding speech. 'And here Mandelshtam himself has been speaking out against us, the so-called "Right" wing, virtually accusing us of counter-revolution. You should blush with shame, comrades.'[53]

No blushes were, however, forthcoming, and it took considerable courage on Commissar Lunacharsky's part to defend the Art Theatre's production. The accusation of 'virtual counter-revolution' had been made in just this connection. Ceding a number of points to the Leftists, Lunacharsky counter-attacked from an unexpected direction by caustically reminding Orlinsky and Blyum of how *The Days of the Turbins* had been passed by the censorship. He recalled that they had themselves 'signed the permit, and been so confident of their own ideological reliability and authorial talent that they had altered and amended the play in collaboration with Bulgakov'. He then moved the argument on without a moment's pause to a more intellectual level, to the threat posed by Left extremism to Russia's existing cultural forces.

I find all of Agitprop's proposals acceptable. But this is not enough for the comrades. They want to take things further. In the process some of them have shown their teeth, or it might be better to say their claws. It was particularly evident in the case of Blyum and Kerzhentsev that they do not believe the old art is worth a bent kopek. [. . .] For them the academic theatres are simply incorrigible class enemies. They are enemy strongholds which are still holding out, and to which we need to send political commissars to subjugate them finally. On the one hand this shows them up as pessimists who have little faith in the power of the proletariat and our state to re-educate these extremely important detachments of the intelligentsia by persuasion and a proper approach. On the other hand it demonstrates a throw-back to War Communism.

Lunacharsky did not mince his words in frankly predicting that in art the 'infantile disease of Leftism' would have disastrous consequences.

We hesitate to let them off the leash because all that we have put so much effort into conserving could be smashed to smithereens. [. . .] The theatres are not such obstinate class conglomerations that you need a sledgehammer to break them up.[54]

Lunacharsky's arguments cut no ice with his opponents and 'MAAT-baiting' continued undiminished. More than that, at the end of the 1926/27 season *The Days of the Turbins* was removed from the repertoire of the Moscow Art Theatre. The conflict took a new turn in the autumn and the matter was taken to the highest level, as it had been when *The Turbins* had been passing through the censorship machinery initially. In response to an anxious telegram from

Nemirovich-Danchenko in Hollywood enquiring about the fate of the production, Olga Bokshanskaya reported on 15 September 1926 that it would hardly be possible for the Commissariat of Enlightenment to represent the Theatre successfully. 'After all, last year it was ultimately not Narkompros but the Politburo that passed the play for performance, so presumably we shall have to address ourselves to that quarter this year also.'[55]

The document we might expect from what Bokshanskaya wrote is not to be found in the archive, but there is a letter from Stanislavsky to Avel Yenukidze, Chairman of the Central Executive Committee of Soviets, explaining the situation clearly and simply. 'Uncertainty is the theatre's worst enemy. It saps the actors' energy and causes endless difficulties and delays. In view of all that has been said, I appeal to you to intercede on our behalf for permission to stage *The Turbins* and *Armoured Train*.'[56] (Vsevolod Ivanov's play *Armoured Train 14–69* had by this time been characterised as 'an attack by the kulaks and intelligentsia'.)

On 11 October the Praesidium of the Collegium of the Commissariat of Enlightenment confirmed a resolution allowing the production to go ahead, as Lunacharsky promptly reported to Stanislavsky: 'You already know of course that you have permission to stage *The Turbins* for this year at least.'[57] The qualifying 'at least' attested that the battle was not yet over, and this was soon confirmed. The appearance of Bulgakov's play on the Art Theatre's autumn playbill was met by a co-ordinated broadside from the Leftists.

> 'The aristos are of good cheer.
> Their *Days* will see a second year'

quipped *Krokodil*'s satirist, while the indefatigable Blyum condoled with the Art Theatre who, by retaining the production, 'had set themselves apart from the joy of millions of people' and 'had not laid on the altar of the October festivities a worthy offering'.[58] (The USSR was preparing for the tenth anniversary of the October revolution of 1917.)

What the Art Theatre did 'lay on the altar of the October festivities' was *Armoured Train 14–69*. Now the cartoonists had something new to draw: the heroes of *Days of the Turbins* perishing beneath the wheels of the armoured train. In autumn 1928 there was renewed talk of taking *The Turbins* off, but Stanislavsky, again enlisting Yenukidze's support, succeeded in winning a reprieve, if with the proviso that it was to be retained only 'until the next new production'.[59]

The controversy around *The Days of the Turbins* took a new turn and reached new heights of shrillness after the publication of *Flight* and the announcement that the Art Theatre was considering producing it. Some of RAPP's most prominent dramatists now attempted to have all Bulgakov's plays taken off all the stages of Moscow. Bill-Belotserkovsky wrote to Stalin urging just that. In February 1929 Stalin replied with a letter which was to set the tone for the whole of the subsequent period, in which he laid down his views on the state of the theatre in the USSR as a whole and what he thought of the state of theatre criticism. *The Days of the Turbins* was not only not swept away but actually taken under Stalin's wing. He had been one of the play's most attentive spectators, attending performances no fewer than fifteen times. Stalin defended the Art Theatre with the simple and patently unchallengeable political argument that *The Days of the Turbins* was 'a demonstration of the all-conquering power of Bolshevism'.[60] Admittedly Bulgakov was simultaneously denied any part in the production's success, which was put down wholly and exclusively to the actors. In the end, however, even Stalin's odd line of defence failed to save the production, and in March 1929 the history of *The Days of the Turbins* was interrupted for almost three years.[61]

Bulgakov summarised the whole saga in his own way. In 1927 when the campaign against *The Turbins* was at its height he had begun writing a play commissioned by Tairov's Chamber (Kamerny) Theatre, utilising the plot of one of his barbed early articles. In autumn 1928 the Repertoire Committee recommended the play for production, and on 11 December Alexander Tairov staged it under the title *The Crimson Island*. It was a dramatised pamphlet, a rejoinder to the Art Theatre's critics, and Bulgakov's final contribution to the theatre discussion of the 1920s.

A Parody and a Pamphlet

Before we turn to Bulgakov's contribution to that debate let us look at another play of 1928, published by *Teakinopechat'*, recommended for staging, and long since forgotten. This was *The White House*, a play written by two young literary hopefuls, Vladimir Bogolyubov and Ivan Chekin. It boasted two subtitles, 'What They Left Unsaid' and 'A Social Drama of the White Guardists'.[62] The play was never performed either then or later, but it sheds an interesting light on the battles of the 1920s in the theatre. It is a play written specifically to take *The Turbins* to task on every issue raised in the theatre debate. Its authors were out to neutralise the social and artistic impact of the Art Theatre's production.

The White House questions and parodies Bulgakov's plot, characters, approach to the theatre, and means of expression. Its co-authors went beyond parody, taking Bulgakov's theme and resolving it in accordance with the prescriptions of the Art Theatre's critics. In this respect at least the *Anti-Turbins* was heir to a hallowed tradition. Gogol's *The Government Inspector* had been ideologically made over in Tsitsianov's *The Real Government Inspector*. Molière's comedies had spawned plays designed to refute them, as Bulgakov was to relate with a clear input from his own experience. The interest such items hold is that they are a condensation of the norms and concepts which the original has violated. *The White House* is a negative which, if we reverse it, enables us to understand what was crucial in the context of the times in *The Days of the Turbins* and the Art Theatre's production of it.

The dramatis personae of *The White House* are Bulgakov's heroes marginally renamed, and include Alexey Zurbin; Ignaty Shcherbinsky; Igor from Zhitomir; Maria, Alexey's sister; and even Mikhail Bulgaevsky, an infantry captain. Among the episodic characters our attention is immediately caught by Fyodor, the batman after whom the critics had so hankered.

We deliberately omitted one detail from the account of Bulgakov's speech at the debate on *The Days of the Turbins* and *Lyubov Yarovaya*, and this we now require. 'I imagine very briefly two scenes with a batman,' Bulgakov had fantasised. 'One written by me, the other by Orlinsky. In mine Alexey Turbin would say, "Vasily, put the samovar on." The batman would reply, "Yes, sir," and disappear for the rest of the play. Orlinsky would need a different batman, so let me say quite clearly that Alexey Turbin is a good man. He would never dream of knocking his batman about or giving him it in the neck as Orlinsky would like.'[63]

The White House begins 'behind cream net curtains' with the stage direction 'Alexey is swearing at his batman'. He shouts, 'I will not tolerate conniving! Stand to attention! Heels together! You have two buttons undone!'

Instead of Myshlaevsky the man taking a bath is the cadet Igor from Zhitomir, and Maria asks him to show himself, promising him 'a maternal kiss on the forehead'. Igor emerges. 'Maria kisses him on the lips and laughs for a long time.' Having summarily dealt with the lecherous sister to their satisfaction, the authors of this 'social drama of the White Guardists' give a parodistic 'Bulgakovian' stage direction: 'Approaching music. A march'. With a march playing in the background, which Bulgakov really was fond of, a dialogue ensues between Zurbin and his sister, a typical White Guardist family heart-to-heart.

Alexey. We must give Bulgaevsky some underwear.
Maria (sotto voce). We can't possibly. We have none to spare.
Alexey. But the man needs some.
Maria. You've hardly any yourself. Give him some and that's the last we'll see of it.

Alexey. Maria! Whites are honest! As honest as Don Quixote.
Maria. Right. (*Exit*)

Adhering to the original plot chronology in their parody, the authors set their heroes down for a dinner among friends. Igor from Zhitomir immediately neutralises Lariosik with his admissions.

I am a cadet . . . And I have a good feeling here in your courtly setting . . . Let's face it, back home . . . What is there back home? My big, fat, momma making out with the ex-owner of, forgive me, a beer hall, a quarrel over . . . forgive me, over a set of dirty underwear . . . but here . . . in your house . . . there is no dirt, no jealousy, no greed.
Bulgaevsky. A good White must have something to believe in.

Even the absent momma in Zhitomir, who sends a touching sixty-three-word telegram, is unmasked and annihilated by her class associations with the owner of a beer hall.

Alexey's parodied monologue runs:

We must show them our teeth, as Ivan the Terrible and his avenging *oprichniks* showed theirs to the boyars of the capital and the high-born Morozovs of Moscow. We must bite through the red movement's arteries. That is incumbent upon us, our sacred duty. We are the Whites. The White House is ours. Implacable is the punitive sword in the hands of the Whites! Prepare for the storm! Furl the sails. The Whites are justice. The Whites are the law!

Bogolyubov and Chekin not only parody Bulgakov's themes, but also his favourite presentational techniques, in particular with an abundance of inappropriate literary references and quotations, musical reprises, guitar singing, and so forth.

The first act ends with a bang, literally realising Bulgakov's hypothesis of how Orlinsky would have written the batman scene. Zurbin, seeing Fyodor carrying underwear into the bathroom to a captured red, punches him in the face and shouts in a rage, 'To the kitchens, pleb!'

We shall spare the reader a detailed paraphrase of the other two scenes. In their free flight of fantasy the co-authors unwittingly created a monstrous cartoon. At one moment Zurbin and Bulgaevsky seize government money and flee shamefully from the battlefield. At another a simple woman meets Reds who spring up from who knows where, and tears a piece off her own skirt to serve as a banner. At one point Igor the Cadet sees the light, and runs towards the triumphant people with cries of 'Take me from them . . . Traitors . . . Thieves

. . . I am no parasite, please believe me . . . I was tricked . . . Ensnared . . .'. Bogolyubov and Chekin climax the play with the stage direction 'The Internationale, crescendo', evidently believing this to be a touch distinctively their own as against the Internationale 'far away, but coming closer' in the finale of *The Days of the Turbins*.

In his fictionalised biography of Molière Bulgakov would relate the unprecedented barrage of criticism which met *L'Ecole des femmes*. Two irate young littérateurs, Claude de Villiers and Jean de Visé, wrote an anti-Molière play on the same topic in which they unceremoniously characterised the author of *Tartuffe* as 'a roué . . . a monkey, and a cuckold'. It was then, as Bulgakov admits, that Molière made a fatal mistake.

Forgetting the axiom that under no circumstances should an author enter into any kind of disputation in print on the subject of his own works, Molière decided in a frenzy of rage to attack his enemies. Since he was a master of stagecraft he aimed his blow from the stage, writing and producing in June 1663 a short play called *The Critics of 'L'Ecole des femmes'*.

These disputations, the narrator assures us, brought Molière nothing except weariness and a peculiar state of mind which many years later was dignified with the imposing medical label of hypochondria. 'And on his back,' the biographer remarks in passing, 'he lugged two very indifferent writers to immortality.'

The critical battles over *The Days of the Turbins* brought Bulgakov nothing except a nervous disorder. He developed a tic in his shoulder, began to be afraid of being alone, and also developed a phobia of large gatherings. And on his back, like the author of *Tartuffe*, he lugged two very indifferent writers to immortality. The co-authors of *The White House* were to live long and prosper, writing a great diversity of works, and probably quite forgetting that in 1928 they had knocked out a little play for a joke which set the seal on the campaign against *The Days of the Turbins*. Bulgakov, however, 'in a frenzy of rage', responded with his polemical *The Crimson Island*, a play destined to bring him neither fame nor fortune.

Bulgakov too was a master of stagecraft and replied from the stage. He offered the critics a play written with his own plot but elaborated in full accordance with Blyum's rules. He generously endowed it with the clichés and stereotyped situations which Soviet playwriting had already evolved, beginning with his own *The Sons of the Mullah*. The element of self-parody gives this polemical playlet a lyrical subtext unexpected in a work of its kind.

The Crimson Island incorporated the parodied aesthetics of Left theatre, from Meyerhold's production of Sergey Tretiakov's *Roar, China!* to the Maly

Theatre's production of *Leftwards Our Course!* by Bill-Belotserkovsky. The polemic may have been directed at theatre issues, but it went far beyond that; it cut into the unchallengeable heart of the Soviet Government's new cultural policy which aimed to turn the artist into a helot and panegyrist. That was exactly how Alexander Tairov talked of the play in an interview with the magazine *The Life of Art*.

The action of *The Crimson Island* takes place in a theatre. It is the dress rehearsal of a play by a Citizen Jules Verne in the theatre of Gennady Panfilovich, with music, an erupting volcano and English sailors.

This theatre in the town of N retains all its time-hallowed structures and its hide-bound theatre and stage routines. Falling into the turbulent flood of the revolution it has hastily 'adapted' itself and blithely begun, using the same arsenal of theatrical devices, performing only thoroughly 'ideological' plays.

The dramatist Dymogatsky is a great admirer of Jules Verne, to the extent that he has adopted his name as his pseudonym. Whenever he receives a commission he writes an utterly 'revolutionary' play with members of the bourgeoisie, an erupting volcano, oppressed native peoples, allied interventions, English sailors and so on and so forth, all set against a background of his favourite Jules Verne exoticism.

Both Gennady Panfilovich the theatre Director and Dymogatsky the playwright . . . are falling over themselves to 'adapt' to the new times. Both are filled with an almost mystical dread of a third party, Savva Lukich, because on him depends whether their production gets the thumbs up or the thumbs down.

They will go to any lengths, refashion the play in any way required, to get the thumbs up. They have only just finished the casting, but unhesitatingly arrange a dress rehearsal in full make-up and costumes, with a prompter to whisper the lines, because Savva Lukich is about to go off to the Crimea. Savva Lukich, however, understands important social responsibilities in a distorted, bureaucratic way. Like the Pope he is convinced of his own infallibility, and airily disposes of the fates of the Gennady Panfiloviches and Dymogatskys. With their collaboration he cuts plays to ribbons in a great rush, and is quite unable to see in his bureaucratic blindness that with their co-operation he is imposing a repulsive, philistine, unprincipled, inartistic opportunism. He is proliferating the deformed clichés of pseudo-revolutionary plays which can only bring the revolution into disrepute; plays which can only achieve the opposite of what they intend, which can only fulfil an anti-social function, peddling in place of real revolutionary pathos and power a sugary philistine syrup which is an incompetent and clichéd surrogate.[64]

Evidently Bulgakov had touched a raw nerve with the future director of *An Optimistic Tragedy*, a play of legendary awfulness, to judge from the unmistakable emotion behind this response to his play.

'The action of *The Crimson Island* takes place in a theatre.' The play has two interrelated themes: a parody of playwriting clichés; and an examination of the way in which these clichés come into being, created, as Pavel Novitsky put it in a barbed but at times very perceptive review of the play, by 'frightened lackeys' and 'panegyrists'.[65]

In the parody which is at the heart of the play Bulgakov deploys the whole range of the clichés of diction and situation which had built up in contemporary playwriting. We find both the obligatory subdivision of heroes into 'positive' (the 'red native men and women, countless legions') and 'negative' (the 'blackamoor guard, negative, but conscience-stricken'); and the finale obligatory in this style of playwriting. 'The play concludes with the triumph of the red natives. How else?' It is thus enough for Savva Lukich to see a run-through only of the finale for him to decide the fate of the production.

Bulgakov's scrapbook includes a newspaper cutting from *The Life of Art*, No. 29, 1928. This is Yevsey Lyubomirsky's article 'The Evolution of Cliché in Soviet Playwriting', which examines the range of stereotypes in use in plays about the revolution.[66] These find their way from one play to the next, and extend from the standardised positive hero and the breezy, muscle-bound revolutionary sailor to the ways appropriate to the discrediting of particular sub-categories of the bourgeoisie. 'The *haute bourgeoisie* decays in ritzy bars . . . while the fall of the petty bourgeoisie or the degeneration of certain sections of the workers and peasants takes place in beer halls to the accompaniment of familiar music hall ditties.' We have Bulgakov to thank for pointing out this independent corroboration of his play by a literary scholar.

Among the articles in *The Way Forward for the Theatre*, the account of the 1927 meeting on the theatre, there is the no less curious testimony of Bespalov who spoke in the debate on Lunacharsky's speech. Bespalov reported with some alarm on the 'Mongol raider' mentality of certain proletarian dramatists. Writing a play they 'begin to have qualms that they may not turn in quite what is required. Things reach the point where one of the proletarian writers speaking in front of his fellow-dramatists at a serious meeting could talk about how plays ought to be written nowadays [. . .] "It is absolutely essential to have three characters negative and five positive. That way you keep a proper balance and the play has a chance of being accepted. And when I portray a communist, I know to give him one negative trait and five positive, etc".'[67]

Bulgakov offered the critics of *The Days of the Turbins* a play made to just such rules. The parody was founded on an exotic, miniaturised geographical setting. A major event of world history, whose tragic hypostasis Bulgakov had himself examined in *The White Guard*, *The Turbins* and *Flight*, was here the object of a literary travesty translated to a desert island. There was no mistaking the allusions: the downfall of the ruler, the political meetings, the repelling of an onslaught by English sailors, even the killing, but all on the level of Toytown.

Bulgakov really did seem to be turning all the themes of his dramas inside out in *The Crimson Island*. In that sense we certainly can see it, as Julia Babicheva suggests in her article on the comedy, as a kind of fourth, satire drama, complementing a tragic trilogy on the collapse of the White cause.[68] The tragedy of Turbin or Khludov is transformed into the 'crime and punishment' of the travestied General Likki-Tikki, commander of the armed forces under the tyrannical Sizi-Buzi. 'I beg forgiveness for the fact that as a consequence of my blindness and lack of education I served under the tyrant Sizi-Buzi and was a tool of repression in his hands.'

Bulgakov invents a whole sub-plot involving the servants of Lord Glenarvan who have suffered under their masters and fled, together with the conscience-stricken white Blackamoor Tohonga, from Europe to the desert island. Not a single point made by the critics of *The Days of the Turbins* went unanswered. Bulgakov came up with a play which would leave his critics nothing to complain about.

These latter are represented in the play by Savva Lukich. He does not actually appear until Act Three, by which time the play is almost over, but the action revolves round him from the start. It is Savva Lukich's taste in artistic matters which dictates the form of the play from the outset.

> *Gennady*. Right then, Act One. An island inhabited by red natives living under the thrall of white blackamoors . . . You'll have to excuse me, what natives are we talking about here?
>
> *Dymogatsky*. It's an allegory, Gennady Panfilovich. You have to understand it rather subtly.
>
> *Gennady*. These allegories will be the death of me. Look, Savva loathes allegories. 'Don't you give me allegories,' he says. 'Allegories on the outside, for sure, but inside there such Menshevism that you might as well just give up.'

The overarching theme which draws the whole of this 'dramatic pamphlet' together is the killing of live tissue, the live being reduced to the mechanical and puppet-like. It is a process which extends to all the play's characters, from the director and the actors to Savva Lukich who, Bulgakov makes no bones about it, is cloned from Shchedrin's mechanical 'little organ' in his *History of the Town of Glupov*. The theatre's owner Gennady Panfilovich, 'clean-shaven, ginger-haired, and vastly experienced', has a motto which helps him out whatever the occasion: 'The theatre, my dear, is a temple.' Bulgakov adapts the old comic device of attaching a catchphrase to a character to show the complex being reduced to the elementary, the live to the mechanical. The conductor Likuy Isaevich repeats a single line throughout the play: 'Don't continue. I have it already.' This motif culminates in a demonstration of the device stripped to its bare bones. A dummy parrot is introduced whose voice is another incarnation of Metelkin the assistant director. Deep down Savva is wholly satisfied with the parrot. It is an ideal embodiment of the Soviet artist as a creative unit subordinate to him.

Savva. What a lovely parrot! . . . Hello, polly!
Parrot. Hello, Savva Lukich, workers of the world unite, shaking hands is abolished!

Bulgakov immediately parallels this nonsense with an episode involving the actors.

Savva. . . . Hello, blackamoors!
Blackamoors. Hello, Savva Lukich!
Savva is rattled.

Tairov tried to interpret this stylistic feature of the play within the terms of his own practice as a director. In the interview already mentioned he described his production of *The Crimson Island* to *New Theatre-Goer* as 'a continuation and deepening of the Chamber Theatre's work within the tradition of the harlequinade. I mean by that giving a grotesque, theatrical rendering of what is ugly in life, stripping it bare in all its soullessness, and exposing any tendency to regard it as acceptable and normal.'[69]
Beneath the surface level of Shchedrinian themes and motifs Tairov discerned an ancient and compelling current of the 'comedy of masks'. The play is being written, as was customary in the *commedia dell' arte*, before the eyes of the audience. Bulgakov's theatrical genius manifests itself here in the genre of the improvised buffonade.
Tairov's highly theatrical harlequinade interacted with Dymogatsky's hack play and the 'new entrepreneur' personified by Savva Lukich to produce an unexpectedly explosive mixture. The lax and backward provincial fraternity of the actors is living in another age and wholly unconcerned about the actual meaning of the play they have to act in. The range of available characters, rigidly defined by the kind of roles the actors are prepared to play and their various temperamental demands ('Kill me if you must, but not before Act Two,' Anempodist Sunduchkov, who is playing Sizi-Buzi II, beseeches Dymogatsky) all react unpredictably with new demands which are completely beyond the grasp of these traditional tragic actors, comic actors, and *grandes coquettes*. When, after

viewing the play's finale, Savva announces in dead silence that the play cannot be passed for performance because its outlook is that of the Change of Landmarks movement, the theatre takes his dread pronouncement very calmly. Gennady Panfilovich gives the assistant producer five minutes to come up with a new finale 'incorporating world revolution', which he does. The English sailors return to the island, throw their officers in the sea, and merrily sing 'We are all sons of the people'. Savva Lukich is delighted with the finale and, like Blyum (who was much taken by Sudakov's artless last-minute changes to *The Turbins*), passes the play for performance (but also only for one theatre!).

The role of Savva Lukich was played in Tairov's production by Yevgeny Viber. He was made up to mimic Blyum, a diminutive, amiable grey-haired figure in spectacles stitting on stage on the throne, drinking a cup of tea and enjoying talking about art. It was to this small figure that Dymogatsky, half out of his mind, tearing himself free of the actors, addressed himself in the production's finale. The tacking on of 'world revolution' in five minutes flat was too much even for him. The hack playwright was suddenly overcome with the same searing, unanswerable shame as had once overwhelmed the author of a native play in Vladikavkaz. Bulgakov disrupted the comic action, choreographing the duel between Dymogatsky and Savva Lukich, punctuating it with charged pauses and silences. Lacking words of his own, Dymogatsky resorts to Chatsky's monologue in *Woe from Wit* and hurls it at Savva Lukich from the bottom of his heart, changing only one word: 'the times of *Kolchak* and subjugation of the Crimea'.

Gennady Panfilovich, 'clean-shaven, ginger-haired and vastly experienced', takes up Griboedov's text in horror, as if declaiming: 'We're going to end up in the trough, Sergei Sergeich, I'll be off.' Dymogatsky is calmed down and pulled to one side. The actors give the finale their all and jubilantly look forward to a successful production. The order is given to take *Oedipus* off and put up posters announcing the new première. Savva Lukich finally brings down the curtain with an 'Amen!' granting universal absolution.

Bulgakov was not the only playwright to address 'the theatre question' in those years. Mayakovsky in *The Bath-House* and Vsevolod Vishnevsky in *The Last Decisive* did the same. Konstantin Rudnitsky tells us:

It is instructive to compare the parodied scenes in *The Last Decisive* and the monologue of the producer in *The Bath-House* ('Come over here, Comrade Capitalism . . . Convey class domination in your dance . . . Fanciful working masses, revolt symbolically! . . . Put your fanciful worker's feet on fancifully overthrown Capitalism') with the ideological efforts of the producer in *The Crimson Island*, and to compare Mayakovsky's Pobedonosikov and

Bulgakov's Savva Lukich. Fuelling both these dramatists, and Vishnevsky too, we find the same sense of outrage and hatred of pseudo-political hack work, 'vampuka', the vulgarised and profaned agitka-play, and the imbecile caprice of loudmouths in authority and ignorant 'arbiters' of aesthetic taste.[70]

Konstantin Rudnitsky is a major historian of the Soviet theatre and there is a good deal of truth in what he says. There were, however, also significant differences in what these three antagonistic dramatists had to say on 'the theatre question'.

Bulgakov's response took him into forbidden territory. *The Crimson Island* was subjected to harsh, extremely hostile criticism, and Bulgakov not only made it clear he was aware that some were inclined to read deeper political implications into his play, but even dared to encourage them. He approvingly quoted the place in Pavel Novitsky's review where he claimed to detect in *The Crimson Island* the 'malign shadow of the Grand Inquisitor crushing artistic originality, promoting servile, absurd, lickspittle dramatic stereotypes, and crushing the individuality of actor and playwright alike'. He also quoted with evident approval the phrase in the same article about 'a malign, dispiriting power which fosters helots, lickspittles, and panegyrists'. Only a simpleton could have taken this 'malign, dispiriting power' to refer only to one or other of the Leftist critics or jealous fellow playwrights who had unexpectedly had such overwhelming power conferred upon them. For all their aggressiveness, the members of RAPP were mere puppets. The strings were pulled by the supreme puppet-master. In his letter 'To the Government of the USSR' Bulgakov, as the author of *The Crimson Island*, put his views completely unambiguously.

It is not for me to judge how clever my play is, but I readily admit that a malign spectre is indeed conjured up in it, and that it is the spectre of the Main Repertoire Committee. That Committee it is which breeds helots, panegyrists and frightened lackeys. That Committee it is which kills creative thought. It is destroying Soviet playwriting and will eventually be the death of it.

These are not views which I have confined myself to whispering in dark corners. I put them in a dramatised pamphlet and had it staged. The Soviet press rallied to the defence of the Main Repertoire Committee, describing *The Crimson Island* as a lampoon on the revolution. This view cannot be seriously entertained. The revolution is not lampooned in the play for many reasons of which, as space is limited, I shall indicate one. It would be *impossible* to write a lampoon of the revolution because of its exceptional grandeur. A pamphlet is not a lampoon, and the Main Repertoire Committee is not the revolution.

When, however, the German press writes that *The Crimson Island* is 'the first call in the USSR for freedom of the press' (*Molodaya gvardiya*, No. 1, 1929) it is writing the truth. I admit it. Fighting censorship of any kind and irrespective of the regime under which it operates is my duty as a writer, no less than calling for freedom of the press. I am an ardent supporter of freedom of the press, and firmly believe that any writer who claimed not to need it would be like a fish stating publicly that it did not need water.[71]

The translation of an article from the *Deutsche Allgemeine Zeitung* of 5 January 1929 survives in Bulgakov's archive in which the foreign affairs correspondent attempts to compare Bulgakov's play and Tairov's production of it with Pirandello. He categorises *The Crimson Island* as a 'dramatic capriccio' inseparable from a life 'where every free word is an act of orginality, and every joke against the rulers an act of courage'. He tried to guess what it was in Bulgakov's play that 'can have appealed to an apolitical director like Tairov', and touches on several features of the production. There is 'a rapid succession of extraordinarily colourful stage tableaux: the casting of the play; putting on the grease paint in the dressing rooms; dramatic and idyllic scenes on the tropical island; the English lord's feudal castle; the fiery volcano; the fighting on the barricades and the love scenes; the urbane atmosphere, and the proletarian joy of fraternising. A wealth of impressions for the ear and eye, a most curious Russian sketch.' There then follows the conclusion which Bulgakov quoted in part in his letter:

This time the Russian audience, which usually talks endlessly at theatre performances about the acting and direction, was wholly absorbed by the meaning. On the crimson island of the Soviet Union, surrounded by an ocean of 'capitalist' countries, contemporary Russia's most talented writer has timorously, through self-mockery, raised a strangled voice for intellectual freedom in the play.[72]

The pamphlet's meaning was understood in his own way by the individual who was already beginning to determine the fate of artists and theatres. In his reply to Bill-Belotserkovsky in February 1929 Stalin harshly criticised Svidersky, the head of the Main Committee for the Arts, and in the same breath put down also the Main Repertoire Committee, for being guilty of 'the most incredible mistakes and distortions'. First among the incredible mistakes singled out was *The Crimson Island*, which had been passed for performance in the 'Chamber Theatre, which really is bourgeois'. Drawing his letter to a close, Stalin sought to allay Bill-Belotserkovsky's fears: 'As far as rumours of liberalism are concerned, let us rather not talk about this. Leave it to the wives of Moscow merchants to busy themselves with rumours.'[73]

In Stalin's letter *The Crimson Island* was dismissed as 'waste paper'. Put this together with his definition of *Flight* as a play evoking 'pity, if not indeed sympathy, for certain strata of the anti-Soviet émigré circles' and Bulgakov's fate was sealed. The years of 'liberalism' were over. The country was entering the Year of the Great Leap Forward.

'The action of *The Crimson Island* is set in the theatre.' Tairov's straightforward assertion is pregnant with meaning. The play stands at a crossroads in Bulgakov's prose and play writing. It is the culmination of several stormy and fruitful years of work for the stage, and anticipates his work in the coming decade. In *The Crimson Island* we can already sense the accumulated knowledge of a man with a good understanding of actors, directors, and the whole psychological mechanism of the theatre and those who people it. This is the starting point for Bulgakov's work on the manuscript of *Black Snow: A Theatrical Novel*. This is the starting point for a switch-over in his study of 'the theatre question' to a historical approach and the example of the fate of Molière.

In his review of the Chamber Theatre production Pavel Markov pointed out a serious blunder on Tairov's part. Instead of recreating life in the theatre in a remote provincial backwater, Tairov moved the action of the play to the metropolitan stage. In so doing, he destroyed the most effective features of the play.

Its atmosphere of provincial dereliction is indeed a major aspect of Gennady Panfilovich's theatre. Bulgakov gives an alarmingly persuasive portrait of the awfulness and the unoriginality, the self-centred actors coasting along, their horizons bounded by their petty intrigues and their greed for leading roles. That is not the end of the story, however. Not by a long chalk. Bulgakov sees and understands everything just as it is, yet for all his sober-minded lack of illusion the future author of *Black Snow* does manage to reveal something of the mysterious and enticing secret of the world of the stage. He recreates the phenomenon of theatre with an amazement and delight inseparable from irony and mockery. With the wry wit of a philosopher of the theatre Bulgakov takes us through how the dress rehearsal is organised for a sad little hack play, with a stage set put together from what is available. Uncle Tom's cabin has been remodelled as a wigwam, and the backcloth has been adapted from *Ivan the Terrible*. The erupting volcano has been made by boring a large hole in a Mount Ararat surplus to requirements, and discarding Noah's ark. Bulgakov conducts us on an ironical tour of all the circles of the theatrical hell. He shows the parts being allocated, the producer's wife landing a plum role, the squabbling, the grease paint, the grumbling and backstabbing, a Gothic temple being lowered on to the stage instead of the pagan one. Bulgakov throws the stage and all its pitiful machinery wide open for all to see. He shows the audience the lighting being set up, the orchestra tuning up, the French horn panting in at the last minute ('I was buying some socks'). All is amateurish, chaotic, senseless. But only until a certain moment. Now that moment arrives. Likuy Isaevich, whose father 'lived in the same house as Rimsky-Korsakov', signals the orchestra, the overture begins, and the curtain slowly rises. Bulgakov slips in an apparently chance stage direction, but one in which he is wholly himself:

'On stage there is magic. The sun beats down. A tropical island sparkles and shimmers.'

That magical spectacle was to be the last the theatre saw of the author of *The Days of the Turbins* in the 1920s. Even as Tairov's actors were enjoying themselves in his parody the fate of Bulgakov's new play, already announced as a forthcoming production by the Art Theatre, was being decided. Its title was *Flight*.

4

'A Flight in the Mists of Autumn'

Before the Festivities

The fact that Bulgakov was writing a new play for the Art Theatre depicting 'episodes in the struggle for Perekop' was publicised in the press in March–April 1927, at the height of the campaign against *The Turbins*.[1] He was commissioned by the Art Theatre to provide a play titled *Pariahs (The Knights of Serafima)* in April, which we may take as indicating that work on *Flight* was by then in progress.

Bulgakov's writing of *Flight* came about in an entirely natural way and was a necessary part of his development as a playwright. The theme he had begun in *The White Guard* and *The Days of the Turbins* demanded further development and a culminating resolution. The controversy which had attended the Art Theatre's production of *The Days of the Turbins* made its mark on this new play in impelling Bulgakov to give a yet clearer and more unambiguous answer to questions which were still troubling him and his age. He now examined the road to Calvary of those members of the Russian intelligentsia who had thrown in their lot with the White cause from a different, but no less important, angle, posing the question of guilt and personal responsibility for the bloodshed. The new play brought together the images of the 'red crown', the brother sent to his death, the worker sentenced to hang by a verbal, irregular order, and the general warned that he will be haunted by an innocent man he has killed.

During the reading of *Flight* at the Art Theatre Stanislavsky made a pencil sketch which depicts a dour figure with enormous fists slouched over a table. Alongside him, in a halo of luxuriant hair, sits a lean opponent. Theatre historians explain the drawing as showing the impression the scene of Golubkov's interrogation in the counter-espionage section made on Stanislavsky. Olga Radishcheva, who works in the Art Theatre Museum, has interestingly pointed out that the bags under Golubkov's eyes are exactly the same as those Stanislavsky put in his own self-portraits, sketches for his make-up and so on.

Stanislavsky welcomed Bulgakov's new play but was barely able to put in any work on it himself. In the winter and spring of 1928 he was busy rehearsing and directing first Leonid Leonov's *Untilovsk* and then Valentin Kataev's *The Embezzlers*. At the end of the season he was working on a revival of *The Cherry Orchard* with a new cast. When the new productions were being allocated it was Vladimir Nemirovich-Danchenko, back in Moscow at the end of January from Hollywood, who was given *Flight*.

Nemirovich-Danchenko's sole source of information on what had been going on in the theatre in Moscow had been his correspondence. The whole saga of the writing and staging of *The Days of the Turbins* had passed off without his involvement. It was only in December of 1926 that he got to read the play in America, and while he saw it as demonstrating 'a great deal of talent', he rejected the last act outright. He saw the production's 'material success' as deriving from the topic of the White cause and 'the splendid acting of the young company'.[2]

Only in February 1927 did Nemirovich-Danchenko have a chance to read himself into *The Turbins'* reviews. He was amazed. He wrote to Olga:

What a hate campaign *The Turbins* have been subjected to. In all this there are elements of sincere conviction, and even some aspects which merit respect. There is also a good deal that is simply venomous (Blyum) or repulsive. . . . The whole affair redounds to the credit of Lunacharsky and those who took up the cudgels in defence of *The Turbins*, and who stood up for a free (freer) approach to the repertoire.[3]

Nemirovich-Danchenko had gone abroad just as the Art Theatre was on the verge of radical restructuring. Stanislavsky had been left in sole charge for the best part of three years, with a degree of administrative power he had never had before. His principal concern and most difficult artistic problem had been to get the old and young companies to grow together organically.

Bringing the generations together proved far from simple and at times painful. The younger actors quite rightly saw *The Days of the Turbins* as *The Seagull* of their generation, and the very different and conflicting attitudes within the company polarised round it. On 5 November 1926, just one month after the première of *The Turbins*, the Collegium for Artistic Affairs and Repertoire sent Stanislavsky a letter categorically denying 'rumours which have reached the Collegium regarding antagonism on the part of the younger section of the company towards the older'.

The Collegium has resolved: . . . rumours regarding antagonism on the part of the younger section of the company towards the older may have arisen principally in connection with the production of *The Days of the Turbins*, which have brought the young actors acclaim. The younger actors are very proud of this production, but its staging could only have come about by building on the achievements of the old Moscow Art Theatre. It is a vivid illustration of the way in which the older group in the Theatre is passing on its traditions to the younger actors. [. . .] The younger actors of the Theatre object strongly to the rumours being spread and refute them, finding them hurtful and offensive.[4]

After reading this highly diplomatic resolution, drafted by Markov, Stanislavsky noted on it, 'I am very touched and encouraged . . . Given this attitude I look to the future with great optimism.'[5]

'Rumours', which in other organisations are of no great significance, have a very measurable, and not infrequently catastrophic, impact in the theatre. The ferment in the company continued. The 'parliamentary' structure did not prove adequate to resolving the conflicts, and by spring 1928 had collapsed. A Council of Sixteen was created, with a young 'Six' chosen from its ranks for the day-to-day handling of affairs. Initially a 'Five', the 'Six', as Prudkin admits, 'sovietised MAAT'.[6] The main fruit of their endeavours was a dramatic increase in the number of playwrights working for the Theatre. Bulgakov was followed by Leonid Leonov, Valentin Kataev and Yury Olesha. The tentacles of the repertoire-builders stretched out in all directions, extending from Erdman to Bill-Belotserkovsky, to the occasional perplexity of Stanislavsky.

As Markov was to comment many years later, the young leaders were often insensitive to the subtleties of the old stagers' feelings and wounded their self-esteem. This led to internal dissension which was particularly dangerous when the Theatre was being subjected to harsh criticism from outside.

An offshoot of these administrative changes in the Theatre was the appearance of a so-called 'Privy Council'. In autumn 1928 the conflict within the Theatre came to a head. With the support of the most senior of the old stagers, the leader of the young actors under Markov complained to Stanislavsky that the Privy Council was disrupting the normal functioning and progress of the theatre. The theatre press picked up this hot gossip and splashed it all over the newspapers. The season started off with Vsevolod Ivanov's *Armoured Train 14–69*, a new departure for the Theatre, and promptly ran into the sand because of the internal difficulties and disagreements. Spring 1928, the moment Bulgakov presented the Theatre with *Flight*, was in every respect an uneasy and troubled time. Stanislavsky had had high hopes of *Untilovsk*, but neither the audiences nor the critics understood or liked it. It had to be taken off after twenty performances. The production of Kataev's *Embezzlers* caused a certain amount of irritation, reassured nobody, and did not even last twenty performances. *The Gerard Sisters*, a melodrama adapted by Vladimir Mass from *The Two Orphans*, was well received by the public but far from solving the Theatre's problems of repertoire, which in one sense it only made worse. *Armoured Train 14–69*, which stridently confirmed the Art Theatre's new status as a *Soviet* theatre, was in effect a selling of the pass by Stanislavsky. In summer 1927 we come across an unexpected admission in a letter to his wife: '*Armoured Train* had been half-banned. Too bad they didn't kill it off completely.'[7]

Tairov's Chamber Theatre and the Meyerhold Theatre were also having great problems with their repertoire. In May 1928, just at the moment when the fate of *Flight* hung in the balance, Meyerhold, who had once been hoping for a play from Bulgakov, sent Mayakovsky a telegram begging him to come to his rescue with a contemporary play. 'For one last time I must appeal to your level-headedness. The theatre is facing extinction. We have no plays. We are forcibly prevented from resorting to the classics. I do not want to degrade the repertoire.'[8]

In these circumstances the new play from Bulgakov was both a lifeline and a severe threat to the Art Theatre. Certainly it solved problems in terms of the repertoire and preventing any lowering of the Theatre's artistic standards, but not everybody by any means welcomed the idea of repeating all the Theatre had been through in the aftermath of *The Turbins*. Pavel Markov's archive includes a letter in which Vasily Luzhsky expresses strong reservations about including *Flight* in the repertoire and defending it against all comers. 'Let us rather wait for something from another playwright,' he counsels the Literary Director, following this with a detailed if idiosyncratic analysis of *Flight*. 'I have just finished reading *Flight*. It is worse than *The Turbins* or *Untilovsk*, worse than *Getting Late* . . . or *The Mandate!*' The latter title appears only to have been included for the rhyme. In all of *Flight* Luzhsky found nothing to praise except Barabanchikova's phrase 'General Krapchikov is no general – he's an arsehole'. (p. 156) He found the play 'a well-written historical diary . . . a dramatised diary'. Bulgakov's stagecraft was just more of the same: 'more music, White Guards, the Koran, and marches'. Luzhsky felt all trace of action vanished in the Fifth Dream, the 'cockroach races'. He even proposed not to stage the play but to seat the actors round a table and read it directly in front of an audience 'as only the actors of the Art Theatre know how. It would be economical and angry.' He concludes his letter with an outspokenly negative summary assessment of *Flight* as a re-run of a lot of typical Bulgakovian, prosaic, 'twitchy, monocly twaddle'.[9]

Despite this warning from the worldly wise Luzhsky, the Theatre adopted the play and sent it off to the Repertoire Committee. On 18 May the Repertoire Committee officially replied, banning the play on much the same grounds as *The Days of the Turbins*.

The Theatre's repertoire crisis was compounded by a crisis in relations between the different internal factions, which were aired through the press.

In May and June, his biographer tells us, Stanislavsky made notes about the situation in the Theatre and his own situation.

The conditions I work under have changed . . . I am glad to see Nemirovich back (I'm tired). I welcome the Six (I'm old). But still I argue and quarrel with the Six [. . .] All the playwrights are late delivering their plays. *Flight* has been banned. *Blockade* – ?! [. . .] The expectations of the Art Theatre are rising – world wide. All the young playwrights have been hauled over the coals. Nobody wants to write . . .[10]

In the same biographical chronicle Irina Vinogradskaya adduces another illuminating entry of this period: 'There is extraordinary nit-picking on the part of the press, indeed of all the Leftists. There are demands for the development of dramatic literature, but the critics destroy it.'[11]

The reorganisation and wrangling within the Theatre took a heavy toll of Stanislavsky. In late September he wrote to Ripsime Tamantsova from Berlin, 'For some reason I just can't be bothered with the Theatre. I don't know why myself. All the events of the past year have now settled and crystallised, and left such an even-smelling oxide in my heart that I don't know what to do with myself.'[12]

This was Stanislavsky's mood on his return to Moscow on 15 October 1928. He arrived just as the battles over *Flight* were reaching their height. A week before his arrival the play had been discussed at a meeting of the Theatre's Council for Artistic Affairs. In addition to Vladimir Nemirovich-Danchenko, Ilya Sudakov and Pavel Markov, the participants had included Alexey Sviatsky, Head of the Main Committee for the Arts, Vyacheslav Polonsky and Maxim Gorky, who had returned to Moscow from Italy at the end of May 1928. Gorky's presence made what would otherwise have been just another incident in theatre history something out of the ordinary.

Gorky had been taking a keen interest in the development of the young Soviet literature. While still living in Italy his eye had been caught by Bulgakov's prose and playwriting. He shared his delight at discovering a new talent with his correspondents. 'I am following the growth of the new literature in Rus with tremendous excitement. There is much to rejoice at. A wealth of new shoots springing up! Splendid. Our country needs thousands of writers, and here they are appearing . . .' he wrote to Alexander Demidov.[13] In a letter to Dalmat

Lutokhin he mentions Bulgakov's writing as being among those works which show that 'Russian literature is growing sturdily'.[14]

Other observers had different ideas of how Russian literature should be growing. Gorky's stance as someone who wanted to rally the new forces proved controversial. The views of a writer whose vantage point was 'Villa Gorky, Capri' seemed hopelessly *passé*. A famous poetic epistle to Gorky, published in the first issue of *New Left* for 1927, had reiterated a familiar claim to a monopoly of insights:

> Only we,
> however you praise the hacks,
> know what the future intends
> and
> carry the history of literature
> on our backs
> – we and our friends.[15]

The question of who was 'carrying the history of literature' was far from academic. Back in 1926 when the *On Guard* brigade were just embarking on their division of writers into sheep and goats Gorky had made his position clear to Gladkov.

You ask whether I am fully with you. I cannot be fully with people who turn class truth into caste truth. I never will be fully with people who say 'We are the proletarians' with the same feeling as other people in the past said, 'We are the nobles'. I no longer see 'proletarians' in Russia. What I see in the person of the workers is the true masters of the Russian land, and the teachers of all who live there. It is high time to recognise the former truth, and to take pride in it. But the latter truth demands care in the treatment of every man, in order that everyman should not have the right to say that the worker is not the organiser and leader of the new life but just as much a tyrant as any other dictator, and stupid into the bargain.[16]

From 'Villa Gorky, Capri' Gorky could see that the history of literature was being carried also by writers the Leftists dismissed out of hand. Writing to Romain Rolland in November 1925 he had looked into the future. 'The young writers in Russia are very interesting and give grounds for great hopes . . . Books have already appeared which will find a place in the history of literature, for example, Leonov's *Badgers*, and the stories of Bulgakov, Zoshchenko and others.'[17]

Gorky's support for Bulgakov, even from Italy, counted for a great deal.

Bulgakov and Gorky never did get to sit together in Italy on the warm rocks by the sea as Gorky had hoped. Life was to draw them in different directions. A few years later Gorky was turned into one of the Stalin regime's sacred cows, and it was almost as difficult to get in touch with him as with Stalin. This, however, does not detract from the events of autumn 1928 when the struggle was on to save *Flight*. Gorky spoke out on the play's behalf vigorously and without hesitation. Already in the summer Markov informed Stanislavsky that Nikolai Teleshov had passed on information from Gorky 'as yet unconfirmed but giving solid grounds for optimism regarding the inclusion of *Flight* in the repertoire'.[18] Nemirovich-Danchenko sent a telegram to the same effect to him in Berlin. 'Continuing *Blockade*, want immediate start simultaneous rehearsals *Fruits of Enlightenment* and *Flight*, which being passed performance.'[19]

This was the first result of Gorky's intercession. On 9 October he attended a meeting of the Council for Artistic Affairs in order to round things off. Markov first read the May resolution of the Repertoire Committee accusing Bulgakov of idealising the White cause. Sudakov then reported on the subsequent nego- tiations, explaining that, with the involvement of Bulgakov, agreement had been reached under which the Theatre undertook to 'clarify' the character Khludov. 'In *Flight* as it is at present Khludov returns to Russia only at the prompting of his conscience (muddled Dostoevskian notions). [. . .] Khludov should be drawn back to Russia by his knowledge of what is now being done there and because he realises the senselessness of his crimes . . .'. Golubkov and Serafima, Sudakov further reported, should return 'not because they want to see the snow on Nevsky Prospekt again, but because they want to live in the RSFSR'.[20]

Evidently Gorky, for whom this form of theatrical horse-trading must have been something of a novelty, found Sudakov's account thoroughly dispiriting. He started off by responding to it.

It is evident from Sudakov's report that he has been unduly influenced by the Main Repertoire Committee's fiercely worded resolution. Charnota is a comic figure. As for Khludov, he is a sick man. The hanged orderly was only the last straw which broke the camel's back and brought his moral sickness to a crisis.

I can find no evidence of idealisation of the White generals on the part of the playwright. This is an absolutely excellent comedy. I have read it three times. I have read it to Rykov and other comrades. It is a play whose profound satire is cleverly concealed. I should like to see the Art Theatre stage a play of this kind. Sudakov's remarks plainly result from a misunderstanding. He has evidently taken a fiercely worded resolution which completely misses the point of the play too much to heart.

When Bulgakov read the play here his audience, a sophisticated audience, laughed heartily, which shows how well the play has been made.

Flight is an excellent play and will, I assure you, cause a sensation.

Gorky's attempt to persuade his old friend Alexey Rykov, the Chairman of the Council of People's Commissars, to intercede on behalf of *Flight* was probably counter-productive. Given the political equation in the autumn of 1928 Rykov was already in no position to help the Art Theatre.

Alexey Svidersky was no less forthright. 'The overarching theme of the play is flight,' he said. 'Serafima and Golubkov flee from the revolution like blind puppies, as thousands of others fled during this phase of our life, and the only reason they return is precisely because they want to see Nevsky Prospekt and the snow. That is the truth of the matter, and everybody knows it. If we were to put their return down to a desire to contribute to the industrialisation of the country that would be untruthful and therefore bad.'[21] Svidersky went on to raise a wider question of theatre policy which, he argued, ought to proceed from an understanding of the nature of a work of art. 'It is a mistake to adopt a negative attitude towards any really talented play, even if it is less than perfect, because it gets people debating. Even now Bulgakov's play has people talking, even though nobody has yet had a chance to read it.'[22]

The discussing of unread plays is of course problematical, but Svidersky was absolutely right. The only thing he failed to foresee was that he himself and the Main Committee for the Arts would be the principal casualties of the discussion, the Committee subsequently being described in an article by Alexey Seliva-novsky titled 'The Patrimony of the Art Patrons' as having 'sprung to the defence of the most reactionary play of our days, Bulgakov's *Flight*'. This, however, was still in the future, and on 9 October the arguments of Gorky, Svidersky and Nemirovich-Danchenko, who drew the discussion to a close, seemed eminently sensible. The central and provincial newspapers (as far away as Vladivostok) reported the discussion, evidently recognising that it had a significance beyond the immediate concerns of the Art Theatre.[23]

On 11 October *Pravda* published an official announcement that 'The Moscow Art Theatre has adopted Bulgakov's *Flight* for production'. Gorky's comment that the play would cause a sensation was also printed.

It was an important victory for the Theatre, and one which it was to enjoy for just ten days. On 13 October 1928 *Pravda* reported that Gorky, who had 'become acclimatised in recent years to the warm weather in Italy' and who was suffering from tuberculosis and myocarditis, had returned on medical advice to recuperate over the winter in Sorrento. There and then the opponents of *Flight*, who had been temporarily thrown into disarray, regrouped and struck the Art Theatre and Bulgakov a crippling blow.

Two weeks after the triumphal meeting of the Council for Artistic Affairs, ten days after Gorky's departure, and four days before the Art Theatre's thirtieth anniversary, the May resolution of the Main Repertoire Committee banning *Flight* was confirmed. On 22 October an enlarged session of the Repertoire Committee's Political and Art Affairs Council again read and discussed the play. The Art Theatre's interest was represented solely by Sudakov, while the tone of the meeting was set by Raskolnikov, Averbakh, Kirshon, Orlinsky and Novitsky.

The newspaper reports indicate that the reading of the play was an unconventional duet, the first half of *Flight* being read by Sudakov, and the second by the Council's chairman, Fyodor Raskolnikov. According to the newspaper report, 'Two very different attitudes to the play were already evident in the way they read it . . . For Sudakov its meaning, its underlying theme, is the "cockroach race" of people dispersed by the dread tornado of revolution to the four corners of the earth. For him the heroic outbursts and monologues of Bulgakov's characters are of minor significance. He reads them as if already anticipating the cuts the producer will have to make, glossing over one thing, skipping another altogether.' Raskolnikov, however, is said to have read the script 'with heavy irony, emphasising all the stereotypes, the artificial and thoroughly phoney phraseology of the saintly martyrs of the White Guard'.

A heated discussion ensued. Svidersky repeated, if anything more robustly, the view he had put forward at the Art Theatre. 'We cannot judge a play on the basis of the lessons of former school teachers of Russ. Lit. who try to pigeon-hole the heroes as "negative" or "positive types". Let the play stir up impassioned debate and controversy. So much the better. *Flight* will be the best production of the season.'[24]

Sudakov spoke last. Following the tack which had worked with *The Turbins*, he set about explaining how he would stage the production and re-work the script. Afterwards he had to explain himself to Bulgakov. 'I was speaking at the end of the meeting where they were out for blood and I believe I sincerely and honestly defended the interests of the Theatre and the playwright, no more, no less.'[25] As evidence Sudakov sent the transcript of his speech, excerpts of which Bulgakov glued into his scrapbook. 'Your speeches here drive me to despair,' Sudakov had said. 'You are suffocating the theatre and making it impossible for it to function.' He went on to explain that Khludov was the only strong figure in the play and 'all the others are cockroaches. Take Charnota. Who is he? A fraud, a pimp, a cardsharper . . . He is a complete shit, a degenerate who has sunk as low as it is possible to sink. Korzukhin, Lyuska, Charnota,' Sudakov continued his speech in defence of the play, 'are truly the dregs of humanity.' His arguments in favour of Khludov were no more flattering. 'What more proof of victory do you want when you have conquered the White General Slashchov and got him working for you in the Military Academy here in Moscow?'[26]

On 24 October it was officially announced in the press that *Flight* was being removed from the repertoire. This was immediately followed by a cannonade of editorials and articles in *Komsomolskaya pravda* and elsewhere: 'Flight Back to the Past Must Be Stopped', 'Flight of the Cockroaches', 'Strike Down the Cult of Bulgakovism'.[27] Speaking in Leningrad Pyotr Kerzhentsev claimed *Flight* had been passed for performance 'under pressure from the Right Wing' and that rectifying the error had been a matter of great urgency.[28] *Worker's Moscow* published a report of a meeting of RAPP under the title, 'An End to the In-Fighting: *On Guard* against the Cult of Bulgakovism'. The title of the meeting was 'Who We Shall Fight and What We Shall Fight For in 1929'.[29]

The target had been chosen, but even within the RAPP leadership there were differences over *Flight*. Stepan Sheshukov cites an interesting document in his book *The Furious Zealots*. On 30 October 1928 Sergey Kanatchikov was urgently summoned to a meeting of the Communist fraction of the RAPP secretariat. As RAPP's representative on FOSP (the Federation of Associations of Soviet Writers) he was accused of loss of vigilance and of having committed an 'enormous ideological error'. The error was that not only had the accredited representative of RAPP not spoken against *Flight*, he had actually voted in favour of publication of excerpts from the play. Kanatchikov did his best to defend himself. 'About *Flight*. I went to the reading of this play. I can see nothing anti-Soviet in it. It made a good impression. The twelfth issue of *Red Virgin Soil* is short of material and Vsevolod Ivanov suggested printing excerpts from *Flight*. I saw no reason why they should not be printed and voted in favour'. Vladimir Kirshon parried, 'Odd that a RAPP worker should be voting for space to be given to *Flight* when it is obviously counter-revolutionary.' As a result a resolution was passed to 'request the Central Committee to relieve Comrade Kanatchikov of his representation of RAPP on FOSP'.[30]

These were the decidedly tricky circumstances obtaining as the Moscow Art Theatre prepared to celebrate its thirtieth anniversary. The date of 28 October 1928 became not only a celebration but also an affirmation by the Theatre of its artistic and social beliefs. The anniversary itself became a battlefield, with the Leftists preparing for what they saw as a vitally important ideological showdown.

Pavel Markov was later to recall how agitated the Theatre's founders were and how Stanislavsky delivered his speech. At first he even learned a script by heart, but when the evening arrived he had a lump in his throat and said not what he had prepared but what he truly felt. He thanked the Government for allowing the old stagers of the Art Theatre to come to an understanding of the revolution in their own way, not hurrying them or obliging them to dye themselves red at the cost of their integrity.

We have come gradually to an understanding of the age, and gradually too our art has begun an organic evolution. Any other way would simply have pushed us into turning out pseudo-revolutionary hack work. We wanted to approach the revolution differently. We wanted not merely to observe how people march with red flags, but to look deeply into the revolutionary soul of the country.[31]

   This sounded, of course, both rather solemn and rather provocative. Neither did Stanislavsky leave any doubt about whom he was addressing in the part of his speech which dealt with the new playwriting.

I have said in the past and will say again that we are seeking closer ties and a union with contemporary writers, who give cause for great optimism. We have links with many writers, among whom there are some extremely talented people with a splendid feel for the stage . . . We must be patient and show good will if the most talented writers are not to be frightened off or pushed aside.[32]

   Those who saw frightening off and pushing aside as their main aim in life were not slow in replying. A meeting was held in the Communist Academy to discuss 'The Anniversary of the Moscow Art Theatre before the Tribunal of Marxist Theatre Studies'. In his paper on 'The Sociology of the Moscow Art Theatre Anniversary', Pavel Novitsky described Stanislavsky's speech as expressive of a 'deep organic alienation of spirit and outlook from our age on the part of Stanislavsky and his theatre'. Attempting to drive a wedge between the Art Theatre's twin leaders, Novitsky, who was extremely well informed about the Theatre's internal tensions, drew an administrative conclusion: 'There is nothing more to be hoped for from Stanislavsky. Nemirovich-Danchenko's reliance on the younger actors is much more promising.'[33]
   Blyum and Orlinsky, the bloodthirstiest of all 'MAAT-baiters', went further and volunteered the view that 'there have been and are no waverings in the Art Theatre. Its class orientation is firm. There is more of the cult of Bulgakovism in the Art Theatre than there is in Bulgakov himself.'[34]
   The Art Theatre was in no position to resist this onslaught. Gorky was now far from Moscow, and Stanislavsky's producing of the first act of the long-unstaged *Three Sisters* at a gala performance on the day after the anniversary ended badly. Suffering severe pains in the region of his heart, he barely made it to the end of the act. 'Professor E. Fromholdt was called from the audience and found Stanislavsky prostrate on a divan, looking very pale and still in his make-up and wearing the army uniform of Vershinin . . .'[35]
   Illness took Stanislavsky from the Theatre for two years. Those two long years were the most unpropitious in the whole of Bulgakov's life.

Eight Dreams

The fact that the Art Theatre was unable to produce *Flight* affected not only Bulgakov. It was an irremediable misfortune for the Art Theatre itself. If no one can say for sure what the production might have been like, it is beyond question that after *The Days of the Turbins*, *Flight* opened up exciting avenues for major creative innovation by both the Theatre and its Author and pointed them in a new direction. Because of this we shall find it rewarding to change the nature of our narrative of Bulgakov at the Moscow Art Theatre and take a closer and more detailed look at this play, which perhaps to this day has not been properly understood by the Russian theatre.

On two obvious levels *Flight* is a direct sequel to *The Days of the Turbins*. It follows on in time, in terms of the working out of the historical themes; and in the transformation of certain characters devised with particular actors in mind. From Golubkov's first lines, for example, we recognise the voice of the 'hopelessly civilian' Lariosik with his incorrigibly convoluted, self-defeating and typically intelligentsia manner of speaking:

Can you hear it, Serafima? [. . .] How weird this all is! [. . .] We've been on the run right across Russia for a month now, and the further we go the more incredible it seems . . . [. . .] When all that terrible fighting was going on this morning I actually felt homesick for Petersburg – I did, you know! Suddenly, quite clearly, I saw the green-shaded lamp in my study . . . (p. 154)

The 'green-shaded lamp' is an important and recurrent motif in Bulgakov's biography. He was to tell Popov that it derived from his childhood memories of 'the figure of my father writing at his desk'. The prompter's copy of *Flight* contains another more direct allusion to *The White Guard* and *The Days of the Turbins*. Golubkov introduces a shared geographical setting for all Bulgakov's characters when he asks, 'Have you ever been to Kiev, Serafima?'

The parallels and similarities which are only to be expected in works by the same author should not of course blind us to the real differences which separate *The Days of the Turbins* and *Flight*. The new play uncompromisingly presented themes which had been played down or even cut from *The Days of the Turbins* in the course of production. The play touched on that biographical obsession of the revolutionary years, the images of bloodshed and the murdering of the weak and defenceless which haunted Bulgakov and were not, in fact, to be laid to rest even by *Flight*.

The Days of the Turbins was a play created jointly with the Art Theatre. It has the Art Theatre's poetics firmly stamped on it. *Flight* was the product of

Bulgakov's imagination unconstrained by pre-existent traditions of playwriting. In *The Turbins* Bulgakov was in many ways the junior partner, raising himself to the level of the Art Theatre and learning to think in terms of the stage. In *Flight* he was offering the Theatre something in a different league, which incorporated his own original and daring approach to theatre.

The Days of the Turbins revolves round the state of the Turbins' home life. *Flight* revolves round the state of the world. *Flight* operates on two quite distinct levels: an external, plot level: the flight of Golubkov and Serafima to the Crimea to seek shelter under General Khludov's wing, and from there on to Constantinople; and a second, inner level: the movement and flight of history itself. The two planes intersect in the play's fifth 'dream', the cockroach races, which not only do not halt the action but give it its symbolic meaning.

In *Flight* Bulgakov became a fully fledged dramatist in his own right. The Chekhovian system, which in the 1930s Osip Mandelshtam described as 'ecological', exploring the problems people face as a result of living together or in painful proximity to each other, is not an important dramatic factor in the play.

In his new play people's proximity or the fact of their living together are not crucial or decisive factors in their lives. The daily round is destroyed, leaving only bare existence, a rarefied atmosphere uncongenial for human lungs which Bulgakov's heroes have to learn to breathe.

When *Flight* was only just becoming part of our theatrical and literary canon, Veniamin Kaverin tentatively and questioningly defined its genre as 'satirical tragedy?' or 'a comedy?' The one thing he was sure of was that *Flight* defies the set features of genres and cuts across their conventional boundaries. 'At one moment we are dealing with a psychological drama, the next with a phantasmagoria which almost defies any realistic conception of the world around us.'[36]

In *Flight* Bulgakov tried to find a radically new generic form with which to piece together a picture of times which were drastically 'out of joint'. There is a bitter irony in his recollection in the play of the motivation of human relations in times now irrevocably past: 'You are educated men!' the lecturer from St Petersburg University cries from force of habit to the thieving counter-intelligence agents hastily lining their pockets as the old era comes to an end.

Bulgakov's search for a new answer to the problems raised in *The White Guard* obliged him to describe a world whose laws were not at all those of the family, home and hearth. In *Flight* he tried to recreate his favourite characters' destiny when they were removed from their familiar surroundings and milieu. He took them far away from the house with cream blinds and immersed them in a chaotic, headlong torrent. He tried to measure the logic of the personal, familiar, and run of the mill against a logic which was impersonal, extraordinary, and unreal. He tried to find a new artistic focus to pull the atomised destiny and biography of the Russian intellectual together into a drama.

The definition of the play's genre as 'Eight Dreams' is found in the earliest known versions of *Flight*. This points to a major and fundamental aspect of Bulgakov's vision as an author. There is no gradual building up in the play, no tipping of the scales which leads to change. Much psychological motivation is simply omitted. We are presented with a world in flux, displaced, wrecked, disordered, reminiscent of some lurid dream. 'You hurtle through time and space in disregard of the laws of reality and reason, and dwell only on those points your heart ponders.' The words of Dostoevsky's 'comical man' give some sense of the concept and structure underlying *Flight*.

Dreams can have varying significance in Bulgakov's poetics. A dream can be the blessed vision of a normal life, desired and aspired to, an opportunity to vary what life presents and alter its catastrophic course. It can be a making manifest of concealed and repressed drives, the wish fulfilment of a longing for peace and rest which is very far indeed from what waking reality affords. A dream, finally, can be an endless, anguished circling round one of those points which the heart ponders. This latter is the plane on which Bulgakov was attempting to create Doctor Alexey Turbin's dream in the first version of *The Turbins*, his ailing mind riveted by the sight of a bloody figure lying in the snow, while a brutal cry, 'Trimai iogo!', assails his ears. Bulgakov dropped the dream in the course of re-working his play with the Theatre, accepting that it was 'wholly untheatrical'.

The dreams in *Flight* are of a different order. They are the dreams not of the play's characters but of its author. His is the consciousness which 'hurtles through time and space', freely pulling out and yoking events in a way impossible under the prevailing conventions of stagecraft. As if circumventing Chekhov, Bulgakov turns to the free theatre practice of Shakespeare, itself a product of the need to describe a world 'out of joint' and in process of being set right again. In their own way his endeavours also drew on the general drift of theatre thinking in the 1920s, in particular Meyerhold's theatrical compositions which were inspiring a new playwriting, as Boris Alpers has described.[37] Bulgakov may have been in opposition to many of his contemporaries in the theatre, but for all that he was a child of his times in the way he grew and developed as a playwright. It would be nonsense to attempt to tear him out of his context.

If Bulgakov had inevitably and rightly to accept an artistic compromise with *The Days of the Turbins*, with *Flight* he offered the Art Theatre a play in which the psychological refinement of the existing Chekhovian tradition is wholly fused with the new artistic licence required to describe a world in crisis. He brings in a Shakespearean mode to represent man at the mercy of historical events.

Bulgakov plunged headlong into the realm of the 'literature of serious laughter', to use a term on which Mikhail Bakhtin is the authority. It is worth noting that Bakhtin himself, like Bulgakov and a number of his other contemporaries, arrived at his formulations by way of the social psychology and cultural situation he experienced in his youth, and during the revolution and civil war when his philosophical views were forming and being formed. An era when the traditional ideas and way of life were being destroyed, and new forms of 'proximity and living together' were appearing and becoming set, was to prove a fruitful source for Bulgakov's 'last, sunset novel', *The Master and Margarita*, and for Bakhtin's principal work on the culture of demotic laughter. In this sense, *The Days of the Turbins* is a work of the 1920s, while *Flight* looks ahead, paves the way, and senses the imminence of a new period.

The playwright's dreams in *Flight* do not, as in the first version of *The Turbins*, illustrate events. They fix a temporal perspective which separates the world he is depicting from his contemporary reality. The stuff of his dreams is the stuff of history, and it has passed on now into history. The epigraph from Zhukovsky immediately invites us to adopt this new perspective:

> Renown's a still and radiant shore.
> Our task is thither striving.
> Now rest the man whose flight is o'er!

When Vyacheslav Polonsky spoke at a discussion of *Flight* at the Art Theatre he voiced his doubts about the play's general tone, encapsulating it fairly precisely when he said *Flight* was written 'as if the battle were already over'.[38] To some extent Polonsky was right. Bulgakov really was addressing himself not to the past but to the future. For the Leftists, still seared by yesterday's passions, the tone was unacceptable. It was probably their total incomprehension of what Bulgakov was saying in *The Turbins* that is behind the style in which *Flight* was written, with its rare tension and undisguised lyricism. A whole system of expressive means has been devised to enable the authorial voice to be directly heard in the non-narrative, 'objective' form of drama.

The epigraphs to the dreams and the lengthy stage directions which introduce them were pointers to an important artistic principle. Many producers, Sudakov included, have tried to find ways of incorporating this allusive prose into the script of their productions. Luzhsky even proposed that Kachalov should read the stage directions aloud. Bulgakov's directions contain important information for a proper understanding of the play. Most striking of all is his insistence on indicating the hour at which each dream takes place. The first stage direction-cum-monologue specifies, 'Outside a cheerless October evening, sleet'.

(p. 153) Everything that subsequently occurs in the play is explicitly associated with departing day, sundown, and twilight. We can recognise in this a particular feature of Bulgakov's grotesque and of his personal outlook, expressed through categories of time and space. The 'cheerless October evening, sleet' of the First Dream is followed by the 'darkness' of the Second, with the faint blue electric lights. The stage direction introducing the third scene again emphasises: 'Dim lighting. Autumn twilight'. The Fourth Dream is introduced with the word, 'Twilight', while in the Fifth, where the part of *Flight* set in emigration begins, 'Lights go up on Constantinople in late afternoon sunshine'. In the Sixth Dream 'The setting sun picks out the balustrade of a minaret. Shadows of approaching evening. Silence.' 'An autumn evening in Paris' begins the action of the Seventh Dream. The Eighth and final Dream, is preceded by a stage direction which brings the motif to its climax: 'Through the French windows are seen a minaret, the domes of Constantinople and the top of Yanko's booth. The sun of autumn is setting. Sundown, sundown . . .'

Bulgakov's insistence on this calls for an explanation. We find the theme of sunset and twilight recurring in his very earliest works. For the sick, conscience-stricken hero of *The Red Crown* twilight is 'a terrible and portentous time of day when everything is extinguished and becomes unclear'. Obsessed with a moral predicament to which there can be no solution, a situation very close to that in *Flight*, the hero of the story describes twilight as 'a weighty hour of reckoning'. In *The White Guard* the twilight of 14 December 1918 portends defeat, destruction and the sunset of the Turbins' life. In the novel Bulgakov even developed a symbolic 'clock of life' of the house. According to this symbolic system twilight was 'the most depressed and hopeless time on the human clock-face' (p. 184). At this time 'as twilight approached the mood in the Turbins' apartment grew sadder and sadder' (p. 187).

Pushkin is mortally wounded in the play *The Last Days* when the 'crimson winter sun' is setting, and is brought to the house on the Moyka Canal, as is three times emphasised, 'at twilight'.

In *The Master and Margarita* 'It may have been the twilight which seemed to cause such a sharp change in the Procurator's appearance. He appeared to have aged visibly and he looked hunched and worried.' (p. 351)

Flight contributes one further meaning, linked to the play's central symbol: 'I once went into the kitchen when it was getting dark – there were cockroaches on the stove. I lit a match – it spluttered – and they all ran away.' (p. 187)

Flight's 'dusk of evening' colouration derives from a particular feature of the grotesque in Bulgakov. The unique events which occur in the play and its mixing of the tragic with the farcical, the serious with the comical are descended from a variety of the grotesque found in German romanticism. This is the grotesque of departing day, twilight, the night, as distinct from the sun at noon which characterised the outlook of the renaissance. We are confronted by a form of the grotesque which somewhere along the way has shed its traditional lack of rebelliousness. In this respect *Flight* is a direct precursor of *The Master and Margarita*, a typical work of romantic grotesque. The novel runs true to type with its conception of time, the events of the plot beginning at Patriarch's Ponds 'at the sunset hour of one warm spring day' (p. 13) and finishing on the Saturday 'at sunset' and in 'the twilight of an oncoming storm' (p. 417).

It is worth emphasising the originality of the playwriting technique which Bulgakov developed in *Flight*. There is no sharp dividing line between the main text of the play and the stage directions. The sections typeset in italicised Brevier have a wholly specific role to play in artistic and practical terms. Bulgakov was not by any means the first dramatist to attempt to lay down the *mise-en-scène* and indicate the overall stage treatment of his play. Modern dramatists from Ibsen and Chekhov on had been dragging drama up to the standards achieved in the rest of literature by the judicious use of stage and other directions before theatre practice caught up with them.[39] The wholly subjective, non-script prose deployed in *Flight* incorporated the experience of a fully mature Author of the Theatre, fresh from his close involvement with directing the cast of *The Turbins*. Bulgakov's accompanying stage directions to his characters' dialogue, some short, some long, are often along the lines of a director's suggestions, aiming to channel the actor's imagination. The first version of *Flight* was especially generously endowed with such suggestions. Korzukhin, for example, beginning his game of cards, was to smile at Charnota as if 'to a child walking by the Cathedral of Christ the Redeemer'. Bulgakov was staging his drama on paper. He had a clear idea not only of every piece of stage business of his characters, but also of the director's overall composition of the stage picture. In *Flight* there is an exceptionally detailed emotional score for the future production conveyed in a poetically condensed form; what since the time of Chekhov the Art Theatre had been calling 'mood' or 'tone'.

Setting the play's mood, Bulgakov virtually does away with such conventional stage directions as 'Enter' or 'Exit'. In *Flight* people 'disappear', 'vanish', 'sink into the earth', 'appear', 'rise out of the earth', 'rise to dizzy heights', 'get the bit between their teeth', 'bare their teeth', 'hurtle in', are 'crazed with horror', 'materialise from a hatchway', 'emerge from the wall', 'soar above the booth'. All of which gives the play its peculiarly phantasmagorical tone and colouring.

This world is viewed as a unity of time and space, and as a symphony of accompanying sounds. Bulgakov was never again to compose as detailed a musical score for his other plays. He fine-tuned and perfected it over many years, returning to it whenever there was a hope, however faint, that it might be produced. In autumn 1933 Yelena Sergeevna Bulgakova recorded in her diary, 'M.A. yesterday. At Patya Popov's. Annushka sang to guitar. M.A. constantly requesting gypsy waltzes – needed for *Flight*.'[40]

The muffled chanting of the monks rises from the crypt, hooves clatter, a bell tolls, a gentle waltz played by a military band accompanies the sailing of Charnota's cavalry, the armoured train clanks and bangs, its whistle emitting a hoarse, martyred shriek, the silence of the grave, the gentle trilling or deafening shrilling of telephones, the demented Hermann's aria from *The Queen of Spades*, and the strange symphony of Constantinople in which the Russian song 'The Moon is Shining' mingles with Turkish melodies, the bass voices of the vendors of buffalo milk respond to the tenor cries of lemon sellers, accordions play dashing marches and water drips quietly, a barrel-organ plays 'Parting', the thin voice of a muezzin floats out from a minaret, and a Russian choir belts out the song of the Twelve Robbers. The function of all this polyphony is to convey the continuum of life, and to universalise a plot about the emigration to the level of an epic.

Bulgakov's montage of time, place and sound is there to perfection in the very first stage direction of *Flight*. The upper reaches of the stage setting, the barred window, the brown face of a saint in a fresco, the faded wings of the seraphim and gilded haloes on the icons convey a high biblical symbolism. On a second level the space of the church interior is like a theatre set for Noah's Ark. Then there is the crypt from which the prayer rises, 'Holy Father Nicholas, martyr and saint, pray for us'. Heaven and Hell, Noah's Ark and a monastery, the muffled prayer rising from the crypt on a cheerless October evening with sleet, monks betrayed by their unworthy shepherd who, along with their abbot, 'vanish underground' (in the first redaction it was even more pronounced: 'into the bowels of the earth'). Thus in the play's initial stage direction we are introduced to a world which is spent.

The twilight of an epoch heading for extinction blurs the boundaries between life and death. It creates an abnormal situation, which is the customary setting for grotesque realism within whose field all manner of transformations and mystifications are possible. A pregnant woman becomes General Charnota, a chemist from Mariupol turns into an archbishop. In this same twilight Charnota presents himself to Serafima's former husband Korzukhin in Paris in bright yellow underpants.

It is difficult, of course, to imagine now how effectively the Art Theatre might have translated the Eight Dream convention to its stage. Yelena Bulgakova's diary entry for 15 October 1933 is very interesting and informative in this respect:

Second meeting on the music for *Flight*. M.A. says 'Must get it right,' i.e. musical numbers must not sound too vulgar and real, which the Art Theatre tends towards. But neither must it lapse into theatrical Leftism which never is effective, especially not in the Art Theatre. Sudakov does, however, seem to be getting the hang of what the Dreams in *Flight* are all about. He wants the epigraphs to each scene read out, for example by Prudkin who plays Golubkov. M.A. says it's not a bad idea, but unlikely to succeed at the Art Theatre.

Judging from the minutes of the rehearsals, Bulgakov had grounds for concern. Matters concerning the play's poetics plainly took second place to analysis of the characters' personalities. Not unexpectedly, Khludov proved a major problem.

We know that the prototype for Khludov was Yakov Slashchov, a general of the White army who returned to Russia early in 1922. In 1921 he had published a memoir and documentary history of the 'defence and surrender of the Crimea' in Constantinople, *Ya. Slashchov-Krymsky: I Demand To Be Judged Publicly and by Society*. In 1923 Slashchov published a different version in Moscow under the title *The Crimea in 1920*, with an introduction by Dmitry Furmanov. It makes sense to compare some of the motifs in *Flight* with this memoir evidence.

The young general put military honour above all else. He despised the intelligentsia for its dithering (and hated the HI – 'Holy Intellectuals' – Party). He despised equally the mob at GHQ and the 'nits in the rear' ('When you've finished crushing the red bastards, I strongly advise dispossessing the bastards in the rear'). He was fearless ('I have looked death in the eyes often enough'). He loathed Wrangel and his incompetent hangers-on who were pushing everything towards inevitable disaster. He knew only one way to restore order: hang, hang and hang again. The complicated and malign figure delineated in the pages of Slashchov's memoirs made a deep impression on Bulgakov.

A whole range of twists and turns of the plot in *Flight* were suggested by Slashchov's books. The saga of the counter-intelligence officers stealing everything they can get their hands on under cover of the regime ('A dying order always makes use of such vermin', as Slashchov put it); the nature of the Commander-in-Chief's relations with a popular general of whom he was jealous; the appearance among the troops of Bishop Benjamin trying to organise a crusade ('I had some difficulty believing in this padre's bravery'); the halo of 'Saviour of the Crimea', 'Russia's last hope' ('We must not forget that only Slashchov is holding the front together. The soldiers love him and trust him alone, and all the filth in the rear *is afraid only of him*.' Slashchov himself added the italics to a genuine document of the time): all these touches were incorporated to a greater or lesser extent in the play. Khludov's first line in the play – ' . . . comma. But the Red army commander Frunze did not feel inclined to act the part of a simulated enemy as if we were on manoeuvres' – almost literally repeats Slashchov's caustic tirade, 'But the reds did not feel inclined to act the part of a simulated enemy' (p. 165).

Slashchov's books were primarily the confessions of a professional soldier who was unable at times to conceal a general's arrogance, even when it was emphatically in his own interests to do so. Like Charnota, who relishes the 'beautiful fight' at Kiev, Slashchov recalled his military achievements with pride: 'This battle laid the basis for my holding of the Crimea and extended the Civil War by a full year. Mea culpa, but so it was.'[41]

Through Slashchov's documents and bulletins muffled signals were nevertheless now and again to be heard which for Bulgakov were of supreme importance.

At that point I had faith in virtually nothing. It was a period in which I was passing from despair to hope and when I resolved more than once to throw everything in and clear off . . . It was a dreadful period when I could not say in a definite and straightforward way what it was I was fighting for . . . I found out what was going on in the rear, and a nightmarish state of spiritual division and perplexity took hold within me which was enough to drive a man mad.'[42]

This was what hooked Bulgakov. The brink. A man groping his way forward. In *Flight* Slashchov's madness became the madness of the old world, suffering as book-learning prescribed, and as its own deeds caused it to. Bulgakov transformed the real-life destiny of Slashchov into the tragedy of a conscience which could not simply put the bloodshed behind it, and was unable because of that to shrug off its predicament.

Nothing short of 'muddled Dostoevskian notions', that was, as not a few in the Art Theatre and beyond its walls were quick to point out. Neither did the direct borrowings from Shakespeare's *Hamlet* escape them. 'Over the top' was Nemirovich-Danchenko's reaction, when *Flight* was discussed on 9 October, to the appearance of the hanged orderly's ghost to Khludov. Sudakov promised to rectify the Dostoevskian notions in the stage version, interpreting them as 'pangs of conscience'. The most important aspect of the play is not, however, the perfectly obvious literary parallels, or the impulse Slashchov's book gave for the writing of the play. That impulse; the experiences of Bulgakov's wife Lyubov Belozerskaya, who had herself completed the flight from St Petersburg via Kiev to Constantinople, Paris, Berlin and back to Moscow; the stories of Arkady Averchenko; Alexey Tolstoy's *Ibikus* and sundry other literary sources cannot detract from the crucial fact that in *Flight* Bulgakov found the answer to the question which had been troubling him from the outset, when he was formulating and engaging with the main themes of his writing.

The hero of *The Red Crown*, written in 1922, turns to the hanging and flogging general and prophesies:

Then I became embittered by the torment and wished with all my heart that he should come to you one time at least, and put your hand to his crown. I assure you, you would not have been able to take it any more than I could, not for an instant. But then, who knows, perhaps you too are not alone during the hours of night? Perhaps you are haunted by that grimy, soot-blackened man hanged from a lamp-standard in Berdyansk? If so, we are justly punished. I sent Kolya to help you hang him, but it was you who hanged him, who gave the verbal instructions, without so much as an official order.

The hero of *The Red Crown* does not exonerate himself of blame. He accepts the guilt of not having saved a man, not having helped, not having had the courage even to say what typhus-stricken Serafima or Krapilin, the orderly who is 'so good at talking', dares to shout out. In order to speak the truth you have to forget yourself, take leave of your senses, not consider what you are doing. ('When people here *do* know what they're saying, you can't get a word of truth out of them,' as Khludov morosely jokes (p. 174).) Krapilin needs to forget himself and soar to lethal heights for the truth to pour from his throat in the heat of the moment.

Lethal heights – this is the setting for free human action, the realm of the moral absolute in which it is 'easy' for an ancient philosopher to exist. 'Telling the truth is easy and pleasant,' Yeshua tells Pilate in *The Master and Margarita* (p. 39). For a simple human being these heights prove lethal. The woman who 'does not know what she is saying' is thrown by Khludov into the clutches of the counter-intelligence officers. The orderly who is 'good at talking' is hanged from the lamp-standard on the platform. Analysing what is the key predicament in *Flight*, Marietta Chudakova draws an important conclusion. 'Thus we have here a close investigation (in two variations, even) of the psychological predicament whose insolubility caused the hero of *The Red Crown* to lose his reason: the possibility and consequences of directly confronting a lethal power.'[43]

This is the point in Bulgakov's writing which ultimately leads to that unresolvable argument on the path of moonlight between Yeshua and Pontius Pilate. And Khludov, no less than the Procurator of Judaea, secretly knows the truth, and has a tormenting thirst to hear it spoken. ('Go on, soldier, go on.' (p. 176))

It was very important for Bulgakov that Khludov should be perceived as a genuine man of intellect, wrestling to the best of his ability with the ancient conundrums of Russian culture. In his pen portrait of the character in the very extended stage direction which precedes the Second Dream, Bulgakov quite unambiguously employs historical analogies to universalise traits in Khludov which go beyond the standard attributes of a general. 'The man has a bone-white face [. . .] Khludov is as snub-nosed as Paul the First [. . .] his eyes are old. He is wearing a soldier's greatcoat, belted nonchalantly like a country-gentleman wearing a dressing-gown. Mittens on his hands. Khludov is unarmed.' (p. 164)

In the choking smoky atmosphere of a railway station, beside the black hooded corpses of the hanged, to the tender strains of waltzes played by a brass band ('A waltz to which people once danced at high school balls') and the demented mumbling of a station-master carrying a frightened little girl in his arms, the finale of Russia's battle of ideas is acted out.

This final act is accompanied by a freely interpreted biblical commentary which carries considerable weight in a play about a culture *in extremis*. Epigraphs from the Bible, the parodied treatment of the plot, Christian themes and images disturbingly challenged by other perspectives all contribute in a major way to the overall meaning of *Flight*.

In *The White Guard* the biblical perspective is stated in the epigraph and sustained right through to the end of the novel. 'As he read the shattering book his mind became like a shining sword, piercing the darkness. [. . .] He saw the fathomless blue mist of the centuries, the endless procession of millennia. He felt no fear, only the wisdom of obedience and reverence.' (p. 295)

This culminating of a theme by a quotation is a feature of the Russian literary tradition. Bulgakov deepened it with the passing of time, eventually even daring to attempt the creation of his own 'gospel' in parallel to the canonical version. In *Flight* the biblical theme is split: Bulgakov differentiates his own viewpoint sharply from the 'official' or widespread naive interpretation of current events in terms of ancient prophecy. In the very first dream, set in the monastery, Bulgakov undermines the dogmatic, state-approved view of what was taking place by articulating it through one who proves to be an 'unworthy shepherd'. The Archbishop interprets what is going on around him as wholly confirming prophecy: 'They've drawn a blank . . . Truly is it written: "Thou shalt brand them with a mark on their hand and on their brow" . . . Did you see their five-pointed stars?' (p. 156)

This apocalypse for home consumption is discredited and parodied when the

Shepherd ignominiously takes to his heels, promptly switching to a more secular idiom: 'Merciful Heavens, this is terrible!' And, almost in the same breath, 'Have you got a wagon I could ride on?' (p. 161)

The Second Dream further develops this colliding of the events of actual history with the characters' bookish notions about them, derived from familiar quotations. There is a deadly irony in the quasi-religious mumbo-jumbo Khludov finds himself surrounded by. The staff headquarters propaganda section is doing its best to raise the flagging morale of the doomed army at the station by visual means. 'A young horseman in white is spearing a scaly dragon. The young man is St George, Bringer of Victory, and there burns before him a coloured, cut-glass icon-lamp.' (p. 164) The military artists' primitive fantasy is debunked by none other than Khludov himself. He pours scorn on the traditional role he is invited to play and rejects it out of hand, interrupting the Archbishop's prayer to St George and reducing it to bathos; 'Excuse me for interrupting you, your Grace, but why bother God now? It's quite obvious that He gave us up long ago. Anyway, why should He be on our side? If you ask me He never was. Our sand has run out, that's all, and now it's the Bolsheviks' turn. Look – St George is laughing at you!' (pp. 171-2)

Throughout the Second Dream Khludov blasphemes consistently over this biblical interpretation. After reading the order to retreat which the Commander-in-Chief brings with him ready prepared, Khludov comments, 'Ah, I see you came prepared. So you knew in advance? Good. Lord, now lettest Thou Thy servant depart in peace . . .' (p. 172) Immediately after this he inspires Korzukhin's confrontation with Serafima, with its allusion to Peter's denial of Christ. Korzukhin denies his wife: 'I know no one called Serafima. I have never seen this woman before in my life.' (p. 175) The Dreams in *Flight* which are set in Russia involve a whole series of denials: Athanasius denies his flock; Korzukhin denies Serafima; and finally, intimidated by the red-hot needle in the counter-intelligence section, Golubkov too denies Serafima.

In the Russian text the Fourth Dream is preceded by an epigraph from Exodus: 'And a mixed multitude went up also with them . . .'. (p. 186) It is here that Bulgakov most sharply challenges the attempt on the part of dogmatic quotation-mongers to establish a biblical parallel to the events taking place. Khludov and Athanasius trade incompatible interpretations of a succession of biblical passages. Athanasius attempts to view the flight from Sebastopol as paralleling Exodus: 'And the children of Israel journeyed from Rameses to Succoth, about six hundred thousand on foot that were men, beside children.' (p. 186; Exodus 12, 37) Khludov, to whom Athanasius had sent a Bible, promptly retaliates sarcastically, 'I can even remember some of it. I read it in the train at night when I was bored. "Thou didst blow with Thy wind, the sea covered them: they sank as lead in the mighty waters . . . ." Exodus, isn't it? "The enemy said I will pursue, I will overtake, I will divide the spoil: my lust shall be satisfied upon them." How's that for a man the Commander-in-Chief thinks is off his head? And what are you hanging around here for?' (p. 186) He caps Athanasius's outraged reponse with 'To him who waits shall be given. Sounds like a quotation from your Bible, doesn't it? Do you know what you'll get if you wait here any longer?' (p. 186)

This dialogue is even more pointed in the 1928 prompter's copy of *Flight*, where Khludov retorts:

Here we are, you and I, calmly quoting the Bible, at the very moment Budyonny is advancing on Sebastopol at a variable trot. Can't you just see it? (*Gives a piercing whistle.*) Hah! What's all this then? A dozy parson still hanging around the Palace? Oho ho! . . . (*Hums The Internationale.*) Spankies for the parson. Up against the wall, and pop goes the parson!

Khludov's sick, insolent comments fired straight from the hip deflate the official religious rigmarole of the Archbishop and Commander-in-Chief. They are incensed by what they see as cynical, criminal clowning. The Commander-in-Chief threatens, 'If you do not change your tone, General, I shall have you arrested.' (p. 187) Khludov's farcical, revealing, contemptuous comments sink the bookish 'quotation culture' in *Flight*. They anticipate the quite different later relations between the characters when they are 'free'. The hierarchy of ranks and titles collapses then, and the atmosphere of biblical prophecy and fortune-telling vanishes without trace.

Bulgakov's approach to the Bible, with its perspective of the 'fathomless blue mist of the centuries', is wholly incompatible with the mentality which dredges the scriptures for quotations to fit the occasion and endorse dogmatic certainty and smugness. This is what he challenges constantly. For Bulgakov the 'Book of Life' truly affirms life, and frees the oppressed mind from the sense that the end of the world is nigh. His faith in the natural order, and his constant wonder at the world around him lie behind his deep hostility towards myth-making, historical mummery and mystification.

The flight of time does not stop with the exodus of the Whites. Bulgakov himself moves forward to a particular kind of historicist vision characteristic of grotesque realism, stressing life's eternal incompleteness, unpredictability and capacity to surprise. This is the significance of the very important aspect of the play which we have been discussing.

In the Dreams set in Russia Bulgakov meticulously prepared the ground for the relations which would develop between his characters after they had left Russia. The last thing he had in mind was to write a play about the émigrés, as certain of his literary contemporaries had supposed. Yelena Bulgakova records in her diary the following conversation between Bulgakov and Alexander Afinogenov, which took place on 9 September 1933 in Pavel Markov's office at the Art Theatre.

Afinogenov. The émigrés just are not like that.
   M.A. It's not a play about the émigrés. What you are talking about is not my play. I don't know anything about the émigrés. I have had my eyes put out.[44]

Bulgakov's characters abroad are not engaged in totting up the good deeds and transgressions of the Soviet authorities, and there is no elucidation of their attitude towards the new regime.[45] Bulgakov's play deals with the significance of the passions and suffering of people in a process called 'history'. It is a play about the price man is paying for the new social experiment.

Right up until the Fourth Dream the heroes of *Flight* are not able to communicate freely. Words of truth can only be blurted out in a state of delirium. Truth is one of the synonyms of memory which, for Bulgakov as for Akhmatova, is a basic ethical concept opposed to the 'mindlessness of the Troubles'. In the Fourth Dream the blind killer Khludov begins to see, and his new understanding is accompanied by a restoration of memory and his first attempts to make sense of what has occurred. He tries to explain himself to the spirit of Krapilin, the orderly he hanged: 'Don't you see, you were just one of many who fell under the wheels and they simply crushed you?' (p. 190) The theme of wheels and the Devil's Roundabout is developed subsequently, but Khludov's attempt at an impersonal historical explanation of his conduct does not resolve his problem or bring redemption. Learning that Serafima is safe, Khludov sees this as enabling him to continue his conversation with Golubkov: 'Well, that's one of them dealt with. Now I'm free to talk to you.' (p. 192)

There is a special quality to the 'freedom' enjoyed by people whose lives have been destroyed and who have been cast out from their own land. It is a freedom which enables them to communicate with each other in a way which would have been impossible in their 'normal' life. Previously they were separated from each other by unbreachable barriers: the general, the private soldier, the university lecturer and the 'campaign wife'. In Constantinople and Paris they find themselves in a 'realm of untrammelled personal contact', to use Bakhtin's expression, which Khludov describes as being 'at liberty'. All now enjoy equal rights or, more exactly, an equal lack of rights. Nobody has power over anybody else. Stripped of his social context and status, man is manifest in his true state. *Ecce homo.* We see this mechanism at work as early as the Fourth Dream when, against a background of total defeat and conflagration, Golubkov and Khludov immediately forget the differences in their social standing and relate to each other with a straightforwardness which would have been unthinkable earlier. 'Come on, Khludov,' says Golubkov, 'let's go while we still can . . .' [. . .] 'Khludov, you're sick. You're delirious.' (p. 192) And so on.

Bulgakov wrote a play not about émigrés but about the passage, the flight of time, the place of free will and choice in history, and the price which must be paid to redeem spilt blood. This is why the cockroach race occupies such a central position in the play's structure. There are none of the principal characters in the Fifth Dream (apart from Charnota), but it dwells on just one of those points which Bulgakov's writing keeps coming back to. When Bulgakov was choosing a scene to read out to friends, this (together with the card game between Charnota and Korzukhin) was the one he most often chose. This is an indication of the special status of this climactic Dream of *Flight*, which so largely stands outside the plot.

For Russians Constantinople is a highly evocative symbol in terms both of cultural history and of religion. Bulgakov three times emphasises the 'towering minaret' in his text, and three times picks out from the 'strange symphony' of this eternal city the sweet voice of the muezzin, soaring to his Lord and Master. Bulgakov describes the mixed languages, faiths, and dialects of this Babel with a documentary precision derived from a great variety of sources. His detailed description of the local colour is, however, only there in order to universalise his theme.

Bulgakov has a dream of the flight of time.

In an extended stage direction, honed to the level of the best of his prose, Bulgakov is specifying the time and place of the action. Before all else, however, this is a world of sounds: 'Strange symphony of Turkish songs, the Russian tune "Parting" played on a barrel-organ, street-hawkers' cries, grinding of streetcars' (p. 193). After that: 'Constantinople is ablaze in the late afternoon sunshine', and we catch sight of the towering minaret and the roofs of houses.

The central feature is 'a weird structure something like a fairground booth' for the holding of cockroach races. This proves to be the point at which all interests meet, and is decorated with the flags of different countries and signs in 'French, English and Russian'. Among these is one reading 'Russian Game of Chance. Licensed by Police'.

Having just shown a similar, if tragic, 'game of chance', Bulgakov presents a fairground, metaphorical version. The stage set suggests a farcical haunt of thieves, with Yanko popping 'out on to the booth steps like a puppet from behind a screen' (p. 194). It parodies the Tower of Babel and the end of the world. Each person in the huge, multi-racial crowd has his own bet, his own favourite, and is playing to win. Charnota, who sees life itself as a wild game of chance, bets his last lire by pawning his tray of jumping rubber red commissars to Yanko. He stakes the money on the favourite, Janissary, and is locked in to a fateful duel. 'Shouts of Constantinople all around Charnota . . . Streaming heat.'

Charnota stakes all, and the race begins. The 'Russian imperial tricolour flag is hoisted', a steam organ 'strikes up a rollicking march', but Janissary can't co-ordinate his cockroach legs. He is drunk. The rollicking marches, which in Bulgakov's writing usually accompany an outburst of blind, sub-human, instinctive behaviour, are replaced by a dead silence; and then by a fast, wild Russian song in which the scuttling of cockroaches is to be heard. The outcome of a game of chance is unpredictable. As flies to wanton boys are we to the gods. Yanko is running the show. The English, French and Italian sailors who had bet on Janissary start a knife fight and 'the dream dissolves'.

The fifth dream parodies the earlier flight to Khludov in the Crimea ('He'll take care of us . . .'), reducing it to the level of farce and rounding off the historical part of the plot. The 'game of chance' comes to a bloody end. Charnota's enterprise is liquidated for two lire fifty piastres.

Bulgakov gives the cockroach races a central and prominent position where the main themes of the play come together. Some of his most coveted ideas of the 1920s are here stated at their clearest.

The White Guard already presents life as a circuit whose purpose is largely unclear to those running it. 'For so is the enchanted earth arranged that run as he may, he always finds himself fatally back at the crossroads from which he started.' In *Flight* this sad, ironical idea is to be recognised in the theatrical setting of the cockroach races.

The world is represented as an example of random motion, a chaotic displacement of human particles, minute, infinitesimal, but charged with conflicting interests. Not that this in any way deprives life and history of their essential significance. Quite the reverse. *Flight* in many ways anticipates the conception of the 'flight of time' and its relation to man in *The Master and Margarita*. A situation eternal and unchanging, history as a fated 'crossroads', posit the affirmation of values not external to but located within mankind, whether ethical values as in the case of Yeshua, or Bulgakov's supreme value of the free, creative self-realisation of the individual.

There is no denying that the cockroach race episode is laced with a poisonous irony verging on philosophical sarcasm, but here too Bulgakov remains his highly individual self. His 'strange, unchanging, sardonic smile' is not without a kind of constant astonishment at the world surrounding him, which includes a deadly game of chance as an inalienable part of life.

Arkady Averchenko's book of 'émigré short stories' was published in Moscow in 1927 under the title of *The Upturned Anthill*. Quite clearly his trenchant and talented portrayal of the features of life in Constantinople in the stories 'The Russians in Byzantium', and particularly 'The God of Chance', fuelled Bulgakov's imagination. Averchenko, who was renowned as a contributor to the Satiricon and who died in emigration in 1925, also described the sale of 'mother-in-law's tongues' at the bazaar in Constantinople, and cockroach races. 'They have a starting post, a totalisator, jockeys' colours, and they race live cockroaches. A huge crowd of people gathers to watch. There are hot tips on the favourites.'[46]

Averchenko hit on an unexpected angle from which to throw light on the émigrés' extraordinary way of life, which shows most clearly in 'The God of Chance':

The God of Chance is a mighty god! [. . .]
Take away from a man his cards – he will play bingo. Take away his bingo, he will turn in desperation to cockroach racing; take away the cockroaches he . . . But why go on? I once saw a nurse on a bench in the Summer Park in Petersburg cradling a child in her arms. She was pensively pulling out one little hair after another and murmuring, 'He loves me, he loves me not; he loves me, he loves me not'. This is a passion which can make even those not directly involved lose their hair.

Averchenko is describing the 'Constantinople menagerie'. His really are stories about émigrés. Bulgakov's play was about something else: the same way of life, the same human passion, but refracted through the prism of grotesque realism. The sad gaze of Averchenko looked only to the past. Bulgakov's theatrical dream of the cockroach races may have had the same merciless irony underlying it, but it is itself full of artistic passion and faith in the future. It is not the whole world that is coming to an end. History does not come to an end because Charnota loses. Life is always what is ahead. The indestructible, all-conquering urge to live is just as important in *Flight* as it was in *The Days of the Turbins*. In just the same way it is here the crucial bedrock and moral cement which decides everything.

Charnota bets at the cockroach races, and in the Seventh Dream Bulgakov gives him a long scene playing cards immediately after the epigraph: ' . . . three cards, three cards, three cards! . . .'. The theme of the 'Russian game of chance', which Charnota both plays in *Flight* and embodies, is one of the most important motifs in Bulgakov's play and indeed in his writing, and is firmly rooted in the traditions of Russian literature.

Card-playing had a prominent place in *The White Guard* as well. In the fourteenth chapter and in the chapter of conclusions and resolutions, the Turbins sit down to a game of cards. The candles flicker, Lariosik in a sweat, understanding nothing in the game, puts down and buys cards until he trumps his partner Myshlaevsky in a most ignoble manner, cleaning him out (p. 218). The game is described in tones of romantic irony and has a special poignancy in the circumstances of defeat and as they await their fate.

We recall that Bulgakov ended the first version of *The Days of the Turbins* by likening the defeat of the White cause to losing at cards: ' . . . Captain Myshlaevsky, a non-member of the Communist Party, leaves the stage. I have drawn straight spades.'

In *Flight* the theme of gambling is present throughout the play from the First Dream. General Krapchikov, 'no general – he's an arsehole' (p. 156), having put off deciphering a military signal with a deadly message, sits down to play whist with Charnota and declares himself 'short in hearts'. The passion for gambling is stronger than the fear of death. In the first version of the play this motif was even more in evidence. Agonising over the map of the Crimea, Charnota lamented, 'Oh, Krapchikov, Krapchikov! What a hopeless general you are! And where are you now, Krapchikov, to admire your handiwork, a ragged, composite division, headquarters cut off!' When he learns that Krapchikov has been killed and is 'in another world', he sends after him the worst curse he can think of: 'May the devils in that other world beat you at preference.' In the same version, in the Seventh Dream, Lyuska talked to Korzukhin about playing cards. 'Madame Fréjol', herself addicted to gambling, unexpectedly half-reveals her intimacy with the great card-player: 'You played cards with General Charnota?' she quizzed 'the little rat'. 'You should realise that he completely cleaned out all the hussar regiments in North Tauris. He beat Krapchikov! He can play cards, all right! And how!'

Even the 'little rat' Korzukhin, the worst exemplar of his nation, suddenly demonstrates a foible in his duel with Charnota which restores his credentials as a Russian. 'You're a gambler, Paramon! It's your weakness!', the general in bright yellow underpants discovers to his delight (p. 217).

Being a gambler can be an intellectual matter, as with Khludov. It can also, however, be wholly unintellectual and stem quite simply from someone's expansive nature and desire to spread their wings and take the world by storm. In one of the versions of the final act Charnota, as he was seeing Khludov off back to Russia, defined their difference in outlook as follows: 'Just look at yourself.

Don't go infecting me. I'm not a man of ideas. When you hear the word "Bolsheviks" you get that killer look in your eyes, while I don't give a damn . . . They don't make me angry, the Bolsheviks. They're in clover over there now. They won, and good luck to them! I hope it brings them joy.'

A gamble is a gamble, and Charnota defers to the winner.

There are characters in Bulgakov's play who never gamble at cards or cockroach races. These abstainers are doomed to passivity. Others gamble at their expense. That is the predicament of Golubkov and Serafima: Khludov and Charnota gamble on the heads of 'those not directly involved'. Great subtlety attends the establishment of the characters' pecking order in accordance with this criterion. 'Be a good fellow and find something to do. There, go and look at his scrap-book,' (p. 216) Charnota suggests patronisingly to the dispirited Golubkov who does not understand gambling and thereby automatically relegates himself to a lower plane.

Knowing how closely Bulgakov's main themes are bound up with his personal experience, we might surmise that the source of his theme of gambling was not exclusively literary, and indeed memoirists note a passionate gambling streak in his personality. Mikhail Yanshin remembers Bulgakov getting the Art Theatre actors up to all sorts of games, not excluding tiddlywinks. 'He was endlessly inventive in devising all sorts of games, prizes, and competition rules.'[47] He played billiards and chess, and to the last found time to play cards, his preferred game being whist. This had a place in his daily routine, indeed in his very outlook on life.

Yury Lotman has a solidly researched work on *The Theme of Cards and Card-Playing in Russian Literature of the Early Nineteenth Century* where this whole matter is placed in the context of Russian culture in a way which is undoubtedly of relevance to Bulgakov. Bulgakov follows Pushkin in seeing card-playing (and gambling generally) as a metaphor for the relationship between man and destiny, chance, and history. Echoes of *The Queen of Spades* recur throughout *Flight*, while the Seventh Dream, in which Charnota duels with Korzukhin, is dominated by them. Charnota's disastrous gambling loss at the cockroach race and his no less amazing success in Paris are seen side by side. A game of chance is a potential duel with fate. Chance arises in the conflict between chaos and strict predictability, 'a powerful, instantly effective instrument of Providence'. Pushkin's idea seems no less applicable to Bulgakov.

Man throws down a challenge to Fate, trying to beat life at its own game. In *Molière* the Marquis gambles with marked cards with Louis himself, the symbol of earthly power and regulation. In Bulgakov even higher beings are not averse to a flutter, though it might seem pointless for them to tempt Fate given the predictability of the result. But no, even they need the play of possibilities and alternatives. In *The Master and Margarita* the impudent monstrous cat Behemoth takes on Woland, pocketing chesspieces like a Nozdryov. These, moreover, are special chesspieces in that they are alive. The chequered board, it transpires, is the chessboard of life. The cat loses, but still does not want to give in. He gambles to the last, submitting finally 'only because I find it impossible to play when I'm distracted by jealous, hostile spectators!' (p. 294)

Pushkin confessed to his friend, 'The most powerful of the passions is the passion for gambling.' In Russian culture, given the nature of the Russian state as it evolved in history and the limited opportunities it offered for individual initiative, 'the most powerful of the passions' was mythologised. It came to be seen as the model of a way of life where everything was infinitely regulated with no place left for any occurrence not sanctioned by higher authority. Lotman notes that at the time of writing *The Queen of Spades* Pushkin had already ceased to see chance as synonymous with evil and regulation with predictability. 'On several occasions Pushkin contrasts dead, inflexible regulation with chance, likening the difference to that between death and life!'[48] Pushkin intuits a world where everything is chaos and chance is intuited within a world where everything has been so deadened that nothing can any longer happen. Pushkin's paradoxical vision seems closely akin to Bulgakov's sense of reality.

Charnota's triumphal, chance, miraculous win over Korzukhin is an expression of just this side of Bulgakov's outlook. It reflects an understanding of human nature founded on certain ideas firmly rooted in Russian culture. The faith in a miracle happening, in 'sudden, unmotivated redemption', the 'terrible appetite for risk' were features we know Dostoevsky considered fundamental to the Russian mind.

'To change your whole destiny in the course of an hour': this very human urge is integral to *Flight*, a part of Bulgakov's understanding of the complex Russian national character which he projects on to the character of historical events. Nemirovich-Danchenko's contribution to the discussion at the meeting of the Art Theatre's Council for Artistic Affairs suggests that people at the Art Theatre were well aware of the cultural context in which Bulgakov's character existed. '[Charnota] will be laughed at,' Nemirovich-Danchenko said, 'in just the same way that people laugh at the types in Gogol's comedies.'[49]

Bulgakov coloured Charnota's miraculous win with his customary irony. The episode concludes with Lyuska's reminding us that his gambling in Paris is nothing more than a cockroach's last attempt to jump out of a bucket of water. His lucky break will enable him to buy a new pair of trousers, but will have no long-term impact on their destiny. The point is underlined by Bulgakov's sending Charnota back into the clutches of Yanko the Cockroach King in the dénouement, where more likely than not the Devil's Roundabout will bring everything back to its initial hopelessness.

The last three Dreams show the cockroaches being dropped into the water and vanishing into non-being. Bulgakov develops his theme of the cockroaches and the bucket of water with marked, and sometimes excessive, consistency. A stage direction introducing the Sixth Dream runs, '*On one wall is an ornamental water-pipe, from which water drips slowly into a large stone basin*'. (p. 200) A similar allusion accompanies the argument between the former general and his 'campaign wife': '*Enter Serafima with a bucket. [. . .] Charnota and Lyuska do not notice her*'. (p. 201) Golubkov, having found his compatriots and Serafima by chance, keeps sitting down 'on the edge of the water basin'. Bulgakov has him do this on three occasions. A human tragedy turns into a sad farce, which in turn is purified by a radiant, intense lyricism.

The musical score of the last three Dreams comprises marches, the tear-jerking 'Parting', the choir's rendering of the ballad of 'The Twelve Robbers', Hermann's aria from *The Queen of Spades* and finally a sweet oriental prayer carrying from the minaret. Bulgakov worked the score out in fine detail, and its effect is to raise *Flight* above its possible, indeed obvious, interpretation as a play about émigrés on to an altogether different plane: 'Let us pray to God, and sing an ancient lay of bygone times.'

Presenting recent events in the genre of an ancient lay looks forward to Bulgakov's understanding of history in *The Master and Margarita*, with its juxtaposition and paralleling of contemporary and biblical events, its Moscow chronicle and ancient legend. Bulgakov continued to work intermittently on *Flight*, completing the final revision in autumn 1937. The play paved the way for *The Master and Margarita* and was itself inescapably influenced by Bulgakov's developing 'main book'. Echoes of *Flight* are to be heard not merely in such isolated phrases and motifs as 'a flight in the mists of autumn', but also in the concluding, culminating tone of the play.

Comparing the various versions of the play, Violetta Gudkova has noted how the image of 'the woman from Petersburg' was purified and romanticised. In the first version she could still blowsily say of her marriage, 'I got married: then I got unmarried'. In the final version she has the radiant, almost icon-like aspect of a seraph close to the Godhead. Bulgakov elevated the concluding words of Golubkov and Serafima to a level similar to that in the finale of his novel where the Master and Margarita bid farewell to the city before embarking on their flight to 'eternal refuge'.[50]

The image of the 'flight in the mists of autumn' serves rather like an emotional tuning fork for the play, welding *Flight* and *The Master and Margarita* together as a single creative endeavour which derived from very personal sources. On 21 May 1933 Bulgakov inscribed a book to his wife Yelena, 'To my secret friend who came into the light, my wife Yelena. You will make the final flight with me.'[51]

Pressure to tidy up Golubkov's and Serafima's motives for returning to Russia only served to make Bulgakov depict even more feelingly the calling to each other of two voices before they vanished. The result is a poetic duet in which the theme of snow, death, and oblivion predominates. A woman's voice sings:

'What has happened these past six months, Sergey? Were we dreaming? Tell me the answer. Where were we running away to and what for? Lamp-posts on the platform, men dangling in black hoods . . . then this heat and stink and despair . . . I want to see the Nevsky again, I want to see the snow! I want to forget it all as though it had never happened!' A man's voice responds, 'None of it happened, we imagined it all. Forget it. In a month we'll be home, then it will start snowing and the snow will cover our tracks . . . Come on – we're going!'
Serafima: 'We're going! No more dreams!' (p.227)

The snow on Nevsky Prospekt takes us straight back to Chekhov's *Three Sisters*, with their homesickness for an unattainable homeland of the spirit. The snow is both an image of the 'still and radiant shore' of renown, and of 'eternal rest', which so affects the Master before his farewell flight.

Bulgakov pondered long and hard over how to round off Khludov's destiny, refusing simply to cave in to external pressure. His integrity as an artist had to be satisfied in the way the play was amended, and the end result did not in any way offend it, as Bulgakov was to write to his brother in Paris in 1933 upon completing one more version of the final Dream. He conscientiously considered various possibilities. At one moment he left Golubkov and Serafima in emigration, and Khludov with them; another time he had the tormented general do away with himself (which was the 1933 version). In autumn 1934 he finally decided to have Khludov commit suicide at the end, and even wrote 'Final version' on the copy.[52] In the autumn of 1937, however, he again returned to the problem. Yelena's diary contains an important entry in this connection: 'Spent the evening trying to persuade Misha that the first version, without Khludov's suicide, is better. (But M.A. disagrees.)'

This would suggest that the version published and universally acted is not in full accord with Bulgakov's wishes, although both versions express the same theme if in different ways: the theme of a man who can redeem the blood he has shed only through self-annihilation. For Serafima and Golubkov snow symbolises oblivion and hope. For Khludov snow symbolises only death. 'But you'll be shot out of hand!' 'Instantly.' (*Smiles.*) 'On the spot. Cotton shirt, down to the cellar, snow outside . . .'. (p. 223)

History has completed one circle and started on a new one. 'Aha! Do you hear that? The cockroach races have started again!' The Russian choir singing forth the ancient lay of the twelve robbers is drowned by the sound of oriental prayer. The sweet voice of the muezzin prepares the way for the play's final stage direction: '*Constantinople starts to fade and vanishes for ever.*' (p. 227)

A Choice of Genre

While the critics argued abut Khludov's motives for returning, Slashchov met his fate in real life. His tale was rounded off finally in just the manner a literary character had foretold. On 11 January 1929 an unknown young man presented himself at the flat of the Military Academy instructor. 'Are you former General Slashchov?' he asked. 'Yes,' Slashchov replied. The youth then shot Slashchov in the chest at point blank range, and Slashchov fell. The assassin ran away. He was arrested shortly afterwards and subsequently put on trial. It was discovered that his surname was Kolenberg and that he was avenging the execution on Slashchov's orders of his brother in Nikolaev during the civil war. The story is told by Victor Fomin in his memoirs, *Notes of an Old Chekist.*[53]

The assassination of Slashchov provided the occasion for banning the play. The actual reasons, however, went much deeper. Only following the disintegration of the USSR has a crucial document come to light in the Politburo archives which explains what actually happened. The question of whether to allow the production to go ahead was deliberated over by the Politburo and by Stalin himself. On 14 January the Party Areopagus considered the matter of M. Bulgakov's play and referred the question to its so-called troika, chaired by Kliment Voroshilov, the People's Commissar for Military and Maritime Affairs. Voroshilov first consulted Pyotr Kerzhentsev, who at that time was working in the Party Central Committee's Section for Agitation and Propaganda. He then wrote to Stalin, on the notepaper of the Chairman of the Revolutionary Military Council, no less, with a draft resolution banning the production as 'politically inexpedient'. In Kerzhentsev's *aide-mémoire* the reasons for the ban are enumerated with disarming frankness:

To stage *Flight* in the Art Theatre, which is already producing *Days of the Turbins* (at the same time as *The Crimson Island* of the same ilk), is to give comfort to a group within the Art Theatre opposed to the revolutionary repertoire and to surrender positions secured by the theatre with its production of *Armoured Train* [. . .]. This would be a backward step for our entire theatre policy and might lead to the loss for the theatre-going working man of one of our stronger theatres.

Kerzhentsev proposed not only that the play and the production should be banned but that all further work on it should cease forthwith, including 'talks, readings, the studying of roles etc.' On 30 January the Politburo gave further consideration to the matter of *Flight* and resolved to ban both the play and the Art Theatre production. The skirmish over Bulgakov was part of a larger struggle between the liberal and the fanatically orthodox wings of the Party, in which in-fighting and secret manoeuvres were much in evidence. The principal puppet-master, however, very rarely showed himself above the screen. A recently discovered letter sent by Lunacharsky on 12 February 1929 to Stalin shows the People's Commissar of Enlightenment mounting a final onslaught on the Central Committee's Section for Agitation and Propaganda and Kerzhentsev. The letter was provoked by Kerzhentsev's article in *Pravda* on 9 February, blaming the Commissariat for the fact that *Days of the Turbins*, a play which, he roundly declared, perversely misrepresented the revolutionary movement in the Ukraine, was still being performed on the Moscow Art Theatre's stage. The article was timed to coincide with the arrival in Moscow of a delegation of Ukrainian writers. Lunacharsky, outraged by this piece of brazenness in the Party's official newspaper, sent Stalin a top secret memorandum in which he reminded the Leader that *Days of the Turbins* remained in the Art Theatre's repertoire on the explicit instructions of Stalin and the Politburo, that the Section for Agitation and Propaganda was fully aware of that secret instruction, and yet was attempting to defame the Commissariat of Enlightenment 'in the eyes of the entire Party and even, indeed, of the entire country'. Needless to say, what was agitating Lunacharsky was not the fate of Bulgakov. His concern was for his own position. He was fully prepared to follow up the ban on *Flight* with a ban on *Days of the Turbins* if directly instructed to do so by the General Secretary. All he was asking for was instructions.

On the very day Lunacharsky decided to go for broke, Stalin received the Ukrainian writers. The transcript of the meeting reveals a number of startling, but perfectly explicable, things. Stalin himself was subjected to a concerted attack by the fanatics from Kiev, who demanded the sacrifice of *Days of the Turbins*. Stalin tried to defend his favourite play with his familiar argument that, although it was anti-Soviet, it demonstrated the all-conquering power of the Bolsheviks. He failed. The slaves demanded that their master should play by the rules of the system he had himself created. They demanded that he officiate at a bloody ideological ritual. And so he did.[54] Naturally the decision was kept top secret, and a special method was devised for advising theatre circles of the Party bosses' attitude.

Stalin's letter replying to Bill-Belotserkovsky became public knowledge in February 1929. In it he suggested that before *Flight* could be passed for performance a further, Ninth, Dream would have to be written about the victory of the Bolsheviks. In March all Bulgakov's plays vanished from the playbills of the Moscow theatres. In September 1929, just before the beginning of the new theatre season, Richard Pikel stated that 'the conflict over Bulgakov's plays was a struggle between reactionary and progressive groupings within and around the theatre', while offering Bulgakov cold comfort by adding that he was talking 'only about the dramatic works he has written to date'.[55]

Bulgakov's plays did indeed become a focus in the power struggle of different social interest groups as the Great Leap Forward got under way, but what was hanging in the balance was not only the fate of Bulgakov's plays or, indeed, of the Art Theatre. The fate of Soviet culture was being decided for many decades to come. The rooting out of opposition and dissidence in the political sphere was being transferred virtually instantaneously to the sphere of art. The balance of forces which had held throughout the first decade after the revolution and which had been codified in the 1925 resolution of the Central Committee of the Communist Party, was unceremoniously breached in the autumn of 1928. Ruthless tactics and methods which had been employed in the political battles were transferred to literature and the theatre. These now aimed not merely at suppressing opponents' ideas but at destroying the opponents. It was not only 'enemies who refuse to surrender' who, as Gorky advised, were to be destroyed, but even those who were in the process of surrendering. The gloomy prophecies of Bulgakov's pamphlet *The Crimson Island* paled in comparison with the reality.

In the autumn of 1928 other important events in the life of the Soviet theatre were occurring even as the battle raged round Bulgakov's plays. At the end of October of that year Mikhail Chekhov posted a letter in Berlin to Anatoly Lunacharsky in which he tried to indicate with complete frankness the impossibility of the continued existence of an artist or indeed of art itself in the conditions which had developed.

The former leader of Moscow Art Theatre II wrote:

I have been driven from Russia, more exactly from the life of the Russian theatre which I so love and for whose sake I would have endured, and have endured, many a difficulty, deprivation, and injustice. I have finally been driven out by the one simple fact about our day-to-day theatre life which is truly unendurable: its senselessness. It has collapsed with incredible speed, like a great spiral, in to its centre and there it has stopped dead. Those who control the theatre have become completely hostile to all the interests essential to the art of the theatre. Thanks to the efforts of our narrow-minded theatre press questions of aesthetics have become something to be embarrassed about. Ethical questions (without which even 'contemporary' plays are an impossibility) are considered to have been resolved once and for all and therefore of no further interest to society. A whole range of purely artistic moods and colourful spiritual nuances have been lumped together under the heading of 'mysticism' and banned. All that remains for the theatre is to present mundane pictures of revolutionary life and crudely cobbled together propaganda pieces. There is nothing to challenge an actor or stretch him (and no point in his trying to develop), while the public has nothing worthwhile to watch, nothing to delight it, and nothing to stimulate its grey matter.[56]

Mikhail Chekhov addressed his complaint to Commissar Lunacharsky from Berlin. In July 1929 Mikhail Bulgakov raised similar issues, but in a much more uncompromising form, in Moscow. In that month he sent Stalin, Mikhail Kalinin, Alexey Svidersky and Maxim Gorky a letter in which he totted up what his existence as a Soviet writer in the 1920s had brought him.

. . . thus as of the present theatre season all my plays are banned, including *The Days of the Turbins*, which has been performed some three hundred times.

In 1926 I was taken under escort to the OGPU on the day of the dress rehearsal of *The Days of the Turbins* and subjected to an interrogation [. . .]

Now at the end of the tenth year my strength is gone. I can exist no longer, persecuted, knowing that I may no longer be published or produced within the USSR. I have been brought to the verge of nervous breakdown, and request that you intercede on my behalf with the Government of the USSR to have me exiled from the USSR . . .[57]

In early September 1929 Bulgakov sent a further letter to Gorky.

Everything has been banned. I am ruined, persecuted, and completely isolated.

Why keep a writer in a country where his works cannot exist? I must ask for a humane decision: let me leave.[58]

On 15 September 1929 Pikel announced a further great victory for the Soviet theatre from the pages of *Izvestiya*: the destruction of Bulgakov's plays. The same day in the same newspaper Gorky published an article titled 'A Waste of Energy'. Condemning the campaign unleashed from above against Boris Pilnyak and Yevgeny Zamyatin, the author of *The Lower Depths* wrote,

All my life I have fought for a caring attitude towards people, and it seems to me that the struggle needs to be intensified in our time and circumstances. [. . .] We have developed an idiotic habit of raising people up on a pedestal only to hurl them down shortly afterwards into the dust and dirt. There is no need for me to give examples of this absurd and cruel way of treating people. Everybody knows them. I am reminded of the 'kangaroo courts' against petty thieves in 1917–18, which were completely disgraceful dramas staged by philistines. It is just these philistine, suburban, lynch-mob persecutions which come very unpleasantly to mind whenever you see everybody enthusiastically and sadistically setting about a lone individual, in order first to destroy the offender before going on to move into his job . . .[59]

Gorky did not succeed in stopping the persecution of Zamyatin and Pilnyak. On the contrary, he found himself viciously ambushed. He was prevented from publishing a second article on the topic of the literary persecutions, which did name Bulgakov. In this article, titled 'More about the Same', he wrote:

To the best of my knowledge Zamyatin, Bulgakov, and all the others who are being or have been anathematised are not striving to prevent history from doing its job, a fine and great job. There is no blind, organic enmity in them towards those who are honestly doing that great and essential work.[60]

Gorky was only wasting his own energy. The writing of the 'fellow-travellers' was subjected to a carefully thought-out and merciless campaign of attrition. Anna Akhmatova was, in her own words, 'hastily immured in the first convenient wall' and, at the age of thirty-five, issued with an old-age pension. Osip Mandelshtam was similarly awarded an old-age pension 'for his contribution to Russian literature, and in view of the impossibility of making use of the said writer in Soviet literature'. First all those who were still able to make themselves heard had to be destroyed. Then it would be the turn of those practising 'the genre of silence'. 'At the present time, Citizen Podsekalnikov, things that may occur to a live person can be expressed only by someone who is dead.' This line from Nikolai Erdman's play *The Suicide* gives a pretty fair impression of the situation by the autumn of 1929 when the third revolution or, as it was called at the time, the 'revolution from above', was in full swing.

This so-called revolution made its influence fully felt in the theatre. A whole barrage of major embarrassments included the failure of Mikhail Chekhov and Granovsky, director of the State Jewish Theatre, to return from the West; the critical situation of the Meyerhold Theatre, which in the autumn of 1928 was on the verge of liquidation; and finally Stanislavsky's illness and a deep-seated schism within the Art Theatre. In summer 1929 Vladimir Nemirovich-Danchenko wrote from Karlsbad to Sergey Bertenson in Hollywood about how things stood in Moscow. Bertenson was a former member of the Art Theatre who had translated *The Marriage of Figaro*. Nemirovich advised him that on this occasion he had had great difficulty getting permission to travel abroad, and that procedures for obtaining a foreign passport had become extremely complicated.

Even Moskvin and Knipper are having problems. For the time being they have been turned down, despite Moskvin's having spoken to Yagoda himself [. . .] Svidersky told me that 'a certain suspect institution' ('suspect' was his expression: I corrected it to 'suspicious'), had had doubts. They had asked him, Svidersky, whether he was not afraid of my failing to return . . . Could he guarantee that I would? . . .

Svidersky was talking about this later in a private house and is reported as having said, 'I cannot guarantee it, but if he (i.e. I) does not return, I shall close his Studio down . . .' I imagine Svidersky intended that this conversation should be passed back to me and that the Studio would stand surety for my return. What a fool! As if, having decided not to return, I would have continued to be interested in the Studio.[61]

Nemirovich-Danchenko regretfully told Bertenson of the banning, after three months of rehearsals, of *Flight*, and of the bizarre and offensive ideological ordeal he had had to endure in the 1928/29 season. The situation was so bad that 'even an excessively well looked after director has seriously to reconsider the possibility of continuing to work in Moscow'.

So there you are. Let's have a good chinwag while I am abroad (although at Orlov's trial there were hints that even abroad the letters of Russians are intercepted by some sort of GPU agents. I have no secrets from 'it', but it feels better all the same like this, from here).

On the one hand you know, of course, that to date I have nothing to complain about in Moscow. The Government and those associated with it are favourably inclined towards me, all its various factions, whether of the right or the left. They let me live there extremely well. Most important by far is the fact that my real work is there, in the two theatres. If even I were thinking of leaving Moscow, who could that leave who wasn't? [. . .] I am writing away here, with no idea of what I am going to end up saying. There are certain nagging pinpricks of ideas and feelings which I cannot get free of. I shall not dwell on the first factor, Moscow itself. For all my privileges, there could be incidents which would send me in the opposite direction. The destruction of the Musical Theatre for the greater glory of Stanislavsky's Opera Theatre, for example. The Sviderskys of this world know perfectly well that I am susceptible on that score. Or my not being able to stop some new campaign of persecution.[62]

Nemirovich goes on to discuss various possible Hollywood projects in detail as an alternative creative future for himself. He urges Bertenson to stop 'poisoning' himself, overcome his scepticism, and get in the mood for battle:

We must condition ourselves psychosomatically. Constantly! Every step of the way! Smile. Go on, force yourself. Pull a face! The physical re-positioning of the lips affects how you feel inside. The most important thing, though, is to have faith. How can you coax it along in yourself? [. . .] Banish all thought of the *possibility* of failure. You have not yet worked this through *to the end*.

So long! (as they say in the USSR).[63]

This remarkable human document, written at a time of great change, goes a long way to explain things that befell the Art Theatre's director in the 1930s.

Returning in autumn 1929, Nemirovich-Danchenko reported all the latest Moscow news to Hollywood. Lunacharsky had been removed and Andrey Bubnov appointed in his place. Svidersky had been sent off as ambassador to Latvia and replaced by Raskolnikov. The Art Theatre had had a 'Red Director' appointed who was 'exceptionally intelligent, attentive, tactful, and energetic'. Nemirovich also passes on the intelligence that an attempt is being made to introduce a new revolutionary calendar in the USSR, abolishing Sundays and introducing a rotating working week to enable the factories to work without a break. His letters are reserved, and clearly written with unintended readers in mind. For all their reticence, they make it plain how brutally the times were being changed, and the Art Theatre with them.

Nemirovich-Danchenko was trying to understand what place there could be in this new age for himself and his Theatre.

As the literary and theatre battles of the 1920s approach their climax, trying to work out what was going on and who was fighting whom becomes a nightmare. The members of RAPP gave Mayakovsky a hard time. In *The Bedbug*, however, Mayakovsky includes the author of *Flight*, accidentally 'defrosted' along with a bedbug, in a list of outmoded phenomena of which the pure and radiant future has no recollection. He was rubbishing Bulgakov even as the Art Theatre was negotiating with him for a new play. Meanwhile *Evening Moscow*'s satirist excoriated both plays as totally alien to the present day:

> What's the fare next season, eh mugs?
> Cockroach races and frozen bedbugs.[64]

Meyerhold and Mayakovsky might still be hanging out slogans at the first night of *The Bath-house*, continuing their feud with the Art Theatre and its 'psychultery', but the fact of the matter was that this was all water under the bridge. A new period was beginning, with new plots, new heroes, and new ways of thinking. 'The bloodshed was elsewhere,' as Yury Tynyanov, who at this moment was bringing out his biography of Griboedov, *The Death of Vazir-Mukhtar*, would have said.[65]

A new literature and a new theatre were being born, with the artistic intelligentsia trying to find ways of accommodating the demands of 'the present day' and learning to speak its unfamiliar language. The Great Leap Forward embroiled art no less than other aspects of the nation's life.

Literature and the theatre shifted their position, with many of the so-called fellow-travellers thinking again. Yury Olesha denounced his earlier self; Ilya Ehrenburg, 'without recovering his breath', made a start on a 'second day'.[66] Even Pasternak was experiencing a 'second birth', composing his own *Stanzas* in parallel to those of Pushkin to Nicholas the First, fearful of being left an irrelevant fop in the new era, and aspiring to 'work at one with everyone within the ordered rule of law'.[67]

In 1929 Boris Eikhenbaum gave a definitive formulation of the new literary dilemma in his *My Chronicle*: it was not a question of how to write, but of how to be a writer.

Just as the times began to change, Mayakovsky responded by choosing the genre of conversing with his contemporaries and successors *At the Top of My Voice*. He again became exercised by the problem of how to be understood; a problem already stated in a discarded ending to his 1926 poem, 'Home Again!':

> I want my country to understand,
> But if it won't, it's a pain.
> I'll pass unnoticed through the land,
> Slope by, like rain.

Mayakovsky explained in a 1928 article why he had left these lines behind in the draft. 'For all their sense of highly strung romance (My readers reach for their hankies), I plucked them out, these lyrical little rain-dampened feathers.'[68] 'Rain-dampened' lines could be readily enough plucked out, but the problem of being understood remained. The danger of being left as an irrelevant fop, or of passing unnoticed through your own land was real enough.

In Osip Mandelshtam's *Fourth Prose*, written in the winter of 1929–30, the poet classifies all the works of world literature according to whether they were written with or without permission.

The first are crap, the second stolen air. I want to spit in the face of writers who write things for which permission has been given. I want to bludgeon them over the head and sit them all down to a glass of police tea in the Herzen Club. [. . .]

I would forbid these writers to marry and reproduce. How can they be allowed children, when children are there to carry our work forward and prove what we can only surmise. While these fathers have sold their souls to a pock-marked devil to the third generation.[69]

Thus were the lines drawn up in literature as the Soviet Union entered the new decade of the 1930s. The question facing Bulgakov, as it faced a number of his contemporaries, was not how to write but how to be a writer, and how to remain a writer in a new and trying situation. He saw his own destiny in historical perspective. Indeed, this was virtually the definitive feature of the author of *Flight*'s thinking as an artist. He tried to view the situation which had evolved, not narrowly in terms of his own day-to-day biography, but as part of the course of history, 'in the free atmosphere of world culture,' as Pasternak was to say in *Safe Conduct*. For Bulgakov the Year of the Great Leap Forward was to see the birth of the most fruitful ideas behind his later writing. By May 1929 he delivered to *Depths* (*Nedra*) a chapter from a novel of fantasy provisionally titled *The Engineer's Hoof*.[70] This was the period of gestation, and largely also of realisation, of other related projects, a novel about the theatre (*To a Secret Friend*) and his play about Molière (*The League of Hypocrites*).

The times dictate a number of genres, and nobody is exempt from having to choose. What a writer does have is the right to make his choice.

The League of Hypocrites was begun in one of Bulgakov's notebooks whose opening entry bears no direct relation to a play about a French writer of comedies.

The Matter of a White Crow. The Year of Our Lord One Thousand Seven Hundred and Fifteen and of January the five-and-twentieth Day. We, being in the Monastery of Novodevichy, did notice a Bird, a white Crow flying with Magpies. And regarding the Trapping of that Bird we beg Permission of your Highness that it be not forbidden us to catch that Crow in the said Monastery . . .[71]

Marietta Chudakova, who first brought together and published these scraps of evidence from the archives, concludes, 'Bulgakov abandoned the attempt to elucidate the destiny of a playwright in prose close to his own personal experiences [i.e. *To a Secret Friend*]. He turned instead to writing a play about a playwright and the theatre in which very personal material was profoundly changed and sublimated into material from another age and a different genre.'[72]

Bulgakov had no particular wish to be a white crow. He was merely doing his best to carry out the task of a writer, as he saw it, in a fit manner. Despite the very many difficulties of his personal situation he completed his play *The League of Hypocrites* and delivered it to the Art Theatre. He wrote on 16 January 1930 to tell his brother how things stood and about his newly completed play.

I have written a play about Molière. The best experts in Moscow have said it is the strongest of the five plays I have written. [. . .] I have been having no end of trouble with it for the past month and a half or more, in spite of its being about Molière and the seventeenth century, and in spite of the fact that I don't so much as touch on the present day in it. If this play is wrecked I shall be left without recourse. I have to report to you in all seriousness that my ship is sinking. The water is already flooding in as I stand on the bridge. I must go down like a man . . .[73]

On 18 March it became apparent that there was no hope of *The League of Hypocrites* being passed for performance. It was then that Bulgakov wrote a letter to the Soviet Government. Referring to his theatre career he asked them to bear in mind that he was not a politician but a writer, and that he had offered all his output to the Soviet stage.

If even what I have just written is unconvincing and I am to be sentenced to silence for life in the USSR, I ask the Soviet Government to give me work in my area of specialisation and assign me a job as a full-time theatre producer.

I specifically and emphatically request that this should be a *categorical order*, and that I should be officially *assigned* to such a job, because all my own attempts to find work in the only area where I can be useful in the USSR, as an exceptionally well-qualified specialist, have ended in a complete fiasco. My name has been made so odious that my offers to work are met with *fear*, despite the fact that my virtuoso understanding of the stage is excellently known in Moscow to an enormous number of actors and producers, and moreover to the directors of theatres.

I offer the USSR an entirely honest specialist without any hint of wrecking tendencies, [the word is comprehensible against the background of the Shakhty trial and other show trials of those years of 'bourgeois specialists' who were supposedly 'wrecking' Soviet industry] a producer and actor who will undertake to stage conscientiously any play, from those of Shakespeare right through to the plays of the present day.

I request that I be appointed a producer-technician in the First Moscow Art Theatre, the best school there is, under the direction of K. S. Stanislavsky and V. I. Nemirovich-Danchenko, who are great masters of stagecraft.

If I cannot be appointed a producer, I request the post of full-time walk-on actor. If I cannot be a walk-on actor, I request employment as a stage hand.

If even this is impossible, I request the Soviet Government to do with me as it sees fit, but to do something because I, a dramatist who has written five plays, well known in the USSR and abroad, am facing *at this very moment*, penury, homelessness, and disaster.[74]

Bulgakov wrote the letter on 28 March 1930.

On 14 April that year Mayakovsky committed suicide. Before his death he left some lines about water under the bridge and a love-boat wrecked on the rocks of life. In the same note there are several words addressed to the RAPP leader Vladimir Yermilov. The latter had viciously attacked *The Bath-House*. Mayakovsky responded by inscribing a banner with a stanza about critics whose pens only help the bureaucrats, and trying to hang it up in the auditorium of the Meyerhold Theatre. The RAPP leadership demanded that the banner should be removed. Settling his accounts with life, Mayakovsky remembered this churlishness and regretted that he had not been able 'to swear it out' with Yermilov.[75]

The image of the dead poet is etched in Pasternak's *Safe Conduct*: 'Aloof, turning his back on everyone, even lying there, even in that sleep he seemed to be obstinately wanting to be somewhere else and about to leave . . . It was an expression people have when they are at the beginning of life, not at its end. He was pouting and sulking.'[76]

On 18 April Bulgakov received a telephone call from Joseph Stalin. The conversation was later written down, to be published thirty-six years later in the journal *Questions of Literature*.

Stalin. . . . We have received your letter. The comrades and I have read it. You will receive a favourable reply. But perhaps we really ought to let you go abroad? Have we really put your back up so much?

Bulgakov. I have been thinking a lot recently, about whether a Russian writer can really live outside his own country, and it seems to me that he cannot.

Stalin. You are right. I think the same. Where do you want to work? In the Art Theatre?

Bulgakov. Yes. I would like to, but I asked them about it and was turned down.

Stalin. Put in an application. I have a feeling they will agree . . .[77]

The Art Theatre 'agreed'.

Right up until 1991 there were differing accounts in circulation about Bulgakov's letter to Stalin and the phone call from the stocky Georgian in the Kremlin to the author of *Flight*. Lyubov Belozerskaya, Bulgakov's second wife, insisted he did not in fact send 'upstairs' the text which, from the late 1960s, was known as his letter 'To the Government of the USSR', but only a brief note. The question was finally settled only in May 1991, with publication in the magazine *Ogonyok* of various items from the KGB files relating to Bulgakov. The text Bulgakov sent Stalin was indeed the text of the letter we know. We are able to glean some interesting details of this less than straightforward 'case' from a report by a secret agent. The typescript copy of the letter which Bulgakov sent to the GPU bears the resolution of Genrikh Yagoda, at that time the omnipotent head of the secret police: 'He must be allowed to work where he wishes. G.Ya. 12 April.' Yagoda's resolution is quite obviously the result of a conversation with Stalin, and reflects the view Stalin put forward in his telephone conversation with Bulgakov.

Why did Bulgakov's challenging letter evoke such a benevolent reaction? This secret is largely revealed by the agent's report. Here are some excerpts from that inelegantly written report (which was published in full in *Ogonyok* on 20 May 1991).

Everybody is talking in literary and intelligentsia circles about Bulgakov's letter.

It is said the circumstances were in the following manner.

When Bulgakov's position became intolerable (why it became intolerable it will be explained below), Bulgakov in a fit of despair wrote three letters of identical content addressed to Comrade J. V. Stalin, F. Kon (at the Main Committee for the Arts) and to the OGPU.

In these letters Bulgakov wrote in his usual biting and poisonous manner that he had several plays and 400 newspaper reviews, of which 396 were rude and bordering on persecution and practically calling for his physical annihilation. This campaign had made him into a kind of leper, who not only the theatres began to flee from, but also editors and even representatives of organisations he wanted to get a job with. A completely intolerable situation arose not only in a moral but also in a purely material respect, verging on poverty. Bulgakov asked that either he and his family should be allowed to emigrate, or he should be given a chance to work.

The anonymous GPU informer goes on to retell things already well known to the institution employing him. For us, however, his account is of great interest:

A few days passed, and the telephone rang in Bulgakov's flat.

'Is that Comrade Bulgakov?'

'Yes.'

'One moment. Comrade Stalin is going to speak to you.' (!)

Bulgakov was absolutely certain this was a practical joke, but he held on.

Two or three minutes later he heard a voice on the telephone:

'I apologise, Comrade Bulgakov, for not being able to answer your letter promptly, but I am very busy. Your letter interested me a great deal. I should like to talk to you personally. I do not know when this will be possible because, I repeat, I have a great deal of work, but I shall advise you when I can see you. At all events we shall try to do something for you.'

At the end of the conversation Bulgakov immediately rang up the Kremlin and said somebody had just phoned him from the Kremlin and said he was Stalin.

Bulgakov was told it really was Comrade Stalin. He was terribly shocked.

The agent goes on to relate the reaction in the Main Committee for the Arts to this conversation, and that the Moscow Art Theatre has signed a contract with the disgraced dramatist without more ado. Finally he gives an assessment of how news of the call has been received in literary and theatre circles in the Soviet capital. This last element is crucial.

That's the whole story, as everybody is saying, like a beautiful legend, a fairy-tale and which many people think is just incredible.

It is necessary to note what is being said about Stalin at present in literary and intelligentsia circles.

The impression is as if a dam has suddenly burst and everybody around has seen the true face of Comrade Stalin.

After all, there was, it seemed, no other name about which so much more malice had been woven, the opinion that he was a fanatic who was leading the country to ruin, and who they thought was responsible for all our misfortunes and so on, as a blood-thirsty being sitting behind the walls of the Kremlin.

Now what they all say is,

Stalin really is an important person after all and who would have thought, simple and approachable. One of the actresses at the Vakhtangov Theatre said at O. Leonidov's,

Stalin went to *Madame Zoyka* twice. He said with an accent, 'It is a good play. I do not understand, I simply do not understand why it is passed for performance one moment and banned the next. It is a good play. I see nothing bad in it.'

. . . The main thing is they are saying Stalin is nothing to do with the economic crisis. His line is correct, but they are all bastards that are around him. It was those bastards that were persecuting Bulgakov, one of the most talented Soviet writers. Various literary phoneys have been doing well out of hounding Bulgakov, and now Stalin has clipped their ear.

It has to be said Stalin's popularity has taken a really unusual form. He is being spoken about warmly and lovingly, telling the legendary history of Bulgakov's letter over and over again.

Thus was the Stalin legend gradually created, with the Bulgakov episode, as we see clearly from the report of this implicated informer, a small link in a well-thought-through chain of actions.

Bulgakov's conversation with Stalin took place on 18 April 1930, just a few days after Mayakovsky's suicide. Stalin was neutralising the impact of that pistol shot with his charitable hand-out to Bulgakov. Bulgakov did not at first recognise what was going on. He lost every point in his conversation with Stalin except one: he did get a job at the Art Theatre.

On 4 September 1930 Stanislavsky sent Bulgakov a letter of good wishes from Badenweiler. He found such an exalted parallel for the dramatist's arrival at the Theatre that contemporaries must surely have been in some astonishment.

My very dear Mikhail Afanasievich,

You cannot imagine how glad I am that you are joining our Theatre!

I have had occasion to work with you only at a few of the rehearsals of *The Turbins*, but even then I sensed a director in you (and perhaps also an actor?!).

Molière and many others have combined these professions with writing!

I welcome you from the bottom of my heart. I sincerely believe it will all be a great success, and look forward very much to working together with you as soon as possible . . .[78]

The dramatist's ship might have sprung a massive leak but it did not sink. On this occasion too life proved unpredictable. 'Chance is a powerful and instantly effective weapon of Providence,' Pushkin had said. It brought Bulgakov to the safe haven of the Art Theatre. Two years later the heroes of *The Turbins* would again be stepping up to the footlights, giving back to Bulgakov a part of his soul. A further two years on Bulgakov would be recalling in a letter to Sudakov the naive but wise words of Lariosik, as appropriate as any to the celebration of the four-hundredth performance of *The Days of the Turbins*:

We met at a difficult and terrible time, and we have all been through a very great deal, myself included . . . And my frail barque . . . Well it's no good dwelling on sorrows . . . Time has moved on. We're all alive, the play is alive, and more than that: now you're even preparing to start rehearsals on *Flight*.[79]

'Time has moved on. We're all alive, the play is alive . . .'. It was a kind of personal summing up of the first decade after the revolution. Bulgakov entered the new epoch as an assistant producer of the First Moscow Art Theatre and, simultaneously, as a consultant to the Theatre of Working Youth, the *Teatr rabochei molodezhi*, abbreviated in common parlance to TRAM.

5

'Cover me with your Iron Greatcoat'

An Enchanted Place

On 6 August 1930 assistant producer Mikhail Bulgakov of the Moscow Art Theatre wrote a significant letter to Konstantin Stanislavsky which inaugurates his 'Theatre Period'.

Returning from the Crimea, where I have been restoring my shattered nerves after two years which have been very difficult for me, I am writing you a simple unofficial letter. [. . .] After being deeply depressed by the loss of my plays I felt much better when, after a long pause and already in a new capacity, I crossed the threshold of the Theatre you created to the renown of our country.

Receive your new producer, Konstantin Sergeevich, with open arms. Be assured that he loves your Art Theatre.

Return to Moscow and walk once more across the cloth bordering the auditorium.[1]

The mention of the cloth bordering the auditorium is a secret sign for those initiated into a mystery. The theme of the theatre and the theatre world in general as a closed circle, a kind of redemptive enclosure, which Bulgakov had been aware of earlier, became one of his most persistent ideas at this time.

From May 1930 and throughout the long decade of the 1930s, Bulgakov was to find himself in that 'enchanted place', the theatre. In an almost Gogolian fashion it combines a magical and a workaday location in inextricable and sometimes breath-taking unity. The world of the stage was to be opened up to Bulgakov from the inside, in all its dazzling splendour and its no less dazzling poverty. It would show the dramatist its various facets, at first in the Art Theatre and later also in the Bolshoy when he went to work there. Bulgakov would experience bitterness and deep disillusionment in full measure, but he would never lose the sense that this was a world with a special, elite status and security, almost a kind of grace to it.

In replying to his newly arrived employee Stanislavsky drew, as we have seen, some very exalted and flattering comparisons. He had good reason to mention Molière, who had successfully combined the profession of a man of letters with direct involvement in the theatre. Bulgakov's life within the Art Theatre did at first seem to mould itself to this classical prototype. Appointed assistant producer in May 1930, he asked Stanislavsky one year later to include him also in the list of actors. He left TRAM, and prepared fully and wholeheartedly to belong to his Theatre. Before, however, Stanislavsky could decide this simple question he had first to address himself to Andrey Bubnov, who had recently replaced Lunacharsky as Commissar of Enlightenment. Bubnov's agreement to Bulgakov's combining the two jobs was duly forthcoming. In his capacity as a producer Bulgakov the writer was soon set to work on adapting Gogol's *Dead Souls* for the stage, a project instituted before he came along. Bulgakov only once justified his status as an actor, appearing as the Judge in *The Pickwick Papers*.

Combining his service to the cause of literature with direct involvement in the work of the theatre proved highly problematical. Three hundred years had passed since Molière had been Director at the Palais-Royal, writing, producing and acting in his own plays. The theatre and literary worlds had moved on and become demarcated. The life of 'comedians', public through and through, open and extrovert, came to contrast markedly and sometimes proved inimical to the solitary and intense labours of the professional writer. It is difficult to imagine Gogol or Chekhov going to work in the theatre, being summoned by slips of paper to the repertoire office or immersing themselves in the hundred and one details and trivia which make up the average theatre day.

With the passing of time a writer's independence, his keeping a certain distance from the theatre, have become a prerequisite for an equal relationship.

Bulgakov involuntarily violated a norm which had evolved over the centuries. Existing simultaneously in two worlds became a source of new creative ideas, but also of a palpable conflict.

The Theatre took Bulgakov over completely. It puts its stamp on his writer's psychology, on his very method of perceiving and experiencing life. In Bulgakov's letters of the 1930s the theme of dual nature is never far away. He spent the first half of his day at the Theatre, and the second at home going over what had taken place during the first half. 'In addition to adapting the work for the stage and the corrections, to whose kingdom there will evidently be no end, there is the directing, and on top of that, the acting . . .'.[2] From Yelena Bulgakova's diary we can see clearly how totally engrossed he was in theatre matters, and that he really did mean it when he said 'I am no longer here'. 'We sat till four o'clock eating mandarins and absorbed in talking about the Theatre.'

Like all true adherents of the Moscow Art Theatre, Bulgakov's wife wrote 'Theatre' with a capital 'T'.

Theatre gossip, and the conflicting interests of the factions within the Art Theatre, fill Yelena's diary to overflowing. All this took its toll of Bulgakov, tiring and irritating him, but he had a living to make.

Bulgakov's work in the Theatre involved far more than the mere producing of plays. Working with the vocalists, preparing gala concerts, talking at open discussions with members of the audience, writing memoranda and reading other people's plays could all at times push his own literary work aside. On 6 January 1931, for example, Olga Bokshanskaya reported to Nemirovich-Danchenko,

Markov has fallen ill with angina [. . .] His illness has had a devastating effect on the pieces for the 'Morning in Commemoration of the 1905 Revolution'. [. . .] Bulgakov was asked today to stop work on [his adaptation of Gogol's *Dead Souls*] and do this instead. Sakhnovsky is terribly upset because he was waiting for the results of Bulgakov's labours with great impatience.[3]

As if Bulgakov's involuntary work on the extremely difficult task of adapting Gogol's epic for the stage were not enough, he was liable to be deployed to wherever there was an emergency, and in the theatre there always is an emergency and it is always 'devastating'. It was enervating work which left no time for peace and quiet, and which crowded out his own literary projects.

Many times Bulgakov looked ahead, anticipating his pleasure when Gogol's work would come to life. Stanislavsky often amazed him at rehearsals, letting him delight in the miracle of theatre. Bulgakov was extremely reserved in his judgements and indeed in any expression of his feelings. He nonetheless wrote Stanislavsky a letter after one of the rehearsals of *Dead Souls* the like of which we find nowhere else in his correspondence:

Dear Konstantin Sergeevich,
I meant to write to you the day after the rehearsal of the party in *Dead Souls* but was, in the first place embarrassed, and in the second out of commission (I had a cold).

This is not a letter on business. Its purpose is to express to you the delight I have been feeling these last few days. In three hours I watched you transform this crucial scene from something stilted which just was not working into something living. The magic of theatre really exists!

It gives me hope for the future and raises me up when my spirits fall. I find it difficult to say what it was that delighted me most. In all conscience, I do not know. Perhaps your comment on the figure of Manilov, 'You can say nothing to him, you can ask him nothing without his instantly landing himself in the soup'. That was the high point. It is a riveting definition in precisely the theatrical sense of the word, and your demonstration of how to convey it was mastery of the first order.

When you are at the rehearsals I do not fear for Gogol. He will come through you. He will come in the first scenes of the performance in laughter, and will leave in the last, covered in the ashes of deep meditation. He will come.[4]

With this letter we are, of course, jumping ahead very considerably. Its chronological place is not until we come to the production history of *Dead Souls*. It is, however, of fundamental importance if we are to understand the question of Bulgakov and the Theatre.

We have hastened to introduce it not in order to soften an impression, or steer a tragic theme towards a happy ending. Bulgakov's relations with the Art Theatre were not by any means spoiled by deliberate ill will or misunderstanding. There was there a real enough, fundamentally insoluble conflict over and beyond the personalities involved. Bulgakov's feverish, ceaseless, devoted work led virtually nowhere.

In such a situation the fact of living simultaneously in two worlds could be psychologically beneficial. When his Molière biography was given the thumbs down in 1933 Bulgakov fell back on his mission in the theatre in just this way.

And so, I wish to bury Jean-Baptiste Molière. That way it will be quieter and better all round. It really is of no consequence to me at all whether my dust jacket decorates a shop window. I am basically an actor, not a writer. Anyway, I am all for a quiet life.[5]

The theatre both protected and limited Bulgakov. It rescued him even as it wounded him. It has to be said that for all their love of Bulgakov, few people in the Art Theatre were fully aware at that time what calibre of writer was imprisoned in that assistant producer's uniform. His considerable self-respect was wounded, for example, when in the greetings telegram Nemirovich-Danchenko sent on the four-hundredth performance of *Days of the Turbins* he found 'not a single letter' referring to the play's author. ('I imagine it is not done to refer to the author. I had been unaware of this, no doubt as the result of my provincial upbringing.'[6]) Even the revival of the production in January 1932, which Bulgakov declared had returned a part of his life to him, brought sadness together with the 'flood of joy'. Bulgakov concludes his letter to Popov about the first night of the revived *Turbins* with the following sadly typical incident:

Then a messenger appeared in the form of a beautiful girl. I have lately perfected an ability which rather takes the edge off living. This is the ability to divine even as someone is approaching what it is he wants of me. Evidently the sheaths on my nerves have been completely worn away, and communing with my dog has taught me to be constantly alert.

In short, I know what people are going to say, and the worst of it is that I also know it will be nothing new. There will be no surprises. I already know it all. I had only to look at the tense, smiling mouth to know that she was going to ask me not to take a curtain call . . .

My messenger said K. S. had rung to ask where I was and how I was feeling.

I asked her to thank him, and tell him I was feeling fine, was standing in the wings, and would not take any curtain calls.

Oh, how my messenger beamed! And said that K. S. thought that would be wisest. [. . .]

They took twenty curtain calls. Afterwards the actors and my acquaintances bombarded me with questions. Why had I not come on stage? What point was I making? It appears that if you do take a curtain call you are making a point, and if you do not you are also making a point. I don't know. I really don't know what to do.[7]

The bitter humour with which Bulgakov describes his predicament in the Art Theatre tells us that he was well aware how peculiar it was. It had come about for many social reasons and was only to a very minor extent contingent on the will of the man who had sent the courier to ask him not to take a bow. Knowing this of course did nothing to ease the situation, and as time went by Bulgakov could only become increasingly sensitive to his place as an assistant producer who was no longer by any means an Author of the Theatre.

When Bulgakov joined the Art Theatre Stanislavsky had flatteringly likened him to Molière. After working there for a few years Bulgakov himself drew a parallel which favoured him considerably less. Someone had advised him to ask the leaders of the Art Theatre for help in a vitally important matter. Bulgakov replied, 'Let Anton Chekhov ask them for help.'[8]

The hurts multiplied and snowballed. One incident led on to another ('as if I am shooting from a rifle which has been nobbled', as he told Grigory Konsky, one of the actors). Bulgakov got on with his theatre work to the best of his ability, treating it on an equal footing with his own writing. Productions might be in rehearsal for years, but Bulgakov turned up religiously, obeying not so much the voice of reason as the imperative of his theatrical second nature. 'If it gets passed, that's splendid; if it doesn't, never mind. I work hard and passionately on these rehearsals,' he reported on *Molière* to Pavel Popov. 'There's no escape if you have the stage in your blood'.[9]

'The stage in your blood.' This formulation goes far to explain Bulgakov's relations with the Art Theatre. All the hurts and pinpricks to a sensitive ego, the whole strange carnival of a life which nevertheless was strictly regulated, all that endless toil which did not lead up to a performance would later be distilled into the classical lines of *Black Snow*. The six long hard years which wore out the working relationship of the writer and the Theatre were to provide the basis and material for one of Bulgakov's most deeply felt and sublime projects. His relationship with the Art Theatre became history and was transmuted into a work of art. The topic was the new position of a playwright in the theatre, and the situation of the theatre itself as it negotiated its passage through a new period in history.

The Art Theatre launched into the 1930s without Stanislavsky. Returning to Russia after a two-year absence he was unable to throw himself into work immediately, and a further year was to pass before he could start work on rehearsing his first works of the new decade, *Dead Souls* and Alexander Afinogenov's *Fear*. For some years Stanislavsky had observed the goings-on within the Art Theatre from afar, and quite major things were going on which affected not merely the surface but the very nature of a theatre which had evolved a very particular identity over the years.

As one decade ended and another began the Art Theatre put on a number of productions from the classical Russian and world repertoire: Dostoevsky's *Uncle's Dream*, Tolstoy's *Resurrection*, Shakespeare's *Othello*. The first two gained themselves a secure place in the repertoire and went on to become Soviet stage classics, but the Shakespeare production flopped. It was rehearsed by Sudakov to Stanislavsky's instructions and rushed into performance in the spring of 1930 to fill a gap in the schedule. It survived a mere ten performances and was taken off even before Stanislavsky returned to Moscow. The worst aspect was that he continued regularly sending advice on a production he believed to be in rehearsal to people who were too afraid to tell him that it had not only been rushed into performance but had already folded.

This was a period when some in the Art Theatre favoured going for 'breadth' rather than 'depth', quantity rather than quality, a policy against which Stanislavsky was prepared to fight to the death.

As one historical period succeeded another the Art Theatre, which was basically conservative in its ways, tried to work out its own response to the sharp increase in the pace of historical change. Emulating industrial factories, it concluded a contract for 'socialist competition' with the Meyerhold Theatre which included among its 'objects', as people said in those years, Nikolai Erdman's play *The Suicide*, which both theatres were planning to produce. As in other Moscow theatres, special creative shock brigades were set up in the Art Theatre. The administration was urging a no-break week, and supporting the slogan that the 'traditional season' should be smashed. The Theatre gave an enormous number of performances (760) in one season, with no rest days. It took part in the far-reaching anti-Easter campaigns, and greeted the metal industry shock-workers from its stage.

'An unwonted spectacle,' a newspaper reported on one evening in the Art Theatre. 'The Chekhovian symbols are covered with metal numbers [. . .] The curtain parts, taking the seagull away with it. The theatre company stand in a line and declaim a welcome to the metal-workers of Moscow:

> We'll cast out the darkness as fast as we can,
> The blow we strike jointly unerringly gauge,
> Together fulfilling the new Five-Year Plan,
> You by the furnace and we on the stage.

The Theatre was certainly changing. There was a youthful ferment. The 'young shoots', as people said at the time, sought their own response to demands to march in step with the present day. Attempts were made to forge an alliance with the powerful RAPP. The Art Theatre staged a production of Vladimir Kirshon's anti-kulak play *Bread*. Joint activity was embarked on with Alexander Afinogenov in an attempt to persuade this talented writer of the practical possibilities of Stanislavsky's Method, which the supporters of RAPP (and Afinogenov) dismissed as subjective idealism. New versions of the 'social command' to playwriting appeared. Pavel Markov spent an entire year trying to improve *A Good Man*, a play about the struggle against the kulaks. It never did make it to the stage. Another play on much the same level, Vagramov's *Take-off*, was produced but flopped. The play concerned the struggle against the locust and was centred around a member of the nobility who had become a Red Army commander. The former aristocrat demonstrated his political maturity twice over, first by returning from a flight (rather than crossing over to the enemy as his detractors predicted), and secondly by beating the locusts.

The Theatre was changing in a hurry, and it made mistakes. All the hectic work on new plays produced no results to speak of. From Italy Nemirovich-Danchenko warned his literary director through his secretary: 'Markov should think carefully about what I have been repeating endlessly: nothing worthwhile will come of all these corrections and reworkings. Not ever! In forty years' experience I can think of no single instance. And look at the plays we are dealing with: *The Embezzlers, Untilovsk* and *A Good Man*.'

Leonid Leonov's play *Untilovsk* doubtless found its way into this list by mistake, but Nemirovich-Danchenko's anxieties were fuelled by real enough facts.

The Theatre was seeking its place in a society which was being turbulently modernised. That society, at least as represented by the theatre critics, continued to attack the Art Theatre in the 1930s as it had in the 1920s. Vladimir Blyum was damning *Othello* and *Resurrection*, and Maeterlinck's *The Blue Bird* for 'affirming faith in a life beyond the grave to Soviet children'. In an article titled 'Captive to the Classics' Osaf Litovsky, whose standpoint Lunacharsky characterised as primitive and uncouth, was still accusing Tolstoy and the Art Theatre of exercising a corrupting influence on Soviet audiences. In the autumn of 1931 RAPP was still convening its secretariat to proclaim a final push against the twin theatre strongholds of academicism and Meyerholdian formalism. Their generalising document on the theatre was much trumpeted in advance. An announcement that RAPP was organising its own theatre was welcomed by a section of the Art Theatre's 'young shoots'. In a succession of manifestos the RAPP leaders continued to recall their brave victory over the counter-revolutionary plays of Bulgakov and to select new victims among the demoralised writers. But the era of the Furious Zealots was drawing to a close, and a change in the status of the Art Theatre was perhaps one of the principal indications that major change was imminent.

On 12 December 1931 RAPP published their militant statement on the theatre with a deadly characterisation of the true nature of the Art Theatre.

On 15 December a short official communiqué announced that the Praesidium of the All-Union Central Executive Committee of the Congress of Soviets had resolved to 'remove the First Moscow Art Academic Theatre from the jurisdiction of the RSFSR People's Commissariat of Enlightenment and transfer it to the jurisdiction of the Praesidium of the Central Executive Committee of the USSR'.[10]

The close proximity of the publication of these two documents must have given the Art Theatre's vociferous opponents food for thought. The Art Theatre was now the Moscow Art Academic Theatre of the USSR.

The change of name was followed by a sharp change in the Theatre's fortunes, one consequence of which was an order to restore *The Days of the Turbins* to the repertoire.

The level at which this decision had been taken was immediately clear to Bulgakov. He wrote to Popov:

In mid-January 1932, for reasons known to me but which I am not at liberty to discuss, the Government of the USSR gave the Moscow Art Theatre a remarkable instruction to revive *The Days of the Turbins*.

For the play's author this is tantamount to having a part of his life returned to him.[11]

Bulgakov may not have considered himself at liberty to discuss the reasons for this 'remarkable instruction', but they are of the greatest interest. On 16 September 1931 Markov informed Nemirovich-Danchenko, who was in Berlin, of an important meeting which had taken place at the Theatre with Gorky's participation. 'He [Gorky] is presently extraordinarily well disposed towards the Theatre and is taking the closest interest in the negotiations to transfer us to another jurisdiction.'[12]

When discussing possible playwrights who might provide the Theatre with a play for the fifteenth anniversary of the October revolution Gorky named 'a basic group of writers' on whom the Art Theatre should rely. He included in it 'Leonov, Vsevolod Ivanov, Olesha, Afinogenov, and Bulgakov'. In the same letter Markov passed on Gorky's comments on the finale of *Flight* and also his benevolent attitude towards *The League of Hypocrites*, which extended to his wishing to 'facilitate the play's production'.[13]

On 26 October Bulgakov told Popov, 'My *Molière* has received a "B" categorisation for universal performance.'[14]

These were signs of a completely changed situation. A most important document is Stanislavsky's appeal to the Government, which he had thought about deeply and agonised over at length. This letter played an important role in securing the Art Theatre's transition to a new 'jurisdiction' and official status.

Recognising and accepting the inevitability of major change, Stanislavsky began by stating that the Art Theatre could fulfil its role in the present day only if it was allowed to retain 'its *essential*, acknowledged, historically tested basis'. By this he meant the presence of 'solid and enduring organisational forms' and 'first-rate dramatic material', that is, the very things which had created the phenomenon of an *art* theatre.[15]

Stanislavsky saw the basis of the Theatre being systematically destroyed. 'A theatre of major artistic forms' was switching to a planned and organised policy of hack work. The 'no-break week', the endless guest performances, the immoderate inflating of the theatre company with people who had no idea why it had been created or what its mission might be, 'indifference to one's obligations which rules out any further development of theatre craftsmanship', a sharp fall in the standards expected of plays for inclusion in the repertoire. Such were the harbingers of the Theatre's 'imminent catastrophe'.

Stanislavsky particularly emphasised the problem of plays for the repertoire. 'The System and the Art Theatre's hard-won experience are of no consequence if we are going to return to those ephemeral plays which littered the stages of Russian theatres thirty years ago.' Fully informed about *Take-off, A Good Man* and the rest, Stanislavsky addressed the Government with measured firmness.

One would have imagined that the primary responsibility of the Art Theatre's Committee for Political and Artistic Affairs might have been to familiarise itself with the nature and

1. Bulgakov's home at No. 13 St Andrew's Hill, Kiev

In the spring the parks bloomed white with blossom. [...] A green sea ran down in terraces to the gentle, dappled Dnieper. Dark nights of blue and black above its waters, the electrically lit cross of St Vladimir suspended high above. [...] Those times were the stuff of legend, when a young generation lived its days in the parks of the most beautiful city in our country knowing no sorrow. But those times were cut short, as suddenly, menacingly, History made its entrance. (Mikhail Bulgakov)

2. Mikhail Bulgakov's father,
Afanasy Ivanovich Bulgakov,
c. 1907

3. Mikhail Bulgakov in
High School uniform, 1909

4. The company of the Solovtsov Theatre, Kiev, early 1990s

5. Three Moscow Art Theatre playwrights:
Valentin Kataev, Yury Olesha and Mikhail Bulgakov, 1924

6. The Moscow Art Theatre's 'young' management,
'The Six': Nikolai Khmelyov, Pavel Markov, Nikolai Batalov,
Ilya Sudakov, Yury Zavadsky and Mark Prudkin

7. Left to right: S. Topleninov, Mikhail Bulgakov, N. Lyamin
and Lyubov Belozerskaya, Bulgakov's first wife, 1926

We set great store by Bulgakov.
He may yet develop into a producer. He is not only a writer,
but an actor too. I am judging by
the way he demonstrated things
at rehearsals of *The Turbins*.
Really he was the director, or at
least it was he who put in those
sparkling highlights which made
the production a success.
(Konstantin Stanislavsky)

8. Mikhail Bulgakov in 1926

9. Konstantin Stanislavsky
in 1926

10. Mikhail Bulgakov
with the cast of
Days of the Turbins,
1926

Days of the Turbins [. . .] has served a useful purpose. It was the first political
play on our horizon to raise serious, socio-political matters. (Anatoly
Lunacharsky)

11. Mark Prudkin as Shervinsky in *Days of the Turbins*

Working on *The Turbins* has been as unforgettable as first love. (Mark Prudkin)

12. The High School scene from *Days of the Turbins*

13. Mikhail Bulgakov
in 1928

14. The sketch drawn by Konstantin Stanislavsky during
the reading of *Flight* at the Moscow Art Theatre in 1928

It is a play whose profound satire is cleverly concealed. I should like to see the
Art Theatre stage a play of this kind. [. . .] *Flight* is an excellent play and will, I
assure you, cause a sensation. (Maxim Gorky)

15. Mikhail Bulgakov in 1932

16. Yevgeny Kaluzhsky as Mizhuev, Ivan Moskvin as Nozdryov
and Vasily Toporkov as Chichikov in *Dead Souls*
by Gogol at the Moscow Art Theatre in 1932

17. Mikhail Bulgakov
as the Judge in
The Pickwick Papers,
1934

'Who is that?' he asked Stanitsyn
in a quick whisper, not recognising the actor. 'Bulgakov.' 'What
Bulgakov?' 'Our Bulgakov. The
playwright. The author of *The
Turbins*.' 'It can't be!' 'It really
is, Konstantin Sergeevich.
Honest to God!' 'But what talent
he's got . . .' and again he roared
with laughter at something as
loudly and infectiously as only
Stanislavsky could. (Vitaly
Vilenkin)

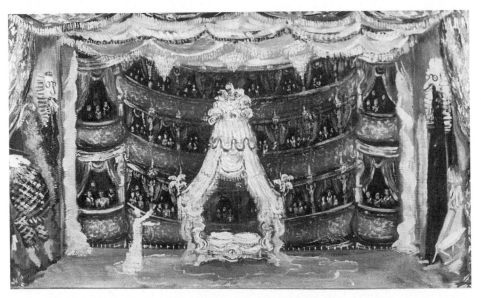

18. Pyotr Viliams's stage set design for Bulgakov's *Molière*

19. Mikhail Bolduman as
Louis XIV in *Molière*, 1936

20. Victor Stanitsyn as Molière

The portrait of Molière in his declining years is excellently painted, a Molière
worn out by disorderliness in his personal life and the burden of fame. The
presentation of the Sun King is equally good and bold, even beautiful. In fact all
the roles are splendid. It is an excellent play. (Gorky)

21. Mikhail Bulgakov in his study,
wearing his 'master's cap', 1936

'Are you a writer?' asked the poet with interest. [. . .] 'I am a master.' His
expression hardened and he pulled out of his dressing gown pocket a greasy
black cap with the letter 'M' embroidered on it in yellow silk. He put the cap on
and showed himself to Ivan in profile and full face to prove that he was a master.
(Mikhail Bulgakov, *The Master and Margarita*)

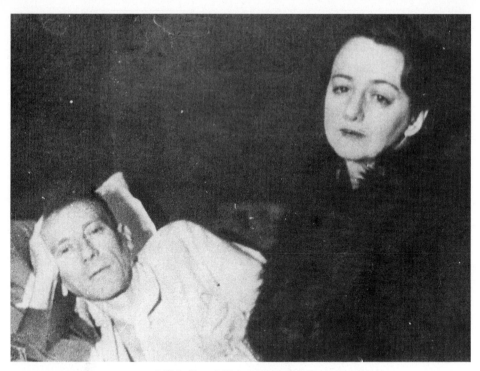

22. Mikhail and Yelena Bulgakov, 1940

23. Seryozha Shilovsky, Mikhail and Yelena Bulgakov,
Pavel Popov and M. Chemishkian, 1940

preconditions of the Art Theatre's work and to form an understanding and appreciation of the Art Theatre's place in the art of our country and the world. Regrettably it reacts uncritically to misconceived strictures of the press. It latches on to the pretext of the need to respond to burning questions of the present day and does its utmost to assist the Main Repertoire Committee in systematically obstructing the staging of plays which have been found by the Theatre. Given the absence of plays combining political reliability with genuine artistic quality, it obliges the Theatre to stage ephemera with a modicum of primitive propaganda which might be more appropriate and would perhaps better achieve their ends in a different place and with different staging. It is ultimately a source of systematically promoted hack work![16]

Stanislavsky sees the measures capable of saving the Theatre from catastrophe as being the 'issuance of precise Governmental and Party directives' on the role of the Art Theatre in the present day as '*a theatre of classical drama and the best, artistically significant plays of the present-day repertoire*', and also the 'removal from it of tasks which primarily require *rushed* work'.[17]

Stanislavsky's letter and Gorky's energetic lobbying resulted not only in the Art Theatre's being taken under direct government control. At the same time the Theatre's Committee For Political and Artistic Affairs was liquidated, its 'Red Director' (Mikhail Heitz) relieved of his post, and the plenitude of artistic and administrative power again restored to its directors and founders, Konstantin Stanislavsky and Vladimir Nemirovich-Danchenko. The struggle against the locusts disappeared shortly afterwards from its playbill, *The Days of the Turbins* was revived, and *Flight* and *Molière* put in rehearsal.

With the dissolution of RAPP a marked change came over the attitude of the Theatre's critics. In autumn 1932 Osaf Litovsky, former scourge of the classics, published an article under the title 'Stage the Classics!'; while that most vigorous of RAPP's 'young shoots', Vladimir Yermilov, coined a form of words which within a few years was to become an obligatory pendant whenever reference was made to the Art Theatre: 'the Greatest Theatre in the World'.

Vilification of Stanislavsky's Method as idealistic and mystical gave way to a gradual discovery of its uniquely redemptive qualities. The Art Theatre became known as an 'Academy of Theatre Art' within whose walls new generations of theatre workers for the provinces were expected to receive instruction. The purpose of their instruction was the '*inculcation of the Art Theatre's Method*', as Vasily Sakhnovsky was to write in autumn 1932 in *Evening Moscow*.

Yury Tynyanov was right when he said a period ferments in the blood, each period in its own way. Art senses this fermentation very early, detecting its slightest manifestations and bearing them within itself. One of the first productions with which the Art Theatre responded to and justified its new status, was *Dead Souls*. The production was shot through with the ferment of change.

'Not a Stage Adaptation, but Something Quite Different . . .'

There had been plans to dramatise Gogol's *Dead Souls* before Bulgakov was put on the task. The Collegium for Artistic Affairs and Repertoire had resolved to work on it as long ago as 1926, at which time Dmitry Smolin was commissioned to adapt it for the stage. His dramatisation survives in the archive of the Art Theatre Museum, a bulky and hopelessly untalented play, one of many unsuccessful attempts to translate Gogol's great epic to the Russian stage.

In May 1932 Bulgakov described to Popov how the task had come his way.

So, dead souls . . . In nine days' time I shall be forty-one. Monstrous, but true.

So here I am, at the end of my writing career, forced into making stage adaptations. A sparkling finale, don't you think? I gaze in horror at my bookshelves. Who shall I have to adapt tomorrow? Turgenev, Leskov, the Brockhaus-Efron Encyclopaedia? Ostrovsky? Fortunately the latter adapted himself for the stage, evidently foreseeing the fate in store for me in 1929–32. In short . . .

1) It is *impossible* to adapt *Dead Souls* for the stage. Take that as an axiom from someone familiar with the work. I am told there have been a hundred and sixty attempts. Even if that is an exaggeration, it is none the less impossible to stage *Dead Souls*.

2) So why did I take it on?

I did not take it on, Pavel. It is a long time since I last took anything on, because I do not control anything in my life. Fate grabs me by the throat. I was no sooner appointed at MAAT than I was given the job of acting as assistant producer for *Dead Souls* (Sakhnovsky is the senior producer, there's Telesheva, and there's me). My first glance at the manuscript of the adaptation, written by a freelance, was sufficient to make my blood run cold. I realised that barely had I crossed the Theatre's threshold before ill-luck had attended me. I had been appointed to produce a non-existent play. Not bad for a start, eh? After that it is all relatively straightforward. After protracted and agonised debate something was generally recognised of which I have long been aware, but of which, unfortunately, many are unaware. In order for something to be acted it must first be written. In short, I have had to write it myself.[18]

Bulgakov's account is clearly jaundiced by the two years of hard work he had put in and which by May 1932 had led nowhere. The early stages of the work were considerably brighter than he suggests here.

The idea of appointing Bulgakov as assistant for *Dead Souls* came from Nemirovich-Danchenko, and it needs to be said it later bore fruit. Bulgakov's close study of Gogol's fate and active engagement with his ideas and emotional charge were all to be absorbed and become integral to Bulgakov's own literary destiny.[19]

As long ago as 1926 Bulgakov had told Popov that Gogol was his favourite author. 'There is no one to compare with him.' Admittedly he also rather oddly explained the failure of the second volume of *Dead Souls* by Gogol's having 'written himself out'. In the 1920s he was primarily interested in Gogol as a satirist. Bulgakov's story 'The Adventures of Chichikov, an Epic in Two Points, with a Prologue and Epilogue' is built around Gogolian themes and the mask-like types he discovered.

In his 'Gogol Period' Bulgakov penetrated to the very source of Gogol's art. He pondered the traits of the Russian national character and the peculiarities of Russian life which, as he put it, caused his literary mentors 'untold sufferings'.

In the 1930s Gogol crops up in Bulgakov's life at the most unexpected moments. Seeking to explain his need to travel and see other countries in his letter to Stalin, Bulgakov refers to Gogol and quotes him: 'I knew only that my travels were not at all for the purpose of enjoying myself in foreign parts, but rather that I should suffer my fill, as if I sensed that I would learn the price of Russia only when outside Russia and would learn to love her only when far from her'.

Through the crystalline prism of Gogol Bulgakov views the features of everyday life in Moscow, his own situation and the whole tangle of fantastic absurdity and oddity. Writing to Popov about the revival of *The Days of the Turbins* he states:

The Muscovite in the street was desperate to know what it was all about. They began to torment me with this question, convinced they had discovered the horse's mouth. Then the City's inhabitants decided they would give their own explanation of what it was all about, since neither the play's author nor anybody else seem willing or able to do so. And what explanations they have come up with, my dear Pavel: explanations such as would turn your hair grey. It culminated in a person with great mad eyes, whom I know well, rushing in to my room in the middle of the night exclaiming, 'What is this all about?'

'What it is all about,' I replied, 'is that the inhabitants of this City, and primarily its men of letters, are acting out the ninth chapter of your novel which I, Great Teacher, have adapted for the stage in your honour. You yourself have said, "In their heads there is commotion, turmoil, inconstancy, their thoughts are in disarray . . . there has formed a humour of little faith, slothful, filled with endless doubting and eternal anxiety." Cover me with your iron greatcoat![20]

The composition of *Dead Souls*, no less than the destiny of its author, was to become an integral part of the composition of *The Master and Margarita*. The image of the Master who is called to reveal the truth to people, who 'guesses' the truth, was directly influenced by Gogol. Bulgakov's novel evolved into what is essentially an epic of the twentieth century, one of whose artistic precursors in Russia was *Dead Souls*.

The Moscow Art Theatre Museum preserves several pages of quotations from Gogol which Bulgakov copied, evidently in the summer of 1930 when he was pondering the role of the First Person in his adaptation. In these we immediately recognise Bulgakov's sense of kinship and continuity with Gogol, a writer misunderstood and rejected by his contemporaries. We recognise a writer prophesying his own future:

From my remote and delightful vantage point I see you plainly, Life. Out with all your shamefulness! Out with all the murderous coldness, a whole world obsessed with trivia! [. . .] Away with the desire for flattery of human pride. There is a clear path for you, poet. [Bulgakov drew a funereal black frame round this word.] You will be called base and inconsequential, and will be denied the favour of your contemporaries. They will take away your heart and soul. All the qualities of your characters they will ascribe to you, and your very laughter will rebound against you. (Tikhonravov VII, 81).

I know that the reputation I leave behind will be more fortunate than I am myself. (Letter to Zhukovsky, 1836?).

From this day forward my words are invested with a higher power.[21]

Bulgakov's literary forced labour brought him much that was acutely relevant to his personal circumstances. The major themes of his adaptation of *Dead Souls* are ultimately those of an artist appealing to those who will come after him, and of a poet whose path is laid down for him and sanctified by a higher power.

Work on the first version took up the whole of the second half of 1930. It was a congenial collaboration with Sakhnovsky who has left a detailed record of those first, happy days of their descent into the world of Gogol.

'The Theatre took on its summer emptiness, and upstairs in our offices there was suddenly any amount of space. It was quiet, there was nobody around. You could walk around thinking, with all the doors open, knowing nobody would come in, or interrupt a discussion, or telephone.'[22] In these days of long unwonted stillness a producer, a dramatist and a literary director armed themselves with Tikhonravov's tenth edition of the works of Gogol and let their imaginations roam, imagining a future production. Markov later went away, leaving Bulgakov and Sakhnovsky to continue the work together. 'I have to tell you,' Sakhnovsky goes on, 'that Gogol's epic astonished us, Bulgakov and me. For many, many months we pondered it together, each of us studying it from his own angle, Bulgakov as a writer and playwright, I rather differently. I have to tell you it astonished us, like Dante's *Inferno* or the drawings of Piranesi . . .'

The most interesting aspect to come through in Sakhnovsky's account is the sheer scale of the enterprise. 'So there we were reading aloud, and re-reading in a whisper to ourselves, that gem of world literature, the sixth chapter which Gogol himself was rather amazed by. [. . .] What strange and terrible cries accompanied the regular measure of these lines, one might almost say the stanzas of this chapter!' The producer and dramatist read their way into the verbal artistry of Gogol and discovered there the same breath-taking scale: alongside the 'Flemish precision in the descriptions of Plyushkin's room and his famous junk pile . . . alongside the gloomy lines of the digressions, there is a staggering Piranesi-like picture which seems truly to be describing the ruins of a park, the ruins of Rome: Plyushkin's orchard . . .'.

Sakhnovsky mentions that while writing *Dead Souls* in Italy Gogol was reading and re-reading Dante and Homer, 'slowly strolling along a shady avenue of trees, an avenue which led to Castel Gandolfo, the country palace of the Pope'.[23]

Bulgakov also found the notion of *Dead Souls* being written in Italy of fundamental significance and it very much coloured his future play.

> The man was writing in Italy!
> In Rome (?!). Guitars, sunshine.
> Macaroni.[24]

What struck him was not so much the guitars or the macaroni, but the fact that Gogol was writing about Russia 'from a remote and delightful vantage point'. He conceived a play which would show the kind of intellectual toil a writer would have to face in deciding to write *Dead Souls*. This was Bulgakov's original twist to the theme, and it enabled him to write not the one hundred and sixty-first adaptation, but a fully-fledged independent play.

After the play's first night Bulgakov spoke in December 1932 at a 'comradely meeting of the Art Theatre company and dramatists'. The journalist from the *Literary Gazette* reports him as stating, ' "My main aim was to create a genuinely dramatic play out of *Dead Souls*, with an underlying symbolic unity and logically developing plot intrigue, a play which would keep the audience on the edge of their seats and intensify their interest as the play unfolded." M. A. Bulgakov described his writing techniques for taking the text of the epic and turning it into a truly dramatic work rather than a dramatised narrative.'[25]

'A dramatised narrative' is how he was to designate the version which resulted after three years of work.

On 7 July 1930 Sakhnovsky reported the production plan of the play he and

Bulgakov had jointly devised to the Theatre's Artistic Council. In the compiling of this plan Bulgakov's role was not yet that of the author of a play. He was supposed to be a producer assisting the re-organising of the extracts Smolin had chosen from Gogol's epic. Sakhnovsky's exposition clearly indicates, however, that what was in train was not a shuffling about of selections but an original play with a very free and independent attitude to the original.

The flights of imagination of senior producer Sakhnovsky and assistant producer Bulgakov were subject to the aesthetic monitoring of Nemirovich-Danchenko who was in overall charge of the production at first. In late July Markov reported to him on the first stage of the work.

You have been kept informed on the progress of work on *Dead Souls* by Sakhnovsky's reports. What has been done is, in my view, very interesting. The character of the play as a comedy is also interesting, as are its wholeness and occasionally startling hyperbole. There is for all that no suggestion of any deviation into mysticism. The roles are also of interest and already taking shape very clearly.[26]

The literary director's caution and caveats are understandable if we bear in mind that in adapting classical prose for the Russian stage the co-authors were trespassing on territory over which Nemirovich-Danchenko himself had enjoyed unchallenged supremacy since the Art Theatre's production of *The Brothers Karamazov*. The authors were also mindful of the Art Theatre's fraught relationship with Gogol in the past. Five years after the first unsuccessful attempt to interpret *The Government Inspector*, Nemirovich-Danchenko had voiced doubts when sketching out a vast plan for the Art Theatre's repertoire as to whether the Theatre's aesthetics were compatible with the nature of Gogol's laughter. 'It would only be possible to adapt a few of the chapters of *Dead Souls* for the stage,' he mused. '[. . .] After *The Government Inspector* I am a bit hesitant about Gogol. The comedy acting of our actors seems to me to be too delicate, too "Turgenevan", for the madcap laughter we find in Gogol. We don't want to lapse into superficiality and caricature.' Linking the difficulties the Art Theatre found in coping with Gogol and Dostoevsky, he went on, 'But for the "cruelty" of Dostoevsky and the exaggerated vision of Gogol we are either not sufficiently robust and big-hearted or too timid, too reluctant to laugh and too given to rationalising. Dostoevsky is bad for our health, while Gogol, true Gogol, does not come to life without an immense, almost Bacchic, inner boldness and naivety.'[27]

This was an established view and those presuming to recreate on stage not just 'a few chapters' but all the main aspects of the entire epic had to tread warily. The play they were planning was much freer than the Art Theatre with its limited experience of Gogol was expecting. Sakhnovsky wrote: 'We found ourselves confronting a very complex issue over what to convey in the production. Should we aim to give a broad picture of Russian life in serene epic rhythms, to convey, what Nemirovich described as, "the tranquil flowing of the great river of Russia", or take our cue from the terrible dynamism of Chichikov, the amasser of assets who had galvanised society with his infectious plans . . .'. In another interview, also given just before the first night, Sakhnovsky again confirmed the fundamental rift between the production he and Bulgakov had conceived and the vision of the Art Theatre's founding Director. 'When the first version of the script was ready, Bulgakov, Markov and I, then later Bulgakov and I, and finally just I, spent over thirty hours in very difficult discussions with Vladimir Nemirovich-Danchenko about how the production and script should be structured'.[28]

The main disagreements may have centred on the representation of Rome and other 'liberties' in the play. Nemirovich-Danchenko was mindful of the company's earlier experiences with Gogol, and particularly anxious to avoid anything that might direct the production away from what was deeply comic towards 'superficial gimmickry'. This was his reason for categorically rejecting the co-authors' proposal that Vladimir Gribkov should play the role of Mizhuev. What proved the thorniest artistic problem, however, was the role which Bulgakov called 'The Reader' or 'The First Person'. In approaching this role Bulgakov had to bear in mind Nemirovich-Danchenko's past experience, primarily with the Tolstoy production. *Resurrection* had its first night in January 1930, very shortly before work began on *Dead Souls*.

In *Resurrection* Nemirovich plumped for introducing the author into the adaptation of his work. The part was no longer merely that of a Reader providing a commentary to particular chapters (as had been the case when the device was first tried in the production of *The Brothers Karamazov*). In *Resurrection* 'The Author', played by Kachalov, was directly involved in the play's action, articulating the characters' thoughts, agreeing or disagreeing with them. Neither was he physically separated from the performance behind a lectern, as he had been in the pre-revolutionary *Karamazovs*.

The authors of the Tolstoy production were not wholly successful in overcoming the problems associated with an adaptation. Even the most kindly disposed reviewers commented adversely on the role substituting for the voice of the author. Lunacharsky, for instance, commented that The Reader was 'simultaneously messenger and chorus' and purveyed superfluous information. The Reader 'guides the audience even when the audience feels no need at all to be guided'. Yershov ran into particular difficulties in the role of Nekhlyudov, as

he was reduced to virtually miming what The Reader was saying. To add to
Kachalov's problems he was also expected to 'progress beyond' theTolstoyan
philosophy. He disputed with Nekhlyudov and at times denounced him,
sarcastically accentuating particular aspects of Tolstoy's prose.

Bulgakov did take account of the experience of the Tolstoy production, but
developed it in an entirely original manner. His need was not so much to
'progress beyond' Gogol (although as we shall see below, there was a problem
here too). He needed to give theatrical expression to the personality of the author
which, in the prose epic, held everything together and from which everything
proceeded. On 18 November 1923 Bulgakov wrote outlining his idea to
Nemirovich-Danchenko.

Dear Vladimir Ivanovich,
   The thinking behind the role of The Reader ('The First Person in the Play') in my
adaptation of *Dead Souls* is as follows:
   Further consideration of the script of my adaptation and in particular of the Plyushkin
scene suggests that it would be possible to expand the role of the First Person in the play,
organically incorporating it in every scene, and making the First Person the play's
compère in the full sense of the word.
   This would necessitate very close and imaginative study both of the text of *Dead Souls*
and of such other secondary materials as Gogol's letters and the writings of certain of his
contemporaries.
   It is already becoming evident that the final orientation of this most demanding role can
only be established at the rehearsal stage. Work on this material must, of course, be
commenced in good time, that is immediately after you give final approval of the script of
my adaptation, which I submit herewith.
   It should be added that the play will evidently gain if the role of the Reader or the First
Person is introduced into it, but it would be essential for the Reader, after starting the play
off, to go on to compère it by involving himself with the other characters in a direct and
lively way. That is, he should be involved not only in the 'reading', but also in the action.
   Your respectful
   M. Bulgakov[29]

Eight days later Bulgakov advised Nemirovich-Danchenko that 'a start has
been made on a preliminary working up of materials for the part of the First
Person in the play. As soon as the contours of this very difficult role begin to
become clear Sakhnovsky and I will immediately be in touch with V. I. Kachalov.
   Creating this role will be an extremely difficult task.'[30]
   Kachalov's participation in the Gogol production indicated that the Nemirovich-Danchenko tradition was being continued. Kachalov was the link-man,
stressing the continuity between *Resurrection* and *Dead Souls*. The demands

Bulgakov would make on him were, however, quite different. He would be acting not a character representing the author's voice but the role of the author, Gogol himself entering into dynamic relationships with his own creations.

Bulgakov set out to give his own answer to the question of whether it was possible in principle for great prose to be given full-blooded life on the stage. It was a question Nemirovich-Danchenko had himself once confronted. After the first night of *The Brothers Karamazov* in 1910 Nemirovich had exultantly told Stanislavsky that he had breached the formerly impenetrable wall which separated the theatre from the 'greatest literary talents', and that a 'colossal bloodless revolution' had taken place. 'An immense process which has been ripening for a decade has reached its culmination.' The potential of the device of the Reader was seen not merely as a new technique for the adapting of prose, but as heralding the collapse of all the conventions of the old theatre. In the face of these new tasks even Chekhov now seemed out of date. A new theatre would be built which would freely avail itself of world literature, not excluding even the Bible.[31]

Nemirovich-Danchenko's optimism proved ill-founded. In the twenty years since the first night of *The Brothers Karamazov* no such fundamental change as he dreamed of had come about in the adapting of great prose for the stage of the Art Theatre or of other theatres. Stage adaptations employing Readers and Compères became commonplace. There was no real progress, however. The theatre was unable to find a dramatic equivalent to the image, intonation, and voice of the narrator which are basic to the nature of the narrative genres.

It was just this knotty problem that Bulgakov had decided to attack, developing the idea Nemirovich-Danchenko had sown in a daring and unexpected way.

The implementation of Bulgakov's solution involved sketching a role for the First Person no less ambitious than if he were the main hero of the play. The First Person had moments of crisis and bathos. He commented on events, introduced them, entered into dialogue with the characters, registered astonishment at their actions and articulated the thoughts darting through their minds. He imparted a particular charge of emotion and meaning to the events on the stage which aimed in some measure to convey the character and structure of Gogol's prose.

In some scenes Bulgakov barely sketched in the varied possibilities for the lively and ingenious involvement of the First Person in the play as a character with his own biography and intense, highly dramatic emotional life. In other scenes he demonstrated it in detail. The First Person was to have his own part of the stage, a corner of Gogol's study in Italy, and this was worked into the complex composition of the scenes in Russia. As Sakhnovsky later related, a stone portal in the style of Piranesi would frame the inner space of the stage, where dim, sepia-tinted vistas would open before the audience, glimpsed 'as if from a veranda, an arbour, or a turn in Plyushkin's orchard, somewhere beyond the stakes and boards of a fence'.

Retaining a hint of Italy in the stage design, Sakhnovsky and Bulgakov envisaged the Reader making his first entrance on to the steps at the sides of the portal against a background of 'a part of the Roman aqueduct or the walls of Sallust's gardens'. He would walk on in 'the kind of suit Russians were wearing in Italy in the 1830s. [. . .] The Reader's dress and general appearance were to suggest a restless, touring personage, someone who had just stepped down from a stage-coach and would in a moment be climbing into a britzka or a post-coach to continue his journey. He was to sit himself on the pedestal of a colossal Piranesi urn many times the height of a man, set down his greatcoat, gloves and hat or top hat, and relate Gogol's thoughts about life which are scattered in such profusion through his poetic digressions, letters, and drafts. The Reader would come occasionally into the rooms, and might sit in Plyushkin's orchard before its owner came, and before the arrival of Chichikov. He could even make his exit through the doors of these extremely realistic and authentic dwellings of the landowners and bureaucrats of Gogol's Russia.'[32]

Bulgakov managed only to sketch in the role which the First Person was to play. This was to be established in detail during rehearsal. Alas, the rehearsals with Kachalov were not a success. Stanislavsky was finally able to involve himself, but to the end remained indifferent to the concept of the First Person. He had his own plans for the production which crystallised only as the new rules of life in the 1930s became clearer. Stanislavsky paid at least as much attention to these as to Gogol and his theatrical translator.

The history of the relationship between Stanislavsky and Bulgakov as the production of *Dead Souls* was being worked on is detailed in the scholarly works of Konstantin Rudnitsky and Alexander Matskin, to which we refer the reader able to read Russian.[33] Chief among the many disagreements which arose was Stanislavsky's fear that the First Person might become irksomely didactic. He reasoned, 'You have just been watching something on stage. You have been laughing at it, and suddenly this gentleman comes out and says, "It's not that simple. You have overlooked this and that."

The audience ends up watching the play and thinking all the time, "That man's going to come out again in a minute."'[34]

Matskin considers other purely aesthetic disagreements. Many were against the idea of staging *Dead Souls* at all, seeing it as a politically alien work. Among the insistent suggestions of members of the Theatre's Council for Political and

Artistic Affairs were that Bulgakov should 'show the decaying of the society of that time' and 'link it with the subsequent decaying of the capitalist order (through the role of the First Person)'. In order to make Gogol more relevant it was suggested also that the role of the First Person should be written 'specially to order (not using Gogol's text)'. In these circumstances Bulgakov and Sakhnovsky faced an uphill struggle to gain acceptance for the role of the First Person as they envisaged it.[35]

The removal of the First Person from the play was a major defeat for Bulgakov. Others followed. The play gradually regressed towards an 'ordinary adaptation', which was what Bulgakov had reacted against at the outset. The prospects for giving prose a new life on the stage sickened and died just as they seemed most promising.

When Bulgakov delivered his script to the Art Theatre's directors for their approval, it was a play whose central role had not yet settled into place or been fully consolidated, a play which contained, as yet unknown to its author, the seeds of the great works he was yet to write, a work of forced labour which had become a labour of love. Despite the diplomatic attempts by Markov and Sakhnovsky to pave the way for it, despite Bulgakov's accompanying cautious letter of explanation, the play caused an uproar. Not only did it break the current conventions of stage adaptation, it also breached the bounds of propriety as far as what was then considered permissible in the interpretation of Gogol's text and the understanding of Gogol himself. The controversy was over whether a play by Bulgakov based on this classic of Russian literature had a right to exist. In May 1932 Bulgakov looked back in his letter to Popov at the alarums of autumn 1930 in an abstract, almost scholarly mood. Popov was a literary scholar and philosopher. He had been astonished by the unheard-of liberties Bulgakov had taken with Gogol's text. 'How could you do it? Couldn't you just have cut it?' Bulgakov explained firmly, 'That, my dear Pavel, is exactly what I did do. It's all I did! I dismantled the entire epic stone by stone. I cut it into tiny pieces.'[36] Bulgakov went on to relate his credo as a dramatist, before concluding:

As you see, this is not the one hundred and sixty-first stage adaptation of *Dead Souls*. Indeed, it is not an adaptation at all, but something quite different . . .

Nemirovich was outraged. There was a great battle, but for all that the play was put in rehearsal in its existent form. It has now been in rehearsal for some two years!

. . . Well now, have they been able to fulfil the plan? You need have no fear, my friend. They have not. And why not? Because, to my horror, Stanislavsky has been ill all winter and unable to work in the Theatre. (Nemirovich is abroad again.)

God only knows what is on the stage at present. The only hope is that Stanislavsky will be up in May and able to look in on the stage. When will *Dead Souls* be performed? My guess is, never. Certainly if performed in its present state it will be a major flop for the Principal Stage.

So what is the problem? The problem is that in order to stage Gogol's captivating phantasmagorias you need to have talented directors in your theatre.

That, my dear sir, is the rub.

But then again, who cares? Who cares who cares?[37]

Bulgakov was tired. He had been reduced to dispirited indifference by two years' work in which he had felt himself less and less a playwright, and more and more an assistant producer of the Moscow Art Theatre.

'Crosses, Crows and Fields: the Russia of Nicholas I'

When first put on, *Dead Souls* received an almost unanimously negative press, yet the play went on to attain a special significance with the passage of time and as the new status of the Art Theatre became generally accepted. Scholars of recent years have been obliged to carry out careful restoration work in order to understand the real place of the production in the history of the Art Theatre, and also in the literary career of Bulgakov who had devoted several years of his life to it.

Vasily Toporkov's memoir-based *Stanislavsky Rehearses*, published in the early 1950s, first established the tradition of virtually writing out the contribution of Sakhnovsky and Bulgakov, and representing the intervention of Stanislavsky in rehearsals of the play in mythical terms. These memoirs are rich in factual observations, but they also propound the view that the production was created in a period 'fraught with special circumstances'. These special circumstances, which required neutralisation by the wonder-working Stanislavsky, were, Toporkov informs us, the predominance of formalistic tendencies in the world surrounding the Art Theatre and also degenerate tendencies among certain directors which expressed themselves in 'the fashionable word "grotesque".' Toporkov did not at that time name the offending directors, although it was obvious that he was referring to Meyerhold and in particular to his production of *The Government Inspector*.

Stanislavsky did not see Meyerhold's production of *The Government Inspector*. Sakhnovsky did, and what is more he made some rather interesting notes about it which show where several of his ideas for the Art Theatre production came from. His Piranesi theme and indeed his stage treatment of Rome in general was largely suggested by Meyerhold's production.

Every episode was structured in such a way that a kind of uncanopied bier advanced out of the darkness towards the audience. Its slow emergence with a group of immobile actors from gradually parting wings in time to the blowing of an ominous, plaintive trumpet, synchronised with coloured spotlights pouring out their rays like the reflections of dying suns, built up a funereal sense of a burial.

The sense was much what you experience when you look at a Piranesi engraving: the ruins of the Colosseum, the Arch of Constantine, or the Flavian Amphitheatre, the funerary monuments of the splendour of Rome; a background now for the extravagant attire of the Renaissance, a sumptuous gold carriage passing by ruins beside gnarled trees and cypresses.

Sakhnovsky was very struck by the sense in Meyerhold's production 'of delirium, the anarchic chaos of life, desperation that reality should be as it is'.[38]

Bulgakov had a different sense of the Roman dimension. 'Guitars, sunshine, and macaroni', a city where everyone is that much nearer the deity and finally, completely suffusing the First Person's monologue in Rome, a special kind of Italian light that contrasted and jarred with the local colour of the scenes set in Russia. As if he were saying, 'Since Gogol is viewing them from his remote and delightful vantage point, so shall we!'[39] For all that, Bulgakov's attitude towards Gogol's Russia was in some ways not so far removed from the impressions Meyerhold's spectacular made on Sakhnovsky. 'The Russia of Nicholas I. "Everything in you blank and bleak and flat; your squat towns stick up like dots or tiny signs barely noticeable amid the plains . . . A plaintive song rolling from sea to sea . . ." Crosses, crows and fields: the Russia of Nicholas I.'[40]

The evidence of several reminiscences suggests that Bulgakov was not enthused by Meyerhold's production. Be that as it may, the Art Theatre was similarly aspiring to convey the whole of Gogol, if in a different perspective from that of Meyerhold. This was to be an Art Theatre production without any 'left-wing deviations', with a properly Art Theatre approach to the embodiment of a dualistic world at once fantastic and spectral and yet infinitely realistic. Sakhnovsky wrote very eloquently about the extraordinary way in which Gogol viewed life, probably taking his cue from Vasily Rozanov. That vision only strengthened Bulgakov's resolve to convey not a 'dance of the dead', but the breathing of real, living people, the breathing of the infinitely alive and melancholy stuff of Russian life. To all intents and purposes he was further developing the ideas the Art Theatre had not taken to in *Flight*, only this time using classical material. The poetics he devised for Gogol's 'captivating phantasmagorias' stamped the first version of the adaptation as part and parcel of his corpus of writing.

In autumn 1930 they were joined by the stage designer Vladimir Dmitriev who at one time had begun working with Meyerhold on *The Government Inspector*, was one of his correspondents, and was full of Meyerholdian ideas on how to stage Gogol. He did not leave all of these behind when he began his collaboration with the Art Theatre. His first idea was to go for a grotesque reproduction of the material environment of the period.

Out of all this material Dmitriev devised monstrous pieces of eccentrically constructed furniture [. . .] Each piece had, as it were, its own highly unprepossessing physiognomy, but when they were set out on stage they gave no sense of backwoods mustiness and provincial obscurity. They implied all Russia was formal and aestheticist, and kept a safe distance from the sour, dank, pit-like slums which were typically found on the estates of the ruling classes or in provincial towns.[41]

Sakhnovsky concludes with a comment which clearly indicates the direction in which Dmitriev's mind, influenced by Meyerhold, was moving.

Despite a certain St Petersburg glossiness and the abstract quality of the decor, which was the invariable hallmark of Dmitriev's designs, he did find an overall key for the production which communicated an individual viewpoint on Gogol's Russia. His design was exaggerated and stylised; there was something spooky about it, and it conveyed a sense of the deadening uniformity and regimentation of Nicholas I's Russia.[42]

In his use of the stage space Dmitriev sought also to convey the phantasmagorical element in Gogol.

The dull, grimy colours of Chichikov's grubby room with its peeling wallpaper and the room where the interrogation took place matched the colour and character of the furniture. Both rooms were irregularly shaped and skewed, and the outline of their walls was indistinct. They were suggestive of Hoffmann.[43]

Sakhnovsky's last comment is very much to the point. It was precisely this interpretation of Gogol that Stanislavsky took issue with. In November 1932, shortly before the first night, he was to put his views on this point very bluntly in a talk to the actors.

Gogol is first and foremost a Russian writer. Ostrovsky is a direct successor of Gogol. Nowadays some people like to see Gogol as a Hoffmann. They try to turn him into a German Gogol. But in Gogol evil has a specifically Gogolian character. [. . .] We are going to approach Gogol our way. Meyerhold's approach was through the stage props. We shall approach him through the actor.[44]

In the transcript of the discussion of the dress rehearsal this very fundamental attitude is elaborated on. 'There is such a thing as Russian evil, boorish, crafty, talented, vile. Do you have it in you? And interesting, enchanting, repulsive, and irresistible'.[45] This was the plane on which Stanislavsky pitched the 'through line of the action' of his new adaptation, which superseded Bulgakov's discredited play. The through line consisted of showing how Chichikov's virulent 'pox-idea' spread through Russia, producing a corresponding reaction in each person it came in contact with, and poisoning with its venom those who fell under the wheels of Chichikov's troika.

Stanislavsky did not hit on this serious and profound interpretation straight away. He tried at first to come to an accommodation with the work already put in by Sakhnovsky, Bulgakov and Dmitriev. He tried rehearsing with Kachalov, and devising a new stage treatment with Dmitriev. New sets for the play were not only sketched but actually made in the workshops in the style of a half-finished picture. It was only in the autumn of 1931 that these amazing sets were abandoned, with their sense of place and feeling for the great spaces and melancholy and undisguised yearning of Gogol's Russia. Victor Simov was invited shortly afterwards to design the production, and implemented Stanislavsky's new emphasis: acting positions were spotlighted and divided off by flounced blinds which, needless to say, gave no hint of Gogolian vastness or Russia.

The adaptation of *Dead Souls* for the stage of the Art Theatre had been envisaged as a wholly unique production conveying the ambitiousness and spirit of Gogol's epic in a new play utilising innovative concepts of stage design. Simov, whom Sakhnovsky even forgot to mention in his notes, needed to be brought in when Stanislavsky moved the production in a wholly unexpected direction. Essentially Stanislavsky, who had his own ideas about Gogol and was primarily interested in perfecting his Method, decided to reorientate the production exclusively on the art of the actor. 'My ideal,' he announced, 'is two chairs and a table.'[46] He went on to be more outspokenly negative about Dmitriev's designs in the first phase, which had had the support of Sakhnovsky and Bulgakov.

Dead Souls turns the Russian soul inside out, and you cannot convey that with furniture. [. . .] Give us colours, give us painting. All these constructions are seen nowadays as risible and pathetic. They have broken with the times we live in and the demands of the public. We're sick and tired of stage constructions.[47]

In the next phase of work Stanislavsky rejected even Dmitriev's painted flats, and moved the stage design towards bald, uncompromising asceticism. The actors were to 'turn the Russian soul inside out' in cameo duets, to which the whole play was ultimately reduced. Stanislavsky resolutely excised all trace of the earlier production with its 'captivating phantasmagorias' and grotesquerie.

We ought not to see this turn of events as evidence of capriciousness on Stanislavsky's part. It was a legitimate expression of the headstrong wilfulness of a genius who had total faith in his own artistic intuition. Bulgakov's play and the work Sakhnovsky had done were suddenly surplus to requirements.

Of course the abrupt change of direction could also be put down to Sakhnovsky's professional incompetence. The production he imagined and decribed in his book *A Producer's Job* is remarkable as literature. But Vasily Sakhnovsky failed to translate his ideas into acting. 'So what is the problem? The problem is that in order to stage Gogol's captivating phantasmagorias you need to have talented directors in your theatre.'[48] Bulgakov's caustic comment was targeted straight at his highly intelligent co-author.

Sakhnovsky was a neophyte of the Art Theatre school. He beavered away with an enthusiasm his actors found dismaying, implementing the rules of the Method when its inventor was already moving on to explore new aspects of the actor's creativity. Toporkov recalls in his book how Sakhnovsky attempted to initiate the actors into the world of Gogol.

We went to the museum to look at various portraits of Gogol. We studied his works, and his letters, and his biography. Sakhnovsky even advised me on one occasion to take a walk in a graveyard. That was to bring home the reality of the fact that we were trading in the dead.[49]

With an actor's contempt for cerebral literary talk, Toporkov summarised the results of his work under Sakhnovsky.

No matter how many graveyards, museums and art galleries we walked around, no matter how many interesting talks we had, it was all too abstract. It just filled our heads with useless clutter and distracted us from our practical work.[50]

Toporkov's book reflects the balance of forces in the Art Theatre in the late 1940s when Sakhnovsky, like Sudakov, was seen as peripheral to the Theatre's history, but it would be difficult to overstate his importance in the Art Theatre in the 1930s. If he was probably not up to actually realising the Gogol production on the level he and Bulgakov aspired to, his contribution in the first stage of the work was exceptional. Stanislavsky succeeded in averting a 'major flop on the Principal Stage' by setting out to create a completely new production with aims not a whit less individual than those of his predecessors, even though what those aims were was not clear to him at the outset.

In April 1932 Stanislavsky told his actors he had had little idea of the difficulties ahead when he started on the Gogol production. 'I had no idea this production would prove a course of instruction even for an old man like myself.' The need for a sharp change of direction in both the interpretation and structuring of the play was also due to the new expectations of the Art Theatre, which now had a special status to justify. Stanislavsky indicated as much in replying to criticism at a 'production and output meeting' at the Theatre to the effect that those involved with the play were guilty of outrageous delays in getting it into performance and of destroying two sets of scenery prepared by Dmitriev. Stanislavsky commented in reply, 'Work on the play began to a plan and with decor then fashionable but now wholly unacceptable.'

Between 'then' and 'now' a mere year and a half had passed, but for Stanislavsky this interval was a historic divide. Changes in the times led to changes in taste. In the same document Stanislavsky comments on the way in which art had evolved. '. . . What was fashionable a year ago is now prized no more than a pair of worn out slippers. A period of renaissance is evidently beginning for genuine art. We must support that in every way we can, and warmly welcome it.'

The final stages of work on *Dead Souls* coincided with the liquidation of RAPP. The theatre was entering a period of renaissance supported by state intervention. The period opened like a new play with new tasks to perform and new rules to play by. Meyerhold responded with his production of *The Lady with the Camellias*. ('It is curious,' Olga Bokshanskaya reported to Nemirovich-Danchenko, 'that Meyerhold has produced *The Lady with the Camellias* in an ultra-realistic manner verging on naturalism.'[51]) The Vakhtangov actors, on the other hand, failed to recognise that times had changed, and caused a major uproar when they produced *Hamlet* in a grotesque vein. Tairov's response was *An Optimistic Tragedy* and Stanislavsky's was *Dead Souls*. The change of theatrical scenery transparently corresponded to a change of political scenery.

Stanislavsky was not, if the truth be known, in a completely fit state to return to active work on the Gogol production. The rehearsals were fraught with difficulties and exhausting even in purely physical terms. *Soviet Art*, reporting the opening of the Art Theatre's 1931 season, noted, 'Stanislavsky gave no speech in reply as his doctors are still not allowing him to get excited.'[52] Konstantin Rudnitsky has calculated that a total of roughly one year was spent rehearsing at his residence at Leontiev Lane, and less than a month on the stage in the Art Theatre.[53] This could not but reflect on Stanislavsky's overall approach to producing the adaptation, which tended increasingly to virtuoso duets between Chichikov and the landowners. Progressively less emphasis was put on blocking out the stage space or devising complex *mise-en-scène*.

Leontiev Lane did indeed gradually turn into a course of instruction, and into Stanislavsky's private theatre. He experimented unrestrainedly, driving to desperation actors who felt they already had the whole thing off pat. He began by treating them for 'dislocated joints'. In his determination to have the actor exist authentically in the role, Stanislavsky was quite capable of going over a single phrase, which the actor regarded as a throw-away line, for two or three hours. He began with engendering the 'little truth', the foundation, heedless of deadlines or the need to get the production ready. He was pursuing perfection with the fanatical obstinacy of a musician with perfect pitch. Stanislavsky's rehearsals at Leontiev Lane became an immensely demanding school for the production's actors. At certain times Bulgakov too became a wildly enthusiastic pupil who, as we already know from his New Year letter to Stanislavsky, began to believe again in 'theatre magic'. It was, however, now that the seeds were sown of the catastrophe of several years later when the rituals of instruction were to take precedence over practical results. The performance would cease to be Stanislavsky's highest priority, the ultimate justification of theatre. The process was to take priority over the result.

Stanislavsky was putting the finishing touches to his Method, of which the Actor was the be all and end all. He was supremely conscious of his duty to the future. Actors lived, then as now, for the moment, impatient for the first night, impatient to act, impatient for applause. The 'course of instruction' was a distraction.

Mikhail Yanshin was involved in the rehearsals both of *Dead Souls* and *Molière*. Many years later he was to recall that many actors were unenthusiastic about Stanislavsky's perfectionism. 'Rehearsing with Stanislavsky was difficult, exhausting, sometimes agonising for an actor . . . We tried to avoid Stanislavsky's rehearsals and having to work with him. Nowadays it is considered rather improper to remember such things, but that is the truth of the matter.'[54] Toporkov gives a striking illustration of this during work in the Studio on *Tartuffe* in the last year of Stanislavsky's life. The actors made a fair stab at acting Molière's scene, but they were not doing it in accordance with the Method of Physical Actions which Stanislavsky was now professing. At the end of the rehearsal 'Stanislavsky said sadly:

Oh well, I suppose the scene is ready. It will do for acting at the Moscow Art Theatre. But you could perfectly well have acted it this way without me. This is not what I brought you all together for. You are repeating things you mastered long ago, when you should be moving forward. I am offering you a Method to enable you to do this. I wanted to make it easier for you to achieve, but you are just digging your heels in and want to settle for what you already know. Oh well, off you go to the Art Theatre. They'll have the play ready for performance in no time.[55]

The seeds of conflict were already there in the rehearsals of *Dead Souls*. Stanislavsky was out for a purely acting achievement, unencumbered by 'production values'. He would not even allow the actors to gesture because he believed that would keep them from searching for inner adaptation. He wanted them to convey Gogol with their 'verbal vision' (and only their verbal vision). 'We don't need staging. Plyushkin and Chichikov are sitting talking, and all that interests me is the light in their eyes.'[56] They were to incarnate the spirit of Gogol in total immobility, devoid of any producer's gimmicks which might upstage the Actor. It was tantamount to demanding that his actors should all be geniuses.

Toporkov recalls an episode at the rehearsals of *Dead Souls* which brings out very sharply how far Stanislavsky's demands on the actors were diverging from what would customarily have been regarded as perfectly satisfactory. Toporkov was rehearsing Chichikov's monologue, which begins with the sentence, 'Oh, I really am Akim the Fool'. Running through the monologue, the experienced actor 'glanced victoriously at Konstantin Sergeevich'.

'Uh-uh. You're not seeing it at all, my dear . . .'
    '???'
'You are saying the words . . . You see the letters that make them up. You see them written in the script. But you do not see what was seen behind them by . . .'
He meant Chichikov, but in his absent-minded way said, 'Chatsky' by mistake. I was completely fazed.
'I don't understand.'
'Well, for example, when you say, "But what if they seize me, and give me a public flogging, and send me off to Siberia . . ." You have to feel that for (this time he called Chichikov 'Khlestakov') . . . you picture behind these words the punishment, the fetters, the convoy, the rigours of Siberia . . . That's what's really matters. Now, start again.'
'Oh, I really am Akim the Fool . . .'
'You are not seeing it . . . and just saying the words. First build up the visions. See yourself as Akim the Fool, then curse yourself for being such a fool. Now, what is Akim the Fool? How do you see him? Right, carry on . . .'
'Oh, I . . .'
'Terrible! . . . Oh, dear. Turning up the tension straight away. Trying to make yourself agitated from the outside in, trying to stimulate the nervous tension and lose yourself in

the fog when you should simply be concentrating, seeing clearly what you are doing wrong, and well and truly cursing yourself. That's all we need. Now, again!'

'Oh! . . .'

'Why "Oh?" Not "Oh", but "Oh, I really am Akim the Fool". Which word gets the stress? If you stress it wrongly you are not seeing what you are saying.'

And once again we face the only too familiar rehearsal crisis.[57]

Toporkov recalls all this like a conscientious committee secretary, but without any sense of how dramatic the event was which he was describing. Bulgakov also witnessed rehearsal crises, but he saw another side. The mocking, gimlet-sharp eye of the future author of *Black Snow* saw in these classroom exercises 'a penchant for ritual which he found alien and unpleasant; a grand old man playing charades, a shamanistic zaniness'. Alexander Matskin, to whom this observation belongs, raises the very relevant question of whether Bulgakov fully understood 'what made Stanislavsky tick'.[58] The question might no less pertinently be asked whether Stanislavsky understood what made a writer tick who had just spent three years working on Gogol's play, and had been waiting roughly the same amount of time to start work on his play about Molière. Be that as it may, these questions did not arise while they were working on *Dead Souls*, and relations between Bulgakov and Stanislavsky were cloudless. Bulgakov regarded Stanislavsky's prolonged illness in the winter of 1931–2 as a disaster.

Because of that illness Stanislavsky was unable to involve himself with the Gogol production for a long time. Sakhnovsky, Telesheva and Bulgakov continued to rehearse it to the plans he had drawn up, but were unable to carry it off. The work wore everybody down and by spring 1932 the production had run into the sand. Obliged to choose between an actor's or a director's production, Stanislavsky had come down in favour of the actor, but this did ultimately demand the intervention of an active and strong-willed director before the play could be ready for performance.

The run-through was a depressing experience. The typescript of Sakhnovsky's book gives the comments of various participants in the subsequent discussion. They are given here, augmented with material from the transcript of the discussion which is in the Art Theatre Museum.

Pavel Markov said, 'The production is overloaded with realistic detail. We need boldness; we need the pace of an incredible happening. The play's dynamism is lost in the long, drawn-out acting of some of the scenes. [. . .] A production depicting Gogol's Russia should convey a sense of how terrible and sad our life is. The production needs to be properly planned.'

Olga Knipper said, 'Gogol is passion, pathos, temperament, taunting. Some of the scenes are cluttered with unnecessary details of everyday life. It is not scathing enough . . .'

Boris Mordvinov said, 'There is no underlying idea to the production. There are remarkable mosaic tesserae, but without an overall picture . . .'

Nina Litovtseva said, 'I can't accept the production without the Reader. We should just glimpse the figures of the epic. The main thing is Gogol, and the Reader who stands for him. There should be a mad rhythm with everything flashing past the audience . . .'

Add to this Boris Livanov's complaint that 'Captain Kopeykin's story is boring'; Leonid Leonidov's comment that 'The rhythm is terrible. We get not a pause but a gap'; and Nikolai Gorchakov's contribution that 'We need a completely different plan for the production: we need a touch of Hoffman and we need the Reader.' The situation becomes abundantly clear.[59]

Bulgakov took no active part in the discussions, but undoubtedly found this conclusion to his many years of work very painful.

In effect the Art Theatre company neither understood nor accepted what he had done. The more thoughtful and serious actors even tried to view the *Dead Souls* dress rehearsal in the more general context of the Art Theatre's relationship with Gogol. In Ivan Kudryavtsev's diary we read that it had been a mistake to confine the adaptation to the first volume of the epic, which contains only 'negative satire and derision'.

And how are you supposed to act that? What is there for the characters to aspire to? Non-theatre people may say Plyushkin aspires to hold on to his wealth and so on, but there is nothing of that actually in the play. It is all off stage. On stage Chichikov will just keep visiting endless characters, most of them miserly, and bore the pants off the audience with his 'Sell me your dead souls' line. This is deeply untheatrical, and the Art Theatre should not put it on.[60]

'Twas ever so in the theatre. Even the most keen-eyed people fail to see the good seed sprouting.

For all that Stanislavsky had faith in the seed he had sown.

In the autumn he gave those involved a final talk before the preview, repeatedly urging them to bear in mind the performance's 'super-objective'. At the preview itself he became over-excited and went home before the final curtain. *Dead Souls* was performed in the state it had reached by December 1932. As fully aware as anyone of the production's shortcomings, Stanislavsky was sure of one thing only: the truth he had sown would spring up in the actors given time. He even hazarded a guess that it would be ten or twenty years before people would understand Gogol. The limited span of a human life did not perturb him in the least.

Stanislavsky has been proved right. His production has survived the decades. The acting duets of Vasily Toporkov and Leonid Leonidov, Ivan Moskvin, Mikhail Kedrov, Anastasia Zueva and Mikhail Tarkhanov went on to become legendary paradigms. There is no call to revise that legend.

Alas, the Gogol Bulgakov had anticipated when he wrote his admiring letter to Stanislavsky at New Year 1932, the Gogol who was to be brought into being in the first scenes of the performance in laughter and to leave in the last covered in the ashes of deep meditation, that Gogol never visited the stage of the Art Theatre. The poignant lyricism of *Dead Souls*, the 'crosses, crows and fields', the vast expanses of Russia which were to have been embodied in Bulgakov's play were dropped from the production. They were left behind in Dmitriev's discarded designs and Bulgakov's drafts; in the ethereally wonderful rehearsals at Leontiev Lane; in a word, in a different theatrical era.

The cultural memory remembers what was not embodied and realised no less vividly than what was. The soil of the Art Theatre on which Bulgakov cast his seed was not stony ground. A few decades would pass and the idea of bringing prose to life on the stage would be realised in several new ways, including those intuited by Bulgakov. His bold 'Cut! Only cut!' would shape the techniques of associative montage and direct transfer of prose to the stage, obviating the need for the writing of a stage adaptation, which most often killed the literature stone dead. It would no longer be considered necessary to chastely conceal the tensions and conflicts between literature and the theatre under the guise of a 'normal' play. Producers would begin to emphasise the great text behind their production, openly accompanying the transplanted prose with the author's comments and great lumps of authentic prosaic earth. Producers would make use of earlier techniques even as they created new expressive means. They would learn a special stage language to enable them to dispense with the compromising and compromised Compères and Readers and First Persons. The theatre's answer to the prose writer's voice and authorship of his material would be the authorship of a fully original theatre performance. The new First Person would be the director of the performance, creating an integrated world of stagecraft and conducting a dialogue with the writer in the language of the stage. Alongside 'dramatic' theatre a 'theatre of prose' would appear to continue the bloodless revolution begun by the Art Theatre. Bulgakov's ideas, ahead of their time, would come into their own as new forms for staging the prose of Tolstoy, Dostoevsky, Saltykov-Shchedrin and the best contemporary writers, including Bulgakov himself.

All this, however, was far in the future, and by that time the link with the events in the Art Theatre in 1930–32 would have been forgotten.

If we return to the period around the first night of *Dead Souls*, we find the critics making their own deeply offensive contribution to the mixed feelings Gogol's 'translator' was experiencing. Vladimir Yermilov was trying to enlist Gogol in the struggle against the kulaks and the necessity of 'tearing off the enemy's masks'. He accused the Theatre of having failed to perform this fundamental and socially necessary operation. He found the production wholly lacking in social ideas 'because it is impossible to classify as an idea the pathetic little thought that Chichikov too is human! (and this is exactly what Bulgakov's play is about)'.[61] Alexander Orlinsky demanded to know what had happened to Captain Kopeykin 'because of whom Gogol was tormented by the Tsarist censorship'. Bulgakov's indefatigable opponent almost managed to discover just the same absence of class background in *Dead Souls* as he had detected in *The Days of the Turbins*. If the latter had lacked servants and batmen, the new play proffered only 'two or three lightning glimpses of house-serfs. That is all that remains of that "Russia".[62]

The most clearly thought out opposition to the Art Theatre's work came, however, from the respected writer Andrey Bely. His article 'Getting Gogol Wrong' trenchantly attacked both Stanislavsky's production and Bulgakov's play. Bely went so far as to deny either of them even an elementary understanding of the text. 'The theatre has latched on to the anecdotal chronology of events in *Dead Souls*, slavishly putting everything in consecutive order while quite overlooking the most important thing, the living idea behind the work.' 'It is unimaginable that anyone should stage a production of Gogol's *Dead Souls* which leaves out Chichikov's awe-inspiring travelling troyka, which fails to convey the sense of incurable melancholy with which Gogol viewed the limitless expanses of the Russia of his day. And what has happened to all Gogol's lyrical digressions?' Bely accused the devisers of the play of 'a deficient understanding of the principal character' which wrong-footed the guiltless performer of the role. Defending *Dead Souls* against the philistine, Bely went on as a connoisseur of the work to demand no less heatedly of the 'author of the script' what had become of Captain Kopeykin, 'that astonishingly significant social figure'. The incensed poet surmised that the root of the problem was that the Art Theatre had failed to hold a seminar for the 'careful, scrupulous study of Gogol's text'![63]

Such were the critics' reactions. Reactions within the Theatre were little better. Olga Bokshanskaya, who was a sounding-box for part at least of the company, reported on 28 November 1932 to Nemirovich-Danchenko, 'The play written by Bulgakov is not what is being performed. Instead there is a succession of breath-takingly good portraits.' A month after the first night when she had had time to formulate a mature judgement the secretary grumbled to her boss, 'It is all really rather dull. [. . .] Poor Sakhnovsky! I pity him from the bottom of my heart.'[64]

Returning from Italy in early March 1933, Nemirovich-Danchenko said in an interview, 'The Art Theatre saw *Dead Souls* as an epic by Gogol, not as a comedy, and this required lengthy, emotion-charged speeches for Kachalov. Unfortunately, things did not work out that way; whether because it was impossible or because the idea did not catch on I do not know.'[65]

'Poor Sakhnovsky' did his best to defend himself and sulked. He began writing *A Producer's Notes*, a kind of 'white book' of self-justification. The actors got involved in arguments with the critics, reminding them of the production history and pointing out that there had at one time been a Reader, and lyrical digressions, and Captain Kopeykin.

Stanislavsky kept mum, considering it beneath his dignity to answer people who 'had lost the ability to watch good acting' and were able only to recognise production gimmicks. Bulgakov too remained tight-lipped, although there was doubtless a good deal he, no less than Stanislavsky, could have said.

In summer 1933 Stanislavsky went abroad for prolonged medical treatment. He was to meet up with Bulgakov again only a year and a half later, after a decidedly eventful period in the life of the Author of the Art Theatre. It took in renewed rehearsals of *Flight*, the beginning of rehearsals for *Molière* and work on *The Pickwick Papers*. Bulgakov was simultaneously writing his biographical novella about Molière, turning over in his mind the idea of writing a play about Pushkin, and finishing work on *Adam and Eve*. All of it rush jobs, all at the same time, all of it raising new hopes.

Neither did Gogol leave Bulgakov in peace. Ivan Pyriev, a film director, commissioned Bulgakov to write a screenplay of *Dead Souls*, and he began a 'romance with the cinema' entirely in the spirit of his romance with the theatre. Here again we encounter Rome, Captain Kopeykin, and the vastness of Russia. And again there were endless reworkings and comments which had to be taken into account.

Everything I was most fond of has been totally rooted out: the scene with the Suvorov soldiers in the middle of the Nozdryov scene; the great free-standing ballad of Captain Kopeykin; the requiem on Sobakevich's estate; and most important of all, Rome with the silhouette on the balcony. I shall be able to save only Kopeykin, and that only after severely curtailing him. But, Lord! How sorry I am to lose Rome! (From a letter to Pavel Popov)[66]

The screenplay never made it into production. Pyriev began filming *The Party Card*, and Bulgakov began to feel like Captain Kopeykin himself. It became his nickname at home, painfully allusive. 'Lyusya [Yelena] has nicknamed me Captain Kopeykin,' he wrote to his friend. 'Savour it. I think it is first class.'[67]

Bulgakov was also invited to contribute to the adaptation of *The Government Inspector* for the cinema, and did so. When it became obvious there was no chance the project would come to fruition he presented Mikhail Karostin, the producer, with 'a souvenir of our shared torments', a set of the journal *Iskra* for 1861 inscribed, 'Stay just as you are, and if people present piggish snouts to you instead of faces, repeat firmly after Gogol, "I see piggish snouts!" '[68]

In the games and New Year jokes of the Bulgakov household there are echoes of Gogolian plots which seemed to inhabit the very air. Here is Yelena's diary description of New Year's Eve, 1934:

We had a Christmas tree. . . . Misha played a march and the children came rushing into the room. [. . .] Next on the programme was a play. Misha had written a script after *Dead Souls*, two scenes, one at Sobakevich's, the other at Sergey Shilovsky's [Yelena's son]. I was Chichikov, Misha was Sobakevich. Then I was Zhenya [Yelena's second son] and Misha was Sergey.[69]

For several years work on Gogol shadowed Bulgakov's work on his own projects. 'I am writing *Dead Souls* for the screen and bringing back a finished piece with me. Then I shall have all the fuss with *Bliss*. Lord, what a lot of work. But my Margarita is bubbling away in my head, and the cat, and the flying . . .'.[70] The scholars have established that 1934, the year Bulgakov wrote this letter, saw the appearance of a new character in his novel. Marietta Chudakova tells us, 'In the supplementary notebook to the novel begun on 30 October 1934 a strangely familiar hero made his appearance: into Ivanushka's room in the mental hospital from the balcony came "a person some thirty-five years old, thin, clean shaven, blond, *with a mop of hair hanging over his face and a sharp (beak-like) nose and walking on tip-toes*".'[71]

When a solution becomes saturated crystals are precipitated in it. Bulgakov had spent years in Gogol's world. He was saturated with Gogol, and the result was this large and unexpected 'crystal' in his imagination. The Master came into being at the point where Bulgakov's own destiny crossed with that of the man with the 'sharp (beak-like) nose'. Bulgakov just could not get the theme of Rome into any of the writing he was professionally obliged to undertake, until it broke through into his own work, one writer's life echoing in another's. The 'iron greatcoat' of the author of *Dead Souls* covered his distant descendant.

Optimistically preparing for a journey abroad in the summer of 1934,

Bulgakov ran in imagination through the moments which would be sweetest. He imagined conversing with the shades of the two great writers who had filled his mind for so many years.

Paris! The monument to Molière . . . 'How do you do, Monsieur de Molière I have written a book and a play about you.' Rome! 'How do you do, Mr Gogol. Don't be cross. I turned your *Dead Souls* into a play. Admittedly it bears little resemblance to what is being performed by the Theatre. In fact, it's nothing like it at all, but at least I tried . . .'[72]

Bulgakov was over-hasty in reporting all these events in his letter to Veresaev in the past tense. His Gogol Period had indeed come to an end, but his Molière Period still had some way to run . . .

6

'A Part of Theatre Lore'

'The Comedians of Monsieur . . .'

Bulgakov's Molière Period dogged seven years of his life. He started work at the Art Theatre with his play *The League of Hypocrites*, and after the final misadventures which befell it, he left. Between those two points many events drew relations between Bulgakov and the Art Theatre into a tight knot. Before the first night in February 1936 Nemirovich-Danchenko said of the production, 'It has been so long in preparation that it has become the talk of the town, a part of theatre lore.' In *The Gorkyan*, the Art Theatre's house magazine, he went on to interpret the legend as a thing born of 'an amazing lack of organisation' of which 'the causes go very deep and are rooted in a maze of contradictions which go far back in our Theatre's history'.[1]

In many respects the picture has been deliberately muddied. About *Molière* a tight-lipped silence was maintained for some fifteen years, and broken only in the early 1950s. This was when Nikolai Gorchakov published his *Stanislavsky Directs*, in which a whole chapter was devoted to the work on *Molière*. The title of the chapter was 'A Play about a Genius', and it offered what purported to be a documented account of what had happened to *Molière* in the 1930s. Here the play's producer tried to show that the blame for the production's failure lay squarely with the play's author, who had wilfully disregarded the Art Theatre's recommendations.

Gorchakov quoted documents, transcripts of rehearsals, letters from Stanislavsky to him and from him to Stanislavsky. His account exuded documentary authenticity and for many years it remained the sole source of information on an unhappy episode. That it was merely an insignificant incident in the Art Theatre's past Gorchakov did not doubt.

But new times came, and with them some rather unexpected revelations.

Gorchakov was found to have described rehearsals he had not attended, events which had not taken place, and to have quoted letters which did not exist. The starting point was not, of course, Bulgakov but Stanislavsky. The Commission for the Study of the Heritage of K. S. Stanislavsky requested the author of *Stanislavsky Directs* to supply them with the original of an important letter for publication. This was a letter he had quoted as Stanislavsky's response to his, Gorchakov's, self-castigation over *Molière*. In this letter, written almost in the tones of a blessing from his deathbed, Stanislavsky supposedly absolved the young producer of blame and chaffed him paternally, before greeting him 'simply and warmly' again at Leontiev Lane. In his book *Controversy over Stanislavsky* Vladimir Prokofiev has now shown that the letter was fabricated by Gorchakov, a talented improviser no longer absolved of blame, whose entire literary edifice does not stand up to scrutiny.[2]

On the ruins of Gorchakov's legend new structures were erected. Various interpretations of a confused plot were propounded and forgotten controversy revived. Some felt it their bounden duty to 'acquit' Stanislavsky: others no less actively 'rehabilitated' Bulgakov. The result was that not only was the matter not clarified but the antagonists painted themselves into a corner, since this 'part of theatre lore' never could be reduced to a question of who was to blame. So many causes and effects were interwoven, so many vested interests and jealously guarded reputations involved, so many conventions of the time revealed that the whole affair grows from being merely an episode in the political struggle in the theatre into a full-length drama with its own complication, peripeteias, crisis and dénouement. In order to understand the meaning of all that occurred let us go back to the sources of the drama, to the autumn of 1929 when Bulgakov completed work on a play which at that time was titled *The League of Hypocrites*.

Marietta Chudakova has established the initial artistic impulse for the play from a study of its manuscripts. The theme of the downfall of an artist is immediately recognisable in excerpts Bulgakov copied out for use in his future drama. 'Molierana. "Ah! mon Dieu, je suis mort!" (*Le Malade imaginaire*).' In the same place there is a factual note of the first performance by Molière's company in the presence of Louis XIV, and excerpts copied out which sketch the basic conflict: the mutual relations between an artist and the power of a monarch. Pondering on Molière's tribulations in connection with *Tartuffe*, the author of *Flight* copied out of Aleksey Veselovsky's work the part-sentence, 'Demands for his punishment for sacrilege were made *with such force*'.[3] Bulgakov heavily emphasised the last words.

Chudakova then goes on to trace the changes, from the first drafts to the play's first version, in the central line of the plot: relations between Molière and the King.

In the first draft of the so-called King scene, Molière was summoned to Louis not as a result of Charron's slander, but in order to talk about his artistic plans. In this scene Molière was still the young writer of comedies, brimming with new ideas, who only the day before had enjoyed the King's favour. Running through the whole scene is Molière's excitement at the prospect of a possible meeting with the King and the hope of gaining his sympathy and interest in his dramatic work, something which could greatly advance his career. The valet solemnly announces, 'Jean-Baptiste, knight de Molière, begs permission to approach!'

Louis (enlivened). You do? I am delighted to hear it![4]

The king guesses what is on Molière's mind. ('I know what it is: writers enjoy talking about their works in private.') The King makes a point of speaking to the dramatist in private, sending out his courtiers. This version did not graduate beyond the draft notebook. Chudakova notes:

In the first connected redaction, we are offered a different, less optimistic version. We see Molière after the banning of his two best comedies:

A Voice. The servant of your majesty, Jean-Baptiste de Molière.

Louis. Ask him to come in!

(Enter Molière. He walks, bowing from afar to Louis, under the gaze of the courtiers. He is much older, his face haggard.)[5]

In this version Bulgakov the biographer catches what Konstantin Paustovsky in his reminiscences of Bulgakov's story-telling calls 'the echoes of live intonations and real situations'.

Louis. Are you being persecuted?

(Molière remains silent).

Louis (loudly). [If anything threatens you, keep me informed.] Gentlemen! Are there among you no admirers of the writer de Molière? (Stirrings.) I personally am numbered among them.

(Hubbub of voices.)

[Courtiers. Absolutely dazzling pieces].

Well, then. My writer is depressed. He's frightened. And [I will be pleased] I shall be grateful to such as let me know of any danger which may threaten him. (To Molière.) We shall apply our poor strength to fight this off. (Aloud.) I rescind the ban: from tomorrow you may perform Tartuffe and Don Juan. (Hubbub.)[6]

In the drafts of the play there are various conflicting versions of this conversation as well as of Molière's destiny, but the final outcome is never in doubt. Molière was doomed. No matter what evidence of devotion he proffered, his downfall was inevitable. His downfall was not only necessary on the level of the plot but in order to meet the exigencies of genre. The sub-title of the first version tells us this is 'A Play of Music and Light'.

The question of *Molière*'s genre was raised more than once during the many years it took for the production to clear the phase of rehearsal and pass into performance. In several interviews before the première Gorchakov, following Nemirovich-Danchenko's lead, insistently classified the play as a melodrama. Mitigating this with the tag 'in the best sense of the word' only emphasised the genre's low prestige in the world in general, and in the Art Theatre at that moment in particular. Nemirovich-Danchenko went on to explain that it was a matter of a 'historical melodrama', a specially challenging genre for the Theatre in its search for the synthesis of 'simplicity and theatrical effectiveness'.[7]

The problem of genre was crucial at Stanislavsky's rehearsals. He saw it as a historical and biographical play, and underlined precisely these aspects in the 'gold and brocade' design of the production. After the first night Vsevolod Ivanov called *Molière* a 'vulgar bourgeois drama', and Yury Olesha found it related to Rostand's *Cyrano de Bergerac*. He even speculated that *Molière* was a contemporary writer's response to the impression that play had once, perhaps in childhood, made on him.[8]

Olesha seems to have hit the nail on the head. In an interview just before the first night Bulgakov himself spelled out, 'I have written a romantic drama, not a historical chronicle. In a romantic drama it is neither possible nor necessary to maintain the precision of biography . . . The King's cooling off towards Molière is a historical fact, but I have sharpened it in the drama into a conflict, etc.'[9]

Peering into a remote epoch, 'the spectral and fairy-tale Paris of the seventeenth century', Bulgakov did not in fact write merely a romantic drama but chose a variant of it which the German romantics called a 'drama of fate'. There was nothing fortuitous about the play's ending on the final question of La Grange, who was beginning to understand the reality of what had happened to Molière, 'Why did it happen? How shall I put it? Was the cause of this the King's disfavour or the evil work of the Black League? (*Ponders.*) The cause was fate. So shall I note it . . .'

Bulgakov's 'play of music and light' proved also to be about the theatre itself, its nature and its mission, and the vagaries of a comedy actor's life. He depicts the theatre as a close brotherhood, a tiny island living in accordance with its own norms; norms which are incompatible with the laws of the 'League of

Hypocrites' or the Palace. Bulgakov reveals the intrinsic incompatibility of high art and the League, of music, light and 'tyranny without redress' (the terms in which, in the uncensored version of Bulgakov's play, Molière cursed the monarchical boot which was crushing him).

The play's main theme centred round the attempts of a writer of comedies and theatre director of genius to accommodate himself to the absolute, capricious, and totally unconstrained tyranny of the King. The end result is foreshadowed in the very first stage direction: 'In the second dressing room hangs a large crucifix with a veilleuse burning in front of it.' (p. 231)

Bulgakov saw the theme of the creative individual as a tragedy from the very beginning of his literary career. In an early sketch *The Muse of Vengeance* (1921), devoted to Nekrasov, Bulgakov said, '. . . when in the torment of creation he approached his cross (for one who creates may not live without a cross). . . .'[10] The one thing flows inevitably from the other. Wherever there is a Master, there will be a cross for him to bear in the form of a Louis XIV or a Nicholas I. This is why the attempts by Molière, the author of *Tartuffe*, not to step out of line, to curry favour and praise the country's ruler, fall foul of the very nature of a creative artist.

Bulgakov develops the theatre theme in *Molière* using the means of romantic drama, which were in harmony with his sense of theatre. The theatre stage is contrasted with the staginess of the King's palace with its sumptuousness and perfidious splendour; the gloom of the cellar in which the League of the Holy Writ meets; the sombre Cathedral with its 'drifting clouds of incense'; and finally the squalid lodgings of the actors themselves, tiny rooms cluttered with the pathetic attributes of a comic actor's life, a life which has only just graduated from the fair-booth and the wagon. The theatre grows away from the stage prop squalor of reality, transforming it into a magic which Bulgakov describes with that by now familiar sense of delight and wonder which we encountered in *The Crimson Island*, which was a direct precursor of *The League of Hypocrites*.

The very meaning and pathos of the play is woven together from such intertwining and developing themes as the green poster on which one can discern only 'LES COMEDIENS DE MONSIEUR' written in bold capitals, the scenery, the candles, the 'gusts of laughter' of a thousand people which can be heard from the other side of the curtain, the curtain itself dividing the contrasted worlds, and finally the sight of the stage thrown wide open, hovering like some living creature above the auditorium.

The stage is 'raised above the level of the dressing rooms'. We see both stage and auditorium at once at their mysterious conjoining along the line of the footlights, from behind the wings, a vantage point beloved of Bulgakov from where, as the reader remembers, he gave his sketch of the revived *Days of the Turbins*. The theatre stage is revealed in all its transfiguring might. This is the plane on which he describes the comic actor's entrance on to the boards. 'Molière advances on to the stage and turns so that we see him in profile. He pads up to the footlights like a cat, almost furtively. He bows, the feathers of his helmet sweeping the floor'. (p. 232) This is how people prepare for battle, the decisive throw which will decide everything. 'The Comedians of Monsieur . . .' show themselves not merely the servants and lackeys of a King but also the means by which a higher creative will which they are unaware of expresses itself; a will concealed in the very nature of their intrepid acting on the well-lit stage.

In the classical theatre of Japan the actors bow to the ground before beginning and after concluding their acting. They bow not to the audience, but to the One who made acting possible. The boards of the stage, as Bulgakov would agree, are not only an illuminated but an illuminating area where more is demanded of the actor than the mere recital of his lines. He must give 'complete and serious self-sacrifice'. Bulgakov constructs *Molière* on the way life and acting flow through and reflect in each other. We see the plots of Molière's plays being born in the depths of an actor's life. The characters, destinies and mutual relations within a small seven-man company encompass the diversity of human nature like the seven notes of a tonic scale. We watch as reality becomes an object of theatre, and theatre becomes a second reality. We see people coming through theatre to an understanding of life, and the universal accessibility of such an approach. Thus Moirron in a fit of rage flings in Molière's face his own definitive character: 'You're mad, father. Just like Sganarelle.' (p. 255)

Molière seems in his own life to be acting out a plot from one of his plays, and this strange and subtle acting fills the drama right through to the final curtain. When the last fateful performance is at an end, 'the last lights are put out and the stage grows dark. Everything fades, except for the lamp by the crucifix. The stage is sombre and empty.' (p. 285) A sombre, empty stage symbolic of death, non-being, annihilation. This is where the theatre symbolism in *Molière* ultimately leads. This is the significance of its festive lights, and the gusts of laughter from a thousand people filling the dark space of the auditorium.

After the first night Yury Olesha reproached his former fellow-contributor to *The Hooter* for not having shown the characteristics of a professional writer in Molière. The author of *Envy* either did not realise, or chose not to notice, that Bulgakov was painting the portrait of a dramatist, a quite different animal both in terms of his skills and his psychology. He did not need to show Molière working: it was all taking place before the eyes of the audience. The psychology of theatre people, on the other hand, the psychology of an actor, a producer, the director of a theatre company! These are depicted in the play with an insight and wit only possible in a writer who has spent a long time feeling his way intimately into the centuries-old, enduring characteristics of the theatre world.

The Palais-Royal theatre in *Molière* is that self-same apartment of the Turbins which Bulgakov so loved, a home which lives in accordance with its own laws. There was good reason why Bulgakov should recall in his novella about Molière that the first title of his theatre company was 'Children of the Family'. A small natural theatre is a very individual republic separate from the rest of the world. It is a home and a family where the soul of each is bared before the others, and where people try to make sense of life on stage, and interpret life by the laws of theatre. In the play we come to recognise the bonds of a brotherhood of actors, not unlike an order of chivalry. Bulgakov quite deliberately likens La Grange, the chronicler of Molière's company, to a radiant knight standing sentinel over the theatre's soul.

How accurate Bulgakov's picture of Molière's theatre was may be judged from the biography of Molière, written by Georges Bordonove.

The company was to become a family for him, which is why he was the godfather at so many christenings and the witness at so many weddings. That is why he brought up the company's orphans so caringly until they were ready to go out into the world. Of course the brotherhood of actors was there long before Molière came along, but it seems more likely than not that it was Molière who strengthened and regularised those still random and precarious bonds, and established the forms in which that brotherhood exists to the present day.[11]

Recreating the image of the theatre brotherhood, Bulgakov's sharp, ironical eye was of course not blind to the vices and sores which undermined the family of actors. He sees how they are seduced by fame and money, how they cling to the boot of their master, how they preen themselves under the unsleeping gaze of dread authority. He sees their vanity and all the other ordinary human vices which luxuriate improbably in the theatre's special micro-climate. Bulgakov starts his play with the great Molière's servile self-abasement as he reels off shrill doggerel in praise of Louis XIV, who then rewards the nimble comedian and his colleagues royally. Bulgakov left in draft a passage in his novella about Molière which is very germane to this topic, and elucidates important aspects of the play which preceded it.

One of the thinkers of the eighteenth century said actors love monarchy above all else in the world. He expressed himself thus, I believe, because he had insufficiently thought the matter through. It would, perhaps, be more accurate to say simply that actors passionately love any power. They can't afford not to! Theatre art can flourish only where there is a strong, stable, monied power. One could give a multitude of examples. I do not do so only because there is no need for it.

Molière's impromptu rhyme in honour of the King arouses unfeigned delight among his actors ('Ah, what talent! "The Sun" – that was a brilliant touch'). (p. 233) No less is Molière's delight at the King's favour in allowing him to make up the monarchical bed. The wily comedian is prepared to endure any humiliation (although to the thinking of that age, to be invited to make up the King's bed was not by any means a humiliation) in order to preserve his theatre and enable his actors to act. There is nothing in the world an actor would exchange for this opportunity. To act is to live: such is the only law and the only meaning of an actor's life.

Bulgakov concentrates this theme in the figure of Moirron, a classic image of the 'actor as such'. The handsome, depraved boy found in Charlatan's harpsichord has drunk in the poison of the theatre since childhood. Moirron knows no other life, no feelings other than theatrical feelings. Having seduced Armande, having been driven from Molière's house in disgrace, he thinks as only an actor can think: 'It would be extremely interesting to know who is going to play Don Juan now.' (p. 255) Brilliant and courageous on stage, he proves in life to be a pathetic coward and nonentity whom knowledgeable people can mould as they please. The heroic lover betrays his teacher, but Bulgakov, and Molière himself, judge an actor's treachery by laws unknown outside the theatre. The actor Judas who betrays his spiritual father differs from the biblical Judas in not wanting thirty pieces of silver as a reward. He asks the King for the supreme and only possible reward, to return to his own world and join the King's theatre company. This is a touch of pure Bulgakov, and one to which the King responds with unexpected insight and subtlety. Louis XIV (at least as portrayed by Bulgakov) knows all about the hidden springs of an actor's psychology. Despising the informer (as Pilate is later to despise Judas and sympathise secretly with Yeshua), he devises a cruel and unusual punishment for Moirron which the straight world and conventional psychology find strange and incomprehensible. Informing the traitor of the 'good news' that his denunciation has been confirmed, he promptly shows his gratitude by advising him to renounce the dubious calling of an actor ('I hear that you are a bad actor'), and finishes the Judas off by offering him a position in the secret police ('Submit your application to the King in person. It will be granted'). (p. 268)

Thus are Moirron's attempts to escape from the confines of the theatre world crowned. He is an actor and, as far as Bulgakov is concerned, there is no more to be said. 'You would be useless as a police spy. You haven't the temperament for it.' (p. 275)

This is probably the reason why Bulgakov's Molière forgives Moirron and takes the prodigal son back into his house. Preventing La Grange from strangling the informer, Molière's magnanimity proceeds from his connoisseur's knowledge of an actor's soul. 'You impudent puppy!' he scolds La Grange, 'Don't talk about things you don't understand!' (p. 275) 'Now that I've had time to think and have grown wiser after what has happened,' he tells Moirron, 'I forgive you and take you back again into my house. Come back.' The paradox continues. When Molière is threatened by the sword, it is Moirron who now shields his teacher. It is Moirron who 'bares his teeth and silently puts his arms around Molière' (p. 280) and later challenges the booing house and the one-eyed musketeer ('You filthy brute!') (p. 284). It is Moirron, the forgiven actor-traitor, who is prepared to do battle (on stage!) with d'Orsigny. It is he who, like Molière going out 'cat-like' to the footlights, 'lopes' towards the hired killer. Cat-like movements are the hallmark of the acting brotherhood; a brotherhood which the very least of the Children of the Family is prepared to defend with teeth bared.

The theatre theme in *Molière* is inseparable from the theme of the writer. Just as the actor in obedience to a higher power subordinates his human destiny to his acting, so the dramatist too is in some way enslaved by his own creation. In Bulgakov's play only *Tartuffe* makes sense of Molière's life and justifies it. There is no price the writer would not pay in order that his writing should not be destroyed. His obligations to his unstaged play take priority over all other obligations. Bulgakov's play of music and light is about the insuperability of the creative principle in life in its unending and unresolvable dispute with the 'League of Hypocrites'. Such is the theme Bulgakov derived from the fate of Molière.

The play was completed in early 1930. Bulgakov had not intended it for the Art Theatre, but naturally the Theatre was aware of it. Stanislavsky wrote to Leonidov enquiring about *Molière* from Nice, and grumbled about the prospect of its being staged by another theatre.[12] On 19 January 1930 a meeting of the Theatre's Committee for Literary Affairs and Repertoire of the Council for Political and Artistic Affairs took place at which Bulgakov read his new play. There was general agreement among those present. 'The play is very interesting, artistically of a very high standard, and brilliantly theatrical. It gives good material for acting.' The objections of certain members of the Council came down to complaining that 'The play is not relevant; it does not reflect . . . the class struggle; it does not make clear the author's attitude to his characters and the causes of Molière's death.'[3]

Sudakov recommended elevating the play 'to the genre of monumental tragedy'. Sakhnovsky tried to explain to the committee members that the Art Theatre could ill afford to ignore Bulgakov's play when many contemporary plays were 'mere run of the mill political journalism'. Pavel Markov was an old hand at this game. He came to the meeting fully armed. 'The play,' he said, 'is brilliant, very strong formally and in terms of the significance of its images. Its main theme is the great tragedy of an artist who is being crushed by the organised violence of the King and the Church. Its relevance extends beyond a particular period: it is typical of the world of monarchy and bourgeois capitalism.' Markov went on to argue on a practical level that the play would enable Moskvin to work again. He reassured the Committee for Literary Affairs and Repertoire by pointing out that the Theatre was expecting a play from Trenyov about collective farms in a few days' time, and that contemporary plays by Olesha and Kirshon were expected in a couple of months. As the correctness of the Theatre's line on repertoire for the coming season was being made unambiguously clear, the 'inclusion of The League of Hypocrites in the said plan cannot be objected to on ideological grounds'.[4]

Bulgakov spoke at the end of the discussion. Olga Bokshanskaya has recorded some of his salient points about the idea underlying the play. Reacting to the comments, Bulgakov made it clear that he had not set out to write 'a play about the class struggle in the seventeenth century, or to create a monumental tragedy or an anti-religious spectacle. He had wanted to write a play about the brilliant, radiant genius of Molière, who was crushed by a black League of Hypocrites with the full connivance of the absolute, suffocating power of the King. A play of this kind was needed by Soviet audiences.'[5]

The meeting came to no conclusion, and referred the matter to a full session of the Council for Political and Artistic Affairs. In the event this proved unnecessary, the question being resolved on 18 March when Bulgakov received notification that The League of Hypocrites was not considered suitable for performance. 'To put it briefly,' he later commented, 'those two lines on an official form buried all that work in libraries, my creative imagination, and a play, a brilliant play, which had been reviewed by numerous qualified experts on the theatre.'[6]

Only in autumn 1931, when the question was being considered of transferring the Art Theatre to a new jurisdiction, was Bulgakov's play reconsidered. On 30 August Olga advised Nemirovich-Danchenko, 'Gorky . . . asked about Molière and, learning his fate, asked to have a copy sent to him.'[7] On 16 September

Markov, who saw Gorky socially, passed on his opinion about the play, which he had now read. 'He has read *The League of Hypocrites* and considers that it should be performed in spite of a certain amount of autobiographical reference. He will actively assist.'[18]

A number of Art Theatre actors were also aware of the 'autobiographical reference'. Ivan Kudryavtsev noted in his diary on 29 April 1932:

Just read Bulgakov's play *Molière* (first titled *The League of Hypocrites*) . . . Bloody good! Sinitsyn, that living embodiment of the Archbishop, went and died while it was still banned. I remember how Mikh. Bulgakov begged for mercy when I started talking about 'autobiographical tendencies'.[19]

Bulgakov had good reason to beg for mercy. He knew from bitter experience the kind of decisions which could flow from discoveries of that kind, and wanted to avoid an inept, superficial interpretation of his romantic drama. At all events, Gorky's comments proved effective. On 6 October the Main Repertoire Committee decided in the play's favour and it received a 'B' categorisation, which meant that it was passed for performance not only in Moscow and Leningrad but throughout the country. This was something new, and the Art Theatre saw it as a sign of important and encouraging changes. Olga promptly reported to Nemirovich-Danchenko that virtually no alterations had been required in the script and that these were 'almost everywhere, with two exceptions, not in the text of the play but in the stage directions'. A further condition was that the title must be changed from *The League of Hypocrites* to *Molière*. She added that 'the play is to be performed in Moscow by our Theatre. In Leningrad the Bolshoy Drama Theatre is after it, and plans to cast Monakhov as Molière.'[20]

On 15 October 1931 Nemirovich-Danchenko's secretary passed on a further interesting piece of information: 'A contract is being signed with Bulgakov for *Molière*. It stipulates that the play is to be produced no later than 1 May 1933 and that, as a result of a decision by K. S. (and that is the only possible arrangement), rehearsals will start only after *Dead Souls* is in performance, when Moskvin is free.'[21]

The situation within the Theatre which caused the production of *Molière* to be postponed was to cause many other problems. The date for its performance, May 1933, which seemed very late to Olga Bokshanskaya, was to be put back endlessly. The work was to lose the essential rhythm, and the Theatre was to miss its chance. But all this was still in the future, and in the autumn of 1931 a Bulgakov play was once again being cast at the Art Theatre. The roles were reallocated several times. The former Korsh Theatre was dissolved and its actors incorporated in the company, among them Mikhail Bolduman who trumped all other Kings.

Bulgakov read *Molière* to the Art Theatre company on 17 November 1931. 'The play was well received,' Olga reports, 'despite the fact that Mikhail Afanasievich was reading with a cold rather than with his usual sparkle.'[22]

In 1932 Nikolai Gorchakov began rehearsals which smouldered rather than catching fire. Moskvin was bogged down with *Dead Souls*, turned up to rehearsals infrequently, and spent a lot of time trying to get used to the play. He was put off by the theatricality of *Molière*, as we learn from an interesting entry in Kudryavtsev's diary.

Conversation with Moskvin – about Molière. How are rehearsals going? Slowly, but we sometimes strike oil. You see, Ivan Mikhailovich (this to me), Bulgakov really is very theatrical in this play. You have to dig down a long way for the truth of life. For instance, he writes, 'Molière beat his breast' (a stage direction), but when you think about it, and try it, he just wouldn't.

Kudryavtsev comments, also quite relevantly,

Bulgakov's *Molière* is unambiguously a tragi-comedy. Moskvin will act a drama (probably domestic). It's so obvious. Our Art Theatre actors have no feeling for that style and genre.[23]

There is no telling now how Moskvin might have acted Molière, but certainly his withdrawal from the production was a severe blow. We need seek no complex or fundamental reasons for it. Often in the theatre serious consequences are set in train by personal and insignificant causes. Some decades later Yelena Bulgakova recalled the chain of events in 1932 in a letter to her brother.

Moskvin was to have been acting Molière, but just at that very moment he was separating from his wife and having a passionate affair with Anna Tarasova. He came to us and said, 'I cannot rehearse. I feel I am publicly revealing everything about myself. Lyubov Vasilievna and I are having exactly the same conversations at home. Everything is repeating. It is an impossible situation. The whole of Moscow will hear what appears to be my own most intimate feelings.

Yelena gives here her own account of the consequences of Moskvin's withdrawal from the part.

It wrecked the production. Stanitsyn, to whom the part was given, is a very good episodic actor, but he is not someone who can carry a whole production on his own shoulders.

Everything went wrong with the balance. Bolduman played Louis XIV brilliantly and that became the leading role. The critics, mainly one particular critic who really hated Misha, made a meal of it.[24]

We have no reason to doubt Yelena's facts, but there are no grounds for laying the whole burden of responsibility for what happened on Stanitsyn. In cases like this explanations based on events within the Theatre do not give the full story, as Bulgakov himself was fully aware.

Moskvin pulled out. Khmelyov was unhappy with the role of the King and wanted the part of Molière. He too quietly withdrew from the production in the end. The designer Nikolai Ulyanov was replaced by Pyotr Viliams, and the scenery which was ready began to be replaced and costumes to be re-made. Stanislavsky was busy with *Dead Souls* and *Talents and Admirers*. In Nemirovich-Danchenko's absence he had also the heavy burden of directing and administering the company, which was in an extremely volatile state. Then Stanislavsky went abroad for medical treatment for more than a year, orphaning the Bulgakov production.

The atmosphere at rehearsals for *Molière* was very far removed from that which had attended *The Turbins*. Gorchakov did his best to carry out the, admittedly very general, instructions he had received from Stanislavsky, but everybody knew he was not really master in his own house. These were the circumstances in which the work gradually became a part of theatre lore and one, moreover, which reflected grave internal problems at the Art Theatre.

Kudryavtsev records a conversation in his diary which he had in early May 1932 with Nikolai Gorchakov, just when the rehearsals of *Dead Souls* were at their most difficult.

Yesterday spoke to Gorchakov about the staging of *Molière* . . . Everybody wants to be the director (Moskvin, Stanitsyn, Livanov, Batalov). Stanislavsky has declared the play a monodrama and insists on carrying through the principles (in the design) which he has worked out for *Dead Souls*. Livanov considers the part of Moirron completely unsuitable for him. Up till now everybody, including me, had thought it virtually written for him. He is upset about the negative traits in the character and keeps trying to make it more 'noble'. Almost everybody is expressing themselves in their own words and adding bits, taking advantage of the tactful (or distraught) author, who just seems thankful to be alive![25]

The author was not only thankful to be alive but waiting patiently for *Dead Souls* to be performed, after which he supposed that *Molière* would go full steam ahead. He was to be disappointed. Just as the time arrived for the première of

Dead Souls, events within the Art Theatre took a turn which was to poison several months of Stanislavsky's life. The impulsive Ilya Sudakov prepared *The Servant of Two Masters* with the actors to earn a bit extra over the summer. The idea then entered his head that there was no reason why it should not also be performed on the Principal Stage of the Art Theatre. He did a run-through for several old stagers, who were prepared to support him. The Privy Council surrounding Stanislavsky at this time presented the whole affair in an extremely unfavourable light for Sudakov. Stanislavsky demanded a demonstration for himself at Leontiev Lane. The performers ran through the musical with neither music nor songs. Stanislavsky had a talk with them in which he rapidly discovered to his own satisfaction that they had no idea what the play's through line of action was (which for him was the absolute priority). Sudakov started a heated argument. People not directly involved succeeded in blowing the row up out of all proportion, until Stanislavsky was obliged to turn to a government commission and Avel Yenukidze to resolve this 'manufacturing crisis'.

Bursting with ideas, plans and urgency, Sudakov was expressing a mood among the theatre's younger members, whose de facto leader he was. The Art Theatre was pulled in two quite distinct and opposite directions, a conflict which Stanislavsky defined as 'breadth versus depth'. Olga now reported monstrous things to Nemirovich-Danchenko.

To put it very crudely, taking everything in its crudest and most extreme forms, there are currently two opposing trends squaring up to each other in our affairs, headed respectively by K.S. and Ilya Sudakov. This probably sounds utterly absurd to you, but that is more or less the situation.[26]

Sudakov proposed one politically commendable play after another. Social relevance spurted from him. He was prepared to rehearse several plays simultaneously, and reassuringly told the startled Stanislavsky, 'It's okay, Konstantin Sergeevich. They'll pass it! They'll pass it!' Markov was to write later, 'The cooling of relations was a gradual process. Stanislavsky insisted on ever greater depth, particularly when working on the classics, while Sudakov was saying, "Okay, lads, let's really go for it!"'[27]

A quarter of a century later Sudakov was to recall how one autumn, probably in 1934, Stanislavsky had called him to Leontiev Lane for a serious talk about the repertoire. His main reproach to the director was that, 'In selecting the repertoire you go by what the Party periphery wants: I go by what the Kremlin wants.'[28] He meant, of course, Stalin. What Stanislavsky was really going by in the 1930s is something to which we shall have to return, but further on in his memoir Sudakov reproduces a dialogue which gives us a very specific insight into the situation in the Art Theatre at the time: '[Stanislavsky] tried to persuade me to take on Erdman's play *The Suicide*. I had great difficulty persuading him that it lampooned our Soviet life.'[29]

The ringleader of the younger actors did not succeed in changing Stanislavsky's mind, but at least he sets out his own understanding of things with considerable clarity.

The time came when Sudakov's exceptional organisational ability and dauntless temperament could no longer be contained within the Moscow Art Theatre. He became Director of TRAM, and a little later was instrumental in procuring the premises of the disbanded Korsh Theatre for the ancillary stage of the Art Theatre. Neither Stanislavsky nor Nemirovich-Danchenko had planned this expansion. The threatened transition of the Theatre from depth to breadth, and the loss of the traditionalists' cosy sense of the Art Theatre building as their family home, became a reality. In January 1933 Stanislavsky wrote to Gorky, not disguising his alarm that the Theatre had 'more than 120 actors, many of them demanding work which we cannot give them and which they are incapable of performing in the Art Theatre'.

The result is a group opposed to our motto of 'Depth', which aspires to 'Breadth', the quickfire performance of numerous plays, and a quite different understanding of what it means to be an actor. I see no option but to partition the Theatre, so that the main Art Theatre should remain free to pursue its accepted line untrammelled. I consider it essential that all our forces should be concentrated within a single theatre without any 'ancillary stages', and I hope with this united company of people who have a shared understanding of art to achieve the necessary results.[30]

Stanislavsky was unable to see this through. In spring 1933 he fell seriously ill and went abroad for treatment, returning to Moscow only in August 1934.

It is hardly to be wondered at that *Molière* was left hanging in the air and shifted to the margin of the Art Theatre's interests. The delay in putting it into production led to other theatres also biding their time. The production planned by the Bolshoy Drama Theatre in Leningrad was torpedoed by an attack by Vsevolod Vishnevsky, whom Bulgakov described in a letter to Popov as 'an open face, goes to work like a Red Navy sailor, currently cruising around in Moscow. During his visit to Leningrad he so terrified the Theatre there the play just fell out of their hands.'[31] Bulgakov's fellow pen-pusher, 'not of course by any means an official playwright', had for reasons 'not of course by any means political' also written an open letter to the Bolshoy Drama Theatre in the Leningrad *Red Paper*.

In this letter, headed 'Where Do You Stand?', he said a play 'about the tragic fate of a court dramatist' was grotesquely irrelevant.

We might understand and sympathise with the motives of those who are putting on *Tartuffe*. 'Let's put on the classics . . .' But why spend time and effort on a drama about Molière when you have the real thing available? Or has Bulgakov outstripped Molière and brought new qualities, exposing the 'interconnections of earlier times' like a good Marxist?
        Answer, comrades of the Bolshoy Drama Theatre.[32]

The Bolshoy Drama Theatre's answer was to drop the play. Bulgakov, who one might have supposed by this time to be quite inured to worse accusations than this, was greatly pained by this literary attack. In his letters to Popov describing the episode in detail there is mention of d'Anthès's murderous shot at Pushkin, the 'knight commander of our Russian order of writers', on whose body 'they found a severe pistol wound. When a hundred years on they undress one of his descendants prior to despatching him on his final journey, they will find quite a few scars from flick-knives, and all of them in the back. The weapon changes.'[33]

In the summer of 1932 Bulgakov, as the author of *The League of Hypocrites*, received an urgent commission for a biography of Molière for inclusion in the series 'Lives of Remarkable People', which Gorky had founded. He again immersed himself in the theatre of the seventeenth century, and clearly brought his experiences at the Art Theatre to bear in describing it. In a manuscript of some sixty thousand words Bulgakov develops an enormous monologue in which he analyses Molière's career as a dramatist in painstaking detail and with evident fellow-feeling. He is interested in everything: the tradition from which Molière's theatre grew; the way he behaved as an author in the aftermath of the banning of *Tartuffe*; the means he found for battling with the royal censorship; and the relationships between the actors in his company. The narrator in the biography comments, ironises, expresses delight and sorrow. Sometimes he volunteers a piece of advice to this man separated from him by three centuries, or defends him from the petty criticism of his descendants. Thrown back because of the unavailability of much of the documentary evidence to relying largely on his own intuition and imagination, Bulgakov generously compensates Molière by giving a dramatist's understanding of the tasks and significance of the new theatre and the ways it should be strengthened. 'Oh, nexus of the passing years! Oh, currents of enlightenment!' the narrator exclaims, and boldly characterises the old theatre as 'Molière's Method'. There is more. Having mastered the basic tenets of Stanislavsky's Method in the practical school at Leontiev Lane, Bulgakov gives a literally Stanislavskian explanation of Molière's first crushing failures. He had been trying to 'create a school which would naturally communicate the script from the stage to the audience in a way which was inwardly wholly justifiable' at a time when the fashionable practice was still declamatory bawling from powerful vocal cords.

In early March 1933, having completed work on the novella, Bulgakov wrote to his brother in Paris,

To my great delight I have at last finished work on *Molière*, and delivered the manuscript on the fifth. It has completely drained me. I no longer remember how many years, including work on the play, I have been living in the spectral and fairy-tale Paris of the seventeenth century. I seem now to be taking my leave of it for ever.

If chance should ever take you to the corner of Richelieu and Molière, remember me to Jean-Baptiste de Molière![34]

Bulgakov was jumping the gun. Another three years were to pass before the first night of his play about Molière. In autumn 1933 he wrote to his brother that the *Molière* business was 'so dragging on (for reasons which are purely internal to the Theatre) that I am beginning to despair of ever seeing it performed'.[35] Six months later the reasons 'purely internal to the theatre' are fully revealed in a letter to Popov.

Molière? Well, yes, we are still rehearsing it. All right then, not very often, not very fast. Just between ourselves, I feel pretty hopeless about it. Lyusya cannot talk about what the Theatre has done with my play without getting angry. As for me, it is a long time since I could get worked up about it. If it were not for the fact that I need a new play on the stage in order to pay the bills I wouldn't give it another thought. If it makes it, fine: if it doesn't, too bad.[36]

As if continuing his narration about Molière, 'sick with that passion for theatre for which there is no cure', Bulgakov adds the already familiar lines: 'but I am putting a lot of hard work and passion into these irregular rehearsals. You can't help it if you have the stage in your blood!'[37]

In the same letter Bulgakov gives a chronicle of life at the Art Theatre at this time: *The Pickwick Papers*, in which Bulgakov was rehearsing the part of the Judge, has got bogged down ('and when it will be performed and I shall be able to let you admire my fine red judge's robes I do not know').[38] There is the usual turmoil in the Theatre and the producers are at daggers drawn:

Sudakov has burst through into the station with *The Thunderstorm*, ignoring all the red lights and crashing all the points, and will charge in ahead of everyone else. We need his

Thunderstorm like we need a hole in the head, but Sudakov is a forceful personality and if you should ever write a play my advice is to try to get Sudakov to stage it.

Mordvinov is rushing along just behind Sudakov, clutching Kirshon . . .[39]

About par for life in the theatre, in fact.

Leontiev Lane

Stanislavsky returned to Moscow on 4 August 1934. He arrived from a Europe where the bacillus of the Fascist plague had already been sown. 'I have seen all I can take of Europe . . .' Stanislavsky told the producer Boris Zon according to the latter's notes. 'Germany is finished. Hitler has sent them all packing. There is no theatre left. Max Reinhardt is in emigration. Bassermann has had to emigrate because his wife is a Jewess. It's an utter disgrace!'[40]

Stanislavsky arrived back with a tremendous appetite for work and with the intention of 'making big changes to restructure everything'. At a meeting with the Theatre company he spoke of the immense responsibility being laid on the Art Theate and concluded, as Alexander Afinogenov reports in *Soviet Art*, 'by making all the actors present raise their hands like Pioneers and promise to do their best to do their duty to Soviet audiences'.[41]

Naturally Bulgakov was at this meeting too. His first conversation since Stanislavsky's return is duly recorded in Yelena's diary.

25 August.
M. A. is still afraid to go out alone. I accompanied him to the Theatre and brought him home afterwards. He told me how the meeting went. K. S. arrived at the theatre at half past two. The actors met him with prolonged applause. He gave his speech in the lower foyer. At first about how bad things are abroad and how good they are with us; how everybody there is half-dead and depressed, while with us there is a sense of life and vitality. 'You meet a Frenchwoman and you wonder where her chic has gone . . .' In conclusion he obliged everybody to raise their hands in a pledge that they would all work well. When he finished he went to the exit, saw M.A., and they embraced. Stanislavsky put his arm round M.A.'s shoulder and they went out together.
'What are you writing now?' [. . .]
'Nothing, Konstantin Sergeevich. I am tired.'
'You need to write . . . Here is a subject, for instance: there is no time to get everything done . . . and remain a decent person.'
Then he suddenly took fright and said,
'But you will twist that the wrong way!'
'There . . . Everyone is afraid of me . . .'
'No, I am not afraid. I would have twisted it the wrong way myself.'[42]

In spite of Bulgakov's rather acerbic way of looking at the world, which comes through in this record, it is not difficult to see that Stanislavsky's return to the Theatre changed things for the better, or at least clarified the situation as far as *Molière* was concerned. However, before tackling creative problems Stanislavsky, as was his wont, tackled the administrative problems. The Art Theatre was embarking on yet another of its 'little revolutions' which crowded out all other questions, including the question of Bulgakov's play. Olga, alive to every nuance, sent an autumnal news bulletin to Nemirovich-Danchenko full of rumours about possible personnel changes:

The sole Deputy Director is to be Yegorov. He will have an Assistant Director for Management, and management of the artistic side will be in the hands of three individuals: Podgorny, as Manager of the Company; Sudakov, as Manager for Pushing through New Productions; and Kedrov, as Manager for Through Line of Action in Plays and Rehearsals in Progress. Kedrov has been dubbed Dictator of Through Line of Action, probably K.S.'s label, or perhaps somebody has been parodying him.[43]

Under these confused circumstances the repertoire plan for several seasons ahead was being decided, and *Molière* was once more designated as one of the imminent premières. On 19 September Olga communicated 'a hot tip from Sudakov' that the intention was to stage a new play by Afinogenov, *The Portrait*, and *Three Sisters* on the Principal Stage, with *Molière* scheduled for performance in January 1935. In the same letter she reports that Sudakov is trying to persuade Stanislavsky to give Bulgakov's play to the ancillary stage:

The problem is that K.S. has decided that *Molière* should be a grand and stylish production, and should therefore be played on the principal stage. Sudakov and the other producers would like to have it performed on the ancillary stage, without so much grandiose theatricality. The more so since the repertoire for the principal stage is already overcrowded and there is no space in it for *Molière*.[44]

Even as all this was going on, in September 1934 Bulgakov was trying to arrange a meeting with Stanislavsky. On 21 September Yelena recorded in her diary:

M.A. rang Stanislavsky this morning.
'You don't seem well, Konstantin Sergeevich.'
'I am unwell, but not for you.'
Then they talked about the sets for *Molière* and K.S. asked M.A. to ring tomorrow to arrange a meeting.[45]

We do not know whether this meeting took place. What we do know is that on 31 October Stanislavsky had his first preview of part of the work Gorchakov and Bulgakov had been labouring on for so many years. They showed him the Cathedral scene at his home in Leontiev Lane. Stanislavsky talked to Koreneva about the through line of action . . . and the little truths. He talked to Sosnin about the role of Charron, which 'is entirely based on an enormous emotional charge'.

Despite having received this important support and patronage Gorchakov was unable to conduct any rehearsals in November. Both Stanitsyn and Bulgakov were fully occupied with the last pre-performance stages of *The Pickwick Papers*. At the dress rehearsal, which Stanitsyn directed in the presence of Stanislavsky, Bulgakov showed his acting ability to great effect. Yelena wrote in her diary:

His costume is red robes with a long, curled, white wig. In the interval afterwards he told me he had terrible stage-fright. He knocked the stool over with his robes when he went to sit on it. He had to start the scene hanging on to the rostrum with his elbows until someone helpfully put the stool back in place.[46]

Vitaly Vilenkin was present at the rehearsal. He recalls:

We came to the Court scene. The presiding Judge in his heavy grey wig with his fat crimson nose and beady eyes spread his elbows as he prepared for the questioning. This Judge was famous for hating all animals, and could not stand any figures of speech involving the animal world. As ill-luck would have it the rhetoric of the officers of the court was fairly bursting with animal metaphors. The Judge's famous line 'Stop that animal talk, or I shall withdraw permission for you to address the Court!' resounded with such unfeigned fury that the whole auditorium was convulsed with laughter, and Stanislavsky most of all. 'Who is that?' he asked Stanitsyn in a quick whisper, not recognising the actor. 'Bulgakov.' 'What Bulgakov?' 'Our Bulgakov. The playwright. The author of *The Turbins*.' 'It can't be!' 'It really is, Konstantin Sergeevich. Honest to God!' 'But what a talent he's got . . .', and again he roared with laughter at something as loudly and infectiously as only Stanislavsky could.[47]

The first night of *The Pickwick Papers* took place at the beginning of December, and Bulgakov had the pleasure of showing off his judge's robe to his friends for several months. His dressing room became a kind of club every evening. 'All the young actors gather there. They so admire Misha. It really is very pleasant!' Yelena confided to her domestic chronicle.[48] In Grigory Konsky's memoirs we read how the author of *Molière* set about making himself up.

Giving my hand a quick, firm squeeze, inclining his head to one side while doing so, he would sit down at one of the mirrors, switch on the light and look for a long time at his reflection as if trying to see something unusual in it. [. . .] He would examine himself with his light eyes so seriously and attentively, the way a doctor does when trying to make a diagnosis.[49]

All actors are edgy as they wait for it to be their scene. Some play chess, others tell jokes. Bulgakov organised word games. For every win a symbolic twenty kopeks was paid out. On one occasion he rejoiced the heart of his perpetual rival, Boris Livanov, with the following stroke of morphological originality: 'Hey, Livanov, here's twenty kopeks for you.' 'What for?' 'I dreamt I had been killed and you came into the canteen and said, "Big guard dog. Poor 'gakov!"' All yours!'[50]

Poor ''gakov' was, however, very much still about. In December 1934 he began thinking his way around a play about Pushkin. By late December the basic outline of the play was already established. On 28 December Yelena noted:

Nicholas 1 is already there, and Alexandrina. The strongest impression in my mind today is the scene at Heckeren's when the blind Stroganov arrives to decide whether D'Anthès should duel with Pushkin or not.
The symbolism is of eyeless death killing him with its code of duelling.[51]

The year came to an end with new ideas for plays and the expectation of changes for the better in the near future. 'The year is drawing to its end. Lord, if only things continue as they are.'[52]

This was written by Yelena on 31 December 1934, and on 4 January 1935 there was a new alarm. It was rumoured in the Theatre that *Molière* was to be set back and Afinogenov's play put on instead.

We spent the whole day today going over *that* conversation with Olga Bokshanskaya yesterday. All it came down to was that a date had been fixed for the reading of Afinogenov's new play which, according to Olga, Nemirovich had said was a 'charming sketch'. She added that one ought to take pity on Afinogenov on purely humanitarian grounds. His *The Lie* had not been performed, his *The Portrait* had not been performed, and he still went on and on writing with pure Bolshevik dynamism . . .
I listened to her, said nothing, and gave her a withering look.[53]

Fortunately, Olga had jumped the gun. Nobody had postponed *Molière*. On the contrary, the rehearsals suddenly took off. Pyotr Viliams, having replaced Ulyanov, started designing the new sets, and showed his sketches at the end of

January. 'Very, very good!' Yelena notes. 'Especially the King's staircase, the theatre in the last act, and the graveyard.'[54]

Stanislavsky subsequently did away with the graveyard where the meeting of the League was to take place. Viliams took his cue from Stanislavsky's desire to build on the play's theatricality with grand and sumptuous decor. Nikolai Ulyanov, still in charge of designing the costumes, also gave new instructions. Mme Repina, the wardrobe mistress, recalled, 'In the end we received official instructions to make them of brocade, "so that everything should shine like the sun".'[55]

The production had already been in preparation for four years, with great pauses and standstills in between. These not only disrupted the rhythm of the work, but also meant that the play was exposed to the constant changes in the political and artistic climate. We find a stern note in Afinogenov's diary about Meyerhold's *The Lady with the Camellias*, a dramatic U-turn by the leader of 'October in the Theatre' which had astonished Moscow with its melodrama in sophisticated and luxurious packaging:

The Lady with the Camellias . . . is the subtle poison of decay. This is how the old world lured people, with sparkle, velvet, silk, and shiny things . . . And the audience clap with delight and shout bravo . . . That's just the way that after the fall of the Paris Commune the bully-boys and their wives and prostitutes lived it up . . . And now this is being presented as a pearl of something. You are expected to take it as your standard and learn from it . . . Nonsense and tommy-rot! . . .[56]

What matters is not that Afinogenov misinterpreted what he had seen. The fact is that he is perfectly correct in recording a U-turn in theatrical taste. Viliams, the new designer of *Molière*, set out to create 'not verisimilitude on the stage' but 'a purely emotional background for a melodramatic, romantic production'. He conceived a single basic set with a revolving centre, framed by a portal which was given a different treatment in successive scenes. The detail changed: 'gilded women and regal lilies for the scene with the King; statues of Harlequin and Pulcinello and a portal of rags for the scene in the theatre and Molière's dressing room; painted wooden church carving and a golden portal in the scenes in the Cathedral and with the League'.

Viliams deployed his art to recreate a period when the absolutist state was developing. His stipulation that everything should 'shine like the sun' was a particular aspect of the larger and more important task of conveying, as he wrote at the time of the première, 'the atmosphere of heavy, powerful majesty of the period'.[57]

The great comedian with his cat-like movements and his stutter was to be framed within the gilded portal of the King, with which the ancient masks of the Italian theatre sought vainly to compete. In autumn 1934 a re-jigging of the production was begun which was to give it a completely different slant.

On 4 March 1935, after several months of intensive rehearsal (if Gorchakov was ill Bulgakov took the rehearsals on his own), the cast of *Molière* assembled at Leontiev Lane. The next day they were to run through the performance in the presence of Stanislavsky. It was a crucial moment, with everybody's nerves on edge. Lidia Koreneva raised the temperature by arriving half an hour late. In the screened section of the 'Onegin Hall' they went through the whole performance, except for Molière's death scene which was not yet ready.

In March 1926 the Turbin cast had run through *The White Guard* for Stanislavsky at the Comic Opera Theatre. That had been a moment of destiny in the lives of the Moscow Art Theatre's younger generation and in Bulgakov's theatrical career, a moment which the actors remembered as one of the happiest days of their youth in the Theatre. The run-through on 5 March 1935 decided nothing in the lives of the actors and producers taking part. It decided nothing in the future of the Art Theatre, already firmly established within the system of Stalinist culture. For Stanislavsky the production was also not in any sense epoch-making: as we have seen, the last thing currently on his mind was new productions or simply getting plays on to the stage for the sake of it. They came to Stanislavsky to enable him to give the production a final polish before the first night and formally approve the long-suffering and long-sat-on play for performance. Stanislavsky's state of health meant that he could not come to the Theatre to see the stage sets. He had been unable to conduct even a single rehearsal on stage, to arrange the production or set up the lighting plan, all of them part and parcel of a director's responsibilities. Everybody was aware that the run-through at Leontiev Lane was an odd affair, and that taken together the circumstances boded no good.

The run-through of *Molière* decided nothing in the lives of those involved in the production with one exception: the play's author.

The minutes of Stanislavsky's talk to the performers taken by his assistant producer Vladimir Glebov have survived. From these it is clear that the run-through was something of a damp squib. Stanislavsky damned them with faint praise for not having given up on a production which had dragged on far too long, and for pulling it through in spite of all the obstacles. 'The first impression is positive, both from the acting, and . . . the play is interesting . . . And . . . I'll tell you the "buts" next time.'[58]

The 'buts' related mainly to Stanitsyn's acting of Molière.

All the time I was watching I was waiting for something . . . On the surface everything is spot on and professional. There's a lot of ebullience, and yet something is lacking. At one moment, for instance, there was a suggestion of something, but then it didn't happen. Something was not fully coming out. The acting is good, and it is a very stageable play. There is a lot that is good about it, and yet it leaves you feeling somehow dissatisfied.

After expressing these general misgivings Stanislavsky came to his major 'but', and with it our tale of Bulgakov's relationship with the Art Theatre takes a sharp turn for the worse.

In this play I do not see Molière as the person of enormous strengths and talent that he was. I keep expecting more from him . . . If Molière was just anybody . . . but he was, after all, a genius. It is important that I should feel him as a genius, misunderstood, trampled underfoot and dying.[59]

In all likelihood Bulgakov did not disagree. There was, however, another dimension to the matter. Stanislavsky had found the performance lacking a main nerve, a line of argument, a 'through line of action'. He directed his fire not at the actors, particularly Stanitsyn, but at the playwright. It seemed to Stanislavsky that the play did not fully motivate or simply provided insufficient script for a clear understanding of what it was that befell Molière. 'I do not see the League foaming at the mouth at the mention of *Tartuffe*. I do not know who has left this out, the actors or the author. There is a lack of a clear central theme.' This virtually rubbished all Gorchakov's work as producer, even though Stanislavsky several times more confirmed that he saw the possibility of a 'major successful production'. He offered a choice: if additional work was put in on the production it could be performed on the principal stage. 'If it remains as it is, it's for the ancillary stage.'

It was the playwright who was to put in the 'additional work'. Bulgakov begged for mercy. 'For heaven's sake, this has been dragging on for five years. I'm worn out.' Such emotion cut no ice with Stanislavsky. 'I quite understand. I myself have been writing a book for the last thirty years, and have got into a state where I can no longer make head or tail of anything myself. [. . .] There comes a time when an author ceases to understand himself. It may be cruel on my part to demand additional work, but there's no getting round it.'

Bulgakov tried to explain that 'the actors have to convey Molière's genius on the basis of the script', and that it was not a matter of inserting additional sentences. Bulgakov's objections merely elicited new counter-arguments from Stanislavsky. It seemed to him that there was too much 'physical assertiveness' in the role of Molière. 'He turns out a kind of fighting-cock. In the First Act he is fighting, trying to give Bouton a beating; in the Second Act he is beating Moirron; in the King's ante-chamber he has a duel.' Bulgakov explained his fieriness as an attribute of the period: 'You find the blood and fighting shocking, but I see it as being valuable . . . It seems to me it keeps the audience in a state of tension, wondering whether he's going to get killed. They fear for his life.'[60] Bulgakov's arguments were not invariably persuasive, but it was in any case impossible to bring Stanislavsky round with arguments. He could be persuaded only by being presented with an artistic fact, as he had been in the case of *The Turbins*. There had been no comparable 'artistic fact' in evidence at the rehearsal on 5 March.

They parted with a sense of not having talked their disagreements out, and of being unsure what to do next. Revisions would have to be made, and Bulgakov would have to persuade himself they had to be made. He never worked against his conscience as a writer.

Five days after the run-through of 5 March Yelena noted the result of a second meeting, which had taken place in 'the small opera room at Leontiev Lane'.

Stanislavsky started by stroking M.A.'s sleeve and saying, 'I need to smooth your feathers.' Someone had evidently warned him how angry M.A. had been at being criticised in front of the actors. [. . .] But today M.A. came home in a better humour than last time. A less than good-looking actor is playing one of the Cardinal's monks. M.A. was amused by Stanislavsky's joke that he would be more at home with Plainsong than Evensong.[61]

Four days later Bulgakov himself was describing in a letter to Popov the awkward situation which had developed after Stanislavsky suggested 'in the presence of the actors (after four years work!)' that he should re-script the play's central character.

A predatory gleam appeared in the eyes of the actors and they all started asking for larger parts.

I was so angry. I was sorely tempted to throw the script on the floor and tell them to get on and do their own writing about geniuses and non-geniuses rather than trying to tell me how to do it. 'I can't possibly manage. Why don't I do the acting instead?' But that would never do. I bottled it up and tried to defend myself.

Then, three days later the same thing all over again! He started stroking my arm and said I needed my ruffled feathers smoothed. Then he started on about it all again.

In brief, he wants me to put in something about Molière's importance for the theatre, and find some way of showing what a frightful genius he was, and such like.

It is all so primitive and pathetically bad and unnecessary! And so here I am sitting staring at my copy of the script unable to bring myself to put pen to paper. Not to write it in would be to declare war, throw away all that work, bring down an absolute barrage of inanity, and harm the play into the bargain. But putting green patches on a pair of black dress trousers! . . . God only knows what I ought to do![62]

The 'green patches' which Bulgakov dutifully readied on 15 March, the day following the above letter, are preserved in the archive. They are headed 'Inserts for the play *Molière*, made at the insistence of the Theatre'. Bulgakov wrote several new lines for La Grange and Armande, provided a new dialogue between Molière and the King (in two versions), tightened up the dialogue between Molière and Madeleine, and added a few extra lines for Archbishop Charron. All the inserts have a forced quality almost never found in Bulgakov's writing. Here, to prove the point, is a small example from the new dialogue between Molière and Madeleine, who has just told him she is leaving the company:

Out of spite? I don't believe what you are saying. I can only have been wrong about you. You bring our personal relations into this and want to destroy what you yourself have helped me create? Think carefully, Madeleine. Are you satisfied now?

Bulgakov was evidently trying with this 'patch' to drive home the point that Molière put his theatre above all else.

It was another theatrical crisis in a long and ancient tradition. The director, a creative individual, in the course of devising his own aesthetic world starts writing a rival 'script' for the production. Stanislavsky had an astonishingly powerful imagination, wilful and stubborn. He had never been the dramatist's slave, and certainly not his obedient copyist. Not with Chekhov, not with Gorky, not with the classics. He took a play on the basis that he was its co-creator, and allowed himself complete freedom of self-expression in mastering it. His vision as director was often at variance with that of the playwright. He irritated Chekhov, for example, who concluded Stanislavsky simply had not read his play. The theatre of the twentieth century has been born in the natural conflict and contradiction of those two creative wills, of the playwright and the director, with the director simply not willing to settle for an executive, or even an interpretative role. Directors, much abetted by Stanislavsky and the Art Theatre, began everywhere to feel themselves in control of the production, its sole and sovereign master. If the playbills of the Art Theatre did not read, as they did at the Meyerhold Theatre, 'production devised by Stanislavsky', there was never any doubt but that it was Stanislavsky whose voice was decisive, and his creative will which was freely exercised whether the work in question was a classic or a contemporary play.

Despite the fact that the Moscow Art Theatre, more than any other Russian stage, was an author's theatre, the rivalry between the director's and the playwright's understanding of the play was fraught with potential conflict. The more acutely aware the two parties were of their responsibility to art the greater was that potential. It is enough to recall the bitter, decades-long rift between Gorky and Nemirovich-Danchenko which followed their disagreement about the meaning and direction of *Summer Folk*. Or the profound disagreement between Stanislavsky and Chekhov in their respective understandings of *The Cherry Orchard*. Or the dispute between the Art Theatre and Leonid Andreev, which was never healed.

Bulgakov had shown himself a genuinely theatrical writer in his work on *The Turbins*, accepting and developing truly creative suggestions in a dialogue with his producers. He did not cling to the letter of his script, and showed an admirable understanding and appreciation of the process of give and take in the theatre, the polishing of a production which breathes life into a play. He was quite prepared to make alterations forced on the production by external circumstances, as he did several times with *Flight*, provided the changes did not go against what he described as his conscience as a writer. With *Dead Souls* he accepted the necessity of abandoning his own original idea and subordinating himself to the will of Stanislavsky, considering that he had no right to dictate where the director of the production was the supreme authority.

From the outset *Molière* was a different story, with director and dramatist at loggerheads in their thinking. They differed in their understanding of the very phenomenon of genius in a writer, in how they interpreted the age of Molière, and in what they saw as its relevance for contemporary audiences. No amount of unruffling of feathers or brilliant acting out by the director himself or disquisition by him on his own ideas about Molière could shake Bulgakov. Even Stanislavsky's allusions to his earlier experiences with Chekhov failed to impress the author of *Molière*. Bulgakov explained his difficulties to Yelena: 'Imagine someone started curling Seryozha's ears with a pair of tongs right in front of you, assuring you it was a good idea, that Chekhov's daughter had had her ears curled too and you ought to be pleased.'[63]

For all that, Bulgakov tried swallowing his pride and made a start on adapting the play. His work on *Pushkin* was entering its final phase. He put it aside, and started sewing green patches on to black dress trousers.

Patches, of course, were not what Stanislavsky needed. He needed Bulgakov to embrace his own concept of Molière's genius, and then to produce a script on the high level Bulgakov was capable of. To his surprise, and the irritation of the actors, he got patches.

Nor was this all. As Stanislavsky rehearsed the production new ideas came to him. He decided it was important to introduce actual excerpts from Molière (in Armande and Moirron's 'rehearsal'), in order to demonstrate, inevitably, the quality of Molière's genius. The actors naturally got a predatory gleam in their eyes at the prospect of extra lines (and what lines!). Gorchakov tried to protest that Molière's style clashed with Bulgakov's, but the rehearsal was going great guns, Bulgakov was not there, and everybody was having fun giving free rein to their imaginations.

Stanislavsky was conducting the rehearsals in accordance with a new Method which took physical movements as the key to the actor's living his role on stage. The Art Theatre actors had not worked with Stanislavsky for several years, and had virtually finished rehearsing the play before they ever came to Leontiev Lane. They were very reluctant to accept his suggestions. They had after all mastered the script already, and nobody wanted to start all over again. The situation gradually took a strange turn. As he started working on each scene Stanislavsky would turn it into a class in acting technique, while Gorchakov was conducting parallel rehearsals on the ancillary stage using the settings and costumes of the old model. Gorchakov began skipping rehearsals at Leontiev Lane and Bulgakov, with no option but to amend the script, took time off and tried to force ideas out of himself at home. Seeing no end to the rehearsals, the actors too began discreetly sabotaging them. We read in Gorchakov's book, with its whimsical cocktail of fact and fiction, that after that first run-through at Leontiev Lane Stanislavsky arranged a major rehearsal the following day specially for Bulgakov at which he planned to give him a practical demonstration of all the play's weaknesses and faults. He wanted to show the play in outline to persuade Bulgakov to continue work on the text. 'As often happens in the theatre,' Gorchakov tells us, 'the following day the play's three main actors, Stanitsyn, Yanshin, and Bolduman, were all unexpectedly taken ill and the demonstrative rehearsal had to be replaced by another centring 'not on the main theme of the play, the figure of Molière'.[64] In fact, as we can see from the rehearsal diary, this all happened not 'on the following day' but a month later on 4 April, and those who did not materialise included Stanitsyn, Yanshin, Livanov, Garrel, Gerasimov, Kurochkin, Larin and Shelonsky. The rehearsal diary records tersely, 'Absent owing to illness (cold)'. The suspect infection which had scythed down all the main actors at a stroke was later to reappear in *Black Snow*, where it is unambiguous. If we cannot regard a novel as documentary evidence, Bulgakov's caustic commentary on Patrikeev's suddenly succumbing to a cold is certainly worth considering as psychological evidence. 'His cold won't last long,' Bombardov explains to Maxudov. 'He's feeling better already and yesterday he was playing billiards in the club. As soon as they finish rehearsing that scene his cold will get better. You wait and see – the others will soon start getting colds too. My guess is that Yelagin will be the first.' (p. 168)

Stanislavsky, in a pedagogical world of his own, seemed sublimely unaware that it was time for the production to be staged. With his mind on higher things he had no time to notice that the actors were psycheing themselves up for the first night, and that, after more than three years of rehearsing, the last thing they wanted was to busy themselves with studies and training exercises. For its director Bulgakov's play was an opportunity to convince himself once more that his new Method was correct and powerful. Stanislavsky saw it as completing the vault of the acting Method to which he had devoted his life. 'I have not yet found the way to your hearts,' Stanislavsky lectured the actors at a rehearsal on 15 April, 'but when the penny drops you will be amazed how simple it all is.'[65] The penny had, however, a long way to drop.

Stanislavsky lost no opportunity to show the actors the path to the truth of organic existence in their role, from the 'little truth' of physical action to the emotion. He would sometimes spend hours trying to show the way a costume had been worn, how people had bowed, or held a plumed hat, or used a walking cane. The rehearsals turned into training sessions, brilliant acting improvisations by Stanislavsky himself, lengthy reminiscences which only irritated Bulgakov. It goes without saying that Stanislavsky failed to re-educate the actors and convert them to his theatrical faith in a single month. No amount of getting them to sit on their hands (in order not to block inner action with gesture), no amount of simulated licking of imaginary envelopes could change the outline of the parts they had already arrived at. Worse, what had already been achieved began to disappear. Unable to respond to Stanislavsky's stratospheric demands, stopped at literally every word of their performance, the actors began withdrawing into their shells. 'If you have to think about your hands and stage clichés all the time it is difficult to actually act,' the aggrieved Yanshin complained after being constantly dressed down for touches he had been trying out for years, and which worked every time. 'Acting in front of you is terrifying,' Stanitsyn complained, completely at sea.

Stanislavsky was unstinting in the generosity with which he lavished wonderful suggestions on the actors, trying to find the perfect key in every scene to unlock the potential of the part. He suggested to Stanitsyn that in the scene with Charlatan and his harpsichord which magically played itself Molière experienced a 'childish excitement in the presence of talent in just the same way Gordon Craig could register delight and hoot with laughter at some piece of talented acting'. He could show Sosnin, who was acting the part of Charron, how an ideological fanatic would move, referring back to 'that dim-wit Blyum' who had so hounded *The Days of the Turbins*. Here as an example is how Stanislavsky opened up the scene between Charron and Madeleine in the Cathedral:

Only don't cry [this to Koreneva]. Your eyes are fixed on one particular spot in the emptiness. You can see the Devil the whole time. You are almost out of your mind . . . The Archbishop treats her like an invalid. That will be a better image than something melodramatic. Nobody knows how to caress like the Jesuits and the blind. No wonder they have most success with women.

Stanislavsky worked scrupulously with Stanitsyn and Livanov, showing endless delicate insights into the nature of acting and human relationships, and into the nature of the actor: 'Look at Moirron the way Tolstoy could – right through him, straight in the eyes.'

Stanislavsky went through the role of Armande with Stepanova in immense detail, and here too he created the wholly individual texture of a life: 'She's a really French Madonna who knows how to dance the can-can when she has to.'

'My theory now is to clear away all roles and start from that.' It seemed to Stanislavsky that if an actor could find the correct physical movement he would automatically find the correct emotion. Clearly there was a danger in such an approach of disregarding the dramatist's script, and this was precisely what happened. Livanov stated at several rehearsals that the playwright's words were merely a hindrance to him, and that rehearsing without a script resulted in 'better nuances'. It was easier to act the telephone directory than certain modern plays, he complained. Running through all the rehearsals now was the view that the words were 'wrong', and that the whole thing needed re-writing. Gorchakov did his best to stand up for the play he had been rehearsing for so many years. Stanitsyn tried sometimes to soften Stanislavsky's heart by telling him what a state Bulgakov was in. 'He's been very ill lately. His nerves really are in a bad way. He's afraid of going outside alone. Somebody always comes to fetch him from the Theatre. One time I was in a car with him. I was amazed how pale he went every time we were driving across streets with a lot of traffic.'[66]

All their efforts were in vain. The deeper Stanislavsky got into the play the deeper was his disagreement with Bulgakov, not merely over details but over his basic understanding of Molière and his tragedy. 'What is a genius. How does he differ from an ordinary person? Everything about a genius is very clear,' Stanislavsky said at rehearsals, and reminisced about Tolstoy. It would have been more straightforward to have taken Stanislavsky himself as an example of someone who had never in his life known humiliation or the awareness of 'blinding impotence which you have to keep to yourself'.[67]

The problem of how to end the play also came up at the rehearsals in Leontiev Lane, and it was possibly here that the deep disagreement between playwright and Theatre surfaced most acutely. Let us turn to the talk Stanislavsky gave to Gorchakov and the actors during the rehearsal on 17 April, the rehearsal which provoked the final breakdown in relations between playwright and director:

K.S. . . . Let's look at what the Archbishop has to say in the last act.

Sosnin. He has only one line: 'Death has found . . .'

K.S. Is that the end of the play?

Gorchakov. No. La Grange has a few words after that.

K.S. The curtain . . . falls . . . The King has gone . . . The boxes are empty . . . La Grange appears . . . how is that going to look from an ideological viewpoint?

Gorchakov. We could change the ending: it gets dark, everybody leaves. The scene rotates. Bouton is sitting there, La Grange comes and writes. That would be an epic ending.

K.S. That would be too pessimistic an ending.

Gorchakov. Yes. They would say it was too academic.

K.S. Suppose after the Archbishop's lines La Grange says, 'He is dead, but his work . . .'

Gorchakov. People are always saying an artist's works do not die with the artist. I would suggest the ending as it was before, with the announcement, 'Go home please for today. Performances will be continued tomorrow . . .' Or it could end like *Kean*, 'The sun has set . . .'

K.S. The Kean ending is an ending to theatrical applause; the other ending is too sad. Perhaps we really should end with the announcement: 'He is dead, but his name and his works live on. Performances will continue tomorrow.' I think that's not bad. If we keep to that line throughout we shall end up with a good play. Bulgakov robs himself of a lot of good effects. If he would just accept what is being suggested it would be a good play. He is scared of making it too profound. Philosophy makes him nervous.[68]

We see here a complete divergence between the Theatre's intentions and those of the playwright. It had been largely anticipated in Bulgakov's biography of Molière, in the infinitely sad words he addressed to his hero over the heads of all those subsequent biographers and interpreters: 'But you, my poor and bloodied Master! You did not want to die anywhere: whether at home or not at home!'

We cannot fully understand the arguments at Leontiev Lane, and in particular the discussion about possible finales to the production of *Molière*, without an awareness of how intellectual fashion was changing. The more time passed, the more Bulgakov's image of Molière was at variance with the new ideas about writers of the past. The Leontiev Lane rehearsals were taking place at a time when, apart from everything else, the 'rehabilitation' and later canonisation of the classics was taking place. It was a time of anniversary gala evenings and genuflection before the geniuses of past ages. In 1935 the USSR celebrated the seventy-fifth anniversary of the birth of Chekhov, whose plays had been described by the Repertoire Directory in 1929 as 'extremely insignificant from the viewpoint of their social significance' [*sic*]. New genres of biographical plays and films about the great figures of the past, writers, scholars, and military leaders, were gradually appearing. The patriotic opera was revived.

Different periods cast their picture of the past in words, music, iron and bronze. It is not monuments we see before us but different eras looking at each other and speaking to us in their different languages. Andreev's statue of a sorrowful Gogol ringed by the characters he had created was no longer needed by one age and transferred to the 'reserve collection' of the courtyard in front of the outbuilding in which the writer died. Meanwhile on Gogol Boulevard a new, majestic Gogol rose who speaks to us about the time of his creation no less eloquently than Andreev's Gogol tells us about his.

The switch of Gogols took place in the early 1950s, but the systematic adulation of the classics was a phenomenon of the mid-1930s, paralleling the cult of the 'Wise Leader of the Peoples'. This bizarre superimposition of such different concepts was something the Art Theatre had no option but to take into account.

'The sumptuous majesty of the period' which Gorchakov and Viliams were trying to evoke in *Molière* did not sit happily with the image of the dramatist which came to Bulgakov's mind in the late 1920s. His vivacious, crafty, and seductive Gaul was left stranded in a different cultural setting and a different period in the theatre. A persistent refrain at the rehearsals at Leontiev Lane was how wide of the mark and out of date Bulgakov's ideas about the destiny of the artist were.

Vladimir Glebov, who kept the minutes of rehearsals, might well have marked 17 April 1935 with a black cross in the style of La Grange. Bulgakov was absent from this rehearsal, having taken sick leave. On 13 April Yelena recorded what her sister, Olga Bokshanskaya, had passed on: 'Olga told me that when Stanislavsky heard Bulgakov had not come to the rehearsal because of a headache he remarked, "Perhaps he's got a headache because his play needs to be re-written." '[69] He was at least partly correct. Bulgakov's labours over the re-writing of *Molière* are never referred to other than as a pain in Yelena's diary. On 17 April the League scene was being rehearsed. Stanislavsky was getting on with a director's routine task of checking the playwright's logic and trying to give greater stage impact to one of the play's most important episodes. This time the restructuring went further than previously. Part of the script from the scene of

Molière's dinner with the King was shifted to the League scene. One-Eye, the murderous musketeer d'Orsigny, was to meet Moirron among the participants of the meeting (the young swashbuckler might, Stanislavsky fantasised, have joined the League out of spite). Those engaged in the rehearsal fantasised different endings involving changes in the behaviour of Moirron and the Archbishop. In short, a new scene was devised which Bulgakov was then invited to incorporate in his play. The dramatist's response to the excerpt from the rehearsal minutes sent from the Theatre on 22 April (it was handed to Yelena at a performance of *Dead Souls*), was to send in a peremptory formal letter reminiscent in tone and content of the early letters he had written during the various crises with *The Days of the Turbins*. He suddenly reasserted his self-respect as an author, so long restrained and repressed, in twelve lines which, as he must have known, could well have sealed the fate not only of the play but of the playwright himself as an employee of the Art Theatre.

Dear Konstantin Sergeevich,

I have today received from the Theatre an excerpt from the minutes of the rehearsal of *Molière* of 17.4.35.

Having familiarised myself with it I must categorically refuse to continue with amendments to my play *Molière*, since the alterations to the League scene outlined in the minutes, and other earlier alterations of the text do, I am persuaded, finally violate the artistic integrity of my play and necessitate the writing of a new play which cannot be written by me since I radically disagree with it.

If *Molière* is not suitable for the Art Theatre in its present form, despite the fact that it was in precisely this form that the Theatre accepted it and has been rehearsing it over a period of several years, I must ask you to withdraw *Molière* and return it to me.

Yours sincerely,

M. Bulgakov.[70]

A similar letter was sent to Gorchakov.

It may not be immediately obvious today why this particular rewriting of the text caused the rupture in relations. Bulgakov had shown himself capable of restraint in more trying situations than this. His enormous experience of the theatre might surely have suggested some compromise move, given that what was going on at Leontiev Lane was seemingly little more than had gone on with *Dead Souls*, and indeed always does when a great director comes into someone else's work and begins to re-structure it in accordance with his own ideas. But what was at issue here was not hurt pride, or headaches, or the negative psychological background which, of course, was a contributory factor. At issue was the fact that the play really was being destroyed, and Bulgakov was incapable of being 'pleased' about what Stanislavsky was proposing instead. He was prepared to risk losing the production in order to save the play.

When he received Bulgakov's angry letter Stanislavsky showed remarkable understanding. It would have been only too easy for him to have downed tools. He did not do so. Indeed he tried to understand Bulgakov's sense of his own integrity as a dramatist. On 28 April, reading the letter before beginning the rehearsal, Stanislavsky made a request of the actors. 'Act it how it is, according to the script. Let us win the victory this way. It is going to be tricky, but it is also going to be more interesting.' At the end of the rehearsal Stanislavsky turned to Livanov, who was going on about how he hated 'this play and this role', and told him 'When Glikeria Fedotova was acting in a play . . . and a certain person (who shall be nameless) started criticising it, she told him that when an actress plays a particular role she must love it, and it is the height of rudeness to belittle that role in her presence. She told him once, she told him twice, and the third time she told him, "I love you very much, but must ask you not to visit my house again." And in front of everyone he was shown the door. That's how firmly we have to keep a grip on ourselves.' Stanislavsky immediately went on to talk about Bulgakov's play and unexpectedly declared, 'This is a good play. No, excellent. There are a few points where we do not see eye to eye, but we shall deal with those with time . . . The play has been rather pushed to one side for various reasons. Rehearsals have dragged on and had to be postponed twenty times.'[71]

That same day, 28 April, Yelena noted in her diary that Stanislavsky 'began rehearsing with the original script'.

Stanislavsky conducted several more rehearsals 'with the original script' on 4,5,9, and 11 May, and there analysed the scene between Molière and Moirron with infinite insight. (See *Six Plays*, pp. 274–5.) The scene of the return of the prodigal son was one where Stanislavsky and Bulgakov were absolutely at one in their understanding of the theatre and the actor's psychology. He explained the significance of the encounter between Molière and Moirron to Stanitsyn and Livanov.

Right, Molière. You say, 'You are a first rank actor'. You've given everything back to him. You kiss him . . . But he thinks you, Moirron, would never make a police spy. You don't have the temperament for it . . . Tell him this now, Molière, as the only friend you have left. Feel how close he is to you and tell him your innermost thoughts. Tell him, the only actor you have left, the only one who can understand you, 'But I shan't be able to act with you much longer. I must give up my art'. 'The others will not understand what it means, but I am telling it to you, I shan't be able to act with you much longer.' There's just the two of you now. He is all you have left. Here you are, two actors.[72]

In spite of everything the rehearsals came to nothing. Again and again Stanislavsky urged the actors to concentrate, not now on the problem of the script but on the matter of acting technique, on mastering a means for penetrating deep into human nature. 'The Method is nature,' he liked to say.

When you understand that you will understand the pleasure of being an actor: coming out in front of an audience, standing there in front of it and having the right to do absolutely nothing. You sit down in front of a crowd a thousand strong, and you sit there as you've never sat before and as you would not sit at home. You just sit down there very, very comfortably. Being alone in public is incomparably more agreeable than being alone in private. If you can do that, you know what happiness is. You move your eyes, and already they've understood.[73]

The actors were not up to such demands. Koreneva tried to explain to Stanislavsky that they had not worked together since 1928, and that then Stanislavsky had been looking for emotions, not actions, and had talked in terms of 'cartridges'. 'You used to say, "Push in a cartridge, take it out, push in another." ' Stanislavsky looked ill at ease. 'That was all wrong. Throw all those cartridges away . . .' He was well aware that it was time to finish work on *Molière*. He knew the play had been worked to death and set back far too often and that everybody was at the end of their tether. But he was also incapable of standing back while serviceable old acting clichés were doled out in place of live emotion, and his new Method, which he believed was a revelation, was cold-shouldered by the actors of his own Theatre. Or even smirked at. 'I am seventy-two years old,' he complained at the rehearsal on 4 May.

I ought not to be talking but I do vocal exercises all the time because this is all I live for. [. . .] I know it all. I am so old and wise that I know exactly what an actor needs. And then I am taken aback when you come to rehearsals. Really I do not know what is going on. I feel I have ended up in some new theatre, with actors I do not know. And I have no faith in the way they are acting. [. . .] I am appealing now to the whole collective: SOS! Save yourselves before it is too late.[74]

At just this time the author was arguing no less angrily and passionately in the privacy of his home that 'no Method, no power on earth can make a bad actor act well'. Bulgakov had given up attending rehearsals, and his information came indirectly from the actors and Gorchakov. Gorchakov for his part took the risky and highly questionable decision at the end of April to bring the private disagreements of those rehearsing at Leontiev Lane into the open. Without warning Stanislavsky in advance, he wrote to the Theatre's Board of Management advising them that Bulgakov was refusing to make any further alterations to the play, and that work could not continue.

Stanislavsky obstinately continued rehearsing, no longer demanding any alterations. He inspected the costumes for the production (together with Gorchakov!), and asked everybody to take care not to worsen relations with the dramatist. He was preparing the play for performance even as the question of who would complete the work of production (instead of him) was being decided behind his back.

On 28 May all these secrets were made public. The rehearsal at Leontiev Lane was cancelled and a meeting of the Board of Management called instead, after which Olga phoned Bulgakov to report that 'the Theatre is eager to stage *Molière*', and that 'there can be no question of returning the play'.[75] This could mean one thing only: responsibility for the whole production was being taken over by Vladimir Ivanovich Nemirovich-Danchenko. He it was who proposed to Bulgakov, through his secretary, the deadline for having the play in performance: 15 January 1936.

Yelena Bulgakova's diary records 28 May as a triply auspicious day. In the morning they discovered from the newspaper that they had a win in the state lottery; the same day they won a court case on taxation of royalties in the Supreme Court of the Republic. On the same day too they heard that 'the play was being taken out of the hands of K.S.' and 'would be staged by other directors'. The entry concludes with a short exclamation, which is accorded a line to itself: 'Victory!'[76]

Twenty years later when Yelena was editing her diaries for publication she pencilled out this naive outburst of joy. Two decades later it was only too clear that the loyal and loving recorder of Bulgakov's life should have marked that day in May with the largest possible black cross. But who can foretell the future? Man is mortal and blind. That day Yelena Bulgakova was blind.

Yet again it seemed as if things were beginning to look up. On 29 May Bulgakov finished the first version of his play about Pushkin, *The Last Days*. Two theatres were vying to produce it, the Vakhtangov and the Moscow Art Theatre. In those same days in May *Madame Zoyka* was being re-written, and Bulgakov was thinking about, and partly undertaking, the conversion of *Bliss* into *Ivan Vasilievich* for Gorchakov to stage at the Theatre of Satire. In the evenings the Bulgakovs went out to first nights at other theatres. They saw Nikolai Pogodin's *Aristocrats* at the Vakhtangov Theatre. The whole family went for a ride on the newly opened Moscow Underground and were delighted by the escalator and the cleanliness of the Underground stations. Bulgakov had a home, a family, he was surrounded by an atmosphere of love, hope, merriment and happiness.

There was music in his house: on his birthday on 16 May he received 'two different vodkas (Yerofeich and Dutch gin), several boxes of cigarettes, sheet music (Wagner's *Siegfried* and the march from *Götterdämmerung*), and Le Sage's book'.[77] The change in the fortunes of *Molière* was seen as wholly beneficial. The arguments at Leontiev Lane were a thing of the past, and never again would Bulgakov cross the threshold of that old house in which he had witnessed moments of purest theatre magic, and experienced moments as bitter as any dramatist can know.

How did Stanislavsky take these changes? What taste was left from this work which had fallen apart on him? We have no way of knowing. There is no direct documentary evidence to enable us to glimpse what he was going through. This was, after all, his last production ever in the Theatre he had created. We have a conscience-stricken letter written three years later by Gorchakov. There is a note by Nikolai Chushkin, dated 24 May 1935, in which Stanislavsky speaks bitterly of loneliness, of not being understood, of 'everybody praising him to the skies for what he did in the past, but reacting with indifference, even mistrust, to his latest discoveries'.[78] Once again the Art Theatre's co-founder speaks of how, in spite of its immense visible success, the Theatre is on the verge of a crisis and can be rejuvenated only through experimental work in Studio workshops. 'We need a new revolution in theatre art. We must go back to basics, experiment, probe, put our trust in people who really believe in the quest.'[79] In the summer of 1935 Stanislavsky set up the last Studio of opera and drama in his life. At the same time, without pausing, indefatigable, in much the same way that Bulgakov was writing his novel, Stanislavsky wrote *An Actor Prepares*, his 'main book', his theatre testament. Leonid Leonidov was to recall meeting K.S. at Pokrovskoe-Streshnevo.

I go into a room. It is on the small side. A Voltaire armchair, sitting in which is a venerable, picturesque old gentleman indescribably good-looking. He has a manuscript in front of him, and his legs are covered with a tartan rug. He is writing. The picture is unforgettable. I thought of how all of us, great and small, were rushing about in the theatre, quarrelling, laughing, crying, 'plucking the blossoms of pleasure' like latter-day Khlestakovs, while he sits alone, our artistic conscience protecting art from vulgarity and distortion; preserving truth, the truth of art.[80]

There is nothing directly linked with the events surrounding *Molière*, only a laconic phrase dropped in Yelena's diary entry for 20 October, when the rehearsals which Gorchakov was now conducting on his own were in full spate. 'Stanislavsky said that he was now one of the Theatre's out of work actors.'[81]

We suddenly catch sight of a less than legendary side to a story that had become a part of theatre lore.

Leap Year

A general meeting was announced at the Moscow Art Theatre for 2 June 1935, just at the moment when the future of *Molière* was in the balance. The agenda was officially prescribed: the members of the company were to study the text of Joseph Stalin's speech to the graduands of the Military Academy. When this had been satisfactorily attended to, discussion turned, as so often in the theatre, to more domestic concerns. Stanislavsky and Nemirovich-Danchenko were absent from the meeting, but Moskvin, Leonidov, Tarkhanov, Tarasova, Sakhnovsky, Markov and many other leading actors and producers spoke. One day proved insufficient to conclude the unofficial business, and the meeting ran over into the following day. The discussion manifestly surpassed all expectations, and its transcript is one of the most gripping documents in the Art Theatre's history in the 1930s.

The crisis over *Molière* acted as a catalyst for a very free and emotional exchange of views. Sudakov spoke first and described the rate at which work progressed in the Art Theatre as 'truly abysmal'. He went on to illustrate what this could mean for individual actors. 'The fact that we have not given Khmelyov a part for four years is destroying him. The fact that Stanitsyn started work on *Molière* when he was thirty-three, and now he is thirty-eight, is destroying him.'[82]

Sudakov had touched a raw nerve. One after another those involved in *Molière* began to speak out. What they had to say was less in the nature of a normal speech at a meeting than of confession. As they became more emotional and heated, one speaker sparking off another, the actors began to pour forth such pain and passion as is rarely encountered even at meetings in the theatre. 'Who knows the whole history of the ordeal we have endured for the past five years?' Lidia Koreneva demanded rhetorically. 'I do,' Stanitsyn replied from his seat, and took up where she had left off. 'They go on about how we should take infinite time to prepare a play . . . Take me, for example. In another two years time I shall be unfit to act in *Molière* on purely physical grounds. I am putting on weight and becoming breathless . . . They built the Moscow Underground in two years. In four years we have built up the USSR's heavy industry and put the whole country on its feet. But here in the Art Theatre we can't get a play ready for performance. I am not highly strung,' Stanitsyn went on, 'but now I am ill. My nerves have gone to pieces. I cannot bear to hear the name of this play. I cannot bear to come to rehearsals. I hate a role I used to love.'

Gorchakov, whatever he might write about *Molière* fifteen years later, here established the real course of events, beginning with how the play first came to the Theatre, and ending with the head-on collision which developed at Leontiev Lane. He put what had happened down to a conflict within Stanislavsky between his ambitions as a director and as a teacher.

When we first showed him the run-through and when he was working with us as a director he said it was very good and could be ready for performance very soon. Then he began working on us, not now as a director, but as a teacher instructing pupils. [. . .] When he did remember that we were working for a theatre which did have an obligation to perform plays he would say there was still a month needed, or even just two weeks before we would be ready to perform, but then he would get carried away with his teaching again and the date for the first performance was put off indefinitely.

Not one word did Gorchakov have to say on this occasion about the disagreements with the playwright or the play's supposed imperfections. On the contrary, he called on the Theatre to be understanding of the difficulty of Stanislavsky's position. He had 'vast ideas, vast interesting hypotheses about the way actors act, and no desire whatsoever to work as a director'. As he himself had said, Gorchakov told his audience, 'When you have reached the top it is no longer all that interesting in the twilight of your years to run around getting some new production ready for performance'. Stanislavsky had told Gorchakov he was afraid that if he were to occupy himself solely with teaching, which was what he liked doing best, the actors would not come to his classes. He was not at all sure they would. 'And that's a problem for you old stagers,' Gorchakov said, turning to the Theatre's founder members, Stanislavsky's long-serving colleagues. 'It is up to you to talk to Konstantin Sergeevich, because at present he is feeling very sensitive, confused, and even tragic. He is facing himself and us with this huge question about creativity and loneliness. He is saying, "Might I really find myself back in the same situation I faced with the First Studio?" '[83]

This revealing document has yet to be properly analysed by theatre historians.

Pavel Markov spoke at the conclusion of the meeting. By this time the highly respected literary director was no longer actively involved in working at the Art Theatre and spent most of his time directing at the Musical Theatre. He had evidently been moved by the actors' confessions, and responded with his own deeply felt and no less striking admission. 'The Art Theatre is sick,' he told the meeting, 'and we are trying to cure it by giving it oxygen. We ought to be saving its life by operating on it.' To his mind the root of the sickness lay in a sharp divergence between the essential nature and mission of this great theatre and the decrepit and 'destructive' way in which, despite all the 'little revolutions' which occurred annually within its walls, it continued to be administered.

We all share a burden of responsibility for the Art Theatre. Each of us who has fled from it feels guilt because everything he does elsewhere he could surely be doing with enthusiasm and at full power in this Theatre. But we have given up beating our heads against a brick wall in the Art Theatre. One critic said Lermontov was not so much disenchanted as suffering a lack of enchantment. When I look today at what is going on in the Theatre I sense not disenchantment but a lack of enchantment. There is no faith, only people doing a job. People turn up to rehearsals, but there is no joy in creating.[84]

The meeting elected a commission of ten members, chaired by Markov, and instructed them to discuss the situation with the Theatre's founders. The transcript bears numerous annotations by Nemirovich-Danchenko which testify to his full understanding of the pain and fear for the future of the Art Theatre which run so starkly through each anguished speech by his Theatre colleagues. We must surmise that it also made a powerful impression on Stanislavsky. It may be that the emotions aroused by reading of this meeting lie behind his letter to Stalin, which historians ascribe to the second half of 1935. Stanislavsky's insistent recommendation that the 'rapid throughput' of the ancillary Theatre should be clearly distinguished from theatre in the genuinely artistic sense was fuelled by a desire to restore to the Art Theatre the traditional homely features of family life lived in accordance with natural law.

The Art Theatre began the 1935–6 season with the première of *Enemies*. The selection of Gorky's old drama puzzled many in the Art Theatre, but proved an inspired choice. *Enemies* became one of the most controversial artistic and political events of the mid 1930s, and again confirmed Nemirovich-Danchenko's unrivalled flair for sensing the onset of a new period. On 9 October Bulgakov met Nemirovich-Danchenko at one of the dress rehearsals. They talked at first not about *Molière* but about *Pushkin*, whose fate was currently being decided at the Art Theatre. This important conversation was vitiated by Olga Bokshanskaya, as we learn from the Bulgakovs' domestic chronicle.

The dress rehearsal of *Enemies*. Olga surpassed herself. When it finished we were standing in the stalls, she, Misha, I, Nemirovich, Sudakov and Kaluzhsky. They had just started discussing the artistic merits of *Pushkin* (*The Last Days*) when Olga suddenly said to Misha: 'You should go down on bended knee and beg Nemirovich to stage it.'

There was a silence.

Nemirovich was embarrassed himself. Misha didn't say a word, and started to take his leave.[85]

Nemirovich-Danchenko was to direct *Pushkin* only after Bulgakov's death. In the autumn of 1935, on the crest of the socio-political success of *Enemies*, the director was preparing *Molière* for performance. It had again been announced in all the newspapers as one of the Theatre's forthcoming first nights, although it has to be said that such announcements no longer cut much ice with theatre people. As if to order, a succession of features and articles appeared in the general and specialist press in which the Art Theatre's innovative methods of working with playwrights were discussed. Particularly painful was Alexander Afinogenov's piece in *Pravda*. The author of *Fear* provided a satirical little scene titled 'The Rehearsal', in which the situation within the Art Theatre was described with manifestly inside knowledge.[86] The 'cast' included an Old Optimist, a Middle-Aged Sceptic, an Actress, a Young Sceptic, and a Bilious Cynic called Boris. The actors were talking among themselves in the half-light of the auditorium after the director had again and again proposed starting everything from scratch because he 'didn't see it, didn't believe it, didn't sense it, didn't feel it'. As if continuing their June meeting, the actors referred to the Stakhanov campaign for prodigiously increased industrial output, the construction of the Moscow Underground in two years, and spoke about a particular psychology developing in the Theatre: 'What's the hurry? There's plenty of time.' 'But life is too short, our acting careers are too short to take it that easy,' the Actress angrily retorted. The Bilious Cynic, who plainly had the article's author on his side, explained everything with crude directness. 'We have got lazy! We have got lazy on our fat state subsidy. We know they love us, and spoil us, and we know they'll wait patiently and forgive us everything . . .' The Old Optimist chides Boris. 'No, that's going too far, Boris . . . Our Theatre has an international reputation.' The rehearsal is interrupted. Some of the actors rush off to a film session while others head for the canteen to continue the discussion. The director gives an interview to a newspaper about the forthcoming productions. 'Busy people are rushing all over the theatre. Nobody has any time. Everybody is overworked, everybody except the Theatre itself.'

At the Bolshoy Theatre on 17 October Yakov Leontiev, a former Art Theatre actor, showed Bulgakov the issue of *Pravda* during the interval in *Faust*. 'Afinogenov blessed the Theatre with a skit about the fact that plays are rehearsed endlessly, even for as long as four years.' 'We were walking on air! Serve the buggers right!' Yelena wrote, her measured chronicler's tone lapsing for a moment.[87]

Afinogenov set the ball rolling. Other articles and skits on the subject of *Molière* were soon appearing. The unfavourable comparison of preparations for the production with the building of the Moscow Underground was particularly liked. A certain Ivan Ditya composed an entire anti-Art Theatre conversation in *Theatre and Playwriting* around it. In December, when rehearsals of *Molière* were in full swing, N. Khor'kov too 'blessed the theatre with a skit' in *Theatre Week* (*Teatral'naya dekada*) which was based on a conversation in the Art Theatre waiting room between Molière, Lyubov Yarovaya, Anna Karenina and Tsar Fyodor Ioannovich (the main characters of all the productions and revivals announced by the Art Theatre). Molière has been kept waiting longer than any of them: 'I was here first. It's been nearly four years. I've spent my last bean in the canteen,' he says, trying to placate the hot-headed Lyubov Yarovaya who thinks she should be allowed to jump the queue in view of her 'services to the revolution'.

Keep your hair on, sweetheart, do us a favour . . . None of this lot need your services. Heard of Gogol, have we? One up on the likes of you, right? Well, see that dent someone's sat in that armchair? Three years he was sitting there before his *Dead Souls* became flesh again. Practically sent him up the wall. 'Right,' he said, 'that does it. I'll burn the first part of *Dead Souls* and all. They've driven me to it.'

Our Russian Zoilos was well informed about the disposition of forces within the Art Theatre, and went to town on the predicament of Stanitsyn:

Poor old Molière here just wets himself thinking about Stanitsyn ('He'll do me over'). He can see four years of rehearsals have left Stanitsyn with a wheeze. 'Me waistline's gone to pot, I've got no airy grace to me any more, I really hate you,' he says. 'I can't stand the sound of your name,' he says. 'You make me want to puke! Four years ago,' he says, 'I really loved you man, like I was a kid. I was crazy dreaming about you day and night!'[88]

Skits do not have to be taken too seriously, but in those same publications in those same months of autumn more serious articles, written by those involved in the *Molière* production, began appearing and fleshing out the points Afinogenov had made satirically. Antonina Stepanova, who played the part of Armande, wrote in an article on 'The Actor and the Repertoire Plan' about the short span of an actor's working life being squandered waiting for parts or for productions to be brought to performance. 'The whole *Molière* saga is a dire warning,' she affirmed from the pages of *Soviet Art*.[89]

Also in October Stanitsyn gave an interview through which the alarums at Leontiev Lane echo clearly. In *Evening Moscow* he repeated that what principally interested him in his work on the figure of Molière was 'his simple human feelings'. 'This is the way the representation of Molière can be lifted out of the usual clichéd buskins of the pseudo-classical hero which the French literary historians and the Comédie-Française force him into in their biographical plays. It seems to me,' Stanitsyn concluded, 'that Molière's genius and the attractiveness of the figure are best revealed this way, through the personal qualities of his character.'[90]

In all this Stanitsyn was mouthing Gorchakov's interpretation of a play he had been rehearsing for years. A few days before the première, in February 1936, Gorchakov had his own outspoken say. He did not pull his punches.

Bulgakov's play enables us to see a different Molière, a man of intellectual passion, bursting with vigour, sometimes intemperate or flighty, a man in love with life and his playwriting. What we set out to capture was not the greatness of a figure in history, the brilliance of Molière's acting, or the *galanterie* of a writer at the Court of Louis XIV. We wanted to identify with Molière as an ordinary human being who lived a life of great dramatic tension as a result of all his personal characteristics, which reflect then in his work as a satirist and an actor and in his life as a member of the seventeenth-century French society.

Knowing no foreboding, secure in the knowledge that the first night was imminent, Gorchakov went blithely on rubbing salt into wounds opened up in the forgotten arguments at Leontiev Lane.

Our Molière is not seen in the pose of a castigating tribune of morality of the era of the Sun King; he does not wear the laurels of one of the world's great dramatists or demonstrate bijoux of the classic craftsmanship of the actors of the Comédie-Française. *He just lives*. He lives a private life of turbulent passions such as, we imagine, was lived by Molière in reality.[91]

The words Gorchakov emphasised almost literally repeat the point at issue in the argument between Stanislavsky and Bulgakov which had flared up after that first ill-starred run-through on 5 March. In answer to Stanislavsky's complaints, when he found no evidence of Molière the genius, that he saw only the 'life of an ordinary human being', Bulgakov had polemically rejoined, 'But the life of an ordinary human being was precisely what I was trying to depict.'[92]

We are, however, running ahead here to the days immediately preceding the première, when this article gave the press wind of the hidden web of interests and stresses playing within the Theatre. The difficult autumn and winter days of the 1935–6 season were yet to come, with Gorchakov and Bulgakov rehearsing *Molière* every day on the stage of the ancillary Theatre, preparing a performance to show Nemirovich-Danchenko. In spite of the success of *Enemies* the atmosphere in the theatre was very mixed. The parish-pump politics seemed to block out completely the larger history which gets into textbooks. In all likelihood the Privy Council lost no time in exploiting the transfer of *Molière* to the patronage of Nemirovich-Danchenko to stir up factionalism within the Theatre. This was evident both in the production itself and the mood of its performers. It soon proved necessary to shorten the production, which ran for more than five hours at its first run-through. Its creators took out a scene set in the room of Molière's nanny and cut back on several minor characters. They had to drop a number of lines from Lidia Koreneva's role as Madeleine. 'The flightiest actress in the history of the Art Theatre', as Vadim Shverubovich described her, flew into a tizz and threatened to run to Maria Lilina, Stanislavsky's wife, for protection. When the lighting technician was asked to put more light on Madeleine, Koreneva shrieked, 'Don't bother. Why should I need any light?' We include all this theatrical chaff here not only because it poisoned Bulgakov's life. Out of these unabashed tantrums a brilliant scene in *Black Snow* was shortly to grow in which Ludmilla Silvestrovna Pryakhina throws herself at the feet of Ivan Vasilievich, and scares his unfortunate cat out of its wits and up the lace curtains.

This of course was only the tip of the iceberg, as we can see from a letter Nemirovich-Danchenko wrote, but did not send, to Stanislavsky on 24 January 1936. This was a common occurrence in their relationship, when a first outburst of anger was quelled by the voice of reason, 'our good breeding', as Nemirovich-Danchenko called it at the end of this very interesting document, which was not to be published until forty-three years after it was written.

The letter, written shortly before the first performance of *Molière*, brings together a disagreement over the most basic questions of artistic principle and the no less acutely felt question of the Theatre's 'administrative and ethical life', which both founders considered immensely important. 'You are of course aware,' wrote Nemirovich-Danchenko, 'no less than I am myself that the principal directive of the Government to the Committee for the Arts is to "effect the reconciliation of these two people. It is a great embarrassment that two people so much in the eye of the whole world" (thus, at least, it has been reported to me) "should be incapable of coming to terms within their own theatre".'[93]

In fact, the reason why these two people so much in the eye of the whole world were incapable of coming to terms over many matters was Nikolai Yegorov, who provides a stunning example of the correlation between the parish pump and the larger history of the Art Theatre. A former accountant with Stanislavsky's family firm, Yegorov had risen to his present post in the Theatre of Deputy Director in charge of the Finance and Administrative Section by the well-trodden path of all such 'theatrical Wolands'. Having breathed and been intoxicated by the backstage air, the humble accountant went on to worm his way into every tissue of the Art Theatre's organism, into every intrigue and 'situation'. Taking advantage of Stanislavsky's lengthy absence he had started referring to himself around the Theatre as K.S.'s Deputy. His name crops up in many of the most important documents of the Art Theatre's history in the 1930s. He was involved in one capacity or another in the Theatre's painful reorganisations, and was ultimately also to play an important part in Bulgakov's theatre career. The figure of Yegorov recurs constantly in the Bulgakovs' family chronicle, and was in turn to provide material for the figure of the 'business manager' of the Independent Theatre, Gavriil Stepanovich. Yegorov, endowed with a high tenor voice and a goatee fit for a musketeer, was to acquire Satanic features in *Black Snow*. Not for nothing does a 'hellish red glow' proceed from under Gavriil Stepanovich's table, and his sly proposal to the dramatist to 'sign our little contract' has more than a hint of the pact in *Faust*.

In his unsent letter Nemirovich-Danchenko analysed the Art Theatre's chronic condition with the insight of a psychologist and theatrical diagnostician of long standing. On the eve of the first performance of *Molière* this had become inflamed, with the assistance of various home-spun Mephistophelian figures, to an extreme degree.

Probably we are both rather over-ambitious. It is endemic among those who make their living in the arts. Throughout these thirty-seven years, as you know well, various individuals have battened on it who have no business being in the theatre in the first place; and it is only your and my boundless love for the theatre, and your and my mutual respect for each other's work, and finally simply our good breeding which have enabled us to preserve the Art Theatre from harm.[94]

The problem of Yegorov is placed in the letter alongside the problem of Sudakov and the Theatre's having gone for breadth rather than depth. Nemirovich-Danchenko seems still to be hoping for some breakthrough meeting with Stanislavsky, like their historic first meeting at the Slavic Bazaar restaurant, at which they might sit down and resolve all the artistic and administrative problems which had tightened into such an intractable knot. The letter was not, however, sent and after the first night of *Molière* a situation blew up which ended the possibility of unravelling the 'web of all sorts of circumstances' for ever.

This is the background against which we have to see Nemirovich-Danchenko's agreement to take over responsibility for completing work on the production of *Molière*. It was a very serious and fraught decision, and it has to be said that Bulgakov did not fully appreciate this. On 31 December 1935 Nemirovich viewed a complete run-through of the production on the ancillary stage. He then talked to the cast, throwing into relief not only the problems directly relating to the production, but also the very real predicament of a director taking over someone else's work for which he did not much care. '. . . I have not slept for four nights trying to work out a way of avoiding mistakes and making myself useful,' Vladimir Ivanovich began. 'My situation with this production is an unusual one. If we were beginning one year ago, or even eight months ago, everything would have been very different. Now it is awkward in every respect.' It escaped nobody that the mention of eight months was a reference to the rehearsals at Leontiev Lane and all the subsequent accretions resulting from Stanislavsky's not seeing eye to eye with the cast and playwright.

Before moving on to analysis of the production, Nemirovich excused several of the most difficult actors from the rest of the rehearsal in order to spare their vanity and avoid wrecking the work completely. 'I want first to excuse Lidia Koreneva. Everything about your part is splendid, and if there should be any points in need of further consideration I shall talk to you about them later.'[95]

Having taken this shrewd psychological precaution, Nemirovich-Danchenko uncompromisingly identified the chief problem which had bedevilled the production for years.

It is the single greatest fault. It has always been present in the Art Theatre, and I have always done my best to combat it. A play is adopted and we immediately start, right from the outset, by not being prepared to trust the playwright. This has been the case with such plays as *Three Sisters*, *A Heart is Not a Stone*, and others. We do not trust the author: this part of his play is banal, that part is not right, and so on. We start re-doing it, and usually everyone ends up acting not the play, or even his part, but what he feels like acting.

Nemirovich-Danchenko made clear to the cast that there was for every play 'a certain limit to the actor's vanity which he may not transgress without serious consequences for the play as a whole. This law has been more evidently in operation in the present work than ever before. Of this I am quite certain.' Nemirovich-Danchenko assured the cast of their future success: 'I have no fears for the outcome of this production. By and large it will be well received.' He went on to analyse the main theme of the play, talking about the nature of the writing and acting professions. Stanitsyn's treatment of Molière evidently impressed Nemirovich-Danchenko no more than it had Stanislavsky, but the two directors disagreed in their understanding of the predicament of an artist. For Nemirovich the crux of the whole history was the fact that a dramatist of genius crushes something supremely important within himself, and his nature rebels against the violence. 'A writer is incapable of compromising with coercion. A writer is incapable of coercing his freedom,' he explained to Stanitsyn. [. . .] 'Take

Pushkin as an example. A writer always has a sense that he is choking something within himself. Personally I consider this feeling a very important element in the figure of Molière.' Nemirovich tries to bring home to Stanitsyn his own understanding of what a writer of genius is by interpreting the first scene of the play, with Molière concocting impromptu verses in honour of the King, as a deeply divided scene. At the very moment when Molière is completely carried away by his flattery, he hates himself to the point where he is ready to murder someone. 'Actors have after all been anarchists in every age . . . Actors breathed freedom with the whole of their being. And the more you choke this feeling in yourself as you are addressing the King, the more you need someone to take it out on. "I'll murder him!" (p. 234) could equally be taken as referring to the King.'

Nemirovich thought aloud through the role of Molière in the plot, clarifying it in his own mind and urging Stanitsyn to take on board all Molière's ambiguity, exceptional passionateness, odd way of treating other people, and the extraordinary sensitivity of his 'apparatus' for perceiving life and people. He was suddenly struck by a comprehensive comparison very near to home: 'Take the example of Stanislavsky,' he said. 'He is by turns mistrustful, intimidating, charming, suspicious, and as trusting as a young girl. An incredible collection of contradictions. Only a very dull critic could fail to appreciate such conflicting passions.'

Thus did Nemirovich umpire and resolve the dispute between Stanislavsky and Bulgakov about the nature of genius and how it should be acted on stage. Alas, his striking formulations were no substitute for good acting from Stanitsyn. The part was not working. Stanitsyn had lost faith in himself and gone to pieces.

One of the surprises of the production for Nemirovich-Danchenko was Bolduman's acting of the King. 'I had not imagined him so imposing. More mobile somehow. You act him as if he never has any fun. Your King is no patron of the arts. For me Louis is all glitter, like a firework. I saw him more like the duke in *Rigoletto*, but the way you act him is very good too.' Gorchakov explained they had had a different approach, and it seemed more 'politically interesting' to present the King as a 'golden idol which crushes everything'. The part of Moirron had come completely unstuck. Running through all the rehearsals with Nemirovich-Danchenko is an excavation to discover what hidden treasures might lie buried in this important theme of the production. Totally distraught, Livanov explained, 'Personally, I have been completely driven up the wall by both this role and the play. In the course of all this rehearsing of *Molière* I have acted my way through forty Moirrons . . . Just when you think you've got everything ready there is an interruption, and then you have to start everything all over again from scratch . . . It's driving me stark, staring mad.'[96]

Well aware of its various imperfections, Nemirovich-Danchenko genuinely saw the production as having an important part to play in the life of the Art Theatre. Presenting *Molière* seemed to him a token of the Theatre's continuing 'honour and good health'.

To judge from Yelena's diary, there was no great excitement in anticipation of the first night in the Bulgakov household. All through January Bulgakov was dictating a translation of Molière's *L'Avare* for the 'Academia' imprint. Occasionally they went out to the theatre in the evening. They saw Meyerhold's production of *The Queen of Spades*, and made the acquaintance of Dmitry Shostakovich, who read Bulgakov's Pushkin play, *The Last Days*, and was keen to compose an opera from it. The Bulgakovs went to *Lady Macbeth of Mtsensk District*; Shostakovich had dinner with them, and played a polka at his hosts' request. Bulgakov ran into new difficulties with his comedy *Ivan Vasilievich*, with some over-eager pen-pusher urging him to have Ivan the Terrible say, 'Things are better nowadays than they were then.' On 28 January an article, 'Not Music but Muddle', appeared, harshly criticising Shostakovich's opera. The Bulgakovs read the newspaper in the morning, before Bulgakov went off to a rehearsal of *Molière*. Yelena conscientiously noted in her diary, 'Shostakovich probably was mistaken in taking on such a gloomy, depressing plot. I can just imagine how he must be feeling!'[97]

The historian of ancient times believed the future casts its shadow long before it arrives. It is merely a question of whether we see the shadow. The events of January and February 1936 are seen in the Bulgakovs' family chronicle in a private sort of way, rather than as the links in a historical chain which seems so obvious when half a century has passed. The article denouncing Shostakovich's *Katerina Izmailova* is duly noted, as is the closure of Moscow Art Theatre II at the end of February; but these events are not perceived as throwing any shadow on the first night of *Molière*. Quite the contrary. On 15 February, the day of the première, the Art Theatre's house magazine *The Gorkyan* came out with a triumphant fanfare in honour of the Theatre's new work. There are articles by Nemirovich-Danchenko, Gorchakov, Viliams and Gremislavsky, and a group photograph of all those involved in the production surrounding Nemirovich. The tone of the articles is optimistic and serious-minded. The Theatre is clearly very taken by *Molière*. Nemirovich-Danchenko writes with a warmth he was rarely able to muster for Art Theatre first nights in the 1930s. 'But I could not have achieved such remarkable results if the material I was dealing with had not been so thoroughly prepared already.' He sees the work's most important result in its rare fusion of simplicity and theatricality. 'When we in addition achieve real speed in our output without detriment to the emotional content we shall have taken a serious step towards purging our art of naturalistic ballast.' Nemirovich finds Viliams's design work bears comparison with 'the best creations of our Theatre'.[98]

In concluding his article the Art Theatre's co-founder speaks of Bulgakov's play, the playwright himself, and his literary career. These are in effect the first serious words to be written about the playwright, who had at last arrived at the first night of his long-suffering play.

I should like finally to say a few words about the playwright. I should like to emphasise something I have said many times before: that Bulgakov is perhaps the most technically able playwright we have. His talent for constructing a plot, keeping an audience in suspense from beginning to end of the performance, painting moving figures, and leading the audience to a special, heightened idea, is wholly exceptional. I believe very strongly that the attacks on him are the result of misunderstanding.[99]

These important things were said for domestic consumption within the Art Theatre and can have had no serious wider repercussions at that time. Of the emotional state of the playwright who had finally made it through to the first night we may best judge from a photograph accompanying Bulgakov's interview in *The Gorkyan*, which is captioned, 'He was great and he was luckless'. The author is shown at the dress rehearsal. He is sitting with his head propped in his hand, and his gaze is infinitely sad.

The first dress rehearsal took place on 5 February 1936. The next morning Yelena noted:

Yesterday, after innumerable torments, the first dress rehearsal of *Molière* took place. That extra excitement of dress rehearsals which I love so much. [. . .] It was not the performance I had been expecting since 1930, but it was a success with the audience invited to it. [. . .] I am astonished how accurately Misha predicted how who would act. Yanshin as Bouton and Bolduman as the King are magnificent. Koreneva, Gerasimov and Podgorny are ludicrously bad. [. . .] Viliams is good. In some places the settings drew applause. The first applause ran through the audience when Larin (Charlatan) finished playing the harpsichord. They applauded the King's line, 'Monsieur le duc, if it is not too much trouble, put Father Bartholomew into prison for three months'. (p. 248)[100]

The dress rehearsals went from strength to strength.

On 9 February Yelena noted with some astonishment, 'Success again, and a major one. Some twenty curtain calls'. The tone changes abruptly after the final dress rehearsal on 14 February. 'The dress rehearsal went marvellously. Again the same number of curtain calls, so the audience must like it. But Pavel Markov said the critics, Kruti, Feldman and Zagorsky, were running it down in the intervals.'[101]

Bulgakov had a presentiment of disaster. The day the first critical article on *Molière* came out he reported to Popov:

Molière has been performed. The dress rehearsals were on 5 and 9 February. They say it is a success. At both I had to come out on stage and bow, which I hate.

Today there was the first swallow in *Soviet Art*, a review by Litovsky. He writes against the play with great spitefulness, controlled to the best of his ability. He lies about the actors, with one exception. . . .[102]

The 'one exception' where Bulgakov had to agree with Litovsky was, sadly, Stanitsyn's rendering of Molière, which merited the short comment, 'the figure is lightweight and unimpressive. The role is on the dry side.'[103] It is, of course, difficult after all this time to recreate the likeness of a production which had such a short stage life, but we have to agree that this truly was *Hamlet* without the Prince. Boris Alpers in the *Literary Gazette* fleshed out Litovsky's jaded characterisation with caustic detail:

Out on to the stage comes an elderly comic actor with a nondescript but self-satisfied expression. He has beady eyes, a twisted, triumphant smile, an unmistakable paunch, and a voice which is fussy and breathless. This greying individual comports himself like a *jeune premier* in the old provincial theatre, and passes quickly from anger to an obsequious smile, from capriciousness to a businesslike tone.[104]

The article appeared on 10 March, the day *Molière* ceased to exist.

More swallows were soon flying in, taking their cue from Litovsky. An article threatening dire consequences for Bulgakov appeared in *Evening Moscow* on 17 February in which Timofey Rokotov announced, 'It is wholly impermissible to construct a play on the allegation that Molière was guilty of incest, an allegation made by the great writer's class enemies in order to discredit him politically.'[105] (The 'allegation' had in fact been used by Goldoni in the first known play about Molière.)

Articles along these lines only serve to fuel interest in a play. On 17 and 24 February *Molière* was sold out. 'The production is a resounding success. Endless curtain calls today,' Yelena noted after the matinée on 24 February.[106] It seemed to be a law of Bulgakov's literary career that great success in the theatre had to be accompanied by a downside with diabolical overtones. This time there were endless telephone calls from people wanting tickets, alternating with requests from people who wanted to borrow money. The theatre's hangers-on dreamed dreams of untold wealth, but in the Bulgakov household there was 'a dreadful mood, a reaction after *Molière*'. The play's success with the public did not fool Bulgakov. 'It is not the production I had hoped for.'[107]

Bulgakov read the issue of *The Gorkyan* of 22 February carefully. It contained comments on the production from Vsevolod Ivanov, Alexander Afinogenov and Yury Olesha. For different reasons, in tones which ranged from irritation to condolence, the playwrights unanimously damned both the play and the production. It was not his fellow playwrights' negative comments which caught Bulgakov's attention. He was well enough used to the fact that they rarely jumped for joy at the sight of another's success. When Lev Slavin came up to congratulate Bulgakov on a fine production the fact was recorded in the diary as something quite exceptional. 'A rare instance from a writer. No playwright has ever praised Misha's works.'[108] What did rivet his attention was the comment by the actor Vladimir Gribkov, printed in the magazine alongside the writers' comments, who accused his theatre of 'irresponsibility over the repertoire' and was the first to declare that 'a play of this kind is not needed at all' on the stage of the Art Theatre.[109]

We shall return to this utterance, which had a major impact within the Art Theatre. Events moved very fast, not over months but by the day and the hour. On 4 March the Bulgakovs saw Osaf Litovsky 'writing something down' in the Management box at the seventh performance of *Molière*. Five days later, on 9 March, his editorial article appeared titled 'Exterior Glitter and False Content'.[110] As she read it, Yelena Bulgakova was herself reminded of the words of La Grange, 'I shall put a black cross . . .' In the same place she noted Bulgakov's reaction:

When we read it M.A. said, 'That's the end of *Molière*. And the end of *Ivan Vasilievich*.'
    We went to the Art Theatre during the day.
    Molière has been taken off. It will not be performed tomorrow.
    Everyone's expressions were completely changed.[111]

'Many people were completely at a loss to explain the Board of Management's hasty decision to remove *Molière* from the repertoire,' Vitaly Vilenkin writes. 'Bulgakov could never forgive the Art Theatre for not coming to his defence.'[112]

If the general outline of what befell *Molière* has long been reasonably clear, it is only now, when access has been gained to various highly secret archives, that we can fully recognise the scope and nature of theatre intrigues in which the highest authorities in the state participated. The latest revelations throw a new light on the source of Bulgakov's grudge against Stanislavsky and Nemirovich-Danchenko, and indeed against the Art Theatre in general for the way it had behaved. Pyotr Kerzhentsev it had been who seven years earlier, as an official of the Central Committee's Section for Agitation and Propaganda, had drawn up the *aide-mémoire* which led to the banning of *Flight*. He had gone on to become Chairman of the Committee for the Arts. Now, on 29 February 1936, he teased out the hidden meaning of *Molière* in a denunciation addressed to Stalin and Molotov. The wily bureaucrat saw Bulgakov's aim as being 'to invite the theatregoer to see an analogy between the situation of a writer under the dictatorship of the proletariat and the "tyranny without redress" of Louis XIV'. Deliberately provoking Stalin, the literary satrap quoted from Bulgakov's play: 'Molière is given such lines as "All my life I've licked his spurs and only thought of one thing – don't crush me. And now he has crushed me all the same." "I haven't flattered you enough? Your Majesty, where will you find another plate-licker like Molière?", "What more must I do to prove I'm a worm?".'

Having thus incensed the dictator, Kerzhentsev went on to propose that

the Art Theatre's second stage should be made to take the production off not by a formal ban but by its arriving at a conscious rejection of what the theatre should recognise as a mistaken production causing it to stray from the line of socialist realism. To achieve this a leading article should be placed in *Pravda* strongly criticising *Molière* along the lines of my comments and the production should be analysed in other organs of the press.

Stalin's laconic comment survives: 'I consider Comrade Kerzhentsev right. I favour his proposal.' The names of all the other political leaders concur in a neat row: Molotov, Kaganovich, Mikoyan, Voroshilov, Kalinin and Ordzhonikidze.

Everything after that was played in strict accordance with the authorised script.[113]

For several months more the theatre watchdogs continued to analyse the failings of the defunct production. Boris Alpers's article was soon followed by 'Meyerhold against the Cult of Meyerholdism', a summary in the *Literary Gazette* of a talk given by Meyerhold on 14 March in Leningrad. 'In Nikolai Gorchakov's production I saw my own excesses at their ripest. There is an intoxicant in the theatre called sumptuousness. The greater the director the more relentlessly he fights sumptuousness. Sumptuousness is a poison which sometimes allows one to conceal a lot that is putrid.'[114] Bulgakov not only cut out and stuck these lines in his scrapbook but also a photograph of Meyerhold himself . . .

Also on 14 March *Soviet Art*, which Litovsky edited, returned to *Molière*, having 'organised' an article by Mikhail Yanshin. Decades later the incomparable performer of Lariosik was to relate that the magazine's correspondent had come to see him, interviewed him, and then printed a text which was completely at variance with what he had said. The article was titled 'An Instructive Failure' and its gist was that 'a hopelessly naturalistic production had been mounted on the basis of a faulty script which distorted historical reality'. The Theatre 'had even closed its eyes to the actors' departing from the script of the play (Moirron) to the detriment of text by Molière himself.' The result 'was an enormous flop, a crashing theatrical failure'.[115]

Nemirovich-Danchenko was completely taken aback by what was being written by individuals directly involved in the production, not least by their tone. He even thought of writing an open letter to the company's actors in *The Gorkyan*.

I should like to write a letter to *The Gorkyan* along the following lines: 'I would be extremely interested, indeed I would go so far as to say I am very anxious to know how our actors view such very out of the ordinary phenomena as V. Gribkov's comments on *Molière* in *The Gorkyan*, and in particular Yanshin's article in *Soviet Art*.

In my opinion this is an absolutely basic question, and one which to some degree raises matters of simple theatre ethics.[116]

Four days later Vladimir Ivanovich sent Olga Bokshanskaya a further note in this connection:

Could I think for a moment that actors have no right to express their opinion about their own theatre? The ethical problem arises from the way in which Gribkov and Yanshin have done so . . . Of anyone expressing himself publicly one expects as a matter of course no more than that he should first have thought carefully and deeply, and that he should be conscientious. Where someone from our own company is involved, however, there are also certain very particular circumstances to be considered, or a special sense of decency which one expects. I was just thinking we might talk about this among ourselves within the company. It is all much more fundamental than it might seem at first sight.[117]

Fundamental it most certainly was. Mikhail Yanshin was unable to forget the saga to his dying day. He was to describe in the 1960s how the episode ruined his relations with Bulgakov.

I met him on more than one occasion after that. Of course I did. But I was probably no closer to him by then than many others. For the last time I met him on Kuznetsky Bridge. I could see he wanted to cross Petrovka but there was a great deal of traffic coming from all directions. He did not like that. He was standing there looking rather distraught, and I called to him and offered to help. We crossed to the other side of the street. He thanked me and went on his way. He was wearing a shaggy grey autumn or winter coat I remember. I looked after him for a long time. I did not know it was the last time I would see him. Yes, I never saw him again.[118]

This account was taken down by a shorthand typist, but there is a tape recording too where we can hear the old actor weeping as he recalls this tale of years gone by.

In this respect also, a production which became part of theatre lore had a far from legendary ending.

Something had to be done, and done urgently. On 4 March Bulgakov read an announcement in *Pravda* of a competition for the writing of a textbook on the history of the USSR. He began work the next day. This was to continue for a fairly lengthy period. In the course of intensively seeking a way out of his literary and biographical predicament Bulgakov met Pyotr Kerzhentsev, the first Chairman of the Committee for Artistic Affairs which had been created in early 1936. Part of what transpired in the course of this very important meeting we learn from a missive Olga sent urgently to Nemirovich-Danchenko.

Vladimir Ivanovich, strictly between ourselves, because I know Bulgakov would kill me if he knew I was talking about him behind his back and without his permission: this morning [16 March] he was summoned to see Kerzhentsev and spent an hour and a half with him. Afterwards he was at the Theatre and told me about the meeting. When I asked what they had talked about he replied that it was about his future work, but he said his mind was in a whirl and he had not even had time to speak to his wife, and so forth. In short, I have the impression he has been given to understand that he should not be too downcast by the article, and that he is expected to continue to work. I asked him whether they were giving him a 'social commission' to work on, but did not manage to get anything definite out of him . . . He may not be so secretive later on, but he always seems to insist on keeping his thoughts and actions under wraps at first.[119]

There was nothing that particularly needed to be kept under wraps, and a few days later Bokshanskaya was able to report that it was indeed merely a matter of his future work. No changes in the fortunes of *Molière* or Bulgakov's other plays were expected.

The Theatre tried to find ways of supporting its dramatist in his hour of need. In May a contract was concluded for him to translate *The Merry Wives of Windsor*, the idea being to bring together parts of *The Merry Wives* and *Henry IV*, with a major role for Mikhail Tarkhanov as Falstaff. The play was to have been produced by Nikolai Gorchakov, but Bulgakov was not destined to have a Shakespeare Period.

In spring 1936 the Art Theatre's new Director, Mikhail Arkadiev (whose arrival had been trumpeted in *The Gorkyan* with an article titled 'An Historic Day in the Life of the Art Theatre') wrote to Stanislavsky and Nemirovich-Danchenko raising the question of the ancillary stage, which had no repertoire. Arkadiev informed them of negotiations with Bulgakov regarding a possible reworking of *Molière*, but his initiative came to nothing. Bulgakov refused point blank to rewrite the play. His career at the Art Theatre was clearly in terminal decline.

In April 1932 when *The Days of the Turbins* had been revived at the Art Theatre, Bulgakov had drawn up a preliminary balance sheet of his literary career in a letter to Pavel Popov. Remembering his mother, the 'radiant queen' who had dreamed of her sons becoming post office engineers, he imagined a conversation with her.

I do not know, of course, whether my late mother is aware that her youngest is a solo balalaika-player in France, her middle son an academic bacteriologist, also in France, and that her eldest has chosen not to become anything at all.

I imagine she does. And at times when in bitter dreams I see again that lampshade, the piano keyboard, *Faust* and her (I have dreamed three times of her in recent nights. Why is she disturbing me?), I want to say to her, 'Come with me to the Art Theatre and I'll show you a play. But that's all I've got to show you. Pax, Mother?'[120]

In June 1936 Bulgakov returned on tour with the Art Theatre to his native Kiev and the graves of his ancestors. As if in fulfilment of prophecy, as if carefully rounding off some cyclical pattern in his biography, Fate allowed him to present *The Days of the Turbins* in Kiev. In Kiev, too, to all intents and purposes, the final full stop was put to his ten-year romance with the Theatre.

Bulgakov and Yelena spent the remainder of the summer with the Art Theatre crowd. In Sinop near Sukhumi, in sweltering heat, they talked together for the last time. Gorchakov sent Bulgakov jokey little notes: 'On special instructions of the Board of Management a choppy sea has today been arranged for our great, beloved Man of Letters and of the People, M. A. Bulgakov.'[121] However, it was perhaps on just such a day, shortly before their return to Moscow, that a far from jocular conversation took place between the two men. Gorchakov wanted to persuade Bulgakov to write a number of new scenes for *Molière*. Bulgakov refused. 'I shan't shift a single comma.' The conversation then turned to *The Merry Wives of Windsor*, which Bulgakov had already started translating. Gorchakov advised Bulgakov to lard the play with quips of his own devising. 'You are unduly chaste, *maître* . . .' The *maître* ended by refusing to continue translating. Long experience led him to disbelieve Markov's attempts (Markov was also in Sinop) to comfort and reassure him that the Theatre would protect his rights. 'The Theatre is incapable of protecting me from anything at all.'[122]

Back in Moscow life continued as before. Nemirovich-Danchenko was still taking the waters in Karlsbad, and Olga was still keeping her hand on the Theatre's pulse for him. On 14 September she sent an urgent communication to the spa: 'Bulgakov seems to have been to see Arkadiev to turn down the translation of *The Merry Wives* and all talk of re-adapting *Molière*. I say "seems" because he is always so secretive you can't find out from him properly why he went to see the Director.'[123]

On this occasion Olga Bokshanskaya's hyper-awareness of Theatre gossip had failed her. The Bulgakovs' 'sister dear, godmother and benefactress' failed to divine that Bulgakov had handed the Board of Management his letter of resignation from the Art Theatre.

On 15 September in the leap year of 1936 Bulgakov moved as a librettist to the Bolshoy Theatre.

He wrote to three of his closest correspondents of the time, telling them about his major change of direction.

To Vikenty Veresaev he wrote, 'I have left the Art Theatre. It is too dreadful for me to continue to work in the place where they wrecked *Molière*. I have torn up my contract to translate *The Merry Wives*. I started feeling hemmed in at Art Theatre Passage . . .'[124]

To Yakov Leontiev he wrote, 'When our "sister dear, godmother and benefactress", who always croons so lovingly and tenderly down the telephone, heard about the Bolshoy Theatre she barked "What?!" so fiercely she made Yelena jump out of her skin. I deduce they are not best pleased about the Bolshoy Theatre.' The letter was written on 5 October 1936, the tenth anniversary of the first night of *The Days of the Turbins*. Bulgakov's ironical imagination conjured up an anniversary deputation arriving from the Theatre bearing 'a valuable tribute in the form of a large saucepan of a precious metal (possibly copper), full of the blood they have been sucking out of me for the past ten years'.[125]

The sarcasm is muted in Bulgakov's letter of the same day to Pavel Popov, where the tone is one of sadness and tragic insight. 'Have a bottle of Veuve Clicquot brought up from your cellar and drink a health to *The Days of the Turbins*. Today marks the play's tenth anniversary. I take off my greasy writer's skullcap to the old lady, my wife congratulates me, and the celebration is concluded.'[126]

Another phase of Bulgakov's life was over and done with, and due, in accordance with an established law of his writing, to be smelted and solidified in verbal form. So it was. On 26 November 1936 Bulgakov put pen to paper. In a thick notebook with an oilskin cover he inscribed the title of his next novel: *Black Snow*. Above that principal title he inscribed another, preferred and therefore twice heavily underscored: 'A Dead Man's Notes'. That attentive reader of the posthumously published papers of the Pickwick Club, Mikhail Bulgakov, former actor, former assistant producer, and former Author of the Moscow Art Theatre, started drawing up the balance sheet of his life within the magic circle of the theatre.

7

Departure

'Invitation to an Execution'

Bulgakov's departure from the Art Theatre seemed to untie one of the largest and most painful knots in his life. Yelena records his saying that he wrote his letter of resignation with 'a kind of almost voluptuous pleasure'. He vowed never to cross the Theatre's threshold again, and kept his vow for several years with the meticulousness of a literalist. When, tired of waiting outside in the street for his wife, he did on one occasion go into the Art Theatre office to fetch her, thereby technically infringing his resolution, he felt obliged to 'make his position quite clear'. From the autumn of 1936 the creator of *The Turbins* never again attended a performance of his own play. He boycotted the Art Theatre's first nights, beginning with *Anna Karenina* and ending with Leonov's *Polovtsian Gardens*. Despite the most pressing invitations he did not attend a single one of the gala performances arranged in autumn 1938 to mark the Moscow Art Theatre's fortieth anniversary. He never once sent congratulations to a member of the Art Theatre who had been awarded a government decoration, commendation or other 'mark of attention', even though these began to pour on the Theatre in the latter half of the 1930s as if from a cornucopia. When Yakov Leontiev, deputy director of the Bolshoy Theatre and a former member of the Art Theatre, asked him to send jubilee congratulations to the Theatre he begged for mercy: 'My dear Yakov Leontievich, say the word and I shall unhesitatingly send congratulations to your filing cabinet; but to the Moscow Art Theatre, cut my throat and hope to die, I cannot. The words will not come.'[1]

In May 1934 the secret police came for Osip Mandelshtam, who was taken away from the writers' annexe in what had formerly been Nashchokin Lane. During the search, Anna Akhmatova recalls, a Hawaiian guitar was playing on the other side of the wall in Semyon Kirsanov's flat. Some weeks passed before the prosecutor communicated to Nadezhda Mandelshtam the decision, passed down from on high, to grant clemency: 'Isolate, but retain.' The decision in 'the Bulgakov case' was to all intents and purposes the same.

'For me being prevented from writing is tantamount to being buried alive,' Bulgakov had written to Stalin in March 1930.[2] He was allowed to write, only not to be published. It was his manuscripts which were buried alive, and this graveyard of creative ideas and unrealised hopes brought down an unbearable depression on Bulgakov and poisoned his life. Bulgakov was, like Mandelshtam, isolated and, unlike Mandelshtam, retained. He was vouchsafed the opportunity of observing the bizarre transformations which befell minds, people, and talents from the sidelines. Predicting political twists and turns, people's actions and reactions became a constant game in the family, and brought its own kind of bitter satisfaction. The theme of how he 'guessed it all', which is so important in *The Master and Margarita*, derived in large measure from Bulgakov's experience of being a literary and theatrical pariah. Forcibly removed from the literary and theatrical process, he received in compensation an incomparable opportunity of observing from the side of the road people and events as they truly were. The apostate become eyewitness.

Events in the latter half of the 1930s were ever more bloody. The family diary records the arrests of Boris Pilnyak, Mikhail Koltsov, Sergey Klychkov, Isaac Babel, Natalia Venkstern, Adrian Piotrovsky, Vladimir Kirshon, Vsevolod Meyerhold, and Bruno Yasensky; the suicides of Jan Gamarnik, Sergey Ordzhonikidze, Panas Lyubchenko; and the execution by firing squad of Marshal Tukhachevsky and other top military leaders. One after another the Executive Directors of the Moscow Art Theatre vanished into oblivion. In June 1937 Mikhail Arkadiev was arrested, and two years later Yakov Boyarsky. The author of *The Master and Margarita* had his imagination fuelled by fantastic newspaper reports, such as the *Pravda* article about 'Rapist-Sadist-Professor' Doctor Pletnyov, the doctor treating Gorky, who had supposedly bitten a female patient's breast. The scholarly annotators of *The Master and Margarita* some decades later were to find real-life sources for what appeared to be Bulgakov's fantasy at its most far out. There is, for example, a puzzling moment in the chapter 'Satan's Rout', where we are told one of the 'new boys' 'made his friend, who was under an obligation to him, spray another man's office walls with poison' (p. 308). This was not something Bulgakov had invented. At the March 1938 show trial Bulanov, an assistant of Genrikh Yagoda, testified that he had attempted to assassinate the new People's Commissar for Home Affairs, Nikolai Yezhov.

When he [Yagoda] was dismissed from the post of People's Commissar for Home Affairs he undertook the literal poisoning of the office and of those rooms adjacent to the office in the NKVD building where Nikolai Ezhov would be working. He personally issued the instructions to prepare the poison, namely to take mercury and dissolve it in acid. [. . .] The office was sprayed by Sivolainen [an NKVD operative] in the presence of me and Yagoda.[3]

Apocalypse became routine and the norm. Real-life situations anticipated also the theme of mercy in *The Master and Margarita*.

Yelena had to be restrained by Bulgakov and Leontiev from rushing over and expressing her sympathy to the denounced Ivan Bersenev and Sofia Giatsintova, whom they met by chance beside the Art Theatre. Her companions held her back and 'said this would only rub salt in the wound'.[4] A code of personal conduct had to be devised for living in these conditions of routine daily terror. You had to be ready for anything; not add to the hurt in your own or someone else's heart; 'never scuttle away like a rat from danger into the unknown'; 'wait till they come to get you'; not express condolences, but help as and when you could. Bulgakov did what he could for Nikolai Erdman, released from exile but without the right to reside in Moscow. Himself persecuted and under surveillance, Bulgakov wrote to Stalin asking that the lot of his friend and fellow-dramatist should be eased.

Looking from the perspective of today at the events of 1937 we may wonder why Bulgakov himself escaped the fate which befell so many others. Was he 'overlooked', or was his safe conduct pass in the form of Stalin's 1930 telephone call still protecting him? Probably the latter. There are grounds for believing Stalin was still aware of Bulgakov's existence, and periodically gave signals which, to judge by the evidence of Yelena's diary, were understood by those with power as updating his condescending permission to Bulgakov to continue to live his life. This probably is the explanation of Bulgakov's exemption from the general misfortune. Not having thrown in his lot with the common herd he had, instead, been fated for a whole decade to endure a fiendish cultural torture. It was not by any means immediately apparent to him that Stalin's permission to live on was simultaneously an 'invitation to an execution': his own. Right through until the autumn of 1939 he deluded himself, opposed, aspired, fell into deep depression, again saw some hopeful sign, only then to recognise more clearly than ever that he had no chance at all. 'M.A. said he felt like a drowned man lying on the shore with the waves rolling over him.' The diary is full to overflowing with entries of this kind.

Bulgakov was not, however, engulfed by the waves of 1937. Indeed, in literary terms it was a year of not a few hopes and aspirations as many of his long-term persecutors were now themselves scythed down. It was an understandable delusion that his prospects might at first seem improved when Leopold Averbakh and Vladimir Kirshon met their downfall; Richard Pikel was branded a 'bandit'; Alexander Afinogenov and Andrey Bezymensky expelled from the Party; Osaf Litovsky retired from his post as Chairman of the Main Repertoire Committee; and Alexey Angarov and many other opponents arrested. The vengeful emotion of a woman at last granted retribution flares briefly in the diary. 'It is heartening,' Yelena notes, 'to know that there is after all a Nemesis for the likes of Kirshon.'[5] The Nemesis of 1937 figures more than once in the pages of the diary, when a burst of satisfaction accompanies the brief report that a long-standing enemy of Bulgakov's has been arrested, or that some careerist playwright has had a play damned in *Pravda*, which commonly heralded arrest and annihilation. 'A fitting end to his career!' or 'Yes, retribution has come.' These emotions, understandable and very human, which found their way into the psychology of Margarita in the novel, were short-lived in Yelena. Bulgakov himself was not seduced by any sense of victory over his downcast literary enemies; rather he recognised a systematically thought-through 'ordering of the acts' which changed his own situation not one iota.

Of the many false dawns of 1937 let us examine one, which may stand for all the rest. Early May saw Bulgakov suffering acutely from the awareness that his life and writing had run completely into the sand. Even more than the Art Theatre before it, the Bolshoy squandered his brains and time on empty, useless labours from which Bulgakov could see no escape within the theatre or elsewhere. On 2 May we read in the diary, 'Today Misha has firmly decided to write another letter about his fate as a writer. I believe he is absolutely right. He can't go on living like this. All along I have been telling him he is devouring himself.'

At just this moment, when Bulgakov's mind was preoccupied with this further 'letter upstairs' and with reading the first chapters to his friends of an as yet untitled novel about Christ and the Devil, the door bell of his flat rang and in came a certain Ivan Alexandrovich Dobronitsky. He told Bulgakov that he had been instructed by 'a very senior person' to report the following to him: '. . . it has now been established beyond doubt that all these scum . . . discredited Bulgakov deliberately in order to make possible their own careers as dramatists', that M.A. was 'of great value to the Republic', and 'its best playwright'. Bulgakov's comments are recorded the following day: 'A very interesting conversation indeed. Dobronitsky kept harping on to the effect that "We have all wronged you, but this occurred because we had such types as Kirshon, Litovsky, and the like working on the cultural front. Now we are rooting them out and must put things right. We must return you to the playwriting front. After all you and we (that is the Communist Party and M. Bulgakov, playwright) find we have common enemies and an additional shared concern: our Motherland." Bulgakov's interpretation follows. He harboured no illusions and saw straight through the situation. 'M.A. says that [Dobronitsky] is very intelligent, knows what he's talking about, and the conversation is, in M.A.'s opinion, a more coherent attempt than previously to get him to write, if not a propaganda play then certainly a play about the country's defence. [. . .] In passing Dobronitsky mentioned that consideration was being given to letting Erdman work again.'[6]

Dobronitsky's tidings confirmed the expectations of half of Moscow. Muscovites, long adept at reading between the lines, were sure that 'now, after all that has happened among the writers and critics, M.A.'s situation is bound to change for the better'. In these months as the former leaders of RAPP were being physically exterminated a conventional wisdom developed which was to run for decades, and which has its adherents to the present day. This addressed the question of 'Who was behind the persecution of Bulgakov'. It was most succinctly formulated in May 1937 by Vasily Rafalovich, newly appointed to the Literary Section of the Moscow Art Theatre (and himself soon to be arrested). Rafalovich accused Afinogenov and Kirshon of all the sins under the sun at a meeting of the Art Theatre's activists. 'With the assistance of Heitz, a one-time Director of the Theatre, the Averbakhians tried to turn the Art Theatre into the theatrical mouthpiece of RAPP.' Yelena recorded Rafalovich's speech in her diary as related by Olga Bokshanskaya. He talked about the harm RAPP had done and 'the sort of people operating in it'. 'Just look,' he expostulated, 'at the sort of things they did. They drove Bulgakov, for instance, into the ground. They strangled him and now, instead of being at the Art Theatre writing plays, he is at the Bolshoy Theatre writing opera libretti.'[7]

Vladimir Kirshon, Alexander Afinogenov and Leopold Averbakh were friends of Yagoda. The latter's downfall soon reflected on their fortunes. Afinogenov was denounced and 'worked over' at meetings at the Art Theatre and confessed his guilt in the style which had become current since the first show trials and the destruction of the 'Formalists'. His contrition as he repented was directed to the same Higher Being Bulgakov was planning to write to. 'The political sense of what has happened to me,' said the author of *Fear*, 'is primarily my political ruin and hence my ruin as an artist. [. . .] My play *The Lie* was prevented from reaching the stage, and provided graphic evidence of the artistic dead-end I had reached. The Party signalled me in good time, but I ignored the warning.'[8] The Party's signal had, of course, taken the form of some blistering comments by

Stalin. These had destroyed a play which revealed with unexpected frankness the legitimising of the forked tongue and two-faced hypocrisy as norms of social behaviour.

There are no grounds for defending the members of RAPP from the charge that they conducted a wholly devastating campaign in the late 1920s against all that was best in Russian literature. But neither is there any denying that the Furious Zealots could never have wreaked such havoc if they had not had the complete backing of the highest governmental authority to seize possession of literature. The *Pravda* editorial of 2 December 1928 stated entirely unambiguously that RAPP and RAPP alone was empowered by the Communist Party of the Soviet Union to represent its interests and implement the Party Line in the realm of art. We should recall that the RAPP leadership was not elected democratically, but directly nominated by the Central Committee of the Communist Party. The brawn of RAPP was used to crush the literary 'fellow-travellers'. It was not needed in the following phase and RAPP itself was then fed no less pitilessly into the efficient mincing machine it had created. Pasternak's lines, written at the end of the 1920s, proved applicable to many of them:

> I know you sweep away a man and never shed a tear.
> You too, martyrs to dogma, are victims of these years.

By all accounts Bulgakov had an excellent understanding of the workings of this sorry mechanism. He did not regard the members of RAPP as primary agents in causing all the woes of contemporary literature, and it was wholly unthinkable for him to join in the gloating at the destruction of these martyrs to dogma. In spring 1937 when Afinogenov was expelled from the Party on the premises of the Art Theatre and a campaign was initiated against Leopold Averbakh and Vladimir Kirshon many writers close in their sympathies to the author of *Flight* suggested to Bulgakov that he should participate in the campaign. Bulgakov refused point blank. On 27 April 1937 Yelena records,

We were walking along Gazetny. Olesha caught up with us. He tried to persuade Misha to come to a meeting of Moscow playwrights which is starting today at which they are going to settle scores with Kirshon. He wanted M.A. to speak and say Kirshon was the chief organiser of the campaign against him. On the whole that is true, but M.A. has not the least intention of making any such statement.

The following day yet another acquaintance 'tried to persuade M.A. to come and speak against Kirshon at the meeting. He said Misha would benefit himself enormously. He was wasting his breath.'[9]

In that last phrase we hear the sound of Bulgakov's own voice. The emotion in it is not that of his loving and tormented wife, but that solid bedrock foundation on which Bulgakov's personality and code of personal behaviour and honour rested.

Throughout 1937 the theatre milieu around Bulgakov was buzzing with rumours of a 'complete 180-degree turn in favour of Maka', as Olga Bokshans-kaya was to put it, exultant at the total humiliation meted out in the Art Theatre to Afinogenov and Kirshon. At the Art Theatre meeting Ilya Sudakov and Pavel Markov had been obliged to repent their error in having 'introduced' these dramatists into the Art Theatre. 'So if you want my advice, you should write a play about Frunze just as soon as you can!' she concluded shrewdly, confidently functioning in accordance with widely held principles regarded as unchallenge-able at the time.[10]

The problem of moral choice was no abstraction for Bulgakov. From the late 1920s when he was first subjected to intense persecution for his writing he had constantly to choose. The choice was often not only between literary integrity and literary expediency, but between life and death. This is the matter with which he had begun his 'Letter to the Government'.

> After the banning of all my works many citizens familiar with my writing began offering the same piece of advice:
>
> Write a 'Communist play' . . . additionally, send a letter of contrition to the Government of the USSR with a repudiation of the views I had previously expressed in my literary works, and assuring it that I would work henceforward as a fellow-travelling writer devoted to the ideal of Communism.
>
> The purpose of this would be to save myself from persecution, poverty and, in the long run, inevitable ruin.[11]

A year later Bulgakov returned to this matter in a further letter to the Soviet Government:

> In the broad field of Russian letters in the USSR I was the one and only literary wolf. I was advised to dye my fur. An absurd piece of advice. Even with its hair dyed or clipped a wolf simply cannot be mistaken for a poodle.[12]

Bulgakov was wrong in supposing himself to be the 'one and only literary wolf'. The political wolfhounds of the period fell upon the necks of many of his literary and theatrical contemporaries. He was right, however, in saying he was one of few who refused to pretend to be a poodle. The forms and means of 'dyeing' prior to rebirth or, as the members of RAPP liked to say, 'restructuring' ('*perestroika*'!) were many, various and ingenious. Not to express an opinion was impossible. Simply keeping one's counsel was not an option. Beneath the collective and individual endorsements of the show trials of the 1930s we find the signatures of, among others, Boris Pasternak, Andrey Platonov, Isaac Babel, Boris Pilnyak, Yury Tynyanov and many, many others. Bulgakov's signature is to be found under none of them. The pressures from those around him and from 'public opinion' were enormous. The advice to dye his fur recurs at regular intervals throughout the 1930s and is resolved finally in the tragic history of *Batum*. Here are some relevant entries from Yelena's diary for 1933:

A phone call from the *Literary Encyclopaedia* to the Moscow Art Theatre: 'We are writing an article about Bulgakov, unfavourable, of course, but we would be interested to know whether he has restructured himself since *The Days of the Turbins*?'

Bulgakov's comment: 'Too bad they did not send a courier. He could have told them, "Absolutely. He restructured himself yesterday at 11.00 a.m. precisely."'[13]

In the evening Bulgakov's sister Nadezhda Zemskaya came and passed on the opinion of a certain Communist, a distant relative of her husband. He said of Bulgakov, 'They ought to send him to Dneprostroy for three months with no rations. That'd regenerate him all right.'

Bulgakov's comment: 'Alternatively, feed him on soused herring and give him nothing to drink.'[14]

Zagorsky came (from Kiev) about something but suddenly felt ill and stayed overnight. M.A. went off to the Popovs and I and Zagorsky talked till dawn about M.A.

Why didn't M.A. accept Bolshevism? You can't afford nowadays to stand on one side writing stage adaptations. For some reason he said something like, 'Towards him there comes from the forest's dark shades, divinely inspired, the magician . . . (the writer M.A.), and resolutely refuses to sing songs to the Bolsheviks.'[15] [This compares with Boris Pilnyak's remark, 'I realised that now you either have to march with the Bolsheviks or you have to pack your bags.'[16]]

In 1937 the situation of a wolf which wouldn't dye its fur or a sorcerer who wouldn't sing the requisite songs was viewed with horror and condolence. What well-intentioned advice on how to redeem himself did Bulgakov not receive. Fyodor Knorre suggested he write on the re-education of robbers in the labour communes of the OGPU. One of the most famous plays of the time, *Aristocrats*, was based on a similar theme. It is tartly characterised in the diary as 'A hymn of praise to the GPU'.[17] People suggested he should write stories for *Krokodil*, or an adventure novel, or an anti-religious play, or one about the defence of the Motherland. He was warned that if he failed to deliver some such play *The Days of the Turbins*, the thread by which his material existence hung, would be removed from the repertoire. The situation is revealed most starkly, perhaps, in a conversation with Vladimir Dmitriev. In reply to his suggestion that Bulgakov should write a propaganda play, Bulgakov asked, 'Who sent you here?' The designer delivered a passionate tirade, at once camp and serious: 'Stop now! You are a state within the state. How long do you think this can continue? You must give in. Everybody else has. You are the only person still holding out. It's just plain silly.'[18]

On 3 May 1937 'M.A. stayed in bed all day. He couldn't sleep during the night . . . One person keeps pestering him about why he does not go to the meetings of writers; another wants to know why M.A. isn't writing what's expected; a third wants to know where M.A. got his copy of *The White Guard*, published in Paris . . .'[19]

On 17 August Ivan Dobronitsky again came to Bulgakov's home and continued his harping. Angarov, a senior Central Committee official Bulgakov believed to have been actively involved in ensuring *Ivan Vasilievich* and *Minin and Pozharsky* came to nothing, had been arrested. This, Dobronitsky insisted, showed that there would be changes for the better in M.A.'s literary fortunes, but 'no less insistently, M.A. refused to believe him'. We can see how Bulgakov now felt about the situation he had found himself in after Stalin's telephone call in April 1930 from his answer to Dobronitsky's question, 'Do you regret not saying in your 1930 telephone conversation you would like to emigrate?' M.A. replied, 'I ought to ask you whether that is something I should regret. If, as you say, writers "fall silent when they emigrate", it might seem to make little difference whether they fall silent in emigration or in their own country.'[20]

Three months later the arrest of Ivan Dobronitsky is briefly recorded, without comment.[21]

For a long time after leaving the Art Theatre Bulgakov steered clear of starting any new plays. He seemed intent on keeping the vow he made in a letter to Vikenty Veresaev in April 1937: 'My last attempts to write for the theatres were the purest quixotry on my part. I shall never repeat that . . . I shall no longer be found "in the front-line of the theatre".'[22]

It was no good. Vow or no vow he had the stage in his blood. At one moment, in the 'hopeful' autumn of 1937, he was back giving *Flight* its final polishing, and the next he returned literally to his quixotry. In 1938 Bulgakov started dramatising *Don Quixote* for the Vakhtangov Theatre. Again there were contracts and promises, changes to be made and disappointments. Starting work Bulgakov chose, as he always did, an epigraph. This time the lines were from Cervantes's dedication of *Don Quixote* to his patron: 'With foot in stirrup, *in that agitation which comes in the face of death*, I write to you, great Señor'. In the words underlined by Bulgakov there is a reflection of his own situation, which was greatly exercising him. He had not settled for a career as historian, librettist, or dramatiser. With his foot already in the stirrup he began looking for a way of addressing the present, which was revealing itself in all its dark and bloody grandeur. It was in the black year of 1937 that he set *A Dead Man's Notes* aside and resolved to complete the novel in which the currents of world history and culture flow through the world in which he lived. Bulgakov set out to find an underpinning for human morality in circumstances of extreme difficulty, and demonstrated the possibility of this on the basis of his own experience of life. He tried to carry through his literary mission with the same total self-identification displayed by the writers he chose as the heroes of his plays in the 1930s. Bulgakov's last years were a time of vigorous and fruitful flowering. He did not give up thinking, but sought to discover the sense of the trials he had been subjected to; he overcame them on the plane of his main book, which he ultimately decided to present to the world as the sum of his life's work. Most of all the pages of his farewell novel amaze us with their serenity and clarity, the luminousness of the mind that wrote them, Bulgakov's ability to see his day and his times as part of the flow of history.

He did not go on to deliver the novel to his society. In autumn 1938, in a perplexing and paradoxical move which would seem to fly in the face of all his life had stood for, and all the understanding he had come to in the novel he had just created, Bulgakov appeared to set out to remake and outgamble his own destiny. Immediately after writing *The Master and Margarita*, without pausing to polish and edit it, he took a fateful decision. He agreed to write a play about Stalin.

Did he take a decision, or did he cave in? The question has been discussed for years from different standpoints. We find completely irreconcilable accounts in different memoirs, particularly those of Vitaly Vilenkin and Sergey Yermolinsky who were close to Bulgakov at the time. They present two entirely different Bulgakovs.

In his *Memoirs with Commentaries* Vilenkin denies the 'rather firmly established legend', that the *Batum* episode shows that Bulgakov was broken, betraying himself under pressure of circumstances, 'unwillingly writing against his better judgement with the sole aim of finally getting his plays published and staged again'. He tells us Bulgakov was 'enthused by the image of the young revolutionary, a born leader, a hero (his word) in the very specific situation of the beginnings of the revolutionary movement and Bolshevik underground in Transcaucasia. He saw it as promising material for an interesting and significant play.'[23]

The proposal from the Moscow Art Theatre was motivated, according to

Vilenkin, by an altruistic desire to help Bulgakov again reach an audience with a work which was perfectly natural for that period and that moment in history.

Yermolinsky in his memoirs puts a quite different complexion on the matter.

Attempts to talk him round continued. Those doing the talking were people far from indifferent to what befell him. They were nice people, very nice people! Without a doubt they were selflessly doing all they could for the flourishing of their theatre. They were putting their all into devising the repertoire, and this, also without a doubt, would be a success for him too! A success for all of them![24]

Not to put too fine a point on it, the Art Theatre is seen here in the role of seducer and Bulgakov in the role of the seduced dramatist who is guilty of faint-heartedness and cowardice, 'one of the worst human sins'.

In all this the question of morality is seen to apply only to Bulgakov. Nobody seems yet to have looked at the other side of the question and asked what the Art Theatre was up to. How did it come to develop such an enthusiasm for staging *Batum*, and where does this fit into the whole history of the Art Theatre in the 1930s? Or are ethical norms something which apply only to individuals, and which should be passed over when discussing an artistic entity? Are they something which cannot be elucidated by research into the history of a theatre, even a theatre which occupies a place in the history of Russian culture no less prominent, let us presume to say, than the plays of Bulgakov?

There is another obvious problem here. If *Batum* was an act of capitulation by Bulgakov, why was the 'surrender' not accepted and ratified by the country's ruler? Why was the play categorically banned without discussion?

No answers have yet been provided to these questions, but without the answers we cannot hope to understand the nature of the drama played out in 1939. *Batum* was a sorry episode for the Art Theatre. It cost Bulgakov his life.

The Art Theatre's Choice

Yelena Bulgakov's diary is the repository of all the most sarcastic and bitter things Bulgakov had to say about the Moscow Art Theatre. Many times the two leaders of the Art Theatre are stated to have ruined him. Every error the Theatre made, every state decoration it received is commented on. The main ups and downs of the Theatre in the 1930s are interpreted or forecast. Shortly after his departure from the Art Theatre Bulgakov noticed that his name had all but vanished from the Theatre's history. In the endless succession of articles and booklets about the Art Theatre, written by many of those the author of *The Turbins* and *Molière* had worked side by side with, there was now never a mention of Bulgakov. When the Art Theatre set off on tour to Paris in August 1937 the original decision to present *The Days of the Turbins* was abruptly changed to presentation of Nemirovich-Danchenko's production of *Lyubov Yarovaya*. *The Days of the Turbins* also failed to make the gala playbill in autumn 1938, despite its having played eight hundred times by then and being firmly established as the major production in the Art Theatre's Soviet repertoire. The 'Theatre, created to the renown of the country' went its own way, while Bulgakov who had given it that attestation as he prepared to join it, went his. Despite the fact that the ways they chose were polar opposites, and despite the deep distress and pain Bulgakov felt as he contemplated the humiliating distortion of what his beloved Theatre stood for, their paths did cross one final time with his play about Stalin.

From the late 1920s Stanislavsky and Nemirovich-Danchenko did not direct their joint Theatre jointly. Their disagreements on an artistic and personal level, assiduously fomented on both sides by individuals adept at fishing in the muddy water of theatrical squabbles, led to almost complete estrangement of the two directors. This alienation had begun much earlier. When Stanislavsky returned with a group of the leading actors from his two-year tour of Europe and the United States, Nemirovich set off in 1925 on tour with his Musical Studio, and then stayed in Hollywood until the beginning of 1928. Arriving back in Moscow he set up a young directorate (known as 'The Six') to counteract the administrative board which had evolved under Stanislavsky. Stanislavsky was strongly opposed to this. In the autumn of 1928 Stanislavsky fell seriously ill, returning to work only two and a half years later. In June 1931 Nemirovich-Danchenko for his part went abroad again, to Germany and Italy, and returned only in time for the start of the 1933–4 season. Stanislavsky then went abroad for a lengthy period of medical treatment in Nice. He returned in 1934, but in the autumn of that same year left the building of the Art Theatre, never to enter its doors again. His information about what was going on in the Theatre was gleaned mainly from members of his Privy Council, who were very good at playing on the weaknesses of his idealistic, childishly trusting nature which, as is so often the case with theatre people, was at the same time deeply suspicious. The 'diarchy' changed in the 1930s from a power once beneficent, which had in the past given the Theatre a great artistic impulse to further development, into an absolutely destructive force. The enmity between the Theatre's two founders gave rise not only to monstrous deformities in the way the Theatre was run but to much more serious consequences also. At the most testing moment in its history the Art Theatre found itself split, divided by an internal squabble. The Theatre's moral strength was sapped and undermined just when it faced problems reaching far beyond its administrative structures to the very foundations of its continued existence as a credible entity.

The question really was whether the Art Theatre could continue to exist as a part of the Russian cultural scene, with its own distinctive and non-negotiable principles. On this level there was no difference to speak of between the situation facing Mikhail Bulgakov, writer, and that collectively faced by the company of the Moscow Art Theatre. When Bulgakov wrote his letter to Stalin, Stanislavsky was writing analogously, stipulating conditions which must be met if the Art Theatre were to continue to exist. Some of these conditions were accepted and implemented. The Art Theatre was taken under state protection and placed under state control. It was placed in a monopolistic and wholly anomalous position relative to the country's other theatres. It too, in its way, was isolated, but retained, creating a kind of 'oasis of socialism' on the theatre front or, as people liked to say at that time, a commanding height.

The function of the new Moscow Art Theatre was to demonstrate the legitimacy and continuity of Stalin's cultural policy to the whole of the civilised world. People in the Art Theatre did not wake up for a long time to the fundamental nature and destructive potential of the threat concealed in favours showered down from the summit of state power. The years of harassment and pressurising by RAPP were so fresh in people's memories that the patronage of the Government, and Stalin personally, were at first perceived as very favourable precisely for the advancement of the Theatre's art. In autumn 1933, a relatively 'herbivorous' period, Stanislavsky sent the Art Theatre a message of greeting from Nice on its thirty-fifth anniversary. Very rapidly and non-judgementally enumerating the main events of the century the Art Theatre had lived through and survived, while remaining true to 'the eternal in art', Stanislavsky concluded optimistically, 'Today, as it celebrates its thirty-fifth anniversary, the Moscow Art Theatre is alive, recognised and carefully preserved by the Central Executive Committee of the Soviets.'[25]

Or so it seemed from that distance. Arriving back in Moscow from his travels three months before the anniversary, Nemirovich-Danchenko had formed a wholly different impression. Finding no 'enthusiasm' in the company's work, he invited it to compare the first five years of the Art Theatre's existence with its last five. He produced a series of facts whose far-reaching significance he probably did not fully recognise himself at the time.

At the time of the production of *Julius Caesar* we had a company of two hundred and fifty: today we are nine hundred and seventy-five. Our administration has expanded and become more complex . . . The Theatre has become a state theatre . . . We now have a degree of financial security unparalleled anywhere else in the world. If you tell people abroad about it . . . they think they are listening to the boasting of a Director with Bolshevik sympathies, or simply rub their eyes in amazement . . . You want for nothing. You are told, 'Get on with your work, create. If you need more money you shall have it. Don't feel under pressure to get a play ready, but provide what is needed for civilised life . . . Don't even feel under an obligation to follow any narrowly political tendency.[26]

The seduction of the Art Theatre was effected in a whole variety of ways. The deluge of money and honours was combined with a promise of unheard-of creative freedom. Stalin's handling of his internationally renowned Directors was a model of circumspection and tact. He wanted to retain them for the greater glory of his reign. When Stanislavsky suffered a heart attack in autumn 1928 the Government awarded him a lengthy period of sick leave on full salary and issued him 3,000 dollars in convertible currency. Reporting this to Sergey Bertenson, Nemirovich-Danchenko unexpectedly came to the conclusion, 'The authorities love Stanislavsky just as they did before. A lot more than they love me, needless to say.'[27]

If the love of the authorities had not been coupled with the possibility of practising their art it would have been tantamount to death for both these men of the theatre. There is no doubt that this was a problem which exercised Nemirovich-Danchenko a great deal. He was much more astute in political matters than his celebrated partner. After the RAPP-led pogrom in the 1928–29 theatre season, Nemirovich-Danchenko again turned over in his mind questions which had seemed irrevocably settled with his decision to return to Moscow from Hollywood. In the summer of 1929 he wrote from Karlsbad to Bertenson about his 'old doubts'. He recalls Hollywood and how he had decided the question of whether or not to return. 'Just as when I weighed America and Russia in the balance at the time I left it was 48 to 52, rather than 20 to 80, so now when I think back, remember how it was, mull it all over the balance rapidly swings to 51 to 49, 52 to 48.'[28]

Nemirovich-Danchenko's arithmetic was not a commercial calculation. His concern was for the single most important thing in his life. Could the Art Theatre continue to exist in Moscow as 'the most civilised institution in Russia'? Could the Musical Studio, to which he was wholeheartedly devoted, also survive? Finally, could he continue to work as a director without obstruction on his own projects, as a free artist, advancing the art of the Moscow Art Theatre? As Soviet Russia braced itself for the Great Leap Forward all these questions confronted the founders of the Moscow Art Theatre no less insistently, if less acutely, than they did Bulgakov. Nemirovich thinks back to the ideological test, 'as repulsive as bedbugs and mosquitoes', he was subjected to in 1929, and for all his hardiness and his awareness that he is 'only too well set up', blurts out a rare admission. 'But surely you must be able to see what I have to choke in my heart! And how frequently!'[29]

Half a century after these events the biographer of Nemirovich-Danchenko accurately encapsulated one of the features of his psychology. He could recognise the beginning of a new historical period as unerringly as he could spot a worthwhile new play. It needs only to be added that this time the 'new play' was an unprecedented tragedy. To this day we cannot tell what it must have cost Nemirovich-Danchenko to choke what his heart told him and adapt with improbable elasticity to the place accorded him and the demands made on him in the theatrical firmament of Stalin's Russia.

Bulgakov saw mainly the outward evidence of this dramatic metamorphosis, noting every last slip Nemirovich made as a leader of the Theatre, as the author of bad memoirs, as a human being. 'Philistine' is the most charitable epithet he can find for one of the country's leading directors, whom he was to meet up with one last time over the staging of *Batum*.

No less dramatic was the situation in Leontiev Lane. Was Stanislavsky, 'isolated, but retained' in his house, aware of what was going on outside? Was hard information reaching him about what was going on in the life of the country? Did he know what was happening to Soviet art and what artists were being turned into, including the actors of the Theatre he had created? To judge by the evidence from many sources Stanislavsky, like Gorky at this period, was not really aware of what was happening. Isolation led to a dangerous dislocation and dulling of his moral sense. He did not see that the instantly implemented, boorish and wholly unjustified destruction of Moscow Art Theatre II was a shameful event which portended the future destruction of the theatres of Meyerhold and Tairov. The campaign unleashed in January 1936 against 'Formalism' was not by any means seen in Leontiev Lane for what it was. Stanislavsky even believed, and there is no reason to doubt his sincerity, that the state's rooting out of Formalism proceeded from an elevated concern on the part of government leaders for true art and a wish to support its healthy tendencies. The fact that the campaign was initiated from above and that even major figures in the arts were ostracised did not change his high opinion of the educational nature of the measure. 'It is not we artists ourselves who have acted in defence of true art, but the Party and Government,' he asserted.[30]

Every word Stanislavsky uttered was now written down. He was deified. The street he lived on was re-named in his honour (a distinction conferred on

Nemirovich-Danchenko only somewhat later). He appeared to overlook the apocalyptic purges of 1937. In an article written to mark the twentieth anniversary of the revolution Stanislavsky spoke of the art of the 'future blessed Soviet world republic'.[31] That unexpected little word 'blessed', so utterly remote from the vocabulary of the time, betokens both Stanislavsky's faith and the roots of the moral aberration and manifest aloofness of Leontiev Lane from everything that was going on in the country.

The history of the Art Theatre in the 1930s is a capricious and highly complex graph combining both major creative success in particular productions with no less major defeat in the inner realm of theatre ethics. The Theatre's moral atmosphere is the thing which is destroyed more rapidly and damagingly than anything else. What crises did the founders of the Art Theatre not surmount in earlier years! They rescued the Theatre at the very moment when it acquired fame and an established reputation by starting to open Studios and bringing in new blood. More than once they rescued it from degenerating into a commercial enterprise and showed themselves equal to resisting the diktat of the market and the rouble. They turned down financial subsidies from the Government of Tsarist Russia, which went some way towards ensuring the autonomy of their theatre policy and their independence from the powers that be. They rescued the Theatre after the revolution when the company was threatening to split. They rescued it in 1924 by merging the Second Studio with the Theatre, whose acting strength provided the backbone of *The Days of the Turbins*. They withstood the furious onslaught of the Leftists and affirmed their right not only to depict people parading about with red flags but also to 'look into the revolutionary heart of the country'. Preserving hearth and home, they pre-empted a split in the company by giving independence to those who no longer could or would continue to live in the family home. As the 1930s approached they resisted the diktat of RAPP and successfully defended their right to remain true to the principles on which a Theatre created to the renown of the country was based.

Only Stalin's favour caused them to come unstuck. They failed the test which resulted from the Art Theatre's being declared a 'commanding height' of the Soviet theatre system. Just as the Art Theatre was being torn apart by internal strife a wholly new situation was developing in the theatre in Moscow. Priorities were being laid down which radically undermined the very foundations of the 'most civilised institution in Russia', and mapped out a very distinctive new role for the Art Theatre. When Nemirovich-Danchenko noticed Meyerhold's name was missing from the list of the first 'People's Artists of the USSR' he sombrely and accurately commented, 'This emphasises the required direction.' The new direction was something it was necessary to conform to. The new official status was something to be ceaselessly earned. And earn it they did. The conquest of the Moscow Art Theatre was one of the major victories of Stalin's theatre policy.

In 1946 Vsevolod Vishnevsky would address the Art Theatre company. The main points of his talk are preserved in Olga Bokshanskaya's diary. As the beginnings of the Cold War cast their chill on the cultural sphere, Vishnevsky called upon the members of the Art Theatre to ponder the wise words of Andrey Zhdanov's report and the resultant punitive resolution against the overly liberal magazines *Star* (*Zvezda*) and *Leningrad*. He naturally also called to mind the sins and errors of the Art Theatre's own past and primarily, of course, the plays of Bulgakov. Amongst other things he quoted something Stalin had said of the deceased author of *Batum*: 'Our strength is in having been able to make even Bulgakov work for us.' It is impossible today to check the veracity of this assertion by Bulgakov's long-standing and inveterate foe, but his quotation seems wholly credible and would explain much not only in the *Batum* saga but in the entire 1930s history of the Art Theatre.

Stalin had been able to make the Art Theatre work for him too. He was not only an assiduous and regular member of its audience but an active commentator on the performances he attended, a kind of internal censor, reviewer, patron and adviser, although more than once he explicitly declined any such role, modestly stating that he was not competent in these matters. 'How to make revolutions, now that I do know.' This remark, made after the preview of *Enemies*, was passed on by Nemirovich-Danchenko to Olga. Stalin involved himself in virtually every aspect of the Theatre, from its repertoire policy to deciding which of its actors should be allowed to take their summer holidays abroad. The leaning towards the 'grand style' which descended on theatre culture in this period, and which was reflected after a fashion in the heavy sumptuousness of *Molière*, was the personal taste of the Leader and correlated with his ideas about the façade appropriate to the new state. He awarded the Moscow Art Theatre his equivalent of 'most favoured' status, and this made itself evident in a number of ways. Official support was given to Stanislavsky's Method. The Art Theatre's most long-standing opponents were not only removed from the scene but dispatched from life itself. Stalin allowed certain liberties to the leaders of the Theatre, but such licence did not extend to the members of the Theatre at large. Stanislavsky might be permitted to extend a helping hand to the devastated Meyerhold, a gesture far from usual at the time. Nemirovich-Danchenko might be permitted to refuse the journalistic hacks an interview on the closure of the Meyerhold Theatre, also a rare act of bravado. But the company of the Art Theatre which Stanislavsky and Nemirovich-Danchenko led was required to publicly welcome the liquidation of the Meyerhold Theatre, which it duly did at

a meeting specially convened for the purpose. In the issue of *The Gorkyan* whose
first three pages were devoted to Stanislavsky's seventy-fifth birthday in January
1938, an entire page was given over to the resolution of that meeting and the
personal statements of the Theatre's leading actors. Whoever drew up the
resolution against Meyerhold on behalf of the Art Theatre went to considerable
lengths to ensure that the blow to the first performer of the role of Treplyov
should be as painful as possible, with a degree of ingenuity found only among
theatre people. After the standard reproofs for Formalism and losing touch with
the Soviet public, Meyerhold was further reviled for having allowed 'nepotism
and favouritism' to flourish in his theatre.[32]

From the mid-1930s the Moscow Art Theatre was to all intents and purposes
above criticism of any description. Typical titles of contemporary articles on the
Theatre read 'The Pride of the Soviet People', 'The Best Theatre of the Land of
Soviets', 'Our Country's Remarkable Theatre', 'The Foremost Theatre of the
Soviet People'. Both the Theatre and its actors were ceaselessly rewarded with
titles, prizes, and the opportunity of holidaying abroad in the summer (while
everybody else was having what Bulgakov in one of his letters to Stalin described
as 'the psychology of a prison inmate' persistently inculcated into them). On
tours within the USSR the Theatre was received with unprecedented lavishness,
with the best hotels and government residences outside the cities put at its
disposal. In 1937 Stalin sent the Art Theatre on tour to Paris, and made sure it
was a truly 'royal reward'. Nemirovich-Danchenko reports to Bertenson,

The episodic actors in all the plays were replaced with available principals, so that all the
actors in the crowd scenes were actually first category actors to a man. This was done in
order to enable those not actually involved in the particular productions to travel to Paris
also. This was Stalin's personal gift to the Theatre. Leonidov, for example, had no role at
all but was allowed to go anyway. And they got to take their wives, Leonidov and
Sakhnovsky, and others. About a hundred and sixty people in all. The vast majority had
never been abroad in their lives before. Can you imagine the impression Paris made on
them!

Stalin's generosity even extended to giving the wives a daily allowance so that
'absolutely everyone was able to buy themselves and their relatives all sorts of bits
and pieces, and the ladies were able to get themselves new outfits. As if that were
not enough, Boyarsky came out to meet the company on the way back (he is the
new Director in place of Arkadiev) and all the goods were allowed through
customs without formality'.[33]

Arkadiev, fleetingly mentioned, had been arrested a few weeks before the tour
began.

There was a price to be paid for gifts from Stalin, and the Art Theatre paid. One has the impression that not a single repressive political action, not a trial, not a single administrative decision sealing the fate of an actor or production passed without receiving the 'unanimous' support of the Art Theatre company. Meetings to approve the execution of the military leaders or the ringleaders of the 'Right Wing-Trotskyist Bloc' or the 'Shadow Centre', meetings to approve a 'Constitution not intended for everyday use' (Pasternak's words), to welcome the anti-Meyerhold or anti-Tairov campaigns all gradually became a normal part of the new social status of the Moscow Art Theatre. Being a 'commanding height' brought obligations.

The theatre world, no less than the literary world, was crushed and demoralised by the state terror. Here too there was no right to remain silent. Reading the Moscow Art Theatre's collective greeting to the General Commissar for State Security, Nikolai Yezhov, or the article from the hall of a show trial bearing the signature of a great Russian actor, you still shudder, decades after the event. Here are the show trial impressions Ivan Moskvin wrote (or had written for him) for *The Gorkyan*. He is describing the accused at the March 1938 trial of Bukharin, Rykov, and others. He records their expressions, the expression of Yagoda, 'the face of a hardened criminal with lasciviously slippery eyes, the mouth of a killer, a poisoner. I look at this loathsome degenerate and murderer, I look at the sly, jackal-like face of Krestinsky . . . and instinctively my fists clench.'[34]

Moskvin could see no difference between Yagoda, the real, hardened killer through whom the Art Theatre actors customarily solicited their foreign passports, and the martyr Nikolai Krestinsky. Neither Stanislavsky's Method, nor his experience of acting in Chekhov's plays, nor the spiritual experience of acting the role of the saintly Tsar Fyodor Ioannovich had prepared him to recognise the real through line of action and subtext of this political Grand Guignol. On the very day Moskvin is describing in *The Gorkyan*, Krestinsky, who the day before had repudiated his self-imprecation, was as we now know taken from Lefortovo Prison and suitably 'prepared' for his required public recantation.

But was it really only Ivan Moskvin who was unable to analyse or see what was happening? We are faced with an acute social sickness on a massive scale whose complex and diverse causes we are still only beginning to elucidate. Nadezhda Mandelshtam surmised that human destiny is not some mysterious external force but the 'mathematically calculable derivative of a man's inner charge and the basic tendency of the times'. That formulation may be applicable during 'herbivorous' times, but in times of crisis, when the shedding of blood 'in all conscience' is freely allowed, when the basic tendency of the times entirely swallows up the life of the individual, nothing less than laborious excavation would enable us to discover a man's inner charge. Some were seduced, some were talked round, some were broken, some intimidated, some genuinely believed, and some were predisposed to slavery and gladly aligned their 'inner charge' with the 'basic tendency of the times'. How are we to mathematically calculate a derivative which simply did not have an individual face?

The public reactions of many members of the Art Theatre company to the Moscow trials and other Stalinist campaigns differ not a whit from those of the greatest writers, composers, and scholars. For some their signature to a resolution of endorsement was tantamount to saving their lives; for others it was a publicly proclaimed gesture of loyalty, 'immunisation against the firing squad', as Mandelshtam says in *The Fourth Prose*. Some signed terse, formal statements; others deployed flowery metaphors of outrage. Few strayed beyond the limits of accepted cliché. Some, like Osip Mandelshtam in 1937, composed odes to Stalin with a rope round their necks. 'Positive' verses were dragged out of others using the terrorist's most powerful blackmailing technique: hostage taking. Anna Akhmatova's rhymed birthday present to Stalin of 21 December 1949 was written after her son was re-arrested that autumn. 'I lived under the wing of doom those thirty years,' she wrote in her *Burned Notebook*, but under the wing of doom a whole generation lived out their lives. 'Reactions' to the show trials were obtained or wrenched from Boris Pasternak and Olga Knipper-Chekhova, Andrey Platonov and Ivan Moskvin, Yury Tynyanov and Mikhail Tarkhanov, Isaac Babel and Nikolai Khmelyov. The cup passed from the lips of very few. No doubt each had his inner charge, but the basic tendency of the times dealt equally with all of them, heedless of their desires or intentions. What was important from the point of view of the basic tendency of the times was that Ivan Moskvin, Deputy of the Supreme Soviet, should 'react' publicly to the trial; it was completely beside the point that that same Moskvin might be privately interceding for someone who had been repressed, or that he was even in the process of writing a letter to the man at the top requesting an explanation of what on earth was going on. Nemirovich-Danchenko might be helping those who had fallen victim, and indeed we know that he did so, because Olga Bokshanskaya retained the postal counterfoils of his transfers of money to the Gulag Archipelago, but this was a deeply hidden detail of one's private life which one took care to keep from public view.

In public, in full view of the peoples of the USSR, practitioners of the arts who were not Party members and who had enormous personal moral authority and international reputations made no move to take advantage of their position. The basic tendency of the times steamrollered them all, flattening into the ground their 'inner charge'.

The measure of the unseen tragedy which took place in the hearts of those who had been turned is unknown to us. How often we prefer to see black or white, reluctant to involve ourselves in nuances in which, more often than not, the essence of human history is contained.

Lazar Fleishman's book on Boris Pasternak in the 1930s contains a remarkable document of importance to our present topic. This is an article by Georgy Adamovich published in the Paris Russian-language newspaper *Latest News* in February 1937. The émigré observer of the Moscow trials seems to have understood something which half a century later we still have not fully grasped ourselves.

Here before us is a list of people all demanding 'merciless reprisals against these swine': a famous professor, a famous poet, a great actress known to all of Russia. Are we to say they are worse than us? Weaker, baser, more stupid? We know that is not the case. We can remember them. We knew them; and if the Revolution had never taken place, if it had not forced them to become raving Marats, it would never have entered anybody's head to doubt the soundness of their principles and the worthy nature of their strivings. Are we perhaps to believe they always inclined to the 'steely Bolshevik attitude to life', as one of the Soviet poets expresses himself? Of course we are not. In a good half of all cases the passport a member of the Russian intelligentsia ended up with was a wholly random matter. Some of them could have found themselves here, some of us could have found ourselves staying there. It never was the case that only wholly uncompromising people crossed the border, while all those who decided to stick it out in the expectation of better times were people who imagined they saw a glimmer of truth in Bolshevism from the outset. No. If not all the separating out was random, a great deal, a very great deal of it was; and there are precious few grounds for supposing that the qualitative, moral composition of the intelligentsia is any different there from what it is here. It is entirely possible, then, that were we ourselves presently in Moscow, we would be signing the same proclamations. The burden of guilt, then, lies on all of us, and we cannot parade the purity of our cotton socks until such time as we can demonstrate that they would have been equally snowy white at any time, in any place, and under any circumstances. We must be fully cognisant of this, if only to have a right to discuss those who are signing their names, living in an atmosphere far different from ours, suffering a different misfortune than our insubstantial, rootless, émigré freedom. But a trouble shared is still a trouble, and it is difficult to say where it weighs more heavily. It would be quite absurd to imagine that Moscow is currently populated with apostates and moral misfits who have lost all human semblance, and that they are demanding an eye for an eye with manic insistence even as they declare their love for 'our own dear Comrade Vyshinsky'. No, these are ordinary people, the same as us; and all we can say is, behold what a thing is man. Behold what he may be compelled to become, or at least appear, in dependence on his situation and environment![35]

The article was tellingly titled: 'Without Tolstoy'.

To pay with your signature and your reputation was to pay a terrible price. No less terrible was to be obliged to pay with your voice and your art. For the Art Theatre this kind of payment began in the new way in which it started to choose its repertoire. The voice of Pavel Markov requires no extraneous comment.

And here we must speak aloud of that genius of our times whose sensitivity to the needs of our Theatre has set it on its proper, creative, socially relevant path. I am referring of course to the proposal of Joseph Vissarionovich Stalin to stage *Yegor Bulychov*, *Lyubov Yarovaya* and *Enemies*. These plays have brought a real solution of the crisis which the Theatre was feeling.

Markov's article was called 'New Directions in the Art of the Moscow Art Theatre'. It was published in *The Gorkyan* on 3 June 1937, in the same issue which contained the report of Alexander Afinogenov's expulsion from the Party.[36]

The Art Theatre had begun fulfilling the 'social commission' of the times even earlier. The Theatre had responded to the tragedy of the forced collectivisation of agriculture by staging Vladimir Kirshon's play *Bread*. Kirshon was the very dramatist who had sought to root out 'those who pander to the Bulgakovs' among his colleagues by analogy with the mass murder in the countryside of 'those who pandered to the kulaks'. In February 1936 *The Gorkyan* reported that the Art Theatre had adopted a new play by Lev Sheynin and the brothers Tur called *A Simple Matter*. There immediately followed an interview, with the dramatists discussing the play's main theme: '. . . the palpable love for their socialist homeland radiated by the popular masses'. The authors 'wanted to portray this omnipresent ardour taking the example of the active assistance given by the broad masses of the people to the investigating authorities in their struggle with the enemies of our Union, the spies, diversionaries and their accomplices'. The central role was the prosecutor, characterised as follows: 'The cardinal distinction between the talented prosecutor of the Soviet land and the no less talented investigative worker of a bourgeois country is the unswerving support he receives from the working masses in his everyday work and his ability therefore to count firmly on this class support.'[37] It seems incredible that the idea for the play should have been discussed by the Art Theatre's producers and literary directors actually in the offices of the public prosecutor, Andrey Vyshinsky.

Sheynin, one of the authors, was a prosecutor for particularly serious crimes attached to the Prosecution Service of the USSR who had already made his mark at one of the 1935 trials. Something equally unprecedented in the history of the Moscow Art Theatre was the announcement that a play had been adopted for the repertoire when only its first act had been written. By way of comparison, and to give a sense of how Bulgakov must have been feeling in the Art Theatre in that year of 1936, we should mention that after *Molière* was dropped, the Board of Management gave instructions that Bulgakov was to be made to return the advance for *Flight*, which had been banned earlier.

A Simple Matter never was staged, but similar episodes occur at every turn of the Art Theatre's history in the 1930s. In late March 1939 Nikolai Virta confided the idea for a new play to the readers of *The Gorkyan*. Titled *The Plot*, it was to be set in the period October 1936–May 1937. Its characters were 'members of the Right Wing-Trotskyist Bloc'. The playwright advised the world at large that he had discussed the outline of his play and how to rework it with Nemirovich-Danchenko who had given him invaluable advice. 'Make it more life-like, more truthful, more convincing.'[38] How odd these traditional Art Theatre requirements sound in that malign context!

The problems were not, of course, only to do with being ordered from above to give theatrical form to performances stage-managed elsewhere. The Theatre's repertoire in this period was formed no less by what was banned. After *Flight*, Nikolai Erdman's play *The Suicide*, which Stanislavsky rated exceptionally highly, was banned. It was virtually impossible to appeal. 'Ask Avel Yenukidze personally whether we should put the play on or whether we have to let it go,' Stanislavsky asked Vladimir Sakhnovsky. 'I was in favour of it in order to save a work of genius and to support a writer of great talent.'[39]

A few years earlier it would have been unthinkable that Stanislavsky should have had the humiliation of asking Yenukidze, the Central Executive Committee of Soviets' curator of the Art Theatre, whether he could put a play on or whether he had to let it go. Already in September 1934 it was regarded as a normal part of the new theatre life.

Work of genius or not, the Theatre let Erdman's play go and removed Bulgakov's *Molière* from the repertoire for good measure. In 1937 they decided against performing *Boris Godunov*, and several years later dropped their ambitious and free interpretation of *Hamlet* when Stalin remarked in conversation with Boris Livanov that it was 'not needed'. In the 1930s it seemed to many people, as even now it still seems to some, that a few plays banned or dropped were as nothing when set alongside the major dramatic successes and all the favours Stalin lavished on his favourite theatre. As it proved, however, those lost plays were of immense significance for the artistic future of the Art Theatre.

Moral defeat is a slippery slope. Before long things were going wrong in the productions the Theatre was most proud of. Nemirovich-Danchenko had to propose changes to *Resurrection* before it would be in a fit state for showing in the United States. He was prepared to replace a majority of scenes with others which it was 'not politic to stage in Moscow: Katyusha in the hospital, Katyusha with the children' and to make a different ending for Nekhlyudov (from the drama *And the Light Shines in the Darkness*). The vice-like obligatory ideological attitudes distorted both the staging and underlying meaning of *Anna Karenina*. By cutting Levin and his moral searchings the Theatre largely deprived Tolstoy's novel of its soul and the production of the opportunity of speaking directly to the contemporary audience about vitally important matters.

Nemirovich found it increasingly necessary to choke his heart. At the same time it was essential for him to preserve his artistic independence. We have evidence which shows that even in 1937 he was thinking about this. Before the Paris tour he tried to imagine how the Russian émigrés in France and a European audience would react to the Art Theatre. He did not underestimate the difficulties Gorky's *Enemies* would face in winning hearts and minds in Paris. ('It will be tedious for those who do not know the language.') He can just imagine the reaction to *Lyubov Yarovaya* and *Anna Karenina*. Nevertheless he thought that on an artistic level at least he should have nothing to worry about. He wrote in an oddly phrased letter to Sergey Bertenson:

The productions are so profound in conception and so noble in the task they attempt. They so avoid being nothing but blatant propaganda that only irreconcilable, inveterate, blunted people with blinkers can take exception to them ... My artistic feeling is completely pure.

He continues, trying to seem to convince not so much his far-off correspondent in the United States as himself:

We show on stage the clash between the factory owners and the workers (in *Enemies*); we show the White Guardists and the Commander-in-Chief (in *Lyubov Yarovaya*); and the Palace, the Grand Duke, and the high society of Russia in the nineteenth century (in *Anna Karenina*). Although these are of course basically extremely social productions, I believe they are presented in an artistic form which is ideal for an artist with good taste who is completely independent.

For all that his art was completely independent, Nemirovich-Danchenko warned Bertenson:

Purely in terms of the realia of everyday life there may well be raised eyebrows; and over the changes away from the relationship between the old Art Theatre and the former citizens of the Russian Empire. Everything has changed beyond all recognition since the 1924 tour. People have changed, the times have changed. We speak different languages now . . . In addition in the last few years there has been such a sharp polarisation into hostile blocs that there will even be mutual suspicion.

Nemirovich's next letter was written after the tour, and he gives an intriguing detailed report on how the plays were received; on the differentiation of the émigrés and their press; on the rumours which swept the émigré community in Paris that the company and their entourage were having nothing to do with émigrés; that Nemirovich had kept the company from meeting Shalyapin and was himself avoiding old friends. He also describes the first night of Gorky's play.

The first performance of *Enemies*. A packed house with 70 per cent of the audience Russian-speaking. The buzz of conversation. A little incident before the start which was to have unfortunate consequences. I was sitting with Yekaterina, our ambassador and his wife in one of the boxes. When I went in I felt people's eyes were looking for me. Somebody bowed. I did not recognise them and did not return it. Then a woman with a lorgnette who was standing in the aisle made a great point of bowing repeatedly. She had two men with her. I did not recognise them, and did not respond. [. . .] It was Teffi and people from *Latest News*. I honestly did not recognise them . . .[40]

When Nemirovich-Danchenko had begun rehearsing *Flight* in autumn 1928 he likened Bulgakov's Golubkov to Bertenson for the benefit of the actors. He had written about it at the time to his friend in Hollywood:

The character of a young hero, a St Petersburg university teacher, an idealist capable of the greatest dedication and chivalry. I described you . . . For a long time we mulled over all the characteristic features of such a type. . . .[41]

In the nine years which had passed since then the idealistic Bertenson had evidently become a realist. In autumn 1937 he noted in his diary:

I read Nemirovich's last letter [reporting on the Paris tour] with incredible sadness. I know him so well, and the ghastly reality in which this remarkable man is obliged to live and work is obvious to me from every line. The very style of the letter makes it obvious that Vladimir Ivanovich was in no doubt that before it came into my hands it would be read by the competent 'all-seeing eye'.[42]

The extent to which the Art Theatre was obliged to isolate itself from the outside world is immediately evident from the fact that Nemirovich was not even able to receive Morris Guest or Leonid Leonidov [two impresarios long associated with the Art Theatre. Guest had organised the Moscow Art Theatre's tour of America in 1922–4]. It is just not credible that he could not find a free half-hour for them, and just as Guest and Leonidov did not believe it, so neither do I. [. . .] The Teffi episode is another give-away. With his refined upbringing Nemirovich would undoubtedly have returned a bow from a lady, even if he did not recognise her. Perhaps the phrase, 'When I went in I felt people's eyes were looking for me' is an allusion to the observant eyes which had his every movement under scrutiny.[43]

Bertenson goes on to relate the impression the performances made on the émigrés.

Unfortunately, it was not only the hide-bound critics Nemirovich writes about who were unimpressed. Those most critical were precisely theatre people, among them Dobuzhinsky. Their general consensus seems to be that even if you couldn't actually say the productions were bad, they certainly were not what was expected from the Art Theatre we loved and respected. The loss of the creative freedom it used to have, when it was not subjected to Party requirements and political pressures, showed principally on the artistic side.

I do not for a moment doubt that Nemirovich is fully aware of all this, and indeed knows it better than anyone and is depressed by it. He foresaw this decline of the Art Theatre a long time ago, but in spite of all his efforts he has been unable to halt it. The tiredness he mentions is clearly not physical, but the inner pain which he was always more sensitive to than physical aches and pains.[44]

What Bertenson, living in America, understood, Mikhail Bulgakov, living in Moscow, preferred not to. For him Nemirovich-Danchenko was a strategist, a tactician, a theatre pragmatist, the author of an article on 'The Triumph of the Stalin Constitution', but not in any sense an artist choking his heart. For the author of *Molière* Nemirovich's repertoire policy, the tour to Paris (to which throughout the autumn of 1937 the Bulgakov household reacted variously with alarm, hilarity, and anger), and the whole dreadful atmosphere within the Art Theatre meant just one thing: the end of the Moscow Art Theatre.

In summer 1936 Nemirovich-Danchenko had tried his hand at fortune-telling. He had written from the spa at Karlsbad to his perennial correspondent in Hollywood.

Enormous changes are in the offing, my dear Sergey. Will we meet again? And if we do, how and where will we again be parted? If twenty years ago we could have looked into the future we would never have believed what we saw. Today's reality would have seemed a phantasmagoria even more recently than that. How I should love to be able to see three years ahead, or five! . . .[45]

His choice of the word 'phantasmagoria' seems to have been made advisedly. Nemirovich was writing three months after the demise of *Molière*, and after the campaign of vilification against Shostakovich and his opera *Lady Macbeth of Mtsensk District*. The opera was also being staged in Nemirovich-Danchenko's Musical Theatre, so that the pole-axe brought down on another theatre could equally well have felled him. Nemirovich was only too aware how quickly favourites change. He could not have failed to notice that the vituperative article in *Pravda* which inaugurated the political persecution of the country's major figures in the arts accused Shostakovich's opera of harbouring exaggerated features of the 'cult of Meyerholdism'. His interest in where and how people would 'again be parted' also implied a special sense which rapidly became evident.

To call the events of the next three to five years merely fantastic would have been a considerable understatement.

In barely more than a month the first lurid political show trial was to start, with Stalin's former political peers Grigory Zinoviev and Lev Kamenev facing sentence of death. They were executed in early September; and on 6 September 1936 the title of 'People's Artist of the USSR' was established. Of the first thirteen people to qualify for this exalted honour, four were from the Art Theatre. In mid-September, on the day Bulgakov left the Art Theatre, *The Gorkyan* published the resolution of a meeting in the Theatre at which the collective thanked 'dear, beloved Joseph Stalin' for the awards and 'promised to continue and deepen our work with Soviet authors in order that the magnificent images of our days, and the splendid features of man in the Age of Stalin, should be seen on our stage'. In the same newspaper those who had received awards, including the founders of the Art Theatre, thanked 'the Best Friend of Actors and the Theatre' for this 'new mark of his attention and encouragement'. In the same issue the Party organiser Ivan Mamoshin (who figures in *Black Snow* as Anton Kaloshin), pointing up the lessons to be learnt from the recent trial, accused the collective of the Art Theatre of insufficient vigilance.

You all remember that shoddy individual Shuvalov, the props man. Chaplin, the Assistant Estates Manager in 1934 and Krogilsky, a technician, have been exiled for counter-revolutionary activity. We had Sakalsky, a former White Guard officer, working here as Assistant Director, and he infiltrated not a few of his kind into the Theatre. This White Guardist was up to his tricks among us for a long time.[46]

In October 1938 the Moscow Art Theatre, by now without Stanislavsky, celebrated its fortieth anniversary. The company was formally photographed with the Party and Government leaders. We see the best actors in the world thronging round a double row of Stalin, Molotov, Voroshilov, Zhdanov, Mikoyan, Khrushchev, Bulganin, and Yezhov. At this celebration Leonidov read out yet another greeting to the 'Best Friend of Actors and the Theatre'. They no longer even had recourse to words of their own. The ritual was accomplished in the simplest conceivable way. Leonidov, renowned for his performance as Mitya Karamazov and Othello, recited the doggerel of Dzhambul:

> Stalin is in our every thought.
> Stalin is in our every heart.
> Stalin is in our every song.
> Your life boils in toil and struggle,
> Stalin, Sun of my Life.
> Thanks be to you!

The episode has more than a passing resemblance to the first scene of *Molière* where the dramatist coins the comparison of King Louis to the Sun, and receives a symbolic thirty sous for his trouble.

Two years later the Art Theatre was to award the Wise Leader its Seagull badge, a distinction awarded to this day to those who have laboured long (at least fifteen years!) and hard for the glory of the Art Theatre. The letter of congratulations to Stalin was signed by Olga Knipper-Chekhova, Vladimir Nemirovich-Danchenko, Maria Lilina and Ivan Moskvin.

Stalin was presented with his Seagull badge in February 1940, and two months later the Art Theatre staged *Three Sisters*, perhaps the last great production in the Theatre's history. The eighty-two-year-old Nemirovich-Danchenko, opening his heart again to its harmony, captured a new music in the old drama, with its presentiments and prophecies of a future then still unknown. The mere evoking of the old way of life in the present day was bound to have a dramatic impact in a Moscow which had so recently been through the terror of Yezhov's secret police. We may be fairly confident that when Nemirovich-Danchenko spoke, as he did many times at rehearsals, of the pre-revolutionary characters' 'longing for a better life' he was not referring to the sickening, force-fed jollity of present-day Moscow with its concomitant nights of terror. It was a different Moscow the three sisters were longing for. The Theatre communed with its past, and Chekhov's script revealed a new dimension of meaning. That is why the suggestion in the old Art Theatre *mise-en-scène* of a too solid, earth-bound, everyday reality had to be discarded; why the windows to the garden, the light, early spring and the avenue of birches were thrown open wide. They returned respect for the Russian intelligentsia and the officers of the Russian army, and the virtues of the way they used to live. These things succeeded in strikingly reminding people how their older brothers and sisters had lived. The aesthetic behind the production was to be 'brave simplicity', and this in turn brought forth its ethics, the steady awareness of the tragic nature of an individual life, the search for faith and a firm support with which to confront the approaching menace of a future in which the play's audience now only too clearly lived. What was to be heard behind Nikolai Khmelyov's delivery of Tusenbach's supposition that in twenty or twenty-five years' time 'Everyone will work'? What personal 'inner charge' was hidden in the comment that at least in present-day Russian life there was 'no torture, no executions'?

'Why do we live, why are we suffering . . . If only we knew, if only we knew!' The supplication of the three sisters in the final scene, the march of the brass band, moving, sad, plaintive, in some measure redeemed the Art Theatre. Its production of *Three Sisters* gave people air to breathe. For several generations actors and audiences did breathe that stolen air of great literature, come miraculously to life in the Theatre.

Nemirovich-Danchenko had tried his hand at fortune telling at the spa in Karlsbad in 1936. In summer 1937 it was Bulgakov's turn, launching cigarette papers into the air from the balcony of his flat in Furmanov Lane with Dmitriev. The stage designer tells us, 'We were trying to tell our fortune by how high and far the papers flew. Then there was a great thunderstorm which we had been expecting for a long time . . .'[47]

We are not told how far the cigarette papers flew. Bulgakov had less than three years left to live, in which he would complete *The Master and Margarita*, write a play after *Don Quixote*, and several more hopeless libretti. Within the same three years Dmitriev's wife would be arrested and disappear in the prison camps, and Dmitriev would design the Art Theatre's pre-war Chekhovian masterpiece. Within those years Bulgakov would force himself to write a play which would prove fatal for him, and re-establish his relations with the Art Theatre, broken off in the autumn of 1936. His play was to have been acted on 21 December 1938, the Art Theatre's sixtieth birthday present to the Best Friend of Actors and the Theatre.

Batum

Bulgakov's telephone conversation with Stalin on 18 April 1930 is common knowledge and has been the subject of much critical scrutiny. Every psychological nuance has been pondered, and the general consensus is that Bulgakov lost hands down.[48] And so no doubt he did. He missed his chance to emigrate, as his older friend Yevgeny Zamyatin did not. He missed his chance of pressing to be published in his own country. What he did succeed in obtaining was a job at the Art Theatre and the right to stay alive. In the Bulgakov household this was evidently not considered something to be sneezed at.

Bulgakov's caller from the Kremlin did not like double-dealers. Evidently the classical directness and daunting openness of the letter from the author of *The Days of the Turbins* made a favourable impression. For the consolidation and ornamentation of his reign the new autocrat had need not only of literary lickspittles like Ponchik-Nepobeda, the hero of Bulgakov's play *Adam and Eve*, and his multitudinous prototypes. He needed to 'domesticate' real writers, something immeasurably more prestigious both within the USSR and abroad. There was good reason for his obsessive interest in Khmelyov's rendition of Alexey Turbin. Stalin told Khmelyov, who was granted an audience, he even dreamed of Turbin at night. (Khmelyov passed this on to Yelena, who noted it in her diary.) He compared the stance of Nikolai Erdman in *The Suicide* ('He does not dig very deep') to Bulgakov's open confrontation ('Bulgakov really rubs you up the wrong way'). Even if apocryphal this story, which was retold to me by Yelena Bulgakov, conveys an important truth. Bulgakov, as his contemporaries were aware, enjoyed the status of a legitimised opposition. It was something which he tried to maintain throughout the 1930s, right up to *Batum*.

The decade between the phone call from Stalin and the writing of the play about Stalin was a period when Bulgakov never ceased to hope that there would be a conversation or a meeting which would bring about a dramatic change in his fortunes. At times his hopes would be raised, only to recede again. There is no doubt that the reckless openness of *The Master and Margarita* is to be explained by the fact that its first reader was intended to be Stalin. 'Desperately seeking some way out,' Bulgakov noted on 23 September 1937. 'A letter upstairs? Ditch the theatre? Finish editing the novel and deliver it? I can do nothing. The situation is hopeless.'[49] The letter upstairs and the novel intended for delivery to the same address express the need to continue the 1930 conversation, a sense of unfinished business in the relationship between the dramatist and the dictator. Throughout the decade the anticipation of a dialogue between opposites continued to tantalise him. Much of his behaviour as a writer during the decade is explicable in these terms. In just the same way Boris Pasternak, whose call from the Kremlin was bestowed on him in June 1934, took what one of his contemporaries characterised as a 'pathological' interest in the stocky Georgian for years afterwards.

For Bulgakov, however, the interest was not exclusively philosophical. With the passage of time the tenuous channel of communication increasingly became a lifeline. The sporadic signals from upstairs confirmed that He knew, He was remembering. In response signals began to be emitted from the Bulgakov flat which were aimed at keeping up the depersonalised dialogue. From the mid-1930s, more precisely from February 1936, Bulgakov began sending signals upstairs that he was preparing to write a play about the Leader. It was an intimation of compromise, and a prayer for deliverance. It would be profoundly mistaken to suppose that the history of *Batum* began in autumn 1938. It began in April 1930 when Bulgakov accepted the possibility of dialogue with the new Pontius Pilate.

Our first indication that Bulgakov had 'finally decided to write a play about Stalin' is found in Yelena's diary entry for 7 February 1936. The date marks the start of the threatening political campaign inaugurated at the end of January by the article 'Not Music but Muddle' in *Pravda*. It seems likely that Bulgakov's mentioning of his intention to write a play about Stalin was less a signal of gratitude for the imminent first nights of *Molière* and *Ivan Vasilievich* than an SOS, in the sharply deteriorating situation in literature and the theatre, designed to rescue them. First, however, the signal had to be correctly transmitted. Bulgakov duly put his secret in the public domain on 18 February 1936 in conversation with Mikhail Arkadiev, the new Director of the Moscow Art Theatre. Yelena notes:

I went to see *Faust*, while Misha went to the Art Theatre for a talk with Arkadiev. Afterwards he came up to the box and told me what had been said. He told Arkadiev how wretchedly the Art Theatre had been and still was treating him. He said the only subject for a play which interested him was Stalin. The conversation was extremely interesting, but Misha doubts he will be supplied with material for his play.[50]

Yelena seems not to have read any significance into the fact that this 'interesting conversation' took place to the background accompaniment of *Faust*.

There can be no doubt but that Arkadiev found a way of transmitting Bulgakov's sensational declaration of intent upstairs. It was, however, too late to help. The juggernaut of cultural repression had already acquired an unstoppable momentum.

Immediately after the criticism of Shostakovich's opera Bulgakov's *Molière* came under attack in a *Pravda* editorial which was the opening salvo in the crusade against 'Formalism' in literature. A week after *Molière* was banned Bulgakov saw fit to mention once more, this time in conversation with the

Chairman of the Committee for Artistic Affairs, Pyotr Kerzhentsev, that he was planning to write a play about Stalin. The signals were clearly far from random.

Answer came there none. Stalin's response was oblique and gave no sureties. He continued the virtual dialogue by permitting Bulgakov's transfer from the Art Theatre to the Bolshoy; and then, when Bulgakov was already ensconced as a libretto consultant, he preserved him from harm with seemingly random mentions of his name in a generally positive context.

On 24 November 1937 Yelena noted that Stalin had been present at the first night of Sholokhov's *Virgin Soil Upturned*. He had been talking to Kerzhentsev and said, '"... and now, do you see, Bulgakov has written *Minin and Pozharsky* ...". Yakov Leontiev was so pleased Misha's name had been mentioned.'[51]

This kind of mention extended the validity of Bulgakov's 'safe conduct'. There is no need for us to labour the importance of such patronage in the terror of 1937 and the succeeding years.

The shadow of the Grand Inquisitor hung constantly over Bulgakov's life. The Art Theatre where he had worked, and the Bolshoy where he currently worked, were both governmental theatres. Both have specially equipped government boxes. Stalin liked the theatre and pronounced plays 'the most important and most necessary form of literature'. He appeared in the theatre frequently, sometimes only as the second act was beginning, and usually without a large entourage. On 29 November 1934 he came, yet again, to see *The Days of the Turbins*. In the box with him were Zhdanov and Kirov. The latter had just two days left to live.

The proximity of the Leader stirs the blood of theatre people, and in the Bulgakov household it raised chimerical hopes of a meeting, a continuation of the conversation, a way out of the dead end. There is an extraordinary diary entry in this connection. Four days after the loss of *Molière*, when the sheer hopelessness of Bulgakov's future prospects seemed beyond doubt, Yelena found herself sitting directly opposite Stalin in the Bolshoy Theatre at *Natalya from Poltava*.

I was sitting right at the edge of the Management box, by the proscenium. Misha was next to me. The box was packed full. Before the beginning of the Second Act Stalin, Ordzhonikidze and Molotov appeared in the Government box. I kept thinking about Stalin, and hoping he would think about Misha and that our fortunes would change. At the end of the performance all the performers were on the stage. There was an ovation for the Government box, to Stalin, in which the whole theatre joined. I saw Stalin applauding in return, and waving to the actors in greeting.[52]

Yelena's telepathy did not help, but right until the last days of Bulgakov's life the sense of anticipation of a miraculous change in his fortunes never left the charmed flat. Was it not this mystical hope that engendered the idea in February 1940, when Bulgakov was dying, of asking Stalin to repeat his telephone call, which had miraculously 'saved' Bulgakov in 1930?

Such is the background to *Batum*.

On 9 September 1938 Pavel Markov and Vitaly Vilenkin paid a visit to the Bulgakovs. Their arrival was preceded by several telephone calls and a good deal of preliminary coaxing directed towards getting Bulgakov to at last resume relations with the Moscow Art Theatre and write a play for it. On 17 August Pavel Markov had had a conversation with him at the Bolshoy Theatre during a performance of *The Captive of the Caucasus*. 'Markov pounced on Misha to propose they should have a serious talk. He: "You really ought to write something for the Art Theatre". Misha spoke about all the evil the Art Theatre had meted out to him.'[53]

On 9 September Markov and Vilenkin visited, and for the first time *Batum* was openly discussed.

They arrived after ten at night and stayed until five o'clock in the morning. They had a fiendishly difficult time of it at first. They had come to ask Misha to write a play for the Art Theatre. 'I shall never do anything so foolhardy. It's against my own interests. It is dangerous. I know in advance exactly what will happen. I shall be set upon. I even know the playwrights and journalists who will set upon me . . .'[54]

All this took a good two hours, and when they went through to eat at about one o'clock Markov was looking as black as a thundercloud. At supper the talk switched to general gossip about the Art Theatre and the mood improved. Everybody expressed common indignation at the Yegorovs in the Theatre, and then they again started in about a play. 'The Theatre is being destroyed, the Art Theatre of course. We have nothing to stage, only the old repertoire. The Theatre is dying, and only a really good contemporary play can save it and bring it back to life.' 'A latter-day *Flight*,' Markov said, 'in terms of its having a topic of major contemporary significance.' He called *Flight* 'the most popular play in the Theatre', and added that, 'Of course only Bulgakov is capable of writing any such play for us.' He talked at great length in, apparently sincere, agitation.

All this was a prelude to the main business: 'Weren't you thinking of writing a play about Stalin?'

Misha replied that sources were the big problem. They would be absolutely essential, but how were they to be obtained?

They suggested getting the source material through the Theatre as well. Nemirovich could write to Joseph Stalin.

Misha said, 'It would be very difficult, although I can already see quite a lot of the play in my mind's eye.'

He turned down the idea of Nemirovich-Danchenko writing. Until there was a draft play on the table there was no point in talking about it or asking for anything.[55]

The following day Bulgakov started a new notebook, and in it he wrote the date work on the new play began, 10 September 1938, and a heading, 'Materials for a Play or Opera about Stalin'. In its first version the play was to be titled 'The Pastor'. On one page there is a list of possible titles in Yelena's hand: 'Immortality', 'The Battle', 'The Birth of Glory', 'The Argonauts', 'The Pilot', 'The Youth of the Navigator', 'Thus It Was', 'The Comet Ignites', 'The Condor', 'A Navigator Steered a Ship', 'Youth of the Helmsman', 'The Master', 'It Happened in Batum'. The list suggests Bulgakov's ideas were not straying beyond the general run of the clichés of the time. The only title in the list which catches the eye is 'The Master'. Bearing in mind that by the autumn of 1938 Bulgakov's novel not only had the title *The Master and Margarita* but that it already existed in its final sequential version, the idea of naming the hero of the new play 'The Master' certainly deserves to be remarked upon.

'Materials for a Play or Opera . . .'. This reflects, of course, anticipation of the problems customarily attendant on work for the Art Theatre, as well as Bulgakov's own pondering of what genre would be appropriate to the theme. That the play, or opera, should deal with Stalin's youth was fundamental to Bulgakov's conception from the moment he had made up his mind about writing it, back in February 1936. Up until mid-1935 the details of Stalin's private life were a jealously guarded secret. The official hagiography was begun gradually and came in measured doses. By autumn 1935 the cult of Stalin was in full flower, historians designating the First All-Union Congress of Stakhanovite Shock-Workers as its apogee. This was the moment when the newspapers were filled with the songs of Caucasian *ashugs* and Kirghiz *akyns* hymning the Leader of the Peoples. In mid-October the newspapers reported Stalin's arrival in Tiflis in his native Georgia. There were features about the Leader's mother, and tales of young Soso's childhood and youth. His years in the revolutionary underground were what Bulgakov was primarily interested in, with his private, deeply concealed aims as a writer. Let us, however, not anticipate.

On 10 September 1938 Bulgakov started the notebook for his new play. In the next few months, however, we search in vain for evidence that he was working systematically on it. In his subconscious the project was taking shape, but with difficulty. It was set back as he worked on correcting *The Master and Margarita*, and more often by the usual endless hassle at the Bolshoy Theatre which reduced him to a state of stupefaction.

On 19 September Yelena notes, 'Weariness at the hopelessness of his situation!'[56] At just this time there were telephone calls from the Vakhtangov Theatre, which had accepted *Don Quixote*, although the Bulgakovs had no faith at all that it would succeed.

How everything recurs! Misha writes a play and there are telephone calls, letters and conversations. Then the play is taken off, sometimes with a great commotion, as with *Molière*, sometimes without, as with *Ivan Vasilievich*, and 'all is still', as Sergey used to sing when he was little.[57]

Bulgakov's 'utterly foul mood', as we can gather from the context, was associated with his moral torments over deciding to write a play about the Gremlin in the Kremlin.[58]

We hear nothing about the new play for the whole of September and the beginning of October. Bulgakov was busy on the libretto of *Rachel*. The diary entries record theatre and general news. There is a brief note that German and later Polish troops have entered Czechoslovakia. 'Czechoslovakia gave up the ghost without a struggle.'[59]

Batum was born, not in a burst of love and infatuation with the Art Theatre as *The Days of the Turbins*, or *Flight*, had been. 'There really is something quite extraordinarily repellent about the present atmosphere in the Art Theatre,' Yelena records.[60] The forced nature of his new work, and its complete alienness to someone who had already finished writing *The Master and Margarita*, only served further to oppress his independent spirit. On 20 October after yet another telephoned invitation to attend the anniversary celebration, and yet another refusal on Bulgakov's part, we read,

After that there was, of course, talk of how Misha should write a play for the Art Theatre. It is perfectly obvious that the Art Theatre needs a play about Lenin and Stalin at all costs and, as the plays by other playwrights are extremely weak, they are hoping Misha will save their bacon.

He and Mikhalsky had a sad and depressing talk about *Flight*, in the course of which Misha said his horizons had been artificially limited and how bad it was that he would never get to see any countries of the world other than his own. Fyodor replied in confusion, 'Not at all, not at all. Of course you will get to travel!' He didn't, of course, believe what he was saying.[61]

Five days before the fortieth anniversary an article by Pavel Markov was published in *Pravda* enumerating the Art Theatre's Soviet authors and their plays. *The Days of the Turbins* was not mentioned. 'Persecution by silence', was the Bulgakovs' commentary, although Olga Bokshanskaya averted the blow from Markov, pointing out that *The Turbins* had been crossed out by the censor.[62]

On 26 October Olga reported the anniversary awards. Yelena's diary entry is emphatically factual, although overlying the 'happy, delighted' voice of the bearer of the news we hear Yelena's own, bitter voice.

Yevgeny Kaluzhsky has been awarded the Badge of Honour, and Olga is to receive a valuable gift. Additionally Nemirovich has been awarded everything which, in Olga's opinion, he deserves. Glinishchevsky Lane has been renamed a street in his honour, and he has been given a fully furnished and equipped dacha.

After all these tales she added, in the same happy voice, 'See you tomorrow, then. You are coming, aren't you?'[63]

Despite his flat refusal to attend the fortieth anniversary celebrations, the author of *The Turbins* was busying himself with the Bolshoy Theatre's congratulations to the Moscow Art Theatre. Probably neither he nor anybody else in the Art Theatre anticipated the impact his, in all honesty, relatively straightforward commission would have. Given the state of Soviet society in autumn 1938, however, Bulgakov's public appearance at the Actor's Club (which was where Moscow was honouring the Art Theatre) had the resonance virtually of a political demonstration. He asked Yelena to stay away ('It's better if you do not meet the Art Theatre people'), so the account in the diary is mediated by Bulgakov himself.

Yesterday Misha came home just after two clutching a chrysanthemum and looking very pleased with himself. He kept me in suspense until dinner-time, and told me everything properly over dinner. When he appeared on stage people began clapping. The applause went on for several minutes, getting louder and louder. He delivered his introduction as master of ceremonies, interrupted by laughter from the audience. They got the point of all the jokes and the humour went down well. Then the programme, Misha's idea, began with the stars of the Bolshoy Theatre singing snippets from Art Theatre productions (*The Cherry Orchard*, *Tsar Fyodor*, *The Ardent Heart*) to various operatic melodies. It was all put together in the form of a meeting to celebrate the Art Theatre's anniversary. Everything was a resounding success, from Reizen's first words, or rather bars, 'For weighty matters, men of Egypt . . .' to the Cossack song from *Virgin Soil Upturned*, which had been given a special text for the Art Theatre.

When it was all over the entire audience stood and gave them an ovation, calling them back endlessly. Then Nemirovich, Moskvin, and Knipper came on stage to thank them for their congratulations, and kiss and embrace the performers. In particular Misha was kissed by Moskvin and Nemirovich. Knipper held out her hand for him to kiss exclaiming, 'Our own Bulgakov! You're one of us!'[64]

For several weeks afterwards the Bulgakovs' telephone never stopped ringing Olga Bokshanskaya:

Surely Misha must have felt the affection and love that were washing over him yesterday from the Art Theatre people in the audience? It was so unexpected when he came on stage. He gave such a brilliant introduction. It brought Molière to mind; he spoke in just the same way, and so on.[65]

The Art Theatre anniversary, although it brought a momentary relief in Bulgakov's life, did not significantly alter his relations with the Theatre. Dmitriev lent Bulgakov the book published to commemorate the anniversary. It did include *The Days of the Turbins*, *Dead Souls* and *Molière*. There was a note beside *Molière* that it had been rehearsed two hundred and ninety-six times and 'had seven performances'. 'I felt as sad as if I had been shown a dead person,' Yelena noted.[66] Two months later she records Bulgakov himself remarking, as he was putting his papers in order one evening, 'You know, all this,' he pointed at the archive, 'takes away my will to live.'[67]

The Art Theatre's stalwarts made another foray on 10 November 1938.

Sakhnovsky and Vilenkin came. Sakhnovsky began by saying, 'I have been sent by Nemirovich and Boyarsky to ask you, on behalf of the Art Theatre, to come back and work for us . . . I am to prostrate myself before you like the morning mist. . . . We are holding out our hands to you. You may strike them. If you do, well then I shall stop holding them out . . . I understand that you have suffered no end of swinish misconduct from the Art Theatre, but it's not as if it were anything personal. They have behaved like that towards many people. In fact they do it to everyone . . .'[68]

For all that, Bulgakov was in no hurry to make a start on the play. He was absorbed with *Don Quixote*, and with the absurd and mind-numbing labour of correcting other people's libretti at the Bolshoy. One moment he would be sitting working on the libretto of *Iolanthe* ('Some good lady has worked up a new piano version, in monstrously bad taste, in order to avoid causing offence with Modest Tchaikovsky's references to the deity'); the next he was talking a full hour on the telephone to 'someone called Brainin', the author of a libretto called *The Extraordinary Commissar*. In one place Yelena, that sensitive seismograph, exactly captures the psychological state of Bulgakov, the persecuted author about to embark on a play about Stalin. 'Misha came back exhausted and in a kind of serene hopelessness.'[69]

On 30 November the first official conference on the new play took place at the Art Theatre. Those present were Bulgakov, Markov, Sakhnovsky and Boyarsky, the Director of the Theatre. The contents of their 'wearisome talk' are minuted. Haggling over the play was paralleled by no less irksome haggling over a flat. We recall that the Bulgakovs lived in an annexe built on top of a block of flats in Furmanov Lane. The flat was not large, its partition walls were extremely thin and transmitted sound extremely efficiently. In addition the Bulgakovs were afraid the block might be demolished. The need to find a house, a flat, a roof over their heads again became an *idée fixe* as it had been in the 1920s. Woland's phrase in *The Master and Margarita* about the people of Moscow, 'They're ordinary people, in fact they remind me very much of their predecessors, except that the housing shortage has soured them . . .' (p. 147) derives from bitter personal experience. This first formal discussion between Bulgakov and the Art Theatre representatives produced an unexpected linkage between the housing shortage and the writing of the new play.

Boyarsky began, 'Right, well now, then, let us look at this possibility of your writing a new play for us . . .' and so on.

To this Misha replied, 'We are beginning these talks from the wrong end. What is needed first for a dramatist who has been shot down on the playwriting front is to be given proper social, primarily living, conditions.'

Sakhnovsky adopted the tone Misha had correctly predicted to me,

'A flat, right?'

Misha replied, 'Right.'

After this he levelled with them about how he had been blasted morally and materially; he reminded them about *Molière*, *Pushkin*, *Flight*; the writ from the Theatre after *Molière* was taken off; his removal from the Writer's Club waiting list for a flat, transparently associated with the cancellation of *Molière*; and their whole record of bullying.

Boyarsky changed tack:

'In practical terms it would be more to your advantage to write the play first . . . The Government comes to our performances . . . our old stagers . . .'

Misha said, 'No. First I need proper working conditions.'[70]

There is a saying that 'You can't sell inspiration, but you can sell a manuscript'. Here, however, the proposal was to sell both. Having resolved to take that step, Bulgakov negotiated just as robustly as his circumstances and relations with the Theatre allowed. Yelena summarises the negotiations with unambiguous clarity: 'What it comes down to is that they want to blithely write off everything they have done to M.A. (and of course not to let him have a flat into the bargain!), and con him into writing the play they need.'[71]

The Art Theatre side tried to paper over the cracks. Markov tried to hold out before Bulgakov the prospect that *Flight* might be staged, but Bulgakov flatly refused even to let them have a copy, dismissing it as just a ploy, one more fiddle the Art Theatre was trying on. 'The Art Theatre has come up with another of its magic tricks.' In reality there was no trickery. It was an attempt, however feeble, by his friends to find at least some kind of carrot to induce him to write 'the play they needed'. Two weeks later the question mark over *Flight* disappeared when Nemirovich-Danchenko brought Sakhnovsky up short when he raised the matter. 'There can be no question of that at present. It is in the interests neither of the Art Theatre nor of the playwright.'[72]

Time seemed to have stopped in a moment of expectation. The diary records ever more arrests of producers, writers, close acquaintances and friends. In the early morning of 20 December Yelena made the following entry:

> I have just checked the thermometer. 26 degrees below zero. [. . .] All the streets are deserted.
>
> Misha has 'flu and a terrible stuffed nose. He won't lie down, of course. He's wandering around the flat, collecting up books and sorting his papers.
>
> At dinner there were just the two of us. We spoke about serious matters. Misha says working in the theatre, no matter which, but in my opinion particularly in the Bolshoy, makes it impossible to work at home and get on with your own writing. He comes back from the theatre and this work on other people's libretti so worn out that he's in no state to do his own work.
>
> Misha puts the question. 'So what is to be done? What should be given up? Is it time to make a fresh start?'
>
> What can I say? Life loses all meaning for me when he is not working and doing his own writing.[73]

Yelena emphasises the exact time of the diary entry: 'Night of 20–21 December, 2.00 a.m.' It is not difficult to understand this clue and decipher the subtext of the night-time conversation. 21 December was Stalin's birthday. 'Make a fresh start' means to resist the blandishments of the Art Theatre and abandon the theatre. Bulgakov talked this over with his closest friends. On New Year's Eve 1938 he discussed it with Nikolai Erdman.

> Yesterday when Erdman started advising Misha, in the friendliest possible way, to write a new play, not to let things get on top of him and so on, Misha told him he was preaching like 'the local archpriest'. The wit and sparkle of their conversation gives me such pleasure.[74]

Bulgakov's friend, himself under surveillance and living in Vyshny Volochek, did his best to raise Bulgakov's spirits. Erdman had long ago lost all sense of responsibility for his own literary destiny. All he wanted was to stay alive. He was conceiving brilliant ideas for new plays and screenplays, but none was to come to fruition. Two years later Erdman was released from his semi-prison and recruited to work in a newly created NKVD team. His team-mates included Sergey Yutkevich, Dmitry Shostakovich and many other major artists and actors obliged to work in the 'organs of state security', among them a young member of the Vakhtangov Theatre, Yury Lyubimov. His friends fixed Erdman up with a greatcoat purloined from the Art Theatre wardrobe. Vested in Cheka uniform he marched up to a large mirror in the NKVD club, viewed his image appraisingly, and pronounced in a sad voice, 'They've come to get me.' This tale encapsulates the tragedy of a human life, and the atmosphere of a period of 'tyranny without redress', as Bulgakov's Molière would have said.

On 16 January, after a long interval, Bulgakov did make a start on his play about Stalin. 'I have just read the first scene (in the play, the second),' Yelena writes. 'I thought it was terribly good! All the characters are really alive!'[75]

The continuation was written in an atmosphere of idolatrous adulation of the Leader whose sixtieth birthday would fall within the year. In autumn 1936 the Bulgakovs had been taken aback when Tairov's production of *The Bogatyrs* in the Chamber Theatre was shot to pieces on the grounds that it 'scoffed at the Christianisation of Rus'. In 1939 jingoism became part of the regime's official doctrine. In February of that year Glinka's opera *A Life for the Tsar*, refashioned as *Ivan Susanin*, was staged at the Bolshoy. For the first time since the revolution a choir thundered 'Hail to Thee!' If Baron Rozen in 1836 had written, 'Hail to Thee Our Russian Tsar! Crowned by God our Sovereign Tsar!' Sergey Gorodetsky in 1939 altered his verses to 'Hail to Thee, O Rus, my Rus! Hail to Thee, our Russian Land!' Bulgakov was one consultant for Gorodetsky's libretto. The other was Stalin, who gave orders on how the opera was to be adapted. On his instructions the final act was changed. The Requiem in the penultimate scene was removed, and the choir's 'Hail to Thee!', which at first threw the audience into confusion, became the theatrical coda of the decade.

Our information on the first night of *Ivan Susanin* is recorded by Yelena from Bulgakov's account. He was interested now in the man in the white tunic no longer solely as a political leader but also as a protagonist of the Bulgakov play.

Before the Epilogue the Government transferred from its usual box into the large central box, formerly the Tsar's Box, and watched the end of the opera from there. When the audience noticed they started to clap, and continued clapping throughout the musical interlude before the Epilogue. When the curtain rose, and particularly at the end when Minin and Pozharsky appeared on horseback, it grew louder and louder and eventually turned into a tremendous ovation. The Government applauded the cast, the cast applauded the Government, and the audience applauded both.[76]

This touching unity of Government, stage, and audience faced the intending author of *Batum* with the ticklish problem of how to avoid being subsumed in the general chorus of 'Hails!', which was becoming thoroughly hysterical. In the same entry about the first night of *Ivan Susanin*, Yelena describes, in the words of one of the Bolshoy Theatre's technical staff, the almost religious ecstasy which seized people at the sight of their Leader.

One old woman, when she caught sight of Stalin, started crossing herself and mumbling, 'There, now I have seen him with my own eyes!' People clambered up on to their seats. They say Leontiev and Samosud were summoned to the box after the performance, and Stalin asked them to convey his appreciation to the whole theatre company . . .[77]

Such was the way an unchallengeable system of priorities evolved in Soviet art. Which were the Fatherland's greatest theatres, who were its greatest poets and playwrights was decided by the arresting of some and the incessant rewarding on a massive scale of others. In the winter of 1939 'all remotely noteworthy' writers and cinematographers received awards. All except Bulgakov. In the Bolshoy Theatre box an unknown lady leaned over and conspiratorially whispered to Bulgakov, 'You are the best.' 'The lady evidently wanted to console Misha for not having been awarded a medal. What on earth would Misha want with a medal?!'[78]

The Art Theatre had somehow to find a way of making its adulation stand out from the general chorus, and that was why it needed Bulgakov's play. He was by far their best bet, but first a reconciliation had to be effected.

In early April Nemirovich-Danchenko gave a speech at the Arts Council of the All-Union Committee for Artistic Affairs in which he spoke, among other things, about Bulgakov. Yelena records him as saying:

'An outstandingly talented dramatist. [. . .] Why have you all forgotten about him? Why do you not employ such a talented dramatist? . . .' Someone at the meeting (I do not know who, but I shall certainly try to find out) shouted, 'He's not one of us!'

Nemirovich: 'How do you know? What works of his have you read? Do you know *Molière*? *Pushkin*? He has written marvellous plays, but nobody stages them . . .'

In the evening I talked to Misha about Nemirovich and about this 'He's not one of us!' I think Nemirovich's speech was helpful, but Misha says it would have been better not made, and that the heckling will cost him more than the speech will give him. Besides, why is Nemirovich only saying this three years after the *Molière* débâcle?[79]

The heckler's 'He's not one of us' was as much as a life was worth, as Bulgakov was well aware. As for what Nemirovich could or should have been doing, Bulgakov was being unrealistic. Nemirovich had freedom within the narrow confines of a role and the given circumstances, which he could present as willed necessity. Not only was he unable to stage a play about Pushkin by a playwright in disfavour; he had been unable even to risk completing rehearsals of a work by Pushkin himself. *Boris Godunov*, with its portrayal of a bloody time of troubles and frighteningly topical theme of a King Herod massacring innocents, had ground to a halt in 1937. Everyone had to choke his heart in his own way, a psychological procedure whose effects Bulgakov was himself to experience in full measure with respect to *Batum*.

Art possesses an inherent autonomy. An author is dependent on language. Words have a conscience of their own, and to wilfully bend them without heeding their inner rightness is a dangerous and sometimes fatal undertaking for a writer. Nadezhda Mandelshtam gives a classic example with her description of how in January 1937 Osip Mandelshtam tried in his Voronezh exile to turn himself into a regular professional and craft an 'Ode' to Stalin in a purely mechanical way. While writing it he did not mumble the words to himself in his usual way. He did not try to catch the inner hum of the verse. He did not subordinate himself to the rhythm of lines which drew you along after them. Instead he sat down at his writing desk, spread a sheet of paper in front of himself and tried, by dint of sheer craftsmanship, to force a few lines out of himself. He failed. He flew into a rage, became utterly distracted, and started pacing around the room. In his soul poetry itself was locked in combat with the Unclean Spirit.

Bulgakov too found the Unclean Spirit of compulsion intolerable. In April 1937, after again being pressurised, the diary records: '. . . M.A. sees no way out of his situation. He is under pressure to write in a way he simply refuses to write.'[80] On 28 February 1938, some months before beginning work on *Batum*, Yelena notes 'M.A. utterly loathes *Adam and Eve*. It was written under duress, in response to demands for plays about national defence.'[81] What might not Yelena have written about *Batum*, blackmailed out of him and bringing him to the initial stages of a fatal illness? Bulgakov was conscious throughout the months he was working on *Batum* of this revenge of language, the writer's block always lying in ambush, the unrelenting sense of imminent catastrophe. It is no coincidence that just when work on his Stalin play was at its height he suddenly conceived the idea of a parallel play about Richard the First. From later memoir notes we know the central figure was to be a certain Richard Richardovich, a high-up in the NKVD who patronises a dramatist. In the first scene (which Yelena outlines) the 'shell-shocked writer starts complaining to Richard about his situation and insisting that he is a genius. He asks for help, indeed demands it, assuring him he can be very useful. Richard replies with a monologue on brazenness, but they then come to terms. The writer has been bought. He promises to write a play on a required topic. Richard promises to help, to pilot the play through the bureaucracy, and come to the first night.'[82] After vertiginous twists and complications involving 'a man with a pipe', Richard is denounced and declared an enemy of the people. The writer is crushed. In return for his pains he has achieved neither fame nor a flat. He returns to his garret.

This play posited various possible outcomes for the writer in his dependence on Richard and the 'man with a pipe'. The saga of the mutual relations between several playwrights with Art Theatre connections and Genrikh Yagoda was still fresh in people's minds, but the play had a more personal source. In May 1939 the feasibility of dialogue and collaboration with a higher murderous power was not by any means of purely theoretical interest to Bulgakov.

Bulgakov wrote his required play about Stalin with long gaps as other work continually interrupted it. Plots crossed and were reflected in each other. On 14 May 1939 important changes were made to the finale of *The Master and Margarita* when, as Marietta Chudakova has shown, Matthew the Levite first appears in conversation with Woland. In the course of this the Prince of Darkness delivers himself of an enigmatic phrase about the Master, which for two decades now has prompted all manner of critical speculation in Russia and throughout the world: 'He has not earned light. He has earned rest.' (p. 406)

In mid-May Bulgakov read the ending of *The Master and Margarita* to friends. Those from the Art Theatre, impatiently waiting for his play about Stalin, were staggered.

For some reason they were tense and rigid as they listened to the last chapters. Everything about it frightened them. In the corridor afterwards Pavel Markov stressed to me in alarm that we must not even think of making it public. The consequences could be disastrous.[83]

On 20 May Yelena records, 'Dmitriev came in this morning to tell us about Vete,' who had been arrested a few months earlier. 'Apparently she is no longer alive.'

'There is a rumour in the City that Babel has been arrested.'[84]

On 21 May, Yelena's name-day, after a break lasting several months Bulgakov again sat down to write his play about Stalin. This stressful work was accompanied by strangely theatrical effects.

Towards eight in the evening it began to grow dark, and at eight o'clock there were the first claps of thunder and lightning. A thunderstorm began. It was very short, and afterwards the sky was lit up with an eerie red glow.

Misha is sitting now (10.00 p.m.) working on the Stalin play.[85]

Two weeks later Bulgakov decided he could describe, and in part also read, several scenes from the play to Vitaly Vilenkin. 'I will never forget Vilenkin sitting there, tense and rigid, listening and trying to make up his mind about it.'[86]

This repeated description of Bulgakov's listeners as 'tense and rigid' is worth remarking. It is not a description one would expect of someone who had come to hear, not some banned work, but a play about Stalin.

The work was moving rapidly towards conclusion. On 9 June Bulgakov met the Art Theatre representatives in Grigory Kalishian's office. 'Tea was on the table, with cherries.' The Acting Director of the Moscow Art Theatre promised the earth, a four-room flat and all the perquisites of a most favoured playwright. In return Bulgakov described the play, which was now complete in draft. The Art Theatre representatives were greatly excited and got rather carried away, already trying to decide who should act the principal role; ' "... this really is a play with a hero, a proper role, not like the others," they declared, damning all other modern plays in passing. I think they really are excited about it.' Again the event was accompanied by portents: 'We had just got to the Art Theatre when a thunderstorm began.'[87]

In the hot July days Bulgakov again and again tried out his as yet unfinished play on family and friends to see how it impressed them. He read new scenes he had completed and described others he had in mind. This openness, rare in a writer, is not difficult to understand. He wanted to know in advance the impression he would make on people whose opinion he valued. On 11 June he read three scenes to the brothers Nikolai and Boris Erdman and outlined the remainder to them. They thought it was 'a great success', Yelena noted. 'They like the form, and the part of the hero.'[88] Nikolai Erdman had just signed a contract for a screenplay. 'We sat on the balcony and imagined hopefully that a lucky break was beginning for our little group.'[89]

The Art Theatre was also strenuously trying to get Bulgakov to sign a contract, but having read the draft he refused categorically, spotting their favourite stipulation: 'The author shall be obliged to make all such alterations and additions as the Art Theatre shall deem necessary ...'.[90]

On 13 June Boris Erdman, returning from the First All-Union Conference of Directors, told of the ovation which had been accorded the sixty-five-year-old Meyerhold. (Meyerhold was arrested a few days later.) Bulgakov and Boris

Erdman talked about the new play all evening. Bulgakov described how he was planning to handle the scene of the shootings at the demonstration in Batum. After this there is another short entry, separated by a line and without any sort of commentary: 'Misha is in a foul mood.'[91]

In the stifling heat the Master was applying his usual imaginative flair in trying to add colour and breathe theatrical life into his play. On 14 June he wrote the scene in the Governor's office. 'What a role!' Yelena exclaims, and half a century later we have to agree that the scene really is well written. The young Dzhugashvili-Stalin is absent from it. The Governor is an imposing, florid figure, the role obviously devised with Kachalov in mind. There is no Soso and everything is as it should be, with Bulgakov's rapier-like wit and light, sparkling dialogue much in evidence. Everything is shimmering brilliance until it suddenly freezes into woodenness with the entrance of the play's 'real hero'. The play is permeated by the poet's battle with the Unclean Spirit.

On 15 June Bulgakov signed a contract in which, for the first time in fifteen years of working for the Art Theatre, he threw out the clause about alterations and additions. The following day Olga Bokshanskaya reported an important talk she had had with Nemirovich-Danchenko.

. . . He couldn't sleep last night wondering why *Molière* had been taken off!!! [The exclamation marks are Yelena's, needless to say.] When Olga had finished singing the praises of Misha's new play to Nemirovich she said what a shame it was he wouldn't see it until September, even though it would probably be finished in July. 'What do you mean September?' he yelled. 'You must send it to me abroad as soon as it is finished. I shall work on it out there and bring back a completed rehearsal plan.'[92]

As we know, Nemirovich began work on *The Three Sisters* in January 1939 and was actively rehearsing it. Some weeks later it was decided that Bulgakov's play would be rehearsed by Vasily Sakhnovsky and readied for performance, as usual, by Nemirovich-Danchenko. Such an important production could not be left in the hands of a junior producer.

On 11 July Bulgakov read the play to the Committee for the Arts. 'They listened with intense concentration. They very much liked it. Then they discussed it, but so briefly that it was clear from the outset there was nothing to discuss.'[93]

The Bulgakovs' telephone did not stop ringing as literary directors of provincial theatres in Voronezh, Kazan, and Kiev put in their pleas. The same old story was ground out bar by bar like the tune of a musical box. Everyone was delighted, everyone was gossiping. Incredible rumours began to circulate.

People latched on to Bulgakov in public places, envied him, and planted such drunken kisses on him that when he got home afterwards he scrubbed his lips with eau-de-cologne, expostulating, 'I bet I've caught syphilis!'[94] Everybody was trying to think up a title for him. Everyone wanted an interview.

Bulgakov discussed the title with the Art Theatre management. Kalishian was eager to have a highly political title. In July there was a rushed retyping and simultaneous polishing of several scenes. 'The play is being read, condensed, and ornamented.' On 22 July Bulgakov decided to call it *Batum*, choosing a title devoid of political overtones. On 27 July a reading was arranged at the Art Theatre, in its new rehearsal accommodation and combined with a Party meeting, a fact as improbable as everything else in the whole improbable history of the writing of the play. Seven years had passed since Bulgakov had last read one of his plays at the Art Theatre. Three years had passed since he walked out of the Theatre. The weather did its bit, the intolerable heat resolving itself in a tremendous thunderstorm, which was interpreted as a good augury. 'They listened very responsively, and gave him a long standing ovation when he finished. After that people gave their opinions and found everything very good. Kalishian spoke last and said the Theatre should stage it on 21 December.'[95]

On 1 August, as the Bulgakovs were advised by the Art Theatre management, the play was sent 'upstairs' from the Committee for the Arts.

On 5 August Nemirovich-Danchenko returned from abroad. Kalishian, trying to build bridges, hinted to Bulgakov that it would do no harm for him to be among those meeting him at the station on his return, 'but of course M.A. will not go'.[96]

On 7 August Yelena records an important piece of news: 'Nemirovich likes the play. He rang the secretariat, presumably Stalin's, to find out what was happening, and was told the play had not yet been received back.'[97]

It was decided that Bulgakov should head an Art Theatre brigade to go to Batum to gather material for the forthcoming production. At this moment, probably, after hearing about the telephone call to the secretariat, Bulgakov suddenly had an acute sense that something was wrong. 'When he woke up this morning,' Yelena noted on 8 August, 'Misha said that, having thought it over during a sleepless night, he had concluded it would be best not to go to Batum at present.'[98]

Preparations continued nevertheless. As in *The Cherry Orchard* the fatal date was fixed for 14 August. A few days before departure Bulgakov went at Nemirovich-Danchenko's request to see him in his new house in what had been known as Glinishchevsky Lane. The entry recording the visit exudes Bulgakov's same undiminished scepticism:

Misha returned at dinner-time and gave me a detailed account of the meeting. A beautiful flat with flowers on the balconies. Nemirovich in a colourful casual jacket, debonair trousers, looking younger. Sakhnovsky and Olga.

'Everything in your play is very good, only the first scene does not work. It needs to be structured round four peripeteias.'

After Misha explained and demonstrated to him how the Rector would speak [the scene under discussion is one where the Rector of the theological seminary expels Dzhugashvili] he said, 'Well, perhaps one peripeteia is all right after all.'

'The most powerful scene is the demonstration. The only thing is the soldiers . . .' (A long peroration about how to deal with a company of soldiers.)

Misha: 'But the soldiers should be off stage.'

He mimes the scene.

And so it went on; but afterwards Nemirovich told Olga Bulgakov himself could stage the play better than anyone.[99]

In the final days before the departure for Batum the telephone rang relentlessly. Everyone wanted to know about the play. The theatre hullabaloo gradually developed, in accordance with an invariable law where Bulgakov was involved, into total pandemonium. Rumours about *Batum* were being spread by Yakov Danilovich, director of the restaurant at the Journalists' Club, that same 'pirate' and 'handsome, black-eyed man with a pointed beard' immortalised in the figure of Archibald Archibaldovich in *The Master and Margarita*. On 13 August, on the very eve of departure, Yelena notes:

Soviet Art is asking M.A. to give them a release about his new play . . . 'Our newspaper believes in keeping abreast of all the latest news in the arts . . . The Committee has been so complimentary about the play . . .'.

I told them M.A. could give them no information before the play was passed for performance.

'Tell you what, why doesn't he write a piece and let me have it. I'll keep it handy and if the play is passed I'll print it, and if not I'll let you have it back.'

I said that was rather like writing a provisional obituary for someone who was only seriously ill.

'Come now! Quite the contrary . . .'[100]

Here too the future was casting its shadow before it happened, but nobody managed to recognise it. 'Can we really be going tomorrow!!! It's too wonderful,' Yelena notes.[101] In a letter to her mother in Riga she summarised the family chronicle of the spring and summer of 1939.

Misha has finished his play and given it to the Art Theatre. He dictated it to me, so you can imagine I was sitting there typing from morning till night.

He is diabolically tired. It was very hard work, and absolutely had to be ready by the deadline. It is a positive kind of tiredness, though. The work was tremendously interesting. There is general agreement it is a great success! [. . .] Now the Art Theatre is sending a brigade headed by Mikhail to Tiflis and Batum for preparatory work for the play. Two designers will be sketching, an assistant producer and the assistant literary director will be collecting music and observing local characters, everyday details of the way of life and so on.[102]

Nemirovich-Danchenko let them have a pile of his own family's Caucasian memorabilia and photographs to assist in the observing of 'local characters'. Bulgakov wrote a jocular note in Yelena's name to Fyodor Mikhalsky with suggested seating arrangements for notable members of the audience at the première in December. It is a brief letter and deserves to be quoted in full.

Dear Fedya,
Herewith the first list (artists, playwrights, composers). Please arrange as follows:
Boris Erdman – Art Theatre Management's Box.
Pyotr Viliams – first row (left).
Vissarion Shebalin – third row.
Nikolai Erdman – seventh row.
Vladimir Dmitriev – dress circle, standing.
Fedya, if Olesha comes looking for tickets, do me a favour. Tell the militiaman he is a ticket tout. I feel like having a bit of sport, Fedya dear![103]

There was to be no sport. Two hours after leaving Moscow, after they had celebrated their departure with brandy and oranges, a postwoman came to the carriage at Serpukhov station with a telegram. Let us recall Maxudov's confession in *Black Snow*:

But suddenly . . . Oh that accursed word! . . . As I leave this world for ever, I bear with me a cowardly, insuperable fear of that word. I fear it as much as I fear words like 'Guess what?' 'You're wanted on the telephone', 'There's a telegram for you' or 'You're wanted in the office'. I know only too well what follows words like these. (p. 121)

The postwoman asked 'Which one of you's the accountant?' and held out an express telegram. 'Misha read it (very slowly) and said we wouldn't be going on.'[104] The telegram consisted of just five words: 'Trip now unnecessary return Moscow.'[105] A few minutes later Vitaly Vilenkin and Platon Lesli were standing on the station platform having barely managed to get off the train with their luggage in time. The Bulgakovs travelled on. 'I will never forget their faces in the window,' Vilenkin recalled forty years later.

The Bulgakovs left the train at Tula, recognising that it was going to be impossible for them to have a holiday. The station was a mass of people, the booking office was shut, and they did not know when there might be a train. They managed to find a car, and after three hours' furious driving got home that evening. 'We wondered in the car what we were coming back to. Total obscurity!' When they got home Bulgakov asked Yelena not to put the light on. Candles were lit. The author of *Batum* 'walked round the flat wringing his hands and saying it smelt as if there were a corpse in the house. His dead play, perhaps.'[106] He guessed it all this time too.

'So That They Know . . .'

Controversy has surrounded *Batum* for many years. People seek seducers and culprits responsible for the disaster. They mull over contributory and attendant circumstances. The author of a recent documentary account of 'The Life and Death of Mikhail Bulgakov' concluded consideration of *Batum* with the sacramental phrase, 'Thus was he brought low.'

One very important question has not been seriously considered. If this play was so opportunistic, why was it so inexorably rejected by Stalin? People have sought the explanation in the personality of its First Reader; they have sought it among his venomous entourage; they have sought it in a supposed lack of persistence on the part of the octogenarian Nemirovich-Danchenko, who is presented as having failed even to persuade Stalin to approve a play to perpetuate and celebrate the name of the Leader down the centuries. Nobody has sought the reason for rejection in the text of the play itself. If they had it would have been seen that the play Bulgakov wrote for 'the man upstairs' was not by a long chalk a banner inscribed to order with other people's slogans. He delivered a play full of quite extraordinary surprises.

What is more, his First Reader understood the thrust of Bulgakov's missive only too well.

After the banning of *Batum* a number of explanations circulated. The first was brought to the Bulgakovs by Sakhnovsky. '. . . the play was very negatively received upstairs. You cannot make a figure like J. V. Stalin into a literary character [Yelena later inserted above the line 'a romantic hero']. You cannot place him in imaginary situations and put fictional dialogue in his mouth. The play is to be neither staged nor published.' The second part of Sakhnovsky's report was even more interesting: 'The writing of this play was seen upstairs as an attempt by Bulgakov to throw a bridge across and establish a relationship.'[107]

Considering the matter logically we can see that the first part of Sakhnovsky's report simply does not tie up with the second. If the play was so flawed and politically unacceptable that it could be neither staged nor published, what sort of bridge-building exercise was Bulgakov supposed to be engaging in? What sort of relationship was he trying to establish? Either an outstanding and thoroughly professional dramatist had failed to express his obsequious feelings adequately, or his feelings were far from obsequious and had so offended the tastes of the recipient that he had decided no amount of comments he might make or amendments he might require could make it palatable. What was it that the First Reader read in *Batum* which deprived it of any chance of life?

For two weeks after the interdict Bulgakov agonised over whether to send a letter upstairs. Stalin's obliquely relayed comment about bridge-building took the feet from him morally. He tried explaining to Vilenkin that he had 'documents which proved conclusively that he had first considered the play in early 1936 when the staging of *Molière*, *Pushkin* and *Ivan Vasilievich* had appeared to be imminent'.[108] He continued reading the play to his friends, but now people began to see it in quite a different light, through the eyes of the stocky Georgian in the Kremlin. The first to spot the surprises Bulgakov had embedded in his birthday present to Stalin was Fyodor Mikhalsky. After hearing Bulgakov read the first half of the play on 31 August, he hazarded a guess that the ban might in part stem from 'the gypsy woman, the birthmark, and the words alternating with the song'.[109] His hypothesis deserves consideration.

The incriminating gypsy woman appears in the tale of Stalin's expulsion from the seminary. The young Dzhugashvili is left without a kopek because he has spent his last rouble on a fortune-teller.

I went to buy cigarettes, right? Come back for the ceremony, and run into this gypsy woman right beside the columns. 'I tell your fortune, I tell your fortune!' She just wouldn't let me through the door. Well, then, so I said all right. She was really good at it. Everything is going to work out like I want it. Absolutely everything is going to come true. 'You will travel much,' she says. At the end she even paid me a compliment, 'You will be great man!' It was certainly worth a rouble.

Mikhalsky was surely right in having doubts about this scene. Was it really being suggested that the Historical Necessity manifest in the figure of The Leader should be swapped for a rouble's worth of fortune-telling from a gypsy? Even his class-mate's answer was two-edged: 'Don't you believe it, my friend. It will all work out much less splendidly than you want. There's more than one kind of long journey, you know, . . . Yes, I feel sorry for you, Joseph, speaking to you as a friend.'

The mention of the birthmark comes in Scene Four. Colonel Treinitz is reporting the distinguishing features of the criminal Dzhugashvili to the Governor: 'Medium build; head, without distinguishing features; voice, baritone; mole on the left ear.' The features are of course uncomplimentary. How could the Leader of the Peoples and Best Friend of Actors have an undistinguished head and a mole on his ear? The mole, as M. Petrovsky has perceptively observed, cross-refers to the distinguishing wart on the pretender Grishka Otrepiev in *Boris Godunov*. Bulgakov, expert as he was on the subject of Pushkin, was certainly not unaware of linking the Tiflis seminarist with the false pretensions of the runaway Russian monk. No less risky than the mole is the subsequent text where the Colonel of Gendarmerie's telegram 'Report impression made by suspect's appearance' receives the dismaying reply, 'Suspect's appearance makes no impression whatsoever'. In the first version of the play the police report was classified as 'Secret' to boot!

There are no two ways about it, Fyodor Mikhalsky hit the nail on the head. Bulgakov had good reason for rewarding him in *Black Snow* with a perfect understanding of people. 'Suspect's appearance makes no impression whatsoever.' Bulgakov's suicidal jibe could also be seen in the context of a comment made by Trotsky which gained international currency. In his first foreign interview after being exiled from Soviet Russia Trotsky had described Stalin as 'our Party's most outstanding mediocrity'.

Finally the 'words alternating with the song'. What is this referring to? There is after all a good deal of singing in *Batum* at various times and places. Mikhalsky's suggestion, which Yelena recorded without challenging it, can only refer to the first half of the play. Checking the singing in the first two acts of *Batum* leads to only one possible conclusion: it was the New Year's Eve scene which Mikhalsky found suspect. Not only is there singing to the guitar, both solo and in chorus, but, alternating with the song, 'Comrade Soso' proposes an enigmatic toast to the New Year in which Mikhalsky justifiably surmised seditious intent on Bulgakov's part.

'There is a story,' Stalin begins, 'that once on Christmas night the Devil stole the moon and hid it in his pocket.

'Well now, it occurs to me that a time will come when somebody will create not a fairy tale but a real-life legend about a black dragon who stole the sun from the whole of mankind; and people went to get the sun back from this dragon, and they did get it back; and they said to the dragon, "Now you can stand there up high and shine for ever! We will not let you free again!" '

There is a dangerous semantic play here based on an overlaying of the themes of Christ and Antichrist. The event is taking place not on just any New Year's

Eve, but on New Year's Eve 1902, as Bulgakov is at some pains to make clear. A new era begins with the appearance of the Antichrist, the 'pocked-marked devil' who steals the sun. In the preceding scene Stalin has informed the young worker Porfiry that his alias is the Pastor, a fact to which the tale gives a special significance. Is not the Pastor expelled from the seminary, the Pastor who has repudiated God, the black dragon? This interpretation gains credence not only from Mikhalsky, but also from the textual history of the New Year's Eve scene. In every redaction except the last Bulgakov used the stilted and officious version of the young Leader's speech given in a collection of articles entitled *The Batum Demonstration*. In this sumptuously produced souvenir edition published in 1937 there is more than one reference to the purely political character of Comrade Soso's New Year toast, and the toast itself is several times quoted. There is not a word about devils hiding the moon in their pockets or black dragons. Most of the time Bulgakov adhered strictly to the factual basis of events in Batum (naturally as they were officially retailed). Here, however, he unexpectedly departs from his rule in one of the play's key scenes. Soso's New Year toast, which is in sharp contrast to the extremely turgid mass of Stalin's speech otherwise, is an outburst of long-repressed poetic awareness. The wizard, in the course of performing his ritual sacrifice, suddenly did something unexpected. In the course of his final polishing and ornamenting of the play, Woland's creator suddenly endowed it with a web of secret signs which quite changed its meaning. If Mikhalsky had heard the second half of *Batum* as well he would doubtless have spotted at least one more astonishing metaphor for the Devil who stole the sun from Mankind. The episode occurs in Scene Eight, which is set in the prison.

The criminal prisoners are beating up the 'politicals'. Stalin seizes the prison bars and shouts through them, 'Hey, comrades! Listen! Pass it on! A warder is beating up a woman! A warder is beating up a woman!' The Governor, the same Governor as had earlier been measuring himself against Dzhugashvili's features of an 'undistinguished head' and a mole on his left ear, rushes to the prison and is treated to a ditty by one of the criminal prisoners.

'The Tsar lives in a palace fine
And stuffs himself on quail!
(*The other criminals join in.*)
But here in prison garb we pine.
The people rot in jail.'

To say the least, the prison scene could only evoke associations in 1939 with Stalin's prison camps. Bulgakov actually underlined and drew a frame round the words 'arrest' and 'prison' as key words on the first page of that notebook in which he began writing the new play in autumn 1938. Nor was that all. He finished the scene and the entire act with an episode which has no like in all the mountains of Stalinist hagiography, in which the statement of the theme of the Antichrist pretending to be Christ is defiantly explicit. The scene ends with Stalin being transferred to another prison. One of the warders pulls out a revolver and sticks it in his back:

Prison Governor (to himself). Oh, you demon from Hell! (*Goes off into his office.*)

When Stalin comes level with the first warder, the latter grimaces.

First Warder. Take that! . . . Take that for everything! (*Strikes Stalin with the scabbard of his sword.*)

Stalin staggers and walks on.

The second warder also strikes him with his scabbard. Stalin throws down his travelling case. The lid flies off. He raises his hands, crossing them over his head in order to ward off the blows, and walks on.

As Stalin comes level, each of the warders does his best to strike him at least one blow. Treinitz appears at the entrance to the gateway and gazes skywards.

Stalin (reaches the gates, turns and shouts).
  Farewell, comrades!
  (*There is silence from the prison.*)
First Warder. They won't hear him.

The episode can of course be interpreted as very flattering for the Leader. On a secondary level the scene alludes to the Way of the Cross, as the former seminarist would have had no trouble recognising. However, through the upper stratum of the biblical allusion there juts a meaning unprecedented for its 'magnificent contempt'. The epithet thrown in Dzhugashvili's face, 'You demon from Hell!', a crucial line not found in any of the earlier versions, and Stalin being beaten by jailers like any of his own innumerable prisoners rather than a demiurge, were 'imaginary situations' which made it unthinkable that Bulgakov's 'Stalinist' play should be staged by the Art Theatre or any other Soviet theatre of that time. And what in any case was meant by 'imaginary situations'? Stalin was not, after all, noticeably disturbed by imaginary situations in other plays or films comparable to Bulgakov's. Quite the contrary. We know he encouraged them, personally sanctioning the most improbable fictions of writers unconstrained by historical veracity. Suffice it to recall Shalva Dadiani's renowned play *From the*

Spark . . ., produced that very autumn. From exactly the same source material (which was strictly controlled) one playwright derived a romantic drama, while another produced an unconscionable piece of fraudulence in which, for example, Lenin and Stalin exchange the following lines of dialogue:

Stalin (introducing himself). I am the Transcaucasian delegate.
Lenin. We have just been talking about you. The Ardent Colchidean, is it not?
Stalin (smiling). Yes, you called me that. Hello, Eagle of the Mountains.
Lenin. Give me your hand . . .

That was the kind of play the Ardent Colchidean was looking for, and the kind of imaginary situations he required his playwrights to come up with. The canons were already unchallengeable and universally known. We need to remember the context of the times if we are to appreciate the deadly gamble Bulgakov had decided to take.

The play is shot through with double meanings. Already in the Prologue Bulgakov offers a fairly straightforward key to deciphering the drama's code with its two poles in time: Russia at the turn of the century, and the new, Soviet Russia writhing 'beneath the tyres of the Black Marias'. 'At a time when all loyal sons of our Homeland stand firm by the pedestal of the monarchical throne of God's anointed Tsar as he tirelessly strives for the good of the vastest nation on Earth,' the Rector addresses Soso Dzhugashvili, 'criminals have appeared among the diverse tribes of those who inhabit the Fatherland: criminals who sow the seeds of Evil in our country.' The Rector goes on to admonish Stalin, lapsing into the familiar rhythmical and grammatical features of the language of the 1930s show trials: 'These debauchers of the people, these false prophets striving to undermine the might of the state, spread their poisonous pseudo-scientific, social-democratic theories which penetrate into every pore of the life of our people.'

There are dozens of lines in the play which contain similar explosive devices. In one place Stalin delivers himself of a veritable tirade to his classmate: '. . . it is the duty of every honest person to struggle against that base phenomenon because of which the many millions of our fellow-countrymen are crushed, living in the shadow of oppression and deprived of their human rights.' He hastens to name the offending phenomenon: 'autocracy'. In another place Stalin waxes indignant about the police raiding 'a peaceful worker's flat where no one is in the least criminal'. At one point Tsar Nicholas II discusses the nature of the laws of Russia with his Minister of Justice, and the Minister informs him that the crime committed by Dzhugashvili is punishable by exile to Eastern Siberia for a period of three years. Nicholas's reply, 'Holy Russia's laws are lenient', is distinctly challenging. In a country choked by repression and 'tyranny without redress' just the factual information on the length of sentences under the Tsar could not but make a strong impression. Those who first heard Bulgakov's reading of the play had every reason to stiffen.

Before it was banned nobody, of course, even allowed themselves to think about allusions, possible parallels or double meanings. If we read the play carefully, however, we shall see that it is not just a matter of individual lines or scenes which offend against the norms of official literature in 1939 (Mikhalsky's list, based only on the first half of the play, can be considerably expanded). The whole play was questionable and challenging. It opened out the Stalinist era and compared it with police practice under the Russian autocracy at the beginning of the century. The latter was obscene, but it was not lawless. It was based at least on some approximation to the rule of law.

A different voice was to be heard breaking through the shell of just one more revolutionary drama with its clichés and innuendo. It is impossible not to hear that voice. It is completely misconceived to attempt to measure the play by the general yardstick, as people still attempt to do. *Batum* is a muffled shout. For an entire decade Bulgakov had been waiting for the promised meeting which never materialised. He had lived through the arrests, the death and exile of his friends. He had had his fill of silence and suffering and delivered a play which, in metaphorical form, again raised some of the basic concerns of his first letter upstairs. Here he was again speaking of human freedom, man's dignity in society, the unspeakable noose of the police state round everyone's neck. His play was a reminder to its First Reader of what it was like to be persecuted, kept under surveillance, to have your name on a blacklist with every avenue closed to you. The wolf's ears of the true artist, which Pushkin just could not hide beneath his jester's cap when he wrote *Boris Godunov* under the eye of Nicholas I, stick out just as glaringly in *Batum*. Only monstrous intimidation can explain the failure of people in the Art Theatre and the vigilant members of the Committee for the Arts to notice anything seditious about the play. They had no right to notice that the emperor had no clothes.

Bulgakov's sense of foreboding that it would all end badly, a feeling which had haunted him through all the months he was working on the play, was caused in part by the kind of play he had conceived. His daring plan came to grief, and in a way which could not have been more damaging to his reputation as an author.

In October 1939, when Bulgakov had already been diagnosed as suffering from a fatal illness, Yelena noted in the diary that the Government had been to the Art Theatre, and 'the General Secretary had said in conversation with

Nemirovich that he thought *Batum* was a very good play, but that it was not to be staged.'[110]

Only the second half of Stalin's reported words is believable. Stalin proved a far more perceptive reader of *Batum* than Bulgakov's theatrical contemporaries or, come to that, their descendants who in the years since Stalin died have kept the play under wraps in an act of 'liberal censorship'. 'Why,' they ask, 'should we sully Bulgakov's wonderful reputation by publishing his opportunistic play?'

In 1931 Boris Pasternak wrote a poem analogous to Pushkin's *Stanzas*, 'A century and more, not yesterday . . .'. At the onset of a bloody decade a poet tried by means of historical parallels to urge clemency on the new autocrat and inspire him by the example of Peter the Great.

> But only now it's time to say,
> Distinguishing two revolutions,
> The start of Peter's glorious days
> Was marred by strife and executions.

This quatrain, apparently so flattering in its bridging of the centuries to the new regime, was seen as seditious for good reason and not permitted to appear in print until the mid-1950s. The Ardent Colchidean had no need in his glorious days of analogies whose flattery was two-edged. He could do without being reminded of strife and executions.

In 1939 as in 1929 Bulgakov had again faced the question of how to be a writer. His new answer found expression in his compulsion to write *Batum*. The Year of the Great Leap Forward was more than a decade removed from 1939. There was a whole era between them. Bulgakov's offer was considered and rejected. Stalin was satisfied with knowing Bulgakov had written a play about him. His remark, relayed by Vsevolod Vishnevsky and which so shocked Olga Bokshanskaya in 1946, 'Our strength is in having trained even Bulgakov to work for us', is a sly interpretation of *Batum* in purely political terms. In fact *Batum* is not only far from falling within the canon of Stalinist hagiography: it incorporates an unthinkably courageous act of defiance.

The blow which fell on Bulgakov was not so much the banning of his play as its interpretation as an offer of collaboration. Such treatment left an ineradicable stain on his literary repute. It was an insult from which he was not to recover. Before *Batum* he was still capable of whistling in the dark. After *Batum* his life as a writer lost all meaning, and with it his human, earthly existence. He began to suffocate 'within these stifling walls'. *Batum* was indisputably a violation of language and a sop to the Unclean Spirit. He had perpetrated an act of violence against himself and it undermined his health. The same thing happened with

Osip Mandelshtam when he wrote his *Ode*. In tensing and readying himself to accomplish the act he unbalanced himself mentally. 'I understand now,' he told Anna Akhmatova. 'It was a sickness.' This is probably the plane on which we should interpret the fathomless lines Akhmatova wrote on the death of Bulgakov: 'And you invited in the monstrous guest and then were left with her alone.'

Bulgakov's slow and agonising death, unlike the easy death of the Master, is directly linked with the saga of his last play and gives it a mystical significance. *Batum* was the instrument of Bulgakov's self-destruction as a writer, depriving him of his 'voucher for a place in the Pantheon'.

Bulgakov's last days were days of suffering. The rejection of *Batum* shook even the worldly-wise members of the Art Theatre. As they started coming back to Moscow at the end of August for the beginning of the season the Bulgakovs were bombarded with telephone calls. 'Overall,' Yelena records, 'I have to say that during this period I witnessed more concern, tenderness, love and respect for Misha than I ever expected to receive.'[111] The members of the Art Theatre advised him to write a new play about Soviet people as a matter of urgency. They advised him to adapt Turgenev's *The Torrents of Spring* for the stage. Samuil Samosud suggested he should turn his play into an opera with music by Shostakovich, only 'you will have to develop a female role'.[112] Instead Bulgakov took up Italian in order to keep his mind occupied.

In early September they decided to go to Leningrad for no particular reason other than to escape the questions, telephone calls and meaningful glances. Yelena complains, 'In the Theatre everyone gazes sympathetically at me as if I were a widow'.[113] They were to have no rest. While they were in Leningrad Bulgakov's health began to deteriorate rapidly. After a visit to the doctor nephrosclerosis was diagnosed. Doctor Bulgakov was in no doubt as to its incurability. Sergey Yermolinsky was to remember the words he said the first day after returning to Moscow. 'He was unexpectedly calm. He described very logically to me everything that would happen to him in the course of the next six months and how the disease would develop. He named the weeks, the months and even the dates, defining all the phases of the disease.' Major events of world history were breaking out and these punctuate the diary on even the most trying days: Ribbentrop's visit to Moscow, the conclusion of the non-aggression pact with Germany, and finally the beginning of what was later to be called the Second World War. After Leningrad the entries on the course of the war became very infrequent. The Germans capture Warsaw, but the Bulgakovs barely register the fact: 'We are stricken by our grief.'[114]

In December Bulgakov at first tried editing *Batum* in the writers' sanatorium at Barvikha, but then for the remaining months of his final illness occupied himself with a final editing of his novel. Marietta Chudakova has published lines from the manuscript (italicised) which were inserted in the novel at just this time:

How sad, ye gods, how sad the world is at evening, how mysterious the mists over the swamps. You will know it *when you have wandered astray in those mists*, when you have suffered greatly *before dying*, when you have walked through the world carrying an unbearable burden. You know it too when you are weary *and ready to leave this earth without regret; its mists, its swamps and its rivers; ready to give yourself into the arms of death with a light heart, knowing that death alone can comfort you.* (p. 426)[115]

Bulgakov's incurable illness became known to his friends. Hoping he was not too late to say something which mattered to him, Pavel Popov wrote on 5 December:

Whether I can see you or not, you are what makes life worth while for me . . . When they asked a certain Russian whether he did not perhaps belong to a tribe of barbarians he replied, 'Since there were Pushkin and Gogol in my nation's past I cannot consider myself a barbarian.' . . . So too, being your contemporary, I do not feel the world is an empty place.[116]

On 28 December, returning from the sanatorium, Bulgakov told Alexander Gdeshinsky, a friend of his youth in Kiev, 'Everyone knows there is only one decent way to die, and that is by shooting. Unfortunately I do not possess the requisite firearm.

From the bottom of my heart I wish you health, to see the sun, to hear the sea, and to listen to music.'[117]

Those last words are one of the fullest expressions of what Bulgakov loved in life.

They saw in the New Year of 1940 at home, by candlelight.

Yermolinsky with a glass of vodka in his hand, Seryozha and I with white wine, and Misha with a measuring glass of medicine. We made an effigy of Misha's illness with a fox's head (from my stole), and Seryozha, who had drawn the lot, shot it. Many telephone calls from people at the Art Theatre (Olga, Vilenkin, Fedya Mikhalsky, Gzhelsky, Knipper-Chekhova, Khmelyov, Nikolai Erdman and Raevsky).[118]

On 6 January, trying to come to terms with the *Batum* saga, Bulgakov returned to the idea of a play about 'Richard the First'. He even wrote down a few words, but then abandoned it finally. 'I just can't write. My head is like a cauldron . . . I am sick, sick.'[119]

January was exceptionally cold. 'I have been completely crippled by the frosts,' he complained to Pavel Popov.[120] Yelena confirms in the diary, '24 January: Forty-two degrees below zero. There is a white shroud outside the window like thick smoke.'[121] On one such frosty day, extremely dangerous for someone suffering from kidney disease, the Bulgakovs went to Povarsky Street to see Alexander Fadeev at the Union of Writers. He had started visiting them when Bulgakov first fell ill. Not finding him in, they stayed to lunch in the restaurant. 'Misha was wearing dark glasses and his cap, which made them all stare. I can't describe the way they stared. We returned in freezing fog.'[122]

Sergey Yermolinsky's book contains a photograph of Bulgakov wearing those dark glasses, and inscribed to Yelena, 'To you alone, my friend, I inscribe this picture. Do not grieve that the eyes are darkened: they always managed to distinguish truth from falsehood.'[123]

As always Yelena eagerly looked for auguries. A blue-tit flew into the kitchen, which should mean good luck. She hoped for a miracle, and even tried to organise one. The Art Theatre finally signed the contract for *The Last Days*, Bulgakov's play about the death of Pushkin. On 8 February Vasily Kachalov, Anna Tarasova and Nikolai Khmelyov, three of the country's foremost actors, wrote to Alexander Poskrebyshev, the head of Stalin's secretariat, about Bulgakov's condition. 'A tragic outcome is expected literally any day. Medical science can clearly do no more.' They suggested that the only thing that could save Bulgakov was a massive, joyful emotional shock 'which would give him new strength to fight his illness, or more exactly make him want to live and work, create and see his future works produced on the stage'.[124] The words are, of course, Yelena's. This is her voice, her doing and it reflects her faith that a miracle could yet happen. The actors asked Stalin's secretary to speak to him and ask him to telephone once more, thereby possibly returning the dying writer to life. This fantastic plan could only have been born in the heart of a woman tormented by pain and prepared to try anything. It could only have been supported by true actors, tempted by a *coup de théâtre* and longing to find some way at least of helping the dramatist who had given the Theatre *The Days of the Turbins* and *Molière*.

Bulgakov's last days are chronicled in the family diary and in Olga Bokshanskaya's letters to her mother in Riga. The following are some excerpts from them.

But it is she alone who has to bear the burden of his blackest minutes, and she who hears his gloomy forebodings. And hearing them she is constantly filled with the most intense desire to fight for his life. 'I won't let go of him,' she says, 'I shall wrest him away and he will live.' She loves him so much. It is quite unlike the usual mutual understanding and marital love of partners who have lived a good few years together, and become rather used to each other, and whose love has become something of a habit . . .[125]

'His reason is beginning to be clouded at times. He suddenly starts saying something strange,' Olga wrote one week before Bulgakov's death, 'but then he comes to himself again.' . . . 'Poor Lyusya [Yelena] looks into his eyes and tries to guess what he is trying to say, since often the words have slipped his memory, and this upsets him . . .'[126]

Bulgakov more than once described the way his favourite heroes died. In Leontiev Lane he argued with Stanislavsky over how Molière should die. He decided to have him die on stage, to a roar of laughter from the pit. Bulgakov, like Pushkin in *The Last Days*, possessed the ability to 'easily find the material word corresponding to that in the mind'. In *The Master and Margarita* he succeeded in conveying the feelings of the Master as he prepared to leave Moscow. In the Sparrow Hills, when the rainbow has arched itself across the sky, its foot in the Moscow River, from that very spot from which the City was to be seen spread out beyond the river, 'with fragments of sun glittering from thousands of west-facing windows, and at the onion domes of the Novodevichy monastery', the Master began to take his leave.

For the first few moments a tremor of sadness crept over his heart, but it soon changed to a delicious excitement, the gypsy's thrill of the open road.

'For ever . . . I must think what that means,' whispered the Master, and licked his dry, cracked lips. He began to listen to what was happening in his heart. His excitement, it seemed to him, had given way to a profound and grievous sense of hurt. But it was only momentary and gave place to one of proud indifference and finally to a presentiment of eternal peace. (p. 423)

There is good reason why the biographies of writers conclude by recounting their last words, often pronounced in that state when consciousness is fading and memory becoming attenuated. We do indeed perceive the death of a writer as his 'last creative act', and just because of that try intently to understand what his fading consciousness gives birth to on that frontier between life and death. Russians know from childhood on that the dying Pushkin gripped Vladimir Dahl's hand and asked him to raise him 'Higher, now, higher!' and then, as if again regaining consciousness for a moment, had time to say, 'Life is ended.' We recall Gogol ordering that he should be brought 'a ladder'; Leo Tolstoy, raising himself a little on the bed in the stationmaster's house at Astapovo and suddenly declaring loudly and emphatically, 'Time to clear off! Time!' and, before falling into his last sleep, saying, 'I shall go somewhere nobody can bother me. Leave me in peace.' On the day of his death Dostoevsky opened the copy of the Gospels he had been presented with by the wives of the Decembrists as he was setting off for hard labour in Siberia and tried to foretell his future. The book opened at the

Gospel according to St Matthew, at Jesus's reply to John, 'Suffer it to be so now'. In Badenweiler one July night Chekhov drained a glass of champagne, smiled and said, 'I haven't drunk champagne for ages,' quietly turned on to his left side and fell into eternal sleep.

There is a barely perceptible echo in these last moments and last words of the spirit of a writer's life. At all events, we have an incorrigible urge to hear and try to find a spiritual testament in these last words and gestures.

We may know from childhood of the last creative act of our classics, but we have no way of knowing the way many of Bulgakov's contemporaries died. We shall probably never read what Osip Mandelshtam said as he took his leave of life, or even know how Isaac Babel died. Mikhail Afanasievich Bulgakov was at least fortunate enough to have a personal fate and to die in bed. On 6 March Yelena recorded his last words.

I told him what I guessed he wanted me to, what it seemed to me he was thinking about. I said, 'I promise you faithfully that I shall make a fair copy of the novel and deliver it to them. You shall be published!' He listened fairly lucidly and attentively and then said, 'So that they know . . . So that they know.'[127]

He died on 10 March 1940, at 4.39 in the afternoon, as twilight was falling, that most terrible and portentous time of the day. Olga wrote to her mother that right up until the last second Yelena was expecting a miracle.

'He was sleeping so peacefully again. His breathing was so even and deep,' Lyusya said, 'that I thought the miracle had happened.' She was constantly expecting one from him, with his special nature so unlike ordinary human beings. 'I thought the crisis had passed, he was beginning to recover, he had beaten his illness. He continued sleeping like that, only at about half past four his face twitched slightly. He ground his teeth and then continued breathing evenly, but ever more weakly. And so, very, very quietly, the life went from him.'[128]

The telephone rang the following morning with an enquiry from Stalin's secretariat: 'Is it true Comrade Bulgakov is dead?'

The dénouement denied in life was granted in death, as in any banal drama.

An obituary written at the Art Theatre was published a day later in *Izvestiya*. It was written on behalf of the Art Theatre company, but written by the individual on whom such tasks devolve. That, of course, was Pavel Markov.

The Art Theatre is today racked with pain.

A man has gone who was close to us, whom we loved as a friend, and to whom we owe many moments of creative joy.

He brought to our stage grand emotions, and with his magnificent understanding of the real nature of the actor's art was able to communicate to us all that was most dear and important in his characters. He was fired with enthusiasm for a production no less than its other contributors. There was no aspect of the stage to which he was indifferent. He was as it were a director-dramatist, and an actor-dramatist. . . .[129]

The cortège made its way to the crematorium by a circuitous route. There were the obligatory halts at the Bolshoy and Art Theatres. As was customary, they went up to the doors of the grey-green building, above which Golubkin's pre-revolutionary bas-relief depicted a swimmer cleaving massive waves. This symbol of the new art had never been more appropriate. At the crematorium the oration was given by Sakhnovsky, and Olga Knipper-Chekhova laid flowers on the coffin. Bulgakov was buried in that same Novodevichy Monastery that the Master had viewed from the Sparrow Hills. They buried him immediately beside Stanislavsky, Chekhov and Gogol. As the years passed this 'Cherry Orchard', as the Art Theatre's plot became known, would harbour the graves of Khmelyov and Dobronravov, Sakhnovsky and Tarkhanov, Simov and Dmitriev, Moskvin and Leonidov. Space had been allocated for precisely sixty-five graves, as the meticulous Olga had reported to Nemirovich-Danchenko. Bulgakov was buried where the Art Theatre's section met that of the Bolshoy. Thus the author of *Molière* found himself locked for ever in the circle of the theatre. There was no music at the funeral at Bulgakov's request.

8

Black Snow or A Dead Man's Notes

'You have to love your Characters . . .'

Almost all the older members of the Art Theatre preserve a few cherished slips of paper listing the heroes of *Black Snow* and who their prototypes were. When I asked Pavel Markov the familiar question of who was who, he took down from his bookshelf a bound manuscript copy of Bulgakov's novel and showed me the first page. It was like a theatre programme listing the cast of a play:

Maxudov	– Bulgakov
Ivan Vasilievich	– Stanislavsky
Aristarkh Platonovich	– Nemirovich-Danchenko
Toropetzkaya	– Bokshanskaya
Menazhraki	– Tamantsova
Yelagin	– Stanitsyn
Patrikeev	– Yanshin
Vladychinsky	– Prudkin
Margarita Petrovna Tavricheskaya	– Knipper-Chekhova
Gerasim Nikolaevich	– Podgorny
Thomas Strizh	– Sudakov
Romanus	– Izrailevsky

and so on, in an orderly column, right down to the Art Theatre's doctors, messengers, assistant producers and security men.

The joy of recognising one's colleagues in a novel is like one of those office in-jokes which cannot be shared with the outside world. Markov knew this as well as anybody. In an article written in the mid-1960s he suggested that the reader's approach to *Black Snow* said something about his intellectual level.

Will the reader see it as a deliberate and systematic humiliation of a great theatre and its great founders? Will he read it as a collection of funny stories? Or will he recognise an ironical and, I stress, saddened and regretful exposé of practices which offended against the very basis of the Art Theatre, and enjoy reading a brilliant work premissed on acknowledgement of the Art Theatre's principles?[1]

Yelena Bulgakova responded by writing Markov a letter of thanks with perhaps the most useful comments anyone had to make on the meaning of *Black Snow*, just then emerging from restricted circulation within the Art Theatre into the larger world of Russian literature.

I am so glad you have written about *Black Snow* putting everything in perspective. I find it equally awful when people tell me, 'I just laughed and laughed!', and when they start asking me who was who. That is not what it is about. They are missing the point. It is about the same tragic theme to which Bulgakov constantly returned: the artist in conflict, whether with Louis XIV or the League of Hypocrites, with Nicholas the First, or a theatre director. It goes without saying that he loved the Art Theatre, that it was his Theatre, that he was its Author. It is all so plain in the novel.[2]

First reactions of Bulgakov's theatrical friends ran true to his expectations. Those who felt they were 'favourably' depicted liked the novel a great deal. In Yelena's entry for 12 February 1937 we read of Fyodor Mikhalsky's reaction: 'Fedya is very flattered (He heard the piece set in the office).'[3] Others were incensed, while others still enjoyed a personal shock of recognition and took pleasure in Bulgakov's ability to give literary expression to the strains and stresses of life within the Art Theatre. We have a note written by Vasily Sakhnovsky on 11 March 1937. The director, immortalised in *Black Snow* by the reference to his decadent Roman profile and pettishly jutting underlip, wrote in anticipation of enjoying the novel, about which the Art Theatre was already buzzing with rumours.

I have heard from Joseph (I speak of Joseph Raevsky), that a novel has flowed from your pen which is devoted to a certain Theatre in which I take an interest. I walked along the street with Joseph, laughing heartily. Absolutely rrrright! Short and tasty pastry is one thing, but short and testy producers and art directors are considerably less appetising![4]

Sakhnovsky's in-joke and his exultantly rolled 'r's tell us only that the novel's real meaning was far from being understood. On 3 May 1939 Bulgakov read excerpts from *A Dead Man's Notes* while visiting Viliams. The chapter 'A

Successful Marriage', with its description of 'Ivan Vasilievich' taking a rehearsal was, as Yelena testifies, rapturously received.

Samosud immediately suggested Misha should read the chapter to the entire Bolshoy Theatre, and say the rehearsal was set in a provincial theatre. He so liked the idea of publicly rubbishing Stanislavsky's Method that he would have given anything for the reading to take place. Of course, Misha declined.[5]

Several decades had to pass before Bulgakov's serious purpose could be seen.

Black Snow takes its individuality from a number of sources, of which the most obvious are the directly literary. The novel is related to a whole range of European works, memoir and fictional, written about the theatre, from the books Bulgakov studied during his Molière Period to the confessional works of the German romantics and Goethe's *Wilhelm Meister*. The passion of Goethe's hero for the box of puppets; his ability to create a private opera complete with thunder and lightning using only glue, scissors, paper and cardboard; finally, his very understanding of the nature of theatre and how it rivals life are all to be found reflected in Bulgakov's novel. To be persuaded of this we have only to compare the description of the 'magical little room' in *Black Snow* (pp. 51–2) with the acting of Wilhelm Meister with his puppet booth and his marionettes:

I examined them thoroughly and went on to the stage and thus hovered above their little world. With a kind of reverence I looked down into the openings, enthralled by memories of how wonderful the stage appears from outside, and felt that I was being inducted into great mysteries.

Let us, however, leave to one side for the moment the question of the literary genesis of *Black Snow*, and take a closer look at sources contemporary to Bulgakov which have attracted less attention from the scholars. From its inception the Art Theatre was given to high jinks and buffoonery. People see, in particular, a link between *Black Snow* and the Art Theatre's early 'skits' whose spirit, if in a slightly altered form, was still in evidence when Bulgakov arrived. They are not the sole influence on the novel's genre, but they undoubtedly contributed.

The Art Theatre's skits were born before the revolution and were a unique way of unclogging the pores of the new theatre art. They were not only a way of letting off steam or taking a humorous break from a life of ceaseless earnest seeking, but also helped to establish the cheery, friendly, creative atmosphere which Stanislavsky and Nemirovich-Danchenko saw as integral to the Theatre's existence. Absolutely nothing and nobody was immune from being subjected to satirical review and reconsideration; no cranny of the Art Theatre enterprise was so sacred that the mockery and parody of the skit might not be turned upon it. A culture of laughter, closely related to a general culture of laughter within the Russian theatre in the early twentieth century, was essential if the young Art Theatre was to be protected from stagnation and dogmatic smugness. The skits were a mechanism for self-purification and self-monitoring in the Theatre's ceaseless search for ways of bringing life and human personality alive on the stage, and its equally ceaseless and exhausting struggle against the cliché and yesterday's artistic truth. On this day of carnival within the Art Theatre the ranks and barriers dividing theatre people, and indeed people of the world outside, were done away with. The company's actors and its august leaders were drawn into comedic action on an equal footing.

'The austere, puritanical Temple of the Seagull had an unwontedly frivolous aspect,' *The Footlights* reported of the 1911 review. 'Comical posters are hanging everywhere. Gigantic masks of Stanislavsky and Nemirovich-Danchenko nod to you. Penny whistles shrill, barrel-organs grind, pipes pipe.'

The reporter goes on to recount in astonishment that Stanislavsky, Yuzhin, and Nemirovich were drawn into the comic acting, only for their entrance to be parodied by actors made up as Stanislavsky, Nemirovich and Yuzhin.

The element of carnival was to survive in the old Art Theatre for decades, if in somewhat dilute form, even when no hint of skittishness remained within its walls. Bulgakov came to the Theatre at a happy time when it was experiencing a second period of youth, and each character in *Black Snow* is measured against this criterion of vivacious spontaneity. Olga Bokshanskaya, who belonged to a later generation in the Art Theatre, could neither understand nor abide Knipper-Chekhova's 'relentless irony', her ability to make light of absolutely everything. No less informative, if from another angle, is the appreciation of the atmosphere of the old Art Theatre by Kachalov's son Vadim Shverubovich in his book *People, the Theatre, and Me.* In the Art Theatre people 'did not like things which could not be laughed at'. That admirably characterises Bulgakov's literary approach in passing judgement on the life of the Theatre.

'Alert eyes' . . . In Bulgakov's writing this is virtually the supreme accolade for any individual. We encounter people in *Black Snow* who have worried eyes, sad eyes, enigmatic eyes, crystalline eyes, steely eyes, unblinking eyes, and finally, fiery eyes like the eyes of a wolf in the steppes. Only two individuals are accorded recognition as having 'alert' eyes: Philipp Philippovich Tulumbasov, House Manager, and Vasily Vasilievich, Assistant Director. In the eyes of both of them, moreover, there is a deep melancholy. Behind Phil's eyes 'lurked a barely perceptible, secret, incurable sadness' (p. 92), while the eyes of the Assistant Director are not only alert, but also worldly-wise.

Fyodor Mikhalsky and Nikolai Shelonsky were not, of course, the only members of the Art Theatre possessed of alert eyes. Among other alert-eyed performers we may single out Grigory Konsky, and Boris Livanov who was notable for his now widely appreciated drawings, caricatures and cartoons, beginning with the justly famous satirical curtain-cum-fresco for the Art Theatre's anniversary skit in 1933.[6] The curtain offered a schematic representation of life in the Art Theatre, barbed in the same way that Bulgakov's novel is barbed. In the centre of the composition a happy couple recline on Mount Olympus, the wife being Stanislavsky and the husband Nemirovich-Danchenko.

Livanov was quite exceptional. He combined a remarkable gift for acting with the ability to capture the fleeting theatrical moment, as he amply demonstrated with his cartoon executed on a backcloth twelve metres by seven. We should not underestimate the impact such versatile virtuosity had on Bulgakov. Every line in *Black Snow* reminds us of his dual nature as an actor and a playwright with the stage in his blood, and of his long-standing addiction to the mentality of the Satiricon theatre.

We know from Yelena Bulgakov's diary and many other memoirs that Bulgakov himself had an excellent grasp of the actor's way of understanding people and situations. When rehearsals at Leontiev Lane were at their most trying, Bulgakov could alter his mood on returning home like a true actor by demonstrating what had been going on at the Theatre. On 7 April 1935 Yelena notes, 'M.A. returns from rehearsals at Stanislavsky's completely drained, [. . .] then has himself and me in stitches by demonstrating Koreneva's acting of Madeleine.'[7] We find a similar entry two days later: 'Misha was in exceptionally high spirits recounting the rehearsal of *Molière*. He acted Stanislavsky, Podgorny and Koreneva, and an absolutely classic Sheremetieva in the role of Molière's nanny, Renée.'[8]

Note how Yelena brings together those two elements of recounting and acting, the writer's and the actor's methods of understanding a human being.

The nature of the humour in *Black Snow* is far removed from the funny story or joke so popular with the acting fraternity. A joke is laughter which has gone cold, second-hand laughter which has been borrowed from someone else. The element of authorship is missing from it. People who told jokes were rewarded more often than not with a smile of condescension from Bulgakov, like a fat actor who clamps a piece of someone else's wit in his teeth and rushes around looking for someone to tell it to. The author of *Black Snow*, Yelena tells us, had no time for jokes of this kind. 'He never told them himself.' All the funny things he came out with were spontaneous, sharp-witted, hot from the stove. They had just occurred to him.

Akhmatova's valediction to Bulgakov, 'You could joke like nobody else', reveals the mode of *Black Snow* with a poet's precision. The dominant element is improvisation, plots which are conjured up and develop before our eyes and which are the key to the novel's humour. What Bulgakov's passion takes away, his irony really does restore.

In talking of the humour of *Black Snow* we have to be clear about one thing. We are dealing not only with a book about the theatre but also with 'A Dead Man's Notes'.

This is laughter bursting out on the verge of the void, a retrospective book about the theatre written by somebody departing this life. The solemnity of the viewpoint suggested by the original title is promptly realised in the Introduction. We are told that two days after putting the final full stop at the end of his notes, Maxudov threw himself headlong from the Chain Bridge in Kiev. This is not only a book about the theatre. It grows to become a book about life, with its confessional overtones, the allusion to Kiev and the encrypting of Bulgakov's pet name 'Maka' in the hero's surname; the intense lyricism of the narrative voice; the vividness and intensity of earthly things seen and felt for the last time; and the pathos of a testament speaking from death ('Oh, that glorious world of the office. Phil – farewell! Soon I shall be gone for ever. Think of me sometimes!') (p. 100) This is the viewpoint from which, sadder but wiser, Bulgakov bestows an author's love on all the characters of his novel without exception, from the 'condor' Gavriil Stepanovich to the implacable guardian of the changing-room Toropetzkaya, from the talentless Pryakhina to that maestro of the petty squabble, the conductor Romanus.

In his early article about the prose of Yury Slyozkin Bulgakov formulated an approach to human beings which he considered unacceptable. He designated it 'je-m'en-fichisme' or, more plainly, 'sod-'em-all-ism'. The contrary principle, evident in his own writing, is propounded very clearly indeed in *Black Snow*. As Maxudov labours to rewrite his play in accordance with the counsels of Ivan Vasilievich, he becomes convinced of the impossibility and senselessness of the endeavour. 'You have to love your characters. If you don't, I don't advise anybody to try writing. The outcome is bound to be extremely unpleasant. Believe me, I know!' (p. 118)

Bulgakov's parting book about the theatre is suffused with precisely this higher love, a love which is fundamentally the same in spirit and substance as the first principles on which the Art Theatre based its art.

In 1921 the young Bulgakov wrote of Nekrasov, 'A great talent cannot live by anger alone. The spirit will remain unsatisfied. You must have love, as darkness must have light.'[9] It is a phrase which anticipates the whole aesthetic and ethical colouring of Bulgakov's future writing in general, and of *Black Snow* in particular.

Maxudov in Wonderland

Black Snow does not confine itself to the world of the theatre. It takes in a number of conflicting and mutually exclusive worlds. Maxudov, sitting by his oil stove during a March snowstorm, recalls his life in two different worlds.

World number one – the university laboratory, from which I remember the fume chamber and retorts on stands. I left that world during the Civil War. [. . .] I then got a job on the *Shipping Gazette*. Why? Let's be frank. I nursed ambitions of becoming a writer. What then? I left the world of the *Gazette*. A new world opened up and when I plunged into it that ghastly party proved it to be unbearable. (p. 48)

Maxudov discovers the realm of literature with its 'very best writers' headed by Izmail Alexandrovich, a world of false appearances and vacuousness, a world in which he has no wish to remain.

'I am going to tell the truth,' I mumbled when it was already broad daylight behind the grubby, unwashed blind, 'the whole truth. I saw a new world yesterday, and it was repulsive. I won't belong to it. It's a strange world. A disgusting world. I must keep this an absolute secret. Sshhh!' (p. 45)

Maxudov enters the theatre as his last refuge on earth. It proves to be the only world in which his existence is possible. On the threshold of non-being Maxudov recalls his first impressions of it with a positively sensuous intensity and vividness. He retraces his path to the theatre in minute detail, hour by hour. He recalls his meeting with Ilchin, the director who proposed he should write a play, as a mystical experience. The talk between director and playwright takes place at twilight, to the accompaniment of the sounds of a thunderstorm, peals of thunder and flashes of lightning.

Maxudov reconstructs the breath-taking intensity of his first encounter with the stage and the auditorium, with its dim emergency lighting emanating from a pair of light bulbs. The Academy Stage of the Independent Theatre, like Molière's stage before it, is present before us in the romantic aura of a place permeated, shot through with magical currents, and with its own separate and self-sufficient meaning. '. . . the curtain was open and the stage gaped. It was solemn, enigmatic and empty. Its corners were filled with darkness, but in the middle, faintly gleaming, there stood a golden horse, rearing up on its hind legs.' (p. 55)

That open curtain is the beginning of a life, its first, sweet link. ' "We are closed today," Ilchin whispered solemnly, as if in church [. . .] "He's seducing me," I thought, as my heart thumped and trembled with anticipation.' (p. 55)

In the enormous world-class city the Theatre is isolated, like some fortress or monastery with its own rule. One of the motifs which occurs most insistently in *Black Snow* is that of the magically circumscribed nature of the theatre, a redemptive hermetic space. The Theatre's domain is watched over by comical but devoted guards. Maxudov soon finds his entry to the Academy Stage barred by a small but agile *muzhik* who waves his arms at him as if attempting to entrap a hen. After this gate-keeper we meet two more who are eternally on duty in Phil's office, and squads of other unsung and seemingly incorporeal gnomes in uniform, ushers and messengers who relentlessly accompany the playwright through the circles of this theatre hell. Before the ill-starred reading of his play, led in total silence like a bull to the slaughter by taciturn servants trained by Augusta Menazhraki, Maxudov suddenly feels that the 'shades of the dead were flitting round me' (p. 122).

The impression of a monastery is emphasised by the 'mediaeval-looking iron' and 'studded' doors, the broadcloth bordering the auditorium to muffle the sound of feet, and finally the premises of the Independent Theatre itself, full of magic within and only outwardly mimicking a thoroughly ordinary urban building. When Maxudov, stunned and enraptured by his first encounter, goes out to the street and looks round, he notices in the centre of Moscow a 'wholly inconspicuous building, hump-backed like a tortoise, with cubic, frosted glass lamps outside it' (p. 59). The theatre realm, unmarked on any map, is directly opposite a shop selling 'Trusses and Corsets'.

It is possible to derive a strict and detailed hierarchy from the topography of the Theatre. There is first the foyer with its memorable portrait gallery, where Nero hangs next to Plisov, the manager of the revolving stage; next there is Gavriil Stepanovich's green silk marquee with the hellish glow from under his rosewood table (where Maxudov has the 'little contract' playfully slipped to him); then the stage and the auditorium in which an electric cable runs like a thin snake to the little director's table with its obligatory ash-tray full of cigarette ends and its carafe of water; then the canyon with the stage sets peppered with enigmatic inscriptions like '1st left rear' and 'Count, back', 'Bedroom, Act III'; then the buffet in which the discussion of all the world's problems takes place; then the 'changing room' which has to be passed through as souls pass through purgatory. Then finally, the Office, shifted out to the very edge of the theatre state, the only noisy place, the point where 'life, as it were, gushed in from the street' (p. 91).

This entire hermetically enclosed and compartmentalised world is directed from two equidistant points: Sivtsev Vrazhek and India. Actual spatial relations are here magically blurred and ignored as if in a fairy-tale.

Sivtsev Vrazhek too has its hierarchical topography, mysterious and puzzling to the uninitiated. Maxudov passes unknown old men and women, opens the door to an enchanted place with the magic password 'Appointment!', and finds himself in the presence of the dread Ivan Vasilievich. The tightly closed nature of the theatre world is splendidly revealed by Aunt Nastasya Ivanovna, who reins in the actress Ludmilla Pryakhina, who has thrown herself at Ivan Vasilievich's feet, with the inhibiting injunction, 'Come back, dear – there's a stranger here!' (p. 108)

The ringed-off world of the theatre lives in a time of its own where the clocks are stopped and the calendar of history has no significance. The romantic Master exists in this strange time and place as the heroes of legend exist in the Russian folk *bylina*. The nature of his actions is predetermined by the place in which he finds himself. At the parting of three ways the folk hero chooses the dangerous, forbidden path. In the 'changing room' of the Independent Theatre or in the apartment of Ivan Vasilievich the behaviour of our hero is subject to strict taboos. There are certain words he must not utter, but utter them he none the less does, and thereby seals his doom. And just as in a fairy-tale he is saved by a miracle, worked by Misha Panin and Thomas Strizh.

Bulgakov's theatre wonderland not only has its own time and place, it also possesses a special language wholly incomprehensible to outsiders. At his first meeting with Ilchin Maxudov realises how hopelessly inadequate his knowledge of this language is. He is unable to communicate with the strange and enchanting new world on equal terms. Just as the excited playwright, hypnotised by the golden horse, is breathing in the aroma of the seductive empty stage, Ilchin whispers exotic promises in his ear. 'And who knows, stranger things have happened – perhaps we can persuade the old man himself to produce it!' (p. 54) Then Ilchin, Misha Panin and Eulampia start talking such jargon that Maxudov is as lost as if he were in the depths of the forest.

My hearers then began talking and although they were speaking Russian, what they said was so peculiar that I was quite unable to understand it.

It was Misha's habit, when discussing something, to walk up and down the room, occasionally stopping abruptly.

'Osip Ivanovich?' asked Ilchin softly, frowning.

'No, no, no,' replied Misha, suddenly shaken with laughter. When the laughing fit was over he remembered his murdered friend and aged visibly.

'Any of the old stagers. . . ?' Ilchin began.

'I don't think so,' growled Misha. [. . .]

'And what about Sivtsev Vrazhek?' (Eulampia Petrovna).

'Yes, and nobody knows how India will react to this sort of thing either,' added Ilchin. (p. 57)

Bulgakov uses the literary device of *ostranenie*, making it strange, to raise his depiction of habitual and familiar theatre routine from the level of recognition to that of cognition. Maxudov enters the theatre with the open heart of a child, seeing everything for the first time and describing it with primal words.

Bulgakov's lyrical hero does not know what the 'Cohort of Friends' is or who Grisha Aivazovsky is. He is unaware that the Independent Theatre is run by two co-directors who have not been on speaking terms since 1885. He hasn't a clue as to what the changing-room or Sivtsev Vrazhek are. He does not understand the magic power of the word 'Appointment!', and has no inkling what a 'nakladka' is. Maxudov reads a playwriting contract for the first time and is amazed to discover that every clause begins with the words 'The Author shall not', and that the only one infringing the document's uniformity begins 'The Author must . . .'.

The Independent Theatre and the entire literary and theatre world of Russia in the 1920s is described as if seen for the first time through the clear-sighted and steady eyes of a writer able to penetrate through to what is essential in the motley masquerade of overly familiar words and structures most people have come to accept unthinkingly.

In his impassioned nocturnal and confessional talk with Bombardov, Maxudov, 'inspired by a last wave of emotion' as dawn is breaking, delivers a monologue about the golden horse. It is a declaration of love for the theatre, but it is also a monologue about cognition overcoming recognition, and how the Russian language can overcome and reveal the hidden springs of the Theatre's jargon.

Smashing a saucer in my enthusiasm, I tried to convince Bombardov how as soon as I caught sight of the horse I had instinctively grasped the secret of the stage and all its mysteries. How long ago in childhood perhaps, or perhaps even before I was born I had dreamed of it and longed for it! And now I had arrived in that magic world!

'I'm a stranger in it,' I cried, 'a stranger in your world – but nothing can stop me! I've arrived – and I shall stay!'

[. . .] 'Kindly stop contradicting me,' I said firmly, 'you belong to it but I'm a newcomer, I can still see it all freshly and sharply!' (p. 140)

The fresh, sharp vision of someone who was still a newcomer enabled Bulgakov to see the 'things which had gone wrong in the administration and everyday routine' of one theatre as 'failings of the theatre in general', as Pavel Markov helpfully suggests. The comment needs a certain amount of explication. It would in all probability be difficult, if not downright impossible, to write a novel about the failings of music, or painting, or literature in general. As regards the theatre, Markov's comment does not seem outlandish. Indeed it hints at a

truth which all writers who come into contact with the world of the stage seem to
seek to express. Already when writing his novella about Molière, Bulgakov
looked back to the experience of his predecessors (especially Paul Scarron with
his *Roman comique*) and measured it against the experiences of a playwright
working in the twentieth century. By the time he was writing *Black Snow*,
Bulgakov had been through a schooling in the theatre such as probably no other
Russian writer had ever experienced. He tried to evoke the contemporary stage
on the basis of traditional models. In *Black Snow* a romantic vision of the ideal
theatre ceaselessly collides with the actual practice of the theatre routine and
outputting of plays, which involve a multitude of all sorts of people.

One of the primary distinguishing features of the theatre is that it is a
collaborative enterprise which stamps each contributor to the common cause
with a hallmark of what is known as 'theatricality'. 'A man of the theatre', 'theatre
mores', 'real theatre writing': these are not rigorous terms, but they go a
considerable way to identify the nature of theatre people and the mechanism by
which the theatre functions. 'Failings of the theatre in general' are, for the most
part, associated with this phenomenon, to which people react in very different
ways and which seems to derive from the very nature of the art of the stage.

We have seen how Bulgakov became a writer for the theatre and an 'Author of
the Theatre'; for all that, he never wholly became a 'theatre person', completely
identified with the world of acting and life behind the scenes.

We do not find in *Black Snow* or in Bulgakov's letters the acid put-downs of the
contemporary stage which occur, for example, in Chekhov's correspondence.
For Chekhov, the author of *Ivanov*, the theatre of his time was a 'world of
blockheads, idiots, sounding brasses and tinkling cymbals', or even more
uncompromisingly, 'a rash', 'an unspeakable disease of the towns'. There too we
constantly find actors characterised as a capricious, vain, half-educated mob
seventy years behind the social progress of the times. Kindred denunciations of
the theatre are widespread in the literature of the twentieth century. They are
nowhere to be found in Bulgakov's writing.

Bombardov is Maxudov's double, his second, sober, 'realistic' hypostasis. We
must assume that the comments of this Virgil as he accompanies the romantic
poet and dreamer through the circles of the world behind the scenes are close to
Bulgakov's own views on the theatre.

There is an ambiguous quality in the novel as regards both the concept of
'theatricality' and the concept of a 'theatre person'. They comprise both the
highest flowering of the human spirit, and the lowest index of humanity in a
human being. A theatre person may, like Phil, be possessed of a heartfelt
understanding of all earthly things, a quality which enables him to pick out in the

sea of supplicants besieging the box office precisely those who are worthy to pass through the gates of paradise. A true theatre person as depicted by Bulgakov's pen acquires supernatural powers. Phil not only allows people into this closed world, but also sees them off to the next. The theatre funeral, the famous Art Theatre ritual with fanfares and a lorry driving up to the doors of the Theatre, is one more aspect of this hermetic world, this realm to which one belongs body and soul. It makes manifest also the hidden but equal relations between the theatre and life itself. All Russia passes before Phil. Bulgakov twice lists those attempting to storm the gates of Paradise in great detail. Phil sorts them all instantly, allocating each his place in the gallery, the dress circle, or the stalls in a manner that would do credit to St Peter himself.

It has to be admitted that very few of those we encounter in the world of the theatre have alert eyes. The average 'theatre person' in *Black Snow* is an individual who interprets real life by the laws of the stage, something Nemiro-vich-Danchenko had established as one of the peculiarities of the actor's psychology. This little-researched attribute renders the 'theatre person' both terribly vulnerable and at the same time pitiless, both victim and tyrant. In order to be able to act on a well-lit stage all the theatre's prodigies of self-sacrifice and all its betrayals occur, ingenious manoeuvres are executed which the mind of a newcomer finds both unacceptable and incomprehensible. Both Stanislavsky and Nemirovich-Danchenko were fully familiar with the 'semi-hysterical theatrical organism'. The two of them struggled throughout their lives against this bottled-up, airless quality of the theatre world which Bulgakov so devastat-ingly evokes in his novel. They fought against self-sufficient 'theatricality' as a blight which kept the theatre from performing its proper social and artistic function. When a theatre person never looks further than the theatre, when the stage is sealed off so that the air and bustle of the outside world cannot penetrate, the theatre begins to suffer the symptoms, not immediately evident but none the less severe, of oxygen starvation. Interest in what is going on beyond its walls withers; a writer with his sense of discovery and novelty is considered to be of no interest. The actors find themselves left only with a deformed and debased form of the acting instinct, a form of acting preoccupied only with itself.

As a newcomer Maxudov cannot even comprehend what is as plain as two times two to the 'theatre person', Bombardov, namely why his play should be acted by the founder members rather than those who should act in it in the interests of good art.

'But I don't think my play's good enough to be acted by the founder members!' I roared. 'Give the parts to the young actors!'

'Oh, very clever!' cried Bombardov pulling a diabolical face. 'Of course – let Argunin, Galin, Yelagin, Blagosvetlov and Strenkovsky act it and get all the applause! Bravo! Encore! Hurrah! Look at us, good people, see how well we act! And the founder members, I suppose, can sit around and watch and look embarrassed – and tell each other they're not wanted any more and that it's time for them to retire to the workhouse? Ha, ha, ha! Oh, clever – very clever!'

'I see!' I shouted in an effort to imitate his satanic voice, 'I see it all!'

'It's obvious,' interrupted Bombardov. 'Look – Ivan Vasilievich told you that you had to turn the fiancée into the mother, didn't he? Then Margarita Petrovna or Nastasya Ivanovna could have played her . . .'

'Nastasya Ivanovna?'

'You're not a theatre person,' said Bombardov with an insulting smirk, but without explaining why he was insulting me. (p. 136)

Maxudov has no inkling of the fact that Ivan Vasilievich has a responsibility to ensure the well-being of the founder members. He has to ensure that they have opportunities to act, since for them not to act means not to live. His responsibility is just the same as Maxudov's responsibility to ensure the survival of his play. The only way out of the vicious circle, which is one of the 'failings of the theatre in general', is by moving outside the logic of the theatre. Nemirovich-Danchenko had seen the way out for the Moscow Art Theatre as being to declare it an 'author's theatre'.

An 'author's theatre', bringing truth to the people, has to impose itself by breaking down the refractory egos of actors and directors alike. *Black Snow* shows the topic of the author in the theatre to be inherently dramatic.

As Maxudov enters the theatre's behind-scenes wonderland he comes first to Gavriil Stepanovich's green marquee and then to Polixena Toropetzkaya's 'changing room'. This immediately introduces the important theme of the relationship between Art and The Office, not Phil's splendid Office, but all the services which are essential for provisioning the creative process. While giving The Office its due, the Art Theatre's founders were always afraid that it would expand and grow from a subordinate, auxiliary force into the power that made the decisions.

Without suggesting that the artistic situation in the Independent Theatre can be directly equated with the realities of the Moscow Art Theatre, let us briefly see how the novel reflects the way in which the subordinate interests of The Office tried, perhaps inadvertently, to exert undue influence on the artistic history of the Theatre, and sometimes to usurp it.

It is no secret that the importance of positions and jobs in the theatre does not coincide with analogous job descriptions elsewhere. For example, in the Art

Theatre in the 1920s and 1930s the modest position of Secretary assumed an almost Woland-like power. Let us consider the role played in the Theatre by that guardian of the changing room, Olga Bokshanskaya.

In a letter of 1931 Nemirovich-Danchenko directly charges Bokshanskaya with 'familiarising yourself with all the psychologies in the Theatre'.[10] This secretary is no mere executive or helper but an investigator of the trends and moods within the Theatre, of all the psychological nuances of 'the most complicated mechanism in the world'.

Olga's letters to her boss are a priceless documentary source on the history of the Art Theatre in the Soviet period. She unwearyingly composed these 'accurate, detailed, well-painted letters', as their addressee characterised them, over a period of decades, conscious of her involvement in the Theatre's history. Nothing could prevent the exemplary working of this smooth-running 'informational apparatus'. The great secretary remains true to herself even in the letter which begins by expressing condolences to Nemirovich-Danchenko on the death of his wife. Missing a line, the epistolary equivalent of observing one minute's silence, she briskly continues her daily account of the Theatre's affairs and psychologies, matters which take precedence over life and death.

Olga's boundless devotion to Nemirovich-Danchenko, against which the personal or congeneric ties of the Bulgakovs' 'sister dear, godmother and benefactress' were as nothing, her theatrical intelligence and unheard of energy, placed her in a special position.

Olga Bokshanskaya suffered from ptosis – paralysis of the eyelid. Her eyes appeared always to be half-closed, something which did not at all prevent her from seeing everything that was going on in the Theatre and bringing out the facts in her own highly skilful interpretation. 'My weak eyes, with my capacity for seeing everything slightly veiled', is how she describes herself. These attributes could on occasion cause her to lose a sense of the proper limits of her office, and she could begin to take on a resemblance to that 'theatre person' incarnated in Polixena Toropetzkaya, whose 'crystalline eyes' glitter at the least whiff of intrigue or scandal.

In *Black Snow* the changing room is one more obstacle in Maxudov's path to his audience.

The battle between the changing room and the cabinet, the opposition between the upper and lower storeys of the Independent Theatre in the topography of *Black Snow*, is really very allusive. Gavriil Stepanovich and Augusta Menazhraki guard the chambers of Ivan Vasilievich as a remote outpost of Sivtsev Vrazhek. Needless to say, these mythical guardians of the theatre wonderland are far removed from their prototypes. Ripsime Tamantsova and

Nikolai Yegorov were people of the highest competence who by force of circumstance, primarily Stanislavsky's inability to attend the Theatre because of severe incapacity, became (together with Nikolai Podgorny) the informational apparatus of Leontiev Lane. The Privy Council also presented events and facts, making judgements on personalities and situations, as it deemed appropriate. Pavel Markov has written very well on this subject in his last book. 'Ripsi', as Tamantsova signed her letters to Stanislavsky, did her work with much less virtuosity than Olga, which did not prevent her from instigating the 'minor revolutions' which periodically traumatised the theatre. Here, by way of example, is a letter sent to Stanislavsky on 10 May 1934. It predetermined events that autumn when he returned after his long absence from Moscow. 'And I am writing this not about myself and Nikolai [Yegorov] but about 99 per cent of the company who are weary, worn out, have lost their way and their faith. We officiate in the Temple of Art, but we cannot see the Art.'[11] Deliberately distressing the great director, his secretary condoles:

You are right, K.S.; when people keep silent it means things are bad for the Theatre. Nikolai is particularly affected by the collapse and dying of the Theatre. A few days ago he told me in conversation that when you return you will have to make herculean efforts to revive the Theatre, and that you will have to change your ideas about certain people so radically that he hates to think how it will affect you.[12]

With petty and premeditated jabs like this, 'theatre people' set in train the mechanism of organisational restructuring which Bulgakov not only witnessed but also fell victim to. The atmosphere in the theatre wonderland reflected and was affected by the general atmosphere of fear and despair of the new empire, whose façade the 'Independent Theatre' was called upon to ornament.

A Place of Transformation

Bulgakov had only begun to describe the essence of theatre with his romantically ironical description of the world behind the scenes which the audience never sees. As far as we can judge, the second part of the novel was to have described the rehearsals and first night of Maxudov's play *Black Snow*. The people born in the playwright's dreams were to come to life in the magic box. The truth he had intuited was to be mastered, appropriated, and broadcast to the audience by a multitude of creative people infinitely remote from the author. The power and grandeur of the theatre is in this collective mastering of truth, this accumulation of human reflectors who first fragment the integral image of truth before bringing it together again and focusing it in the magic crystal of the stage. They never cease to astonish Maxudov. He recreates the turmoil before a rehearsal, from which it seems no sense could ever emerge, in great detail. He describes the quarrelling, the scenes, the squabbles, the mess and the muddle. And then Maxudov's eye picks out among the figures jostling each other on the stage the designer from the mock-up workshop, aloof from it all.

Aurora Gossier . . . walked around the edge of the revolving stage measuring the floor with a yardstick. Her expression was calm, almost sad, her teeth clenched. Whenever she bent over towards the footlights her fair hair shone as though it were on fire, and then dimmed to an ashen colour as she turned away. I reminded myself that all this agonizingly slow procedure would come to an end . . . (pp. 156–7)

The image of the ray of light searching in the darkness of the auditorium for its object, the footlights pouring on to the stage a 'live, hot wave of light', is one of the most poetic and symbolic motifs in this book about the theatre (pp. 150, 151). Art breaks through the musty routine and administrative foul-ups, and calls out to all that is most alive in these creative people and draws it up to the light. Outstanding acting redeems the stifling atmosphere of Wonderland. The radiant vision of Aurora Gossier portends a salvation bought by all Maxudov's tribulations.

The theatre's creative battalions, primarily its actors, emerge from their backstage obscurity into this brightly lit place of transformation. Bulgakov creates a collective portrait of the acting profession on the pages of his theatrical testament, creative and idling, potent and fussy, magnificent and dependent, grand and petty. He depicts the acting instinct, the talent for transformation, as a great and mysterious gift of nature. More than that, Bulgakov places the actors right outside the bounds of traditional moral judgement applicable to the rest of the theatre population. The untalented Pryakhina is an exception, but that is because she is denied the status of an actress. As he describes, for instance, the technical sophistication with which Romanus stokes up a scene, pitting the playwright and assistant director against the director, the director against the actors, and one actor against another, Maxudov notes also the glee with which the actors watch the scandal catching fire. But if Maxudov is scathing in his description of Romanus with his fiery eyes which 'swivel like the eyes of a wolf in the steppes', there is an immediate and abrupt change of tone when he turns to the actors.

It was hot, it was May. Hundreds of times, over and over again, these people, their looks dimly enigmatic in the semi-darkness above the lampshade, had smeared their faces with paint, transformed themselves, whipped up their emotions, worn themselves out . . . Now the season was well on and they were getting tired; they were nervous, moody and inclined to tease one another with more than a little spite. Romanus looked all set to provide a long and entertaining interruption. (p. 156)

The loving and forgiving intonation is one you might use in describing the naughtiness of children. The childishness and naivety of the actor's psychology, much easier to play on than Hamlet's flute, seem almost invariably to accompany the gift of acting. Pushkin's characterisation of poetry which, 'Heaven knows, should be a little silly', is probably even more applicable to the world of the actor. The silliness is an openness and receptiveness to the world, a delight, a sacred 'emptiness' which fills up before our eyes with a wonderfully rich spirituality. Where that comes from is one of the theatre's most arcane mysteries, and one which Bulgakov makes no attempt to solve.

For a real actor the path to the living being of another person is as direct and open as the path to his own. He seems to share the nature of everything on God's earth. A closed-off, foreign other becomes the actor's self. We witness this mysterious and magical appropriation of another person's identity in the scenes in the changing room.

Yelagin drew his hand down one cheek and then down the other and I felt I could actually see him sprouting side-whiskers. He seemed to grow shorter, set his nostrils flaring haughtily and as he plucked a few imaginary hairs out of his imaginary side-whiskers he recited through clenched teeth everything that had been written about him in the letter.

Aristarkh Platonovich instantly materialises in the air before Maxudov's astonished gaze. It is this supernatural power, this black magic of acting that Bulgakov only touches on in *Black Snow*. It is in his novel about the Devil, *The Master and Margarita*, that he gives it full rein. Woland's retinue is an absolutely magnificent company of actors, the best buffoons and clowns in the world, whose task is to reveal the truth to people. The black magic performance in the Variety Theatre is ideal theatre. The world of buffoonery, acting, and transformation stands revealed in Bulgakov's sunset novel as a purifying flame. Griboedov burns, the unclean flat on Sadovaya Street blazes, and the Torgsin Foreign Currency Store goes up in flames.

Woland's theatre passes judgement, testing the human strengths and weaknesses of human beings. Against this background the theatre's wonderland behind the scenes looks all the more pathetic and risible with its petty-minded employees, the Likhodeevs, Rimskys, Varenukhas, Bengalskys and buffet managers palming off a naively trusting public with sturgeon of 'second class freshness'. The Variety Theatre is a mirror image of the topography and morphology of the Independent Theatre.

The power of the actor is a natural phenomenon, an art not subject to systematisation or rational explanation; something which, according to Bulgakov, it is impossible to learn and which, according to Maxudov, it is impossible to teach. Maxudov's mistrust of the acting Method devised by Ivan Vasilievich arises from his doubting the possibility of rationalising a miracle. Maxudov contrasts Ivan Vasilievich, Actor of Genius, with Ivan Vasilievich, concocter of Methods and alchemist searching for a means of endowing every mortal with the magic power of reincarnation. In a moment of recklessness at the end of a hard night's drinking, the figure of Ludmilla Pryakhina materialises in Maxudov's overheated brain 'moaning and waving her lace handkerchief'.

'She can't act!' I croaked, almost speechless with fury.
[. . .] 'And none of your theories are any good! That little snub-nosed man who plays a civil servant, his hands are white, his voice squeaks, but he doesn't need any theory . . . and that one who plays the murderer in black gloves . . . he doesn't need theories – he can *act*!'
'Argunin . . .' I could dimly hear through the blanket of smoke.
'There *are* no theories!' I screamed, drunk with over-confidence, yelling and grinding my teeth. At that moment I suddenly noticed an enormous greasy spot on my grey jacket with a piece of onion sticking to it. (pp. 140–1)

The secret of the theatre, to judge from Bulgakov's novel, is least of all to be found in the hands of directors. Bulgakov mentions the director Thomas Strizh only in passing, a stocky figure with 'fair hair, a determined face and a worried look'. He notes additionally that he was carrying a 'well-stuffed briefcase' and that he also had a very strange way of expressing himself: 'Eulampia has nothing to do with here'. But what sort of a director Strizh is, of that we hear nothing. Neither Strizh, nor Eulampia, nor Poltoratzky, the chairman of the corporation of directors, are communicant in real terms with the mystery of the theatre. Only Ivan Vasilievich belongs, and then only in his capacity as an actor. When he suggests that Maxudov should write a scene in which the hero stabs himself instead of shooting himself, he promptly demonstrates how it might be acted. Despite being offended by the renowned director's complete failure to understand his play, Maxudov nevertheless registers the fact that, as he demonstrates the death of the stabbed hero, Ivan Vasilievich is a genius.

Bulgakov can accept the twentieth-century notion of 'director's theatre', it would seem, only in respect of Woland. In the theatre described in *Black Snow*, at all events, it is only the art of the actor that is evergreen, and he doesn't need any theories. The only person who painstakingly writes down in her school book all Ivan Vasilievich says is Ludmilla Pryakhina, and she is beyond earthly help.

Bulgakov's ironical obscurantism and defence of 'actor's theatre' is reminiscent in its terms almost of the extreme views of Alexander Kugel. It was, of course, fuelled by his experiences during Stanislavsky's rehearsing of *Molière*, which recur in the novel as perhaps the most disturbing and bitter note. Bulgakov transfigures this episode from his biography from the 'personal and petty' into the universally significant. He shows a human being, a writer, a Master who has intuited Truth and who, because of the 'failings of the theatre in general', is prevented from revealing his truth to the public. Trying to rewrite his play as the director advises, Maxudov suffers the infinite torments of self-censorship, but goes through with it in order that *Black Snow* should finally see the light of day. The mutual relations of Maxudov and *Black Snow* repeat the story of the relations between the Master with his novel about Pontius Pilate, and the story of Molière's relations with *Tartuffe*. The Master and Margarita are prepared to make a pact with the Power of Evil, and blithely accept death in order that the novel should live. Molière is prepared to lick the King's boots in order to safeguard his play. The same predicament, in a different convention, is what unfolds before us in *Black Snow*. Needless to say, the March snowstorm, the playing with the magic box, the cell of the lonely Master are all romantic attributes far removed from the historical reality which shaped the life of the Bulgakov who wrote *The Days of the Turbins*. Maxudov and Bulgakov do, however, share the same deep feeling for the mission of literature and their duty as writers: '. . . I saw that without that scene the play was dead. And it *had* to come to life, because I knew that there was truth in the play.' (p. 161)

It is at this point that the main conflict in *Black Snow* originates and grows, as also the main conflict in Bulgakov's writing career. The truth which an artist has intuited cannot be made public solely by his own efforts. He is obliged to bring in middlemen. The Master takes his novel about Pilate to a publisher, and the book's fate is decided by Ariman, Lavrovich and Latunsky who are little concerned to see the truth intuited by the artist going freely out into the world. Maxudov gives his play to the Independent Theatre, whose entire structure replicates the totalitarian state.

Bulgakov has a love-hate relationship with theatre people, a tragic love. There is absolutely nothing platonic about the way he was attracted to the stage. This is a procreative, virile love intent on conception. His truth cannot be born without these people, their stage, that spotlight, and the laughter and tears of a thousand-strong audience filling the blue haze of the auditorium. 'I went back to the Theatre, which I now needed as much as an addict needs his morphine,'

Maxudov confesses (p. 160). Or finally, 'consumed with love for the Indepen-dent Theatre, pinned to it like a beetle to a piece of cork, nothing could keep me from seeing every performance . . .' (p. 169). This is strong language, and with the latter quotation the manuscript of *Black Snow* breaks off abruptly. The text illustrates the extreme predicament in which Bulgakov found himself as an Author of the Theatre.

In the autumn of 1937 Bulgakov abruptly stopped work on his theatre novel. There are no documentary clues to enable us to say for sure why this was.

Possibly he had decided to concentrate on his novel about the Devil, seeing it as a more important literary act as far as drawing up the balance sheet of his life and creative work was concerned. Some argue that he consciously chose to leave *Black Snow* unfinished, like many another book in Russian and world literature. Whatever the explanation, we shall never know how Maxudov would have concluded his objections to Ivan Vasilievich on the actor's gift of reincarnation, never know how the first night of Maxudov's play went, or whether it even took place. We shall never read of how it was reviewed by those sworn friends of the playwright, the theatre critics. The experience of intense happiness, which Bulgakov was capable of feeling to the full in life, and equally able to express to the full in his writing, was never to be vouchsafed the hero of *Black Snow*. Maxudov was not to live to see his first night, and the truth he had intuited brought to his audience.

Black Snow's open ending is felt by the reader to be a significant aspect of the novel's composition, quite apart from the circumstances of Bulgakov's literary biography. The last line, cut off in mid-phrase, catches at the throat like the last line of Marina Tsvetaeva's poem about the homeland she had lost:

> Every house is foreign to me, every shrine is empty
> And all is the same and all is one.
> But if by the roadside I see a shrub
> Especially if I see a rowan . . .

There are pages preserved in Bulgakov's archive in the Institute of Russian Literature in St Petersburg. They are headed 'Notes for a Talk on Shakespeare', but on the back of one of them are several lines which relate not to Shakespeare but to the theatre novel Bulgakov had stopped writing two years previously. In 1939, a few months before his death, Bulgakov unexpectedly returned to the work whose alternative title was *A Dead Man's Notes*. He gives a new version of the place where Maxudov lists the visitors to Phil and his office. Bulgakov tries once more to capture the image of those who are trying to storm the gates of Paradise: 'shorthand-typists, clerks of works, students, electricians, wireless operators, filing clerks, blood donors, plumbers, statistical planners, pederasts, heating engineers, telephone line repairmen, railway engineers, bridge mainten- ance engineers, deputy accountants, time and motion study technicians, transport controllers, quality control inspectors, and morse code operatives'.

It is a curious collection of professions, but it is an image of the City and the World turning to their Theatre.

In the 'Prelude in the Theatre' in Goethe's *Faust*, which precedes the 'Prologue in Heaven', there is a classic definition of the significance of a theatre performance which is valid for all time:

> So make your way in this cramped timber house
> Through all creation's realm to pass,
> And wander pensively and well
> From Heaven through the World to Hell.

Bulgakov passed through all creation's realm within the confines of the cramped timber house, experiencing its heavenly magic and its behind-scenes hell. The fruits of his experience were plays which are performed today all over the world, and an unfinished novel charting with classical lucidity the *via dolorosa* of a modern dramatist who wished to become an Author of the Theatre.

The history of the Stalin era and the Stalinist state, so unlike anything that had gone before, radically affected the character of the Moscow Art Theatre and the life of its greatest Author in the Soviet period. The Theatre 'created to the renown of our country' went one way, while the creator of *The Days of the Turbins* and *Batum* went his. For all their many profound differences those destinies are inextricably entwined and inseparable. Indeed, it is in comparing them and studying the moments where they cross that we can come to an understanding of the full tragedy of the times and comprehend the ineluctable nature of all that befell and was endured by them; two destinies, one collective, one individual, but formed by a single cruel measure.

'History is not in what we wore, but how we naked left the world.'

The memory of what they wore, the Theatre and its Author, and how they naked left the world is a part now of Russia's historical memory. Ultimately both have received in accordance with their deeds and how they kept faith. On this the world is founded, however capriciously the cards are dealt. It was perhaps this awareness that moved Bulgakov in his search for an epigraph for *Molière*. He chose the inscription carved on Molière's monument in Paris. As Bulgakov rendered it, it reads,

> He needs no thing for his renown.
> We need him for our renown.[13]

Bibliographical Note

Archives

The reader will have noticed that this book is largely based on archival materials. Those most frequently quoted are as follows:

Archive of the Museum of the Moscow Art Academic Theatre (MAAT Museum)
Various versions of Bulgakov's play *Belaia gvardiia*, prompt copies of Bulgakov's plays, preliminary materials for the adaptation of *Mertvye dushi* and various versions of the adaptation; production archives of Bulgakov's plays; diaries and letters of members of the Art Theatre, correspondence between V. I. Nemirovich-Danchenko and O. S. Bokshanskaya, letters of P. A. Markov, minutes of discussions of Bulgakov's plays at the Council for Artistic Affairs, minutes of the meetings of the Collegium for Artistic Affairs and the Repertoire, letters of personalities in the Soviet Theatre relating to Bulgakov's plays, etc.

M. A. Bulgakov Archive, Manuscript Section of the Lenin State Library, Moscow, Collection 562 (OR GBL, f. 562)
Original manuscripts of Bulgakov's works, typescript versions of his plays, letters of Bulgakov to his relatives, letters and diaries of Elena Sergeevna Bulgakova (which differ from the published edition), answers by Bulgakov to questions from P. A. Popov (1926), autobiographies of Bulgakov of various dates, etc.

Bulgakov Archive, Manuscript section of the Institute of Russian Literature, St Petersburg, Collection 369 (OR IRLI, f. 369)
Correspondence of Bulgakov and P. A. Popov, letters from various individuals to Bulgakov, scrapbooks of the production history of *Dni Turbinykh, Beg, Mertvye dushi*, the first version of the play *Belaia gvardiia*, etc.

Central State Archive for Literature and Art, Moscow (TsGALI)
Bulgakov's letters to A. D. Popov, transcript of the debate *'Dni Turbinykh i
Liubov' Iarovaia'* at the Meyerhold Theatre, Moscow, 7 February 1927, copies of
Bulgakov's plays with comments by employees of Glavrepertkom, etc.

Others
Documents have also been used which are preserved in the Archive of the
Bakhrushin Central State Theatre Museum, Moscow; the State Museum of
Theatre, Musical, and Cinematographic Art of the Ukraine, Kiev; the Archive
Commission of the Union of Theatre Workers, Moscow; and elsewhere.

Published Sources

There are numerous quotations from the immensely informative *Letopis' zhizni i
tvorchestva K. S. Stanislavskogo*, compiled by I. N. Vinogradskaia, 4 vols,
Vserossiiskoe Teatral'noe Obshchestvo, Moscow, 1971–6, hereafter cited as
'I. Vinogradskaia, *Letopis'* . . .'.

    V. I. Nemirovich-Danchenko. Izbrannye pis'ma, compiled by V. Ia. Vilenkin,
2 vols, Iskusstvo, Moscow, 1979, hereafter cited as *'Nemirovich-Danchenko.
Izbrannye pis'ma* . . .'

    M. O. Chudakova, *Arkhiv M. A. Bulgakova. Materialy dlia tvorcheskoi biografii
pisatelia, Zapiski Otdela rukopisei*, vyp. 54, Gosudarstvennaia biblioteka SSSR im.
V. I. Lenina, Kniga, Moscow, 1976, hereafter cited as 'M. O. Chudakova,
Arkhiv Bulgakova . . .';

    Sergei Ermolinskii's memoirs, 'Mikhail Bulgakov (iz zapisok raznykh let)', in
S. A. Ermolinskii, *Dramaticheskie proizvedeniia*, Iskusstvo, Moscow, 1982, hereafter cited as 'S. Ermolinskii, 'Mikhail Bulgakov . . .'

Bulgakov's Works

Where possible, references in the text are to Michael Glenny's translations of
Bulgakov's works. Page references are given in brackets directly in the text. The
following editions have been used:

    The White Guard, Collins Harvill, London, 1989. ISBN 0 00 271026 9.

    The Days of the Turbins (translated as *The White Guard*), *Flight*, *Molière* and *The
Last Days* (translated by William Powell and Michael Earley), all in *Mikhail
Bulgakov: Six Plays*, Methuen Drama, London, 1991. ISBN 0 413 64530 4.

    The Master and Margarita, Collins Harvill, London, 1988. ISBN
0 00 271513 9.

Black Snow: A Theatrical Novel, Collins Harvill, London, 1991. ISBN 0 00 271139 7.

Other editions that have been used are M. Bulgakov, *Dramy i komedii*, Iskusstvo, Moscow, 1965; M. Bulgakov, *Izbrannaia proza*, Khudozhestvennaia literatura, Moscow, 1966.

Early prose, satirical articles and sketches from the newspapers *Gudok* and *Nakanune* and other works are mostly quoted from their first publication.

Notes

Preface

1. P. Markov, *V Khudozhestvennom teatre. Kniga zavlita*, VTO, Moscow, 1976, p. 231.

1 'This is My World!'

1. Memoirs of Vladimir Nelli are preserved in the State Museum of Theatre, Musical and Cinematographic Art of the Ukraine, Kiev.
2. N. Nikolaev, *Efemeridy*, Kiev, 1912, p. 138.
3. "M. R.", 'Pis'ma iz Kieva', *Teatr i iskusstvo*, SPB., No. 10, 1908, p. 198.
4. I. Vinogradskaia, *Letopis'* . . ., vol. 2, p. 339.
5. Ibid.
6. MAAT Museum.
7. S. Ermolinskii, 'Mikhail Bulgakov . . .', p. 635.
8. Ibid.
9. L. Nikulin, 'Pis'ma iz Kieva', *Vestnik teatra*, No. 25, 1919. The portrait of the cultural life of Kiev at the beginning of the century and in 1917–19 is based on materials in the Kiev press of that period, journalistic reports from Kiev printed in *Teatr i iskusstvo*, St Petersburg; and information drawn from the following books: A. Ia. Kapler, *Dolgi nashi*, Sovetskaia Rossiia, Moscow, 1973; G. K. Kryzhitskii, *Dorogi teatral'nye*, VTO, Moscow, 1976; S. I. Iutkevich, 'Shumit, ne umolkaia, pamiat'', in *Vstrechi s proshlym*, Sovetskaia Rossiia, Moscow, 1982. The author has also drawn on his interviews with Alexei Kapler and Sergei Iutkevich.
10. 'Vospominaniia', in N. Teffi, *Nostal'giia*, Khudozhestvennaia literatura, Leningrad, 1990, p. 330.
11. Ibid.
12. N. Teffi, 'Vospominaniia', p. 349.
13. Ibid., p. 347.
14. M. Bulgakov, 'Avtobiografiia', in *Sovetskie pisateli. Avtobiografii*, vol. 8, Khudozhestvennaia literatura, Moscow, 1966, p. 85. Hereafter cited as 'M. Bulgakov, Avtobiografiia . . .'

15. 'M. Bulgakov. Pis'ma k rodnym (1921–1922)', published by E. Zemskaia in *Izvestiia AN SSSR. Seriia literatury i iazyka*, vol. 35, 1976, p. 458. Hereafter cited as 'Bulgakov, Pis'ma k rodnym . . .'

16. Iu. Slezkin, *Stolovaia gora*, Moskovskoe Tovarishchestvo Pisatelei, 1928, p. 24.

17. M. Bulgakov, 'Pis'ma k rodnym . . .', p. 454.

18. *Mikhail Bulgakov. Pis'ma. Zhizneopisanie v dokumentakh*, Sovremennik, Moscow, 1989, p. 48. Hereafter cited as *Bulgakov. Pis'ma* . . . .

19. M. O. Chudakova, *Arkhiv Bulgakova* . . ., p. 95.

20. M. Bulgakov, *Avtobiografiia* . . ., p. 85.

21. Ibid., p. 94.

22. Diary of the MAAT actor Vasilii Luzhskii, MAAT Museum.

23. I. Vinogradskaia, *Letopis'* . . ., vol. 3, p. 79.

24. K. S. Stanislavskii, *Sobranie sochinenii*, 8 vols, Iskusstvo, Moscow, 1959, vol. 6, p. 118. Hereafter cited as K. S. Stanislavskii, *Sobr. soch.* . . . .

25. I. Vinogradskaia, *Letopis'* . . ., vol. 3, p. 142.

26. *Bulgakov. Pis'ma*, p. 37.

27. I. Vinogradskaia, *Letopis'* . . ., vol. 3, p. 91.

28. Ibid., vol. 3, p. 105.

29. Ibid., vol. 3, p. 174.

30. Nemirovich-Danchenko, *Izbrannye pis'ma* . . ., vol. 2, p. 236.

31. Ibid.

32. Ibid., p. 244.

33. Ibid.

34. I. Vinogradskaia, *Letopis'* . . ., vol. 3, p. 253.

35. Ibid.

36. '"Printsessa Turandot" i sovremennyi teatr', in P. Markov, *O teatre*, 4 vols, Iskusstvo, Moscow, vol. 3, 1976, p. 77.

37. I. Vinogradskaia, *Letopis'* . . ., vol. 3, p. 264.

38. Nemirovich-Danchenko, *Izbrannye pis'ma* . . ., vol. 2, p. 250.

39. New information on the Moscow Art Theatre's tour of the USA is published in my article 'V poiskakh El'dorado', *Moskovskii nabliudatel'*, Nos 11, 12, 1991.

40. I. Vinogradskaia, *Letopis'* . . ., vol. 3, p. 306.

41. Ibid., p. 319.

42. K. S. Stanislavskii, *Sobr. soch.* . . ., vol. 8, p. 41.

43. Nemirovich-Danchenko, *Izbrannye pis'ma* . . ., vol. 2, p. 284.

44. Ibid., pp. 287–8.

45. Ibid., pp. 303–4.

46. 'Pervaia studiia MKhAT', in P. Markov, *O teatre*, vol. 1, 1974, p. 407.

47. I. Vinogradskaia, *Letopis'* . . ., vol. 3, p. 425.

48. *Teatr*, No. 2, 1990, p. 144.

49. L. Ginzburg, *O starom i novom*, Sovetskii pisatel', Leningrad, 1982, p. 373.

50. M. Bulgakov, 'Pis'ma . . .', p. 175.

51. V. Shklovskii, *Sentimental'noe puteshestvie*, Atenei, Leningrad, 1924, p. 8.

52. K. Chukovskii, *Chukokkala*, Iskusstvo, Moscow, 1979, p. 24.

53. Pavel Popov's note is preserved in OR GBL.

54. OR IRLI, f. 369.

55. I. Vinogradskaia, *Letopis'* . . ., vol. 3, p. 480.

56. Archive of P. Markov, MAAT Museum.

57. Ibid.

2 The Magical Little Room

1. OR IRLI, f. 369.

2. Ibid.

3. P. Markov, *V Khudozhestvennom teatre* . . ., p. 229.

4. Ibid., p. 523.

5. OR IRLI, f. 369.

6. MAAT Museum.

7. P. Markov, *V Khudozhestvennom teatre* . . ., p. 523–4.

8. MAAT Museum.

9. From the author's interview with Mark Prudkin.

10. MAAT Museum.

11. OR IRLI, f. 369.

12. MAAT Museum.

13. M. Bulgakov, *P'esy 1920-x godov*, Iskusstvo, Leningrad, 1989, p. 39.

14. An excellent source is Lesley Milne's *Mikhail Bulgakov, Belaia gvardiia. P'esa v chetyrekh deistviiakh. Vtoraia redaktsiia p'esy 'Dni Turbinykh'*, Otto Sagner, Munich, 1983. See also Ia. S. Lur'e, 'M. Bulgakov v rabote nad tekstom 'Dnei Turbinykh'', in *Problemy teatral'nogo naslediia M. Bulgakova*, Leningrad, 1987; and the same author's article in M. Bulgakov, *P'esy 1920-x godov*.

15. I. Sudakov, 'Rezhisser i avtor', *Teatr i dramaturgiia*, No. 3, 1934.

16. MAAT Museum.

17. K. S. Stanislavskii, *Sobr. soch.* . . ., vol. 8, p. 269

18. MAAT Museum.

19. Ibid.

20. Ibid.

21. P. Markov, *Kniga vospominanii*, Iskusstvo, Moscow, 1983, p. 291

22. MAAT Museum.

23. I. Vinogradskaia, *Letopis'* . . ., vol. 3, p. 526.

24. P. Markov, *V Khudozhestvennom teatre* . . ., pp. 229–30.

25. I. Sudakov, *Proshchal'nyi vzgliad na moiu zhizn' v trude i bor'be*, Arkhiv memuarnoi komissii Soiuza teatral'nykh deiatelei Rossii.

26. Ibid.

27. Ibid.

28. P. Markov, *V Khudozhestvennom teatre* . . ., p. 535.

29. Ibid., p. 536.

30. Ibid., pp. 536–7.

31. Ibid., p. 537

32. MAAT Museum.

33. Ibid.

34. Ibid.

35. I. Vinogradskaia, *Letopis'* . . ., vol. 3, p. 549.

36. OR IRLI, f. 369.

37. Ibid.

38. Ibid.

39. Ibid.

40. MAAT Museum.

41. Ibid.

42. I. Vinogradskaia, *Letopis'* . . ., vol. 3, p. 551.

43. MAAT Museum.

44. M. Bulgakov, 'Pis'ma . . .', p. 109.

45. MAAT Museum.

46. I. Vinogradskaia, *Letopis'* . . ., vol. 3, p. 558.

47. MAAT Museum.

48. P. Markov, *V Khudozhestvennom teatre* . . ., p. 289.

49. cf. Mikhail Bulgakov, *Six Plays*, Methuen Drama, London, 1991, p. 26.

50. M. Bulgakov, 'Pis'ma . . .', p. 258.

51. MAAT Museum.

52. Ibid.

53. Ibid.

54. I. Vinogradskaia, *Letopis'* . . ., vol. 3, p. 563.

55. MAAT Museum.

56. Ibid.

57. OR IRLI, f. 369.

58. MAAT Museum.

59. Ibid.

60. Ibid.

61. Ibid.

62. I. Vinogradskaia, *Letopis'* . . ., vol. 3, p. 565.

63. MAAT Museum.

64. Ibid.

65. Ibid.

66. Ibid.

67. Ibid.

3 Finding a Home

1. *Rabochaia Moskva*, 14 October 1926.
2. E. Beskin, 'Kremovye shtory', *Zhizn' iskusstva*, No. 41, 1926, p. 7.
3. P. Markov, *V Khudozhestvennom teatre* . . ., p. 289.
4. *Ezhegodnik Moskovskogo Khudozhestvennogo teatra za 1945 god*, p. 21.
5. Ibid., p. 364.
6. V. Pavlov, *Teatral'nye sumerki. Stat'i i ocherki ob akademizme i o MKhATe (1926–1927)*, Biblioteka *Novogo zritelia*, 1926, p. 86.
7. cf. N. Ashmarin in *Nasha gazeta*, 4 October 1926; Iu. Sobolev in *Repertuarnyi biulleten'*, No. 6, 1927; A. Lunacharskii in *Izvestiia*, 8 October 1926.
8. N. Berkovskii, 'Chekhov: ot rasskazov i povestei k dramaturgii', *Literatura i teatr. Stat'i raznykh let*, Iskusstvo, Moscow, 1969, p. 151.
9. Ibid.
10. From a letter of 22 August 1959 from Boris Pasternak to Stephen Spender, in B. Pasternak, *Ob iskusstve*, Iskusstvo, Moscow, 1990, p. 362, and *Encounter*, August 1959.
11. *Tynianovskii sbornik. Tret'i tynianovskie chteniia*, Zinatne, Riga, 1988, p. 234.
12. B. Raikh, 'K itogam teatral'nogo sezona', *Na literaturnom postu*, No. 11, 1927, p. 66.
13. M. Bulgakov, Autobiographical notes received by Pavel Popov, OR GBL, f. 218.
14. M. Bulgakov, 'Pis'ma . . .', p. 232.
15. OR IRLI, f. 369.
16. IMLI, Archive of Gorky.
17. *Pravda*, 2 March 1929.
18. *Vecherniaia Moskva*, 4 October 1926.
19. *Nasha gazeta*, 5 October 1926.
20. Novoe o Maiakovskom, *Literaturnoe nasledstvo*, vol. 65, Izd-vo AN SSSR, 1958, p. 40.
21. *Pravda*, 8 October 1926.
22. *Programmy gosudarstvennykh akademicheskikh teatrov*, No. 54, 1926.
23. *Novyi zritel'*, No. 41, 1926, p. 4.
24. *Novyi zritel'*, No. 43, 1926.
25. *Vecherniaia Moskva*, 12 October 1926.
26. *Zhizn' iskusstva*, No. 44, 1926, p. 12.
27. *Komsomol'skaia pravda*, 29 December 1926.
28. *Krasnaia gazeta*, 9 October 1926.
29. Quote from a scrapbook of press cuttings compiled by M. Bulgakov. Preserved in OR GBL, f. 562. Hereafter cited as 'Press Scrapbook'.
30. Ibid.
31. Ibid.
32. Ibid.

33. Uriel', 'Bulgakov vzialsia za NEP', *Komsomol'skaia pravda*, 13 November 1926; S. Iakubovskii, 'Uborshchik Zoikinoi kvartiry', *Kievskii proletarii*, 29 October 1926.

34. E. Surkov, *K. A. Trenev*, Sovetskii pisatel', Moscow, 1953, p. 402.

35. Press Scrapbook.

36. K. Marx and F. Engels, *Iz rannikh proizvedenii*, Moscow, 1956, p. 586.

37. *Russkii sovetskii teatr. 1921–1926. Dokumenty i materialy*, Iskusstvo, Leningrad, 1975, p. 29.

38. *Puti razvitiia teatra (Stenograficheskii otchet i resheniia partiinogo soveshchaniia pri Agitprope TsK VKP (b) v mae 1927 g.)*, Teakinopechat', Moscow, 1927, p. 23. Hereafter cited as *Puti razvitiia teatra* . . .

39. B. V. Alpers, *Teatral'nye ocherki*, 2 vols, Iskusstvo, Moscow, 1977, vol. 1, p. 193.

40. A. V. Lunacharskii, 'Dva spektaklia', *Zaria Vostoka* (Tiflis), 6 March 1927.

41. M. Bulgakov, 'Iurii Slezkin (siluet), p. 7.

42. M. Bulgakov, 'Pis'ma . . .', p. 225.

43. TsGALI, f. 2335, op. 1, ed. khr. 5.

44. Ibid.

45. Ibid.

46. M. Bulgakov, 'Pis'ma . . .', p. 171.

47. TsGALI, f. 2335, op. 1, ed. khr. 5.

48. Ibid.

49. Ibid.

50. *Programmy gosudarstvennykh akademicheskikh teatrov*, No. 7, 1927, p. 13.

51. P. Markov, *V Khudozhestvennom teatre* . . ., p. 291.

52. *Puti razvitiia teatra* . . ., p. 171.

53. Ibid., p. 121.

54. Ibid., pp. 229–31.

55. MAAT Museum.

56. T. Lanina, 'Stanislavskii i Enukidze', *Teatr*, No. 6, 1967, p. 11.

57. MAAT Museum.

58. Sadko, 'Nachalo kontsa MKhAT', *Zhizn' iskusstva*, No. 43, 1927, p. 7.

59. MAAT Museum.

60. I. V. Stalin, Letter to Bill'-Belotserkovskii, *Sobranie sochinenii*, vol. 11, Gospolitizdat, Moscow, p. 329.

61. ''Dni Turbinykh', 'Zoikina kvartira' i 'Bagrovyi ostrov' snimaiutsia s repertuara', *Rabochaia Moskva*, 6 March 1929.

62. V. Bogoliubov and I. Chekin, *Belyi dom (O chem oni molchali)*, Teakinopechat', Moscow, 1928.

63. TsGALI, f. 2335, op. 1, ed. khr. 5.

64. ''Bagrovyi ostrov' (beseda s A. Ia. Tairovym)', *Zhizn' iskusstva*, No. 49, 1928, p. 14.

65. P. Novitskii, ''Bagrovyi ostrov' M. Bulgakova', *Repertuarnyi biulleten'*, No. 12, 1928, p. 10.

66. Press Scrapbook.

67. *Puti razvitiia teatra* . . ., pp. 148–9.

68. Iu. Babicheva, 'Komediia-parodiia M. Bulgakova 'Bagrovyi ostrov'', in *Zhanry v istoriko-literaturnom protsesse*, Vologda, 1985, p. 140.

69. *Zhizn' iskusstva*, No. 49, 1928, p. 14.

70. M. Rudnitskii, 'Mikhail Bulgakov', in *Voprosy teatra*, VTO, Moscow, 1966, p. 137.

71. M. Bulgakov, 'Pis'ma . . .', pp. 173–4.

72. Press Scrapbook.

73. I. V. Stalin, *Sobranie sochinenii*, vol. 11, p. 329.

4 'A Flight in the Mists of Autumn'

1. *Programmy gosudarstvennykh akademicheskikh teatrov*, No. 10, 1927, p. 10.

2. MAAT Museum.

3. Ibid.

4. P. Markov, *V Khudozhestvennom teatre* . . ., p. 548.

5. Ibid., p. 549.

6. From an interview conducted by the author with Mark Prudkin.

7. cf. A. Smelianskii, 'Assimiliatsiia', *Moskovskii nabliudatel'*, No. 4, 1991.

8. Vs. Meierkhol'd, *Perepiska. 1896–1939*, Iskusstvo, Moscow, 1976, p. 283.

9. MAAT Museum.

10. I. Vinogradskaia, *Letopis'* . . ., vol. 4, p. 129.

11. Ibid., p. 130.

12. Ibid., p. 140.

13. *Gor'kii i sovetskie pisateli. Neizdannaia perepiska*, Literaturnoe nasledstvo, vol. 70, Nauka, Moscow, 1963, p. 152.

14. IMLI, Archive of Gorky.

15. *Novyi LEF*, No. 1, 1927.

16. *Gor'kii i sovetskie pisateli* . . ., Literaturnoe nasledstvo, vol. 70, p. 85.

17. cf. A. Smelianskii, 'Gor'kii i stilevye poiski poslerevoliutsionnoi prozy i dramaturgii (Gor'kii o Bulgakove)', in *Gor'kii i russkaia literatura, Uchenye zapiski Gor'kovskogo universiteta*, vyp. 118, Gor'kii, 1970, p. 165.

18. I. Vinogradskaia, *Letopis'* . . ., vol. 4, p. 137.

19. Nemirovich-Danchenko, *Izbrannye pis'ma* . . ., vol. 2, p. 360.

20. *Protokol obsuzhdeniia p'esy 'Beg' v MKhAT*, MAAT Museum.

21. Ibid.

22. Ibid.

23. Press Scrapbook.

24. Ibid.

25. *Al'bom po istorii postanovki 'Bega'*, OR IRLI, f. 369.

26. Press Scrapbook.

27. *Komsomol'skaia pravda*, 23 October 1928; *Sovremennyi teatr*, No. 44, 30 October 1928.

28. Press Scrapbook.

29. *Rabochaia Moskva*, 7 December 1928.

30. S. Sheshukov, *Neistovye revniteli*, Moskovskii rabochii, 1970, p. 211.

31. I. Vinogradskaia, 'Letopis' . . .', vol. 4, p. 149.

32. K. S. Stanislavskii, *Sobr. soch.* . . ., vol. 6, p. 250.

33. *Novyi zritel'*, No. 48, 1928, p. 5.

34. Ibid.

35. I. Vinogradskaia, Letopis' . . ., vol. 4, p. 152.

36. V. A. Kaverin, 'Zametki o dramaturgii Bulgakova', in *M. Bulgakov. Dramy i komedii*, Iskusstvo, Moscow, 1965, p. 10.

37. B. Alpers, *Teatral'nye ocherki*, vol. 1, pp. 201–2.

38. MAAT Museum.

39. N. Ia. Berkovskii, *Literatura i teatr*, Iskusstvo, Moscow, 1969, p. 277.

40. *Dnevnik Eleny Sergeevny Bulgakovoi*, Knizhnaia palata, 1990, p. 37. Note that this publication is of the diary as edited by Elena Sergeevna in the 1950s. Our page references are to this edition, but quotation is from the text of the original in OR GBL, f. 562.

41. Ia. Slashchev, *Krym v 1920. Otryvki iz vospominanii*, with an Introduction by D. Furmanov, GIZ, Moscow-Leningrad, 1923, p. 41.

42. Ibid.

43. M. O. Chudakova, *Arkhiv Bulgakova* . . ., p. 61.

44. E. Bulgakova, *Dnevnik*, p. 36.

45. The heroine in Iurii Olesha's play *Spisok blagodeianii* compiles a list of 'good actions' and 'crimes' of the Soviet regime.

46. A. Averchenko, *Razvorochennyi muraveinik*, Moscow, 1927.

47. *Vospominaniia o Mikhaile Bulgakove*, Sovetskii pisatel', Moscow, 1988, p. 270.

48. Iu. Lotman, 'Tema kart i kartochnoi igry v russkoi literature nachala XIX veka', in *Trudy po znakovym sistemam, Uchenye zapiski Tartuskogo gosudarstvennogo universiteta*, vyp. 36, Tartu, 1975, vol. 7, p. 135.

49. MAAT Museum.

50. A comparative analysis of the various versions of *Flight* has been made by V. Gudkova in *M. A. Bulgakov. P'esy 1920-x godov*, Iskusstvo, Leningrad, 1989, pp. 550–6.

51. E. Bulgakova, *Dnevnik*, p. 327.

52. OR IRLI, f. 369.

53. V. Fomin, *Zapiski starogo chekista*, Politizdat, Moscow, 1964, p. 148.

54. A. Smelianskii, 'Istrebiteli', *Moskovskie novosti*, April 1993.

55. R. Pikel', 'Pered podniatiem zanavesa', *Izvestiia*, 15 September 1929.

56. Archive of the Bakhrushin State Theatre Museum.

57. M. Bulgakov, *Sobranie sochinenii*, 5 vols, Khudozhestvennaia literatura, Moscow, vol. 5, 1990, p. 431.

58. Ibid., p. 435.

59. M. Gor'kii, 'Trata energii', *Izvestiia*, 15 September 1929.
60. B. Bialik, 'Eshche o nravstvennoi tochnosti', *Literaturnaia gazeta*, 28 October 1987.
61. K. Arenskii, *Pis'ma v Khollivud. Po materialam arkhiva S. L. Bertensona*, Munich, 1968, p. 41. Hereafter cited as K. Arenskii, *Pis'ma v Khollivud* . . .
62. Ibid., p. 49.
63. Ibid., p. 52.
64. Press Scrapbook.
65. A phrase from Iurii Tynianov's novel *Smert' Vazir Mukhtara.*
66. The allusion is to Il'ia Erenburg's novels *Ne perevodia dykhaniia* and *Den' vtoroi.*
67. Boris Pasternak's poem *Stansy*, in his collection *Vtoroe rozhdenie.*
68. V. Maiakovskii, 'Pis'ma Ravicha i Ravichu', *Sobranie sochinenii*, 12 vols, Pravda, Moscow, vol. 12, 1978, p. 381.
69. O. E. Mandel'shtam, *Chetvertaia proza.*
70. M. O. Chudakova, *Arkhiv Bulgakova* . . ., p. 64.
71. Ibid., p. 85.
72. Ibid., p. 86.
73. M. Bulgakov, *Pis'ma* . . ., pp. 160–1.
74. Ibid., p. 177.
75. A phrase from Vladimir Maiakovskii's suicide note.
76. B. Pasternak, *Okhrannaia gramota.*
77. *Voprosy literatury*, No. 9, 1966, p. 138.
78. K. S. Stanislavskii, *Sobr. soch.* . . ., vol. 8, p. 270.
79. OR IRLI, f. 369.

5 'Cover me with your Iron Greatcoat'

1. M. Bulgakov, *Pis'ma* . . ., p. 185–6.
2. Ibid., p. 199.
3. MAAT Museum.
4. Ibid., p. 214.
5. Ibid., p. 255.
6. Ibid., p. 298.
7. Ibid., pp. 232–3.
8. Ibid., p. 285.
9. Ibid., p. 283.
10. *Izvestiia*, 15 December 1931.
11. M. Bulgakov, 'Pis'ma . . .', p. 218.
12. MAAT Museum.
13. Ibid.
14. M. Bulgakov, *Pis'ma* . . ., p. 212.
15. K. S. Stanislavskii, *Sobr. soch.* . . ., vol. 6, p. 293.
16. Ibid., p. 296.

17. Ibid., p. 292.

18. M. Bulgakov, *Pis'ma* . . ., pp. 239–40.

19. Marietta Chudakova investigates the influence of Gogol on Bulgakov in 'Gogol' i Bulgakov', in *Gogol': istoriia i sovremennost'*, Sovetskaia Rossiia, Moscow, 1985.

20. M. Bulgakov, 'Pis'ma . . .', p. 217–8.

21. MAAT Museum.

22. V. G. Sakhnovskii, *Rabota rezhissera*, Moscow, 1937. Here and subsequently quoted from the fuller typescript copy preserved in the MAAT Museum.

23. Ibid.

24. M. O. Chudakova, *Arkhiv Bulgakova* . . ., pp. 93–4.

25. Pel'son, 'Spektakl' akterskogo masterstva. Tovarishcheskaia vstrecha mkhatovtsev s dramaturgami', *Literaturnaia gazeta*, 11 December 1932.

26. Sakhnovskii, op. cit., MAAT Museum.

27. Ibid.

28. *Sovetskoe iskusstvo*, 15 November 1932.

29. B. F. Egorov, 'Bulgakov- 'perevodchik' Gogolia (instsenirovka i kinostsenarii 'Mertvykh dush', kinostsenarii 'Revizora')', in *Ezhegodnik rukopisnogo otdela Pushkinskogo doma*, 1976, Nauka, Leningrad, 1978, p. 65.

30. Ibid.

31. Nemirovich-Danchenko, *Izbrannye pis'ma* . . ., vol. 2. pp. 40–42.

32. Sakhnovskii, op. cit.

33. A. P. Matskin, *Na temy Gogolia*, Iskusstvo, Moscow, 1984; K. L. Rudnitskii, 'Mertvye dushi, MAAT, 1932', in *Teatral'nye stranitsy*, Iskusstvo, Moscow, 1979.

34. A. Matskin, *Na temy Gogolia* . . ., p. 234.

35. V. G. Sakhnovskii, op. cit.

36. M. Bulgakov, 'Pis'ma . . .', p. 240.

37. Ibid., p. 241.

38. MAAT Museum.

39. M. Bulgakov, 'Pis'ma . . .', p. 240.

40. B. G. Egorov, op. cit, p. 74.

41. V. G. Sakhnovskii, op. cit.

42. Ibid.

43. Ibid.

44. MAAT Museum.

45. Ibid.

46. Ibid.

47. Ibid.

48. M. Bulgakov, 'Pis'ma . . .', p. 241.

49. V. O. Toporkov, *Stanislavskii na repetitsii*, Iskusstvo, Moscow, 1950, p. 61.

50. Ibid.

51. Ibid.

52. *Sovetskoe iskusstvo*, 28 September 1931.

53. K. L. Rudnitskii, '*Mertvye dushi*, MKhAT, 1932', p. 166.
54. Transcript of speech by M. Ianshin, MAAT Museum.
55. V. Toporkov, *Stanislavskii na repetitsii* . . ., p. 153.
56. Ibid.
57. Ibid., pp. 74–5.
58. A. Matskin, *Na temy Gogolia*, p. 247.
59. V. G. Sakhnovskii, op. cit.
60. Ibid.
61. V. Ermilov, 'Teatr i pravda', *Izvestiia*, 22 February 1933.
62. A. Orlinskii, 'Spektakl' odnostoronnego masterstva', *Za kommunisticheskoe prosveshchenie*, 23 December 1932.
63. A. Belyi, 'Neponiatyi Gogol'', *Sovetskoe iskusstvo*, 20 January 1933.
64. MAAT Museum.
65. Ibid.
66. M. Bulgakov, *Pis'ma* . . ., p. 303.
67. Ibid., p. 299.
68. Archive of M. Karostin, communicated by G. Faiman.
69. E. Bulgakova, *Dnevnik*, p. 84.
70. M. Bulgakov, *Pis'ma* . . ., p. 299.
71. M. Chudakova, 'Gogol' i Bulgakov', p. 371.
72. M. Bulgakov, *Pis'ma* . . ., p. 308.

6 'A Part of Theatre Lore'

1. *Gor'kovets*, 15 February 1936.
2. V. Prokof'ev, *V sporakh o Stanislavskom*, Iskusstvo, Moscow, 1976, p. 115.
3. M. O. Chudakova, *Arkhiv Bulgakova* . . ., p. 86.
4. Ibid., p. 90.
5. Ibid.
6. Ibid.
7. *Gor'kovets*, 15 February 1936.
8. *Gor'kovets*, 22 February 1936.
9. M. Bulgakov, 'On byl velik i neudachliv', *Gor'kovets*, 15 February 1936.
10. *Voprosy literatury*, No. 11, 1984.
11. Georges Bordonove, *Molière*, Robert Laffont, Paris, 1967.
12. K. S. Stanislavskii, *Sobr. soch.* . . ., vol. 8, p. 224.
13. Archive of the Bakhrushin State Theatre Museum.
14. Ibid.
15. Ibid.
16. M. Bulgakov, 'Pis'ma . . .', p. 176.
17. MAAT Museum.
18. Nemirovich-Danchenko, *Izbrannye pis'ma* . . ., vol. 2, p. 643.
19. MAAT Museum.

20. Ibid.
21. Ibid.
22. Ibid.
23. Ibid.
24. OR GBL, f. 562.
25. MAAT Museum.
26. Ibid.
27. P. Markov, *Kniga vospominanii*, p. 296.
28. Arkhiv memuarnoi komissii Soiuza teatral'nykh deiatelei Rossii.
29. Ibid.
30. K. S. Stanislavskii, *Sobr. soch.* . . ., vol. 8, p. 321.
31. M. Bulgakov, 'Pis'ma . . .', pp. 225, 227.
32. *Krasnaia gazeta* (evening edition), 11 November 1931.
33. M. Bulgakov, 'Pis'ma . . .', pp. 225–6.
34. Ibid., p. 253.
35. Ibid., p. 270.
36. Ibid., p. 283.
37. Ibid.
38. Ibid.
39. Ibid.
40. I. Vinogradskaia, *Letopis'* . . ., vol. 4, p. 370.
41. A Afinogenov, 'Mogushchestvo teatral'nogo oruzhiia', *Sovetskoe iskusstvo*, 5 September 1934.
42. E. Bulgakova, *Dnevnik*, p. 65.
43. MAAT Museum.
44. Ibid.
45. E. Bulgakova, *Dnevnik*, p. 73.
46. Ibid., p. 77.
47. I. Vinogradskaia, *Letopis'* . . ., vol. 4, pp. 386–7.
48. E. Bulgakova, *Dnevnik*, 2 January 1935.
49. MAAT Museum.
50. B. Livanov, *Kompozitsiia po materialam zhizni i tvorchestva*, VTO, Moscow, 1983, p. 52.
51. E. Bulgakova, *Dnevnik*, p. 353
52. Ibid., p. 84.
53. Ibid.
54. Ibid.
55. *Gor'kovets*, 15 February 1936.
56. A. Afinogenov, *Dnevniki i zapisnye knizhki*, Sovetskii pisatel', Moscow, 1960, p. 226.
57. MAAT Museum.
58. I. Vinogradskaia, *Letopis'* . . ., vol. 4, p. 397.

59. MAAT Museum.
60. Ibid.
61. E. Bulgakova, *Dnevnik*.
62. M. Bulgakov, 'Pis'ma . . .', p. 316.
63. E. Bulgakova, *Dnevnik*, p. 89.
64. N. Gorchakov, *Rezhisserskie uroki Stanislavskogo*, Iskusstvo, Moscow, 1951, p. 542.
65. MAAT Museum.
66. Ibid.
67. Ibid.
68. Ibid.
69. E. Bulgakova, *Dnevnik*, p. 93.
70. M. Bulgakov, 'Pis'ma . . .', p. 320.
71. MAAT Museum.
72. Ibid.
73. Ibid.
74. I. Vinogradskaia, *Letopis'* . . ., vol. 4, p. 409.
75. E. Bulgakova, *Dnevnik*, p. 100.
76. Ibid.
77. Ibid., p. 98.
78. I. Vinogradskaia, *Letopis'* . . ., vol. 4, p. 411.
79. Ibid.
80. Ibid., p. 419.
81. E. Bulgakova, *Dnevnik*.
82. MAAT Museum.
83. Ibid.
84. Ibid.
85. E. Bulgakova, *Dnevnik*.
86. A. Afinogenov, 'Repetitsiia', *Pravda*, 17 October 1935.
87. E. Bulgakova, *Dnevnik*.
88. *Teatral'naia dekada*, No. 36, 1935, p. 12.
89. *Sovetskoe iskusstvo*, 15 September 1935.
90. *Vecherniaia Moskva*, 9 October 1935.
91. *Literaturnaia gazeta*, 10 February 1936.
92. N. Gorchakov, *Rezhisserskie uroki Stanislavskogo* . . ., p. 541.
93. Nemirovich-Danchenko, *Izbrannye pis'ma* . . ., vol. 2, p. 442.
94. Ibid., p. 445.
95. MAAT Museum.
96. Ibid.
97. E. Bulgakova, *Dnevnik*.
98. *Gor'kovets*, 15 February 1936.
99. Ibid.

100. E. Bulgakova, *Dnevnik*.

101. Ibid., pp. 112–13.

102. M. Bulgakov, *Pis'ma* . . ., p. 362.

103. O. Litovskii, 'Dva spektaklia', *Sovetskoe iskusstvo*, 11 February 1936.

104. B. Alpers, 'Mol'er bez Mol'era', *Literaturnaia gazeta*, 10 March 1936.

105. *Vecherniaia Moskva*, 17 February 1936.

106. E. Bulgakova, *Dnevnik*, p. 115.

107. Ibid., p. 111.

108. Ibid., p. 116.

109. *Gor'kovets*, 22 February 1936.

110. *Pravda*, 9 March 1936.

111. E. Bulgakova, *Dnevnik* . . ., p. 116.

112. V. Ia. Vilenkin, *Vospominaniia s kommentariiami*, Iskusstvo, Moscow, 1982, p. 387.

113. OR IRLI, f. 369. See also *Teatr i dramaturgiia*, No. 4, 1936.

114. 'Iskusstvovedy iz PB', *Literaturnaia gazeta*, 19 July 1992.

115. *Sovetskoe iskusstvo*.

116. MAAT Museum.

117. Ibid.

118. M. Ianshin, *Stat'i, vospominaniia, pis'ma*, VTO, Moscow, 1984, p. 52.

119. MAAT Museum.

120. M. Bulgakov, *Pis'ma* . . ., p. 231.

121. OR IRLI, f. 369.

122. E. Bulgakova, *Dnevnik*.

123. MAAT Museum.

124. M. Bulgakov, *Pis'ma*, p. 367.

125. Ibid.

126. Ibid., p. 369.

7 Departure

1. E. Bulgakova, *Dnevnik*, p. 208.

2. M. Bulgakov, 'Pis'ma . . .', p. 117.

3. Sudebnyi otchet po delu antisovetskogo 'pravotrotskistskogo' bloka, rassmotrennogo Voennoi kollegiei Verkhovnogo Suda Soiuza SSR 2–13 marta 1938 goda, Moscow, 1938, p. 494.

4. E. Bulgakova, *Dnevnik*, p. 116.

5. Ibid., pp. 137–8.

6. Ibid., pp. 146–7.

7. Ibid., pp. 149—50.

8. *Gor'kovets*, 3 June 1937.

9. E. Bulgakova, *Dnevnik*, p. 141.

10. Ibid., p. 150.

11. M. Bulgakov, 'Pis'ma . . .', pp. 170–1.

12. Ibid., p. 195.

13. E. Bulgakova, *Dnevnik*, p. 48.

14. Ibid.

15. Ibid., p. 66.

16. *Literaturnaia gazeta*, 5 March 1933.

17. E. Bulgakova, *Dnevnik*, p. 47.

18. Ibid., p. 147.

19. Ibid., p. 142.

20. Ibid., p. 163.

21. Ibid., p. 174.

22. Mikhail Bulgakov, *Sobranie sochinenii*, vol. 5, pp. 557–8.

23. V. Ia. Vilenkin, *Vospominaniia s kommentariiami*, p. 296.

24. S. Ermolinskii, *Dramaticheskie sochineniia*, p. 651.

25. K. S. Stanislavskii, *Sobr. soch. . . .*, vol. 7, p. 347.

26. MAAT Museum.

27. K. Arenskii, *Pis'ma v Khollivud . . .*, p. 42.

28. Ibid., p. 47.

29. Ibid.

30. K. S. Stanislavskii, *Sobr. soch. . . .*, vol. 6, p. 353.

31. Ibid.

32. *Gor'kovets*, 25 January, 1938.

33. K. Arenskii, *Pis'ma v Khollivud . . .*, p. 250.

34. *Gor'kovets*, 25 March 1938.

35. G. Adamovich, 'Bez Tolstogo', quoted in L. Fleishman, *Boris Pasternak v 30-e gody*, Jerusalem, 1984, pp. 388–9.

36. *Gor'kovets*, 3 June 1937.

37. *Gor'kovets*, 2 February 1936.

38. *Gor'kovets*, 11 March 1939.

39. I. Vinogradskaia, *Letopis' . . .*, vol. 4, p. 374.

40. K. Arenskii, *Pis'ma v Khollivud . . .*, pp. 244–5.

41. Ibid., p. 245.

42. Ibid.

43. Ibid., p. 247.

44. Ibid., p. 13.

45. Ibid., p. 251.

46. *Gor'kovets*, September 1936.

47. E. Bulgakova, *Dnevnik*, p. 158.

48. M. Chudakova, 'Neokonchennoe sochinenie Mikhaila Bulgakova', *Novyi mir*, No. 8, 1987, pp. 199–201.

49. E. Bulgakova, *Dnevnik*, p. 167.

50–101. See under the relevant date in E. Bulgakova, *Dnevnik*.

102. M. Bulgakov, *Pis'ma* . . ., p. 470.

103. E. Bulgakova, *Dnevnik*, p. 383.

104. Ibid., p. 277.

105. Ibid.

106. M. Bulgakov, 'Pis'ma . . .', p. 471.

107–114. See under the relevant date in E. Bulgakova, *Dnevnik*.

115. M. O. Chudakova, *Arkhiv Bulgakova* . . ., p. 140.

116. OR IRLI, f. 369.

117. M. Bulgakov, 'Pis'ma . . .', pp. 481–2.

118. E. Bulgakova, *Dnevnik*, pp. 286–7.

119. Ibid., p. 389.

120. M. Bulgakov, 'Pis'ma . . .', p. 485

121–122. E. Bulgakova, *Dnevnik*, 13 January 1940.

123. Sergei Ermolinskii, *Dramaticheskie sochineniia*, Moscow, Iskusstvo, 1982, p. 654.

124. M. Bulgakov, 'Pis'ma . . .', p. 485.

125. Ibid., p. 487.

126. Ibid., p. 488.

127. M. O. Chudakova, *Arkhiv Bulgakova* . . ., p. 141.

128. M. Bulgakov, 'Pis'ma . . .', pp. 492–3.

129. *Izvestiia*, 12 March 1940.

8 *Black Snow* or *A Dead Man's Notes*

1. P. Markov, *Kniga vospominanii*, Moscow, Iskusstvo, 1983, p. 236.

2. MAAT Museum.

3. E. Bulgakova, *Dnevnik*, p. 129.

4. OR IRLI, f. 369.

5. E. Bulgakova, *Dnevnik*, pp. 256–7.

6. B. Livanov, op. cit., p. 124.

7. E. Bulgakova, *Dnevnik*, p. 91.

8. Ibid.

9. Ibid., p. 92.

10. MAAT Museum.

11. Ibid.

12. Ibid.

13. OR IRLI, f. 369.

Index